CRIME, PROTEST AND POPULAR POLITICS IN SOUTHERN ENGLAND 1740–1850

CRIME, PROTEST AND POPULAR POLITICS IN SOUTHERN ENGLAND 1740–1850

JOHN RULE AND ROGER WELLS

THE HAMBLEDON PRESS

LONDON AND RIO GRANDE

Published by The Hambledon Press, 1997

102 Gloucester Avenue, London NW1 8HX (UK)

PO Box 162, Rio Grande, Ohio 45674 (USA)

ISBN 1 85285 076 0

A description of this book is available from the
British Library and from the Library of Congress

Typeset by The Midlands Book Typesetting Company, Loughborough
Printed on acid-free paper and bound in
Great Britain by Cambridge University Press

Contents

Acknowledgements

The essays in this book were originally published in the following places and are reprinted by the kind permission of the original publishers.

1 This essay appears here for the first time.

2 *Social History*, 6 (1977), pp. 713–44.

3 This essay appears here for the first time.

4 *Cornish Studies*, 4/5 (1976–77), pp. 50–55.

5 This essay appears here for the first time.

6 *The New Poor Law*, edited by M. Chase, Middlesbrough Occasional Papers, 1 (Leeds, 1985).

7 *Rural History*, 2 (1991), pp. 35–57.

8 *Southern History*, 1 (1979), pp. 135–53.

9 This essay appears here for the first time.

10 *Outside the Law: Studies in Crime and Order, 1650–1850*, edited by John Rule (Exeter University Press, Exeter, 1982), pp. 102–29.

Preface

The essays in this book were written separately over a number of years by two historians who share an interest in the history of popular protest and of crime. Although we both have published books of a national scope, for example Roger Wells, *Insurrection: The British Experience, 1795–1803* (1983) and *Wretched Faces. Famine in Wartime England, 1793–1803* (1988), and John Rule, *The Labouring Classes in Early Industrial England 1750–1850,* (1986) we also continue to research into the history of the southern (including south-western) part of England. We have both edited *Southern History*. These shared interests have frequently brought us together and cemented a friendship over many years. Chapter 1 is a fully-shared effort. Several of the other essays are either entirely new, or significantly enlarged, versions of material only previously issued in the skeletal form of conference abstracts or review articles.

Our formative years were in the great era of 'History from Below'. Although we acknowledge that it left some 'silences', especially over gender and ethnicity, it still hugely enlarged the historical subject. We have no reluctance in continuing to write within the tradition of George Rudé, Eric Hobsbawm, Edward Thompson and Gwyn 'Alf' Williams. The last two were our respective supervisors at Warwick and at York. Sadly they both died in the period we were putting this book together. We dedicate this book to their memory with enduring admiration and affection.

John Rule   Roger Wells

Hampshire   1996

Abbreviations

BL	British Library
BPP	British Parliamentary Papers
BRA	Brighton Radical Association
BRL	Birmingham Reference Library
CCRO	Cornwall County Record Office
DCRO	Devon County Record Office
ECRO	Exeter City Record Office
ESCRO	East Sussex County Record Office
FLP	Fortescue Lieutenancy Papers, DCRO
Goodwood	Goodwood Papers, WSCRO
JP	Justice of the Peace
LC	Lovett Collection, BRL
KCRO	Kent County Record Office
MP	Member of Parliament
NCA	National Chartist Association
PLC	Poor Law Commission
PRO	Public Record Office
ADM	Admiralty
Assi	Assizes
BT	Board of Trade
HO	Home Office
MAF	Ministry of Agriculture and Fisheries
MH	Ministry of Health
WO	War Office
SC, HC	Select Committee, House of Commons
SC, HL	Select Committee, House of Lords
SCRO	Somerset County Record Office
SP	Sidmouth Papers
WMA	Working Men's Association
WSCRO	West Sussex County Record Office

1

Crime, Protest and Radicalism

John Rule and Roger Wells

In writing about Chartism in 1839, Thomas Carlyle put the 'condition of England' question in a particularly direct form:

> Is the condition of the English working people wrong; so wrong that rational working men cannot, will not, and even should not rest quiet under it?[1]

From Southey at the beginning of the nineteenth century to Engels, it was a question that had been overwhelmingly asked, of the industrialising north and midlands, as well as of London. It was from these areas, where the industrial revolution, population growth and urbanisation produced, enlarged and defined a new working class, that the threat to an older social and political order was seen to derive. By the time Elizabeth Gaskell wrote *North and South* (1854–55) even the shock of the Swing Riots seems to have faded from memory and the southern labourers are portrayed as beyond protest:

> You must not go to the South . . . You could not stand it. You would be out in all weathers. It would kill you with rheumatism. The mere bodily work at your time of life would break you down . . . you've reckoned on having butcher's meat once a day. If you're in work; pay for that out of your ten shillings, and keep those poor children if you can . . . You would not bear the dullness of the life . . . it would eat you away like rust. Those who have lived there all their lives are used to soaking in the stagnant waters. They labour on from day to day, in the great solitude of soaking fields – never speaking or lifting up their poor, bent, downward heads. The hard spadework robs their brain of life; the sameness of their toil deadens their imagination; they don't care to meet to talk over thoughts and speculations, even of the weakest, wildest kind, after their work is done; they go home brutishly tired, poor creatures! caring for nothing but food and rest. You could not stir them up into any companionship, which you get in a town as plentiful as the air you breathe, whether it be good or bad . . . you of all men are not one to bear a life among such labourers. What would be peace to them, would be eternal fretting to you. Think no more of it . . . I beg.[2]

---

[1] Thomas Carlyle, *Chartism* (London, 1839), cited by Raymond Williams, *Culture and Society, 1780–1950* (Harmondsworth, 1961), p. 91.

[2] Elizabeth Gaskell, *North and South* (1854–55; Harmondsworth, 1970), pp. 381–82.

This advice was delivered to a discontented cotton-worker who wished to escape from the unrelenting struggle between labour and capital in Manchester, *the* town of the industrial revolution and, according to Engels, the centre of England's 'social war' between the classes.[3] In the non-industrialising, even de-industrialising, south, the workers' struggle could be more simply considered as the 'struggle to live'.

Mrs Gaskell's insistence on the southern labourer's incapacity for thought suggests a social consciousness with an emphasis on survival more than protest. The 1830 insurrection of the Swing Riots has been traditionally seen as a worrying but exceptional episode for the rural south. So too was the farmworkers' flirtation with trade unionism in the notorious events at Tolpuddle in 1833. Swing and Tolpuddle's exceptionality was not unrelated to the severity with which they were repressed. Carlyle was mainly thinking of the workers in industrial and urban England, historians have not in general treated matters differently. There is an established labour historiography which is distinctly regional in its concentration. Edward Thompson's classic *The Making of the English Working Class*, which far more than any other book set the agenda for working-class history, for all its short chapter on the 'field labourers' is essentially a book about London's artisans and the industrial workers of the north and midlands.[4]

There are some exceptions to this geographical concentration. Eric Hobsbawm and George Rudé's *Captain Swing* is a notable one,[5] while in the serious historical study of crime alongside protest, southern-based studies have played an important part. Neither contemporaries nor historians ignored the desperate poverty of the southern farm labourer. To an extent, but a lesser one than was the case with the new urban-industrial Britain, conditions in rural England were revealed in parliamentary enquiries. It was also described in depressing detail in the *Morning Chronicle* and bludgeoned into the national consciousness by William Cobbett.[6] It is the consciousness, not the condition, of the southern population which has been under-studied. It is in this context that this volume, which is in the tradition of 'history from below' pioneered by Thompson, Hobsbawm and Rudé has been complied. Among the primary objectives of these studies is to show that agricultural labourers and other southern working people had a capacity to fight to redress their grievances and were at a considerable remove from the apathetic victims of Gaskell's stereotyping. Not only did southern workers engage in mass mobilisations, they also participated in the major politically driven movements of the time. Protest against the iniquities of the New Poor Law and recognition of the potential benefits of at least

[3] Frederick Engels, *The Condition of the Working Class in England* (1845; reprinted 1987), pp. 232–33; 'These strikes . . . are the strongest proof that the decisive battle between bourgeoisie and proletariat is approaching.'

[4] E.P. Thompson, *The Making of the English Working Class* (Harmondsworth, 1968). The Penguin paperback of 1968 with its important post-script is the standard edition.

[5] E.J. Hobsbawm and G. Rudé, *Captain Swing* (Harmondsworth, 1973).

[6] Lengthy surveys of the condition of the poor in the provinces were published in the *Morning Chronicle* regularly between 1849 and 1850.

manhood suffrage were not exclusive to workers in London and the large industrial and urban locations.

Historians of traditional forms of popular protest have shown a stronger interest in southern England than have those of labour and radical political movements. The careful mapping of food rioting, the most frequent and widespread form of disturbance in the eighteenth century, by Charlesworth and others hardly permits otherwise.[7] Protest over food prices seems therefore, an appropriate place to begin.

Violent fluctuations in the cost of living were inherent where the productivity of the domestic harvest largely determined the nature of the struggle to live from year to year until after the French Wars of 1793–1815. This phenomenon first became apparent during the urbanisation and nascent capitalism of the medieval period, and war intensified with further urbanisation and rapid demographic growth during the time of the Tudor and early Stuart monarchies. Population stagnation in later seventeenth- and early eighteenth-century England, combined with increases in agrarian productivity (in part stimulated by the introduction of the Corn Laws) saw some amelioration of the fragility of subsistence supplies experienced before 1660. The severe food crisis of 1709 and 1727–29 were precursors of renewed fragility from the 1730s. Recurrent crises happened in 1740–41, 1753, 1756–57, 1766–67, 1772–73, 1792–93, 1794–96, 1799–1801, and 1811–13.[8] Most of these crises were also aggravated by war and even more so by collapses in demand for everyday consumer articles and services, other than foodstuffs, with consequent industrial under and unemployment amongst men, women and children.

Consensus over popular responses to dearth and high food prices have emerged in two areas. First, that the 'food riot' in its various forms constituted the most common form of popular mass mobilisation up to 1815. Secondly, that the objectives of these assemblies conformed to what E. P. Thompson dubbed the 'moral economy of the eighteenth-century English crowd'.[9] If the essence of Thompson's identification is undisputed, differences of historical interpretation remain over a number of points. The first disagreement worthy of interest concerns the universality of this brand of popular mentality, which might be boiled down to whether it was regionally (or indeed culturally) specific, or some peculiar combination of the two. Some historians, including Dale Edward Williams and Derek Gregory, have in their different ways argued that because

---

[7] A. Charlesworth, ed., *An Atlas of Rural Protest in Britain, 1548–1900* (London, 1983).

[8] These crises are briefly outlined and mapped in turn in Charlesworth, *Atlas of Rural Protest*. Those of the early French war years have been analysed in detail in Roger Wells, *Wretched Faces: Famine in Wartime England, 1793–1801* (Gloucester, 1988).

[9] E.P. Thompson, 'The Moral Economy of the English Crowd in the Eighteenth Century', *Past and Present*, 50 (1971), pp. 76–136. This hugely influential article was reprinted in Thompson's *Customs in Common*, (Harmondsworth, 1993), along with an important response to his critics, 'The Moral Economy Reviewed'.

universal riot did not apparently accompany universal dearth, some communities did, while others did not, subscribe to moral-economic values. Williams, in particular, emphasises that only specific types of community, notably proto-industrial ones, recurrently engaged in food rioting. Gregory, who appears to be slightly more sensitive to the universality of the concept, believes, like any historical geographer, that the answer to this question lies in mapping the phenomena across the relevant chronology. In some senses these views echo R. B. Rose's 1961 perception, that food-rioting somehow moved northwards during the eighteenth-century, roughly in tandem with the onset of more rapid industrialisation in the second half of the eighteenth century.[10]

A number of observations must be made on these assumptions. Evidential considerations simply mean that even the majority of food riots need not have left their mark in the documentation, at any point of time since the medieval period.[11] Equally evidentially-based is the fact of the sheer intensity of food rioting in the most desperate times, witnessed by the operations of highly-mobile crowds, drawn from several adjacent communities, who grouped and regrouped on successive days to traverse and interrogate farmers (and others) in relatively broad swathes of the rural hinterlands of market towns, many of which also had a manufacturing component in their economies. Moreover protesters in less-populated villages, and especially those whose economies were overwhelmingly agricultural, appear to have adopted non-overt forms of protest including theft, arson and animal maiming. Above all this included the employment of anonymous threatening letter, whose authors clearly shared moral and economic precepts with the perpetrators. The geography of food rioting recoverable from the sources is not synonymous with populist adherence to these precepts.[12]

We have few quarrels with existing identification of faces in the food-rioting crowd and certainly not with Rose's critical observation that such mobilisations permitted the conjunction of working people from disparate trades, and with

[10] D.E. Williams, 'Morals, Markets, and the English Crowd in 1766', *Past and Present*, 104 (1984), pp. 56–73. His argument seems hardly to survive the response of A. Charlesworth and A. Randall, 'Morals, Markets and the English Crowd in 1766', ibid., 114 (1987), pp. 200–13; D. Gregory, 'A New and Differing Face in Many Places'. Three geographies of industrialisation are in R.A. Butlin and G. Dodgshon (eds), *An Historical Geography of England and Wales* (2nd edn, 1990), esp. pp. 354, 359 and n. 10; R.B. Rose, 'Eighteenth-Century Price Riots and Public Policy in England', *International Review of Social History* (1961), pp. 277–92. See also A. Booth, 'Food Riots in North-West England, 1790–1801', *Past and Present*, 77 (1977), pp. 84–107.

[11] Roger Wells, 'Counting Riots in Eighteenth-Century England', *Bulletin of the Society for the Study of Labour History*, 37 (1978), pp. 68–72; and work in progress by Professor Buchanan Sharp.

[12] See E.P. Thompson, 'The Crime of Anonymity', in D. Hay, E.P. Thompson and P. Linebaugh (eds), *Albion's Fatal Tree: Crime and Society in Eighteenth-Century England* (Harmondsworth, 1975), pp. 255–344; Roger Wells, 'The Development of the English Rural Proletariat and Social Protest, 1700–1850'; and idem, 'Social Protest, Class, Conflict and Consciousness in the English Countryside, 1700–1880', both in M. Reed and R. Wells (eds), *Class, Conflict and Protest in the English Countryside, 1700–1880* (1990), especially pp. 40–45, 155–59. See also J.E. Archer, 'The Wells-Charlesworth Debate: A Personal Comment on Arson in Norfolk and Suffolk', ibid., pp. 82–90.

commensurately disparate status, including labourers, to engage: in some senses this does represent action by an 'inchoate working class'. However, Dr Bohstedt's view that women predominated to degrees of exclusiveness, especially towards the apparent end of the main period of the food-rioting tradition, is as E. P. Thompson incisively put it, a 'myth of Dr Bohstedt's own making'. Moreover, whether feminists like it or not, a male chauvinist society protected women from being shot on such occasions, as the army, regular militia or volunteer, actually fired on the crowd. It also protected them, to a degree, from prosecution as well.[13]

The scale of food rioting reflected the nature and the size of the communities from which the protesters came. Mining communities were usually apart, at a geographical remove, from common targets, such the traders in market towns and ports. Miners' own social cohesion underwrote their capacity to enforce the tactics of 'one and all', to ensure that all males at least effectively struck work and then mobilised to secure moral-economic solutions. Although the plebeian inhabitants of such towns, owing to their own weakness, are frequently recorded welcoming the miners' arrival and capacity for powerful intervention, such phenomena essentially represented one distinct community taking on the dominant power groups in a different one. This is at a considerable remove from Bohstedt's representation of riot as 'community politics', an analysis which he underpins through contrasting the riotous conduct of working-class inhabitants of corporate towns in Devon with their ostensible counterparts in northern cities, especially Manchester.[14] Moreover, Bohstedt's perception, even on his favoured home Devonian territory, ignores the fact that the mobilised did not simply appeal to corporate authority to back them in market regulation, but (like the miners) attacked separate communities by crossing borough boundaries to enforce farmers in their villages to release withheld stocks for the immediate supply of the towns. In a similar way, protesters from Devon towns were quite capable of attacking millers located on rivers and in the estuaries who broke the moral-economic code by despatching grain to distant locations, thereby depriving local towns of what their inhabitants conceived as their rightful food supply in times of crisis. John Allen, the historian of his native Cornish market town of Liskeard, itself lying away from the mining district, recalled that in 1793 the report that 'The French are coming' and 'The Tinners are rising!' produced equal alarm.[15]

[13] Rose, 'Eighteenth-Century Price Riots', pp. 277–92; J. Bohstedt, 'Gender, Household and Community Politics: Women in English Riots, 1790–1810', *Past and Present*, 120 (1988), pp. 88–122; Thompson, *Customs in Common*, pp. 306–10, 314–16.

[14] John Bohstedt, *Riots and Community Politics in England and Wales, 1790–1810* (Cambridge, MA, and London, 1983). For a detailed response to Bohstedt's important work see A. Charlesworth, 'From the Moral Economy of Devon to the Political Economy of Manchester, 1790–1812', *Social History*, 18 (1993), pp. 204–17.

[15] See below, Chapter 2, pp. 17–51. J. Allen, *History of the Borough of Liskeard* (1856), p. 360. For the sense of miners' food riots as 'invasions' of farming districts or market towns see John Rule, 'Some Social Aspects of the Industrial Revolution in Cornwall; in R. Burt (ed.), *Industry and Society in the South West* (Exeter, 1970), pp. 94–96.

Collectively quitting the place of work to take part in food riots did not in itself make for an *industrial* dispute per se: the quarrel not being with the employer. Industrial disputes were, however, far from unknown among southern workers. Both the serge manufacture of the south west and the woollen cloth manufacture of the western counties had traditions of industrial action going back to at least the beginning of the eighteenth century.[16] Royal dockyard workers at Chatham, Plymouth and Portsmouth, who were after all employed in Britain's largest manufacturing enterprises, were also early to organise. Journeymen papermakers in Kent, Hampshire and Thames valley had developed a sophisticated strike strategy by the late eighteenth century, as had millwrights and many groups of urban craftsmen, building tradesmen and seamen.[17] Even 'Luddism', named from the events in the north and midlands of 1811–12, had made an earlier appearance in the southern half of England. The shearmen of Wiltshire and Somerset resisted innovation at every turn and attacked and destroyed machinery a decade before the Yorkshire croppers followed suit. Through the 'Brief Institution' of 1802–3 there was a remarkable trade-union tie-up between cloth-workers across the country.[18] Local newspapers constantly reveal particular incidents of industrial disputes. Dobson's count of those reported in the newspapers of the British Library's Burney Collection for the years 1717 to 1800 'discovers' a total of seventy-five in southern England, twenty-four in eastern, twenty-seven in the Midlands, eighty-eight in the north and 119 in London. It also reveals that significantly more labour disputes were recorded in southern than northern and midland England before 1760.[19] The first chapters of the Webbs' pioneering book of 1894 give pride of place to the workers of the south-western and and western clothing districts in the early history of trade unionism.[20] Unionising proclivities were not of course evenly spread in the south. Cornish miners, inveterate food rioters, seldom struck for purely industrial reasons, and hardly even organised industrially before the 1860s. Against this, it has been shown that the happenings at Tolpuddle in 1833 among farm labourers do not represent so singular an event as they have usually been presented.

Acts of protest over food prices and industrial action were often criminal acts. People could be arrested, convicted and punished for them: gaoled and in some

[16] For an account of early trade unionism in the south-western serge district and in the west country woollen cloth manufacture see J.G. Rule, *The Experience of Labour in Eighteenth-Century Industry* (London, 1981), pp. 158–66; and idem, 'Labour Consciousness and Industrial Conflict in Eighteenth-Century Exeter', in B. Stapleton (ed.), *Conflict and Community in Southern England* (Gloucester, 1992), pp. 92–109. See also the important writings of Adrian Randall, especially *Before the Luddites: Custom, Community and Machinery in the English Woollen Industry, 1776–1809* (Cambridge, 1991).

[17] Rule, *Experience of Labour*, pp. 174, 179.

[18] A.J. Randall, 'The Shearmen and the Wiltshire Outrages of 1802: Trade Unionism and Industrial Violence', *Social History*, 7, pp. 283–304.

[19] C.R. Dobson, *Masters and Journeymen: A Prehistory of Industrial Relations, 1717–1800* (London, 1980), p. 22.

[20] See below, Chapter 2, pp. 17–51; S and B. Webb, *History of Trade Unionism* (London, 1911), pp. 28–55.

cases transported or even hanged. But if protest was often crime, the converse could also be true. Crime levels in the rural south, according to Cobbett, were manifestly the result of poverty and deprivation at the bottom of the social scale. In his eyes the landowner, oppressed by the taxation burden of corrupt government, pressed in turn upon the farmer, who pressed on the labourer: 'this class is made so miserable, that a felon's life is better than that of a labourer . . . what education, what precepts, can quiet the gnawings and ragings of hunger'. Historians have tended to follow this line of direct causation. The Hammonds, in their classic *The Village Labourer*, commented on the 'wretched and squalid lot' of the labourers, and concluded that they were 'driven to the wages of crime' and that their history in this period was 'written in the code of the Game Laws, the growing brutality of the criminal law, and the preoccupation of the rich with the efficacy of punishment'. Hobsbawm and Rudé agreed that rural crime was 'almost entirely economic – a defence against hunger'.[21]

Statistics tend to support the link. Professor Beattie's analysis of indictments, from Sussex and from rural Surrey, indicate a 'a strong suggestion' that property crime in the countryside was to a considerable extent a matter of hunger and necessity, fluctuating in line with the price of food. The link is complex. In times of war the level of criminal indictments was more closely affected by bad harvests than in times of peace. This seems to have been because the young men who always committed a wholly disproportionate share of total crime were not as affected by high food prices as were older people with families to support. When war service absorbed large numbers of the young and unmarried males, then level of committal was more influenced by the actions of those more immediately and seriously affected by rising subsistence costs.[22]

Problems of definition are as troublesome as those of measurement. Historians should presumably concern themselves with measuring and assessing what contemporaries considered as 'criminal', for both law and moral opinion change over time. But not all contemporaries agreed with those who made the criminal law – not surprising when the legislature very largely represented the landed oligarchy. A notion of 'social crime' is necessary to make sense of much activity outside the law. Poachers, smugglers and wreckers, for example, did not normally think of themselves as criminal, nor were they usually so regarded by most of the inhabitants of their communities. Such divergences from 'official' views often derived from the redefinitions of property characteristic of the period. Consider, for example, how enclosure might affect a village. Trespass would acquire a new meaning; fuel gathering from the common could become hedge-breaking or woodstealing (the most common of rural offences). The new type

---

[21] See below, Chapter 10, pp. 237–53. William Cobbett, *Rural Rides* (Everyman edn), i, pp. 297–98; J.L. and B. Hammond, *The Village Labourer* (London, 1948), pp. 183–84; Hobsbawm and Rudé, *Captain Swing*, pp. 50, 54.

[22] See J.M. Beattie, 'The Pattern of Crime in England, 1660–1800', *Past and Present*, 62 (1974), pp. 47–95; and his authoritative *Crime and the Courts in England, 1660–1800* (Oxford, 1986); D. Hay, 'War, Dearth and Theft in the Eighteenth Century', *Past and Present*, 95 (1982), pp. 117–60.

and profit-conscious farmer increasingly refused to allow the age-old right of gleaning after harvest, severely curtailing the real value of women's contribution to cottage economies. In manufacturing and in mining the change from independent producer to wage-dependent worker was accompanied by differing views over the ownership of some kinds of 'property' in raw materials or in product. Perquisite expectations were at the heart of many disputes between employers and labour, from taking 'chips' of timber in the royal dockyards to 'kitting' in the bargains in the copper mines of Cornwall. Kitting was hardly considered criminal by the miners but was considered so by the mineowners and prosecuted as ore stealing.[23]

Historians of rural society have stressed that much crime in the countryside was 'social' in another, thought not unrelated sense, that is that it was specifically committed as a form of protest. The destruction of hedges, the maiming of animals and rick burning can be seen as in great part the work of a discontented rural proletariat against oppressors identified among the farmers and landlords. From this perspective, outbreaks like the Swing Riots were exceptional. Far more often the bitterness of desperately poor and underemployed farm workers, given their isolation and powerless position, could most easily find expression in covert nocturnal action. Incendiarism became the symbol of the discontented countryside. Definitions are always problematical, both because they do not always fit and because particular crimes can be committed for a variety of motives. Hungry men rob orchards, poach hares or steal sheep. So do professional dealers or those intending to supply them. So, too, do those with scores to settle against farmers.[24] Nor was all crime in the countryside perpetrated by its inhabitants. Perhaps Chadwick was right to attribute a proportion of rural offences to vagrants and cores of professional country villains, living by crime just as urban thieves did. Some crimes were undoubtedly the work of gangs operating from the towns.[25] Problems abound in the history of crime, but its serious study cannot be evaded. It is essential for the analysis of social and power relationships as well as of protest forms and it is fundamental in the understanding of the struggle to live.

[23] See below, Chapter 3, pp. 81–89. See below Chapter 8, pp. 153–68, for a discussion of the literature on 'social crime'. For industrial crime see also Rule, *Experience of Labour*, pp. 124–35; P. Linebaugh, *The London Hanged: Crime and Civil Society in the Eighteenth Century* (Harmondsworth, 1992), pp. 158–62; 226–30; J. Styles, 'Embezzlement, Industry and the Law', in M. Berg, P. Hudson and M. Sonenscher (eds), *Manufacture in Town and Country before the Industrial Revolution* (Cambridge, 1983), pp. 183–204. For woodstealing and gleaning see R.W. Bushaway, *By Rite: Custom, Ceremony and Community in England, 1700–1880* (1982), pp. 208–33; and P. King, 'Gleaners, Farmers and the Failure of Legal Sanctions in England, 1750–1850', *Past and Present*, 125 (1989), pp. 116–50.

[24] See below, Chapters 9 and 10, pp. 169–235, 237–53. On rural crime and protest see the essays in Reed and Wells, eds, *Class, Conflict and Protest*; J.E. Archer, '*By a Flash and a Scare*': Arson, Animal Maiming and Poaching in East Anglia, 1815–70 (Oxford, 1990); D.V. Jones, *Crime, Protest, Community and Police in Nineteenth-Century Britain* (London, 1982).

[25] For rural criminals see below, Chapter 9, pp. 169–235; and Roger Wells, 'Popular Protest and Social Crime: The Evidence of Criminal Gangs in Rural Southern England, 1790–1860' in Stapleton, ed., *Conflict and Community*, pp. 135–82.

Although sometimes presented as a simple form of agricultural Luddism against threshing machines, behind the protests of 1830–31 lay a miscellany of motives. By mid November 1830, the English countryside, particularly in the south and south midlands was in the grip of a quasi-insurrection generally known after its mythical leader, 'Captain Swing'. Traditional interpretations of the Swing Riots, especially in its south-eastern origins, have focused on a number of critical grievances of agricultural labourers and to a lesser extent of their employers. The labourers suffered from under- and unemployment, derisory wages and increasingly tight-fisted social benefits, collectively known as allowances in-aid-of wages. In many parishes the traditional, annually elected, unpaid overseers of the poor had been given paid professionals known as assistant overseers, whose principal job was to inspect minutely the individual circumstances of claimants with a view to reducing poor-law expenditure. In regions where the threshing-machine made economic sense to the employers, this was certainly a specific grievance because it radically reduced the availability of wintertime employment. Therefore Swing targetted employers, and the assistant overseers, over the issues of wages, employment levels and poor-law allowances. The employers responded by emphasising their own hardships from the post-1815 agricultural depression and the level of taxation (including the local burden of the poor rate) and, where appropriate, the payment of the tithe. The Swing protesters used a variety of tactics. Crowds confronted vestries responsible for poor-rate expenditure as they ultimately bore the responsibility for decisions made by their officials. Crowds also responded to the farmers' protests over tithe levels by forcing both clerical and lay owners radically to reduce their tithe demands on the farmers. These fierce public mobilisations also involved a considerable number of rural tradesmen, especially journeymen (notably blacksmiths, wheelwrights and shoemakers), who were badly hit by the recession's reduction in the demand for agricultural services. Other rural industrial workers who had suffered badly as the result of recent technological innovation – such as sawyers and papermakers – also played an important part in some locations.

The Hammonds in their pioneering study *The Village Labourer* devoted two chapters to what they famously described as 'The Last Labourers' Revolt.' Their interpretation was largely re-iterated by Hobsbawm and Rudé in their 1969 *Captain Swing*. Although Hobsbawn and Rudé were not exactly unaware of the developing Reform Bill crisis, and dimly perceived that there were political elements to Swing, they minimised them. They also assumed that the revolt was essentially over by the end of 1830 at the very latest, devoting much of the remainder of their book to the horrendous judicial counterblast by the newly-installed Whig government and its Special Commissions of Assize. Rudé's access to transportation records held in Australia enabled him to find out much about the hundreds who were transported, which in turn permitted a much closer identification of the faces in Swing's crowds.[26]

---

[26] Hobsbawm and Rudé, *Captain Swing*, chs 12–14. See also G. Rudé, *Protest and Punishment: The Story of the Social and Political Protesters Transported to Australia, 1788–1868* (Oxford, 1978).

There are a number of critical misinterpretations in Hobsbawm and Rudé's interpretation. The first is the simple fact that Swing's first real manifestation took place with the expulsion of customary Irish migrant labour from the north Kentish cornlands in the Isle of Thanet.[27] Secondly, they drastically underestimated the pivotal role of village tradesmen, inducing masters, in the disturbances in general and in their leadership in particular. Thirdly, they failed to appreciate fully the participation of other victims of technological redundancy in the Swing rising.[28] They recount something of the attacks on rural and small-market town manufacturers of farming implements, notably threshing-machines, and were aware of localised attacks on the widely dispersed paper-milling industry. (They, however, overlooked another critical rural industry, sawing, which had been partially mechanised.)[29] Fourthly, they seriously underestimated the political dimensions of Swing, despite dutifully recounting William Cobbetts's rural riding and lecturing prior to the main outbreak. On the very day, 9 November, when fear of political demonstrations against Wellington's government led to the abandonment of the monarch's annual Guildhall dinner with the new Lord Mayor, a crowd of insurgents comprising agricultural labourers, sawyers and other artisans from north Kent and north Surrey was stopped from crossing Blackfriars Bridge by the new Metropolitan Police. At this juncture London was saturated by troops, reducing those available to deal with Swing in the countryside itself.[30] Finally, Hobsbawm and Rudé's account underestimates both the timescale of the protests: they persisted into 1832, with arson in particular continuing into the years beyond.[31]

Swing was a direct antecedent of the Reform Bill crisis. The latter was not only a matter of demonstrations in the manufacturing districts, intermixed with much political agitation by both middle- and working-class reformers. In addition to the well-known demonstrations in Birmingham, Sheffield, and Newcastle-upon-Tyne, there were others in High Wycombe, the scene of attacks by Swing on the paper mills, and in Maidstone, a highly politicised Swing epicentre, involving people not exclusively plebeian, who publicly congratulated the French revolutionaries of 1830 in a document written in impeccable French. On the House of Lord's rejection of First Reform Bill in 1831 the most famous riotous explosions took place in Nottingham, Derby and Bristol; lesser protests occurred in scores of rural locations, including villages in the neighbourhood of

[27] *Political Register,* 24 March 1832; Wells in Reed and Wells, eds, *Class, Conflict and Protest,* esp. p. 160.

[28] R. Wells, 'Rural Rebels in Southern England in the 1830s', in C. Emsley and J. Walvin (eds), *Artisans, Peasants and Proletarians, 1760–1860* (London, 1985), esp. pp. 128–40.

[29] Hobsbawm and Rudé, *Captain Swing,* pp. 114–15.

[30] Ibid., pp. 76–78, 81, 159, 182–87. In an article written in 1969, however, Rudé did observe that, 'London radicalism radiated out into Kent, Sussex and the West', 'Why There was No Revolution in England in 1830 or 1848?', reprinted in H.J. Kaye (ed.), *The Face of the Crowd: Selected Essays of George Rudé* (New Jersey, 1988), pp. 152–53; Wells, in Reed and Wells (eds), *Class, Conflict and Protest,* p. 161.

[31] See *Political Register,* 16 June 1832.

Winchester, the origin came some of those Swing protesters victimised at the Special Commission held in the city.[32]

William Cobbett celebrated the eventual passage of the Reform Bill at Barton Stacey deep in rural Hampshire. He gave a typically polemical yet almost apologetic public explanation for his choice:

> I have always been of the opinion that we owe the Reform Bill more to the COUNTRY LABOURERS than to all the rest of the nation put together; because if they had remained quiet under their sufferings; if they had not resolved not to be reduced to potatoes, and if they had not acted as they did, in order to preserve themselves from this state of terrible degradation, WELLINGTON would not have been turned out, Grey would not have come in, the Parliament would not have acted on Wellington's insolent declaration, and we shall have had no reform bill at all; though in time we must have had a terrible and violent revolution. Everyman therefore, who really wishes for the settlement of our difficulties to terminate in peace, must feel gratitude to these country labourers.[33]

Cobbett continued that he felt 'this gratitude in a peculiar degree' to the labourers, especially those of Sutton Scotney who, before they rose in November 1830, had in October directly petitioned the king for parliamentary reform by sending an emissary to Brighton; where he was rudely denied an audience. Now in mid June, Cobbett explained that he was an 'utter stranger to the neighbourhood of SUTTON SCOTNEY', a mere 'little hamlet' on the London to Salisbury road, 'which I have never passed through but twice in my life, and knew neither Masons (brothers who were transported), nor anyone else in the three adjacent parishes of Wonston, Bullington and Barton Stacey', from which Henry Cooke, executed at Winchester for his role in Swing, came.[34]

Cobbett then revealed that, in order to attribute Swing to his incitement, there had been a regular canvas amongst the [Swing] prisoners in the gaol at Winchester, to find out whether any one would acknowledge that he was acquainted with me, or had been influenced or instigated to me'. Finally, Cobbett explained, there had been a parallel witch-hunt at Battle in Sussex, the scene of the first Swing Riot in that county and the venue for one of his October lectures.[35] These attempts directly to implicate Cobbett in the Sussex events involved not only local magistrates, but government ministers and even the king himself. Despite this conspiracy, Cobbett was saved from conviction and punishment by the refusal of 'the excellent people of Battle' to bear witness against him. He would have celebrated the Reform Bill's passage there, where

[32] For a general survey see George Rudé, 'English Rural and Urban Disturbances on the Eve of the First Reform Bill, 1830–1831', *Past and Present*, 37 (1967), pp. 87–102.

[33] *Political Register*, 16 June 1832.

[34] Hobsbawm and Rudé, *Captain Swing*, p. 223.

[35] *Political Register*, 16 June 1832; I. Dyke, *William Cobbett and Rural Popular Culture* (Cambridge, 1992), esp. pp. 186–89.

he was known, but chose instead Barton Stacey where he was not, because his 'festival' was to be held 'near to the spot where . . . COOKE lay buried'.[36]

Two early indications of the temper of new post-reform Whig government, their attitude towards the Tolpuddle Martyrs and their enactment of the New Poor Law of 1834 were of great significance. If the prolonged Reform Bill crisis had served to heighten political awareness among all sectors of the southern population, so too did the 1832 Act's deficiencies among democratic elements in southern towns and at least some villages. This was reflected in the political unions functioning in several locations and the perception of many magistrates that the readership of the radical press, most worryingly of the *Political Register*, was expanding into the rural proletariat aided by the proliferating new beer shops. The presence of political unions, reported for example in the *Poor Man's Guardian*, was but one reason behind the Grand National Consolidated Trade Union's attempt to launch an initiative to embrace agricultural workers in trade unionism. Although the famous case of Tolpuddle is traditionally interpreted as an isolated attempt at union organisation in an obscure part of Dorset, at least two of the Martyrs had links with metropolitan radicals and with other political activists in local market towns. This dimension is hardly revealed if events are considered in the light of particular prosecution initiative on the part of the local squire, James Frampton, on an obscure charge of administering oaths. However, Home Office intelligence sources were aware of the GNCTU's initiative and this probably determined Melbourne to go along with Frampton's intent to indict the six farm labourers on a charge severe enough for their ultimate transportation. Contrary to the impression given in many histories of the episode, the Martyrs' fate did not end southern agricultural labourers' attempts to unionise, which continued into the late 1830s.[37]

With the new government of 1832, the Poor Law Commission got into its utilitarian stride. Driven by the publication of its infamous Chadwickian perversion of the evidence, the notorious Poor Law Amendment Act sailed through parliament with the minimum amount of opposition from MPs,[38] yet inevitably arousing Cobbett's finest polemic. He described the proposals as a fundamental assault on the basic tenets of English welfare provisions accepted and guaranteed from the reign of Elizabeth. The new Acts constituted a vicious assault on the fundamental rights of poor people:

> above all things, every man and woman and child . . . looks upon his parish as being partly his; and a sufficiency of food and raiment he looks upon as his inheritance. Never, let what will happen, will these people lie down and starve quietly.[39]

[36] *Political Register*, 16 June 1832.

[37] See below, Chapter 7, pp. 127–51; see also Roger Wells, 'Tolpuddle in the Context of English Agrarian History, 1780–1850', in John Rule, ed., *British Trade Unionism, 1750–1850: The Formative Years* (1988), pp. 98–142.

[38] A. Brundage, *The Making of the Poor Law Amendment Act, 1834–38* (London, 1978), ch. 3.

[39] Dyke, *op cit.* pp. 194–95, citing *Political Register*, 29 Feb. 1834.

The death of William Cobbett in June 1835 prevented him from seeing the accuracy of his prophecy.

Rural discontent, deprivation and desperation were much aggravated by the passage of the Poor Law Amendment Act. This hated measure, which threatened the loss of all non-medical outdoor relief for able-bodied males, put a new imperative on raising wages, while the virtual unity of Whigs and Tories in the parliamentary passage of the Act, provided radicals with a golden opportunity to highlight the politics of the post-reform state and its continuing hostility to working class interests. This radical onslaught over government-inspired poor-law reform, notably disseminated by Cobbett's *Political Register* and Hetherington's *Poor Man's Guardian*, generated widespread popular anxiety which became sheer fear when the assistant commissioners arrived in the field and encouraged local authorities to commence implementation of the Act's principles over the winter of 1834–35, before the new Poor Law Unions had been formed let alone become operative. In this atmosphere defensive trade unionism aiming to prise out higher wages, and to insist on full employment to compensate for the loss of allowance in aid of wages and the host of other payments, together with unemployment pay or parchially organised work-schemes, seemed essential. The resultant struggles served to heighten political consciousness of all those on the receiving end of Utilitarianism in action.[40]

Resistance to the Poor Law in the rural south may not have experienced either the intensity or the relative success achieved in the north at a slightly later date. Nor did the issue generate the ferocity of popular politicisation seen in non-rural and principally industrialising theatres elsewhere. Hence historians' traditional concentration on the midlands and especially the north, which we wish to qualify here. Chartism in its historiographically traditional arenas derived directly from the Amendment Act, as well as from the struggle for Factory Reform. If no such particular industrial issue was present in the south, except perhaps the failure of the agrarian trade unionism of 1835–36, the Poor Law furore served to create a climate in which Chartism took some root in the south.

By the 1830s, Southern England contained hardly any of those large concentrations of industrial workers which were to provide the main context of the movement in the midlands and north, nor did it have London's sizeable artisan population with its long tradition of radicalism. Chartist leaders certainly attempted to radicalise the Cornish miners, but in this they were unsuccessful. Yet, only part of the history of Chartism can be learned from a concentration on the working-class populations of the new industrial Britain and of the capital. An examination of southern Chartism is essential to any assessment of the movement's claim to be a national political movement. There were groups of Chartists in probably all southern towns and in very many villages. It was their

[40] See below, Chapter 6, pp. 91–125. For the poor law in a 'moral economy' context see K.D.M. Snell, *Annals of the Labouring Poor: Social Change and Agrarian England, 1660–1900* (Cambridge, 1985), ch. 3. Contrast the lack of understanding of social relations in the neoclassical economic approach of G.R. Boyer, *An Economic History of the English Poor Law, 1750–1850* (Cambridge, 1990).

presence and activities, reported frequently, despite the regional implications of its title, in Chartism's leading newspaper, the *Northern Star*, which helps to sustain that claim, even though there was no large-scale mobilisation of support. The local geography of Chartism in itself can raise questions over the movement's appeal in particular contexts: why was Chartism, for example, proportionately stronger in Bath than Bristol? in Brighton than Southampton? Why did it take root in Dorset, but not in Hampshire's Test and Stoke valleys, which had been centres of radicalism in the early 1830s?[41]

This book does not pretend to be a comprehensive study, but the essays do collectively constitute a challenge to the geography of some common presentations of the history of popular protest. Patterns of protest change. The shifting economic geography which produced the 'industrialisation' of the north and midlands and of south Wales and lowland Scotland, also entailed a 'de-industrialisation' for the south, separating, for example, the metal miners of Cornwall by hundreds of miles from a comparably dense industrial population.[42] Things were in many and important respects different in the southern part of the country, but that does not justify a reputation for passivity. In a high moment of the confident conservatism of the 1980s a recently launched glossy magazine, *Southern Life*, remarked 'perhaps here in the south we are so well-rooted in the past that radical change does not undermine our way of life'.[43] 1985 was the 150th anniversary of William Cobbett's death. That pugnacious southern journalist had a better understanding of the relationships of protest and history in the context of resistance. He came to see that only a thoroughgoing political reform could purge the country from the adverse affects of radical economic changes:

> There is no principle, no precedent, no regulations . . . favourable to freedom, which is not to be found in the Laws of England or in the example of our Ancestors. Therefore,

[41] See below, Chapters 4, 5, and 7, pp. 67–80, 81–89, 91–125. Contrast the geographical complexity suggested by the sites listed in the appendix entitled 'Location and Timing of Chartist Activity', in D. Thompson, *The Chartists: Popular Politics in the Industrial Revolution* (Aldershot, 1984), pp. 341–68, with the ludicrously simplified map headed 'Main Chartist Areas in Britain', in R. Pope (ed.), *Atlas of British Social and Economic History since c. 1700* (London, 1989), pp. 186. Dorothy Thompson's book can serve as an introduction to the vast literature on Chartism. Among few studies of southern localities are R.B. Pugh, 'Chartism in Somerset and Wiltshire', in Asa Briggs (ed.), *Chartist Studies* (London, 1959), pp. 174–219; D. McNulty, 'Class and Politics in Bath, 1832–1848', *Southern History*, 8 (1986), pp. 112–29; and idem, 'Bristol Trade Unions in the Chartist Years', in Rule, ed., *British Trade Unionism*, pp. 220–36; Alfred Jenkin, 'The Cornish Chartists', *Journal of the Royal Institute of Cornwall*, 9 (1982).

[42] For analysis of de-industrialisation generally see Maxine Berg, *The Age of Manufactures, 1700–1820* (London, 1994), pp. 98–114. For two specific southern cases see Brian Short, 'The De-industrialisation Process: A Case Study of the Weald 1600–1850' in P. Hudson (ed.), *Regions and Industries: A Perspective on the Industrial Revolution in Britain* (Cambridge, 1989), pp. 156–174; and Adrian Randall, 'Work, Culture and Resistance to Machinery in the West of England Woollen Industry', ibid., pp. 175–200.

[43] *Southern Life*, January 1984.

I say we ask for, and we want nothing new. We have great constitutional laws and principles, to which we are unmoveably attached. We want *great alteration* but we want *nothing new.*

The great alteration did not happen in his lifetime. If Cobbett was a national figure and had to seek election in the so-called Reform Parliament for Oldham, rather than in one of the post-1832 constituencies of his native Surrey, much of his writing was nevertheless aimed at southern working-people in general and at agricultural workers in particular. Cobbett tried, with some success, to politicise these people. He would not have been surprised that many of them supported Chartism, nor that the southern movement developed resurgent agrarian trade unionism in Tolpuddle country. Southern protest in the 1830s and 1840s drew on a long history, central to which was the struggle to live.

2

The Revolt of the South West, 1800–1: A Study in English Popular Protest

Roger Wells

In a classic, Edward Thompson finally destroyed the assumption that food riots were merely an automatic plebeian reaction to unfortunate spasmodic conjunctions of high food prices and unemployment. In place of such 'crass economic reductionism' he successfully constructed a functional analysis of the food riot, the 'moral economy' of the eighteenth-century crowd.[1] The salient components might be summarised as follows. Primarily the 'moral economy' demanded pure food, honestly measured, at a fair price. Theoretically marketing was to be a transparent process, publicly executed; transactions should take place in the open market. Any deviation was immoral. The food adulterator equalled the farmer or dealer who hoarded to stimulate prices rises, who used secret marketing procedures to conceal the true level of stocks, or made fictitious sales to manipulate prices. These practices threw the 'natural' price-determining mechanism out of gear. Prices depended on the volume of produce physically in the market place; therefore farmers or dealers who conveyed their stocks to distant markets similarly deprived the local market of its rightful supply, raising prices paid by local consumers. This was based on a perception of ancient law, codified by the Book of Orders in 1630, which gave magistrates considerable powers over markets, producers and dealers. While statute law had been amended in 1772, and the Edwardian legislation repealed, the ideals survived, supported by tradition at every level of society, maintained by various types of market supervision, and ultimately by Lord Chief Justice Kenyon, who ruled that the offences of forestalling, regrating and engrossing, remained illegal under common law after 1773.[2]

This essay offers some refinements to the Thompson thesis, partially within the context of the debate which it initially provoked. The 1790s witnessed growing pressure on the nation's ability to feed itself, especially with cereals, the primary subsistence source. Two major national crises in 1794–96 and 1799–1801

---

[1] E.P. Thompson, 'The Moral Economy of the English Crowd in the Eighteenth Century', *Past and Present* (1971), pp. 76–136. Early commentators on this article took issue only with some of Thompson's underlying assumptions, not with his main thesis: see A.W. Coats, 'Contrary Moralities: Plebs, Paternalists and Political Economists'; and E.F. Genovese, 'The Many Faces of Moral Economy: A Contribution to a Debate', ibid., 54 (1972), pp. 130–33; 58 (1973), pp. 160–68.

[2] Thompson, 'The Moral Economy of the English Crowd', especially pp. 83–88, 99–101, 108–9.

demonstrated the fragility of the grain supply following substandard harvests.[3] Despite the suggestion that the early period of industrialisation saw a 'rising union mentality' with popular demands for wages equal to subsistence costs,[4] the 'moral economy' remained the people's ideal answer to the problems posed, and the crowd their weapon. But mass action, and its control, when examined at regional levels, indicate a range of factors which influence both these subjects. Because the crisis of 1800–1, examined here, was national, and because the government and parliament took important measures to mitigate the worst effects, national policy affected developments. Other factors demand analysis. Regional economic and social structures are two of the most important. To these we must add the food supply at the local and national levels, and the all important question of poor relief. All these are variables. For example, although the models provided by the 'moral economy' were constantly available, differing circumstances decided firstly whether the 'moral economy' was invoked, secondly whether it was implemented, and thirdly which of its components were considered relevant in specific situations. For this reason, contemporary analysis of causal factors is the last but no means least important factor.

The economy of all three counties of the south west, Cornwall, Devon and Somerset,[5] was partly agricultural and partly industrial. Each county possessed significant 'centres of consumption'. In Cornwall the greatest centres were the western mining areas. In Devon and south-west Somerset the major centres were almost all engaged in some branch of the textile industry. Of these, Exeter was the largest with over 19,000 inhabitants. Nineteen smaller centres in Devon varied in sized from Northam with just over 2,000 to Tiverton with more than 6500 souls. Exceptions to the textile rule were Plymouth, with 16,000 inhabitants, and the burgeoning neighbouring parishes of Stoke Damarell and East Stonehouse, the site of the Devonport dockyard.[6] These two parishes held over 31,000 people in 1801, nearly 3000 of whom worked in the Royal Dockyard. Brixham and Dartmouth were the only other places whose populations depended primarily on industries other than textiles.

These towns and urban centres primarily depended on the agricultural produce of the region. The predominance of pastoral farming is a nineteenth-century development; in 1800 arable produce was still the most important. Wheat and

---

[3] The national crises have been subjected to in-depth analysis in Roger Wells, *Wretched Faces: Famine in Wartime England, 1793–1801* (Gloucester, 1988). The prosperity of working-class urban dweller's in Devon's corporate towns has been subjected to a novel interpretation by John Bohstedt, *Riots and Community Politics in England and Wales, 1790–1810* (1983), esp. chs 1–2; however, Devon's urban rioters are isolated from others in the region, notably the miners, and Bohstedt's analysis gives inadequate attention to the critically important context of national crisis.

[4] Genovese, 'The Many Faces of Moral Economy', pp. 164–65.

[5] This study is concerned only with the riotous south-western part of Somerset, south and west of a line from Wincanton to the mouth of the Parret.

[6] In 1801 the town was known as Plymouth Dock. Dock was renamed Devonport in 1824, but I have referred to it by its later name here.

barley were the main crops, but in Cornwall barley clearly predominated. The food supply of Plymouth and the Cornish mining areas depended on some supplementation of indigenous produce by additional supplies from eastern England. Plymouth's total demand increased with the steadily expanding population of Devonport and the frequent anchorage of the Fleet in Torbay served to increase the pull exercised over the fertile agricultural region of south-east Cornwall, thereby depriving the western mining area, and putting additional strains on the region's self-sufficiency.[7] Most of the other towns, including Exeter, whose markets were famous for their ample supplies, relied on the produce of local farmers.[8]

Whereas the Devon and Somerset centres were supplied through their markets, the situation in parts of Cornwall differed. Several towns, including some in the mining areas, had no corn markets. Redruth lost its corn market after the riots of 1773, and the inspector's returns from Truro indicate only irregular cereal sales.[9] Padstow was also without, and the townsfolk and local miners went regularly 'Round to the farmer's houses in the country to purchase their corn'.[10]

During the war miners' employment prospects were good and wages high.[11] Demand for labour in most of Devon's ports, especially Devonport, was also good. But the textile industry had been seriously hit by the war, with the loss of continental markets, notably the Spanish and as early as 1799 it was realised that the serge industry 'will never regain its former extent'. In the event the war saw the 'final collapse' of the Exeter serge industry, and Tiverton was but one town where poor rates soared, 'entirely from the want of labour'. The stoppage of the Baltic trade by the Armed Neutrality in 1800 removed, if temporarily, the remaining overseas market.[12] The march of machinery was also having

[7] J. Drowas, Bristol, to E.F. Hatton, Under-Secretary, Home Office, 14 April 1800, PRO, HO 42/49.

[8] This brief survey is based on J. Rowe, *Cornwall in the Age of the Industrial Revolution* (Liverpool, 1955); J.G. Rule, 'Some Social Aspects of the Cornish Industrial Revolution', in R. Burt (ed.), *Industry and Society in the South West* (Exeter, 1970); R. Fraser, *A General View of the Agriculture of Cornwall* (1794); C.B. Worgan, *A General View of the Agriculture of Cornwall* (1811); M. Overton, 'The 1801 Crop Returns for Cornwall', in M. Havinden (ed.), *Husbandry and Marketing in the South West* (Exeter, 1973); W.G. Hoskins, *Devon* (1954); W.W. White, *History, Gazeteer and Directory of Devon* (1850; new edn, ed. W.E. Minchinton, Newton Abbot, 1968); R. Fraser, *A General View of the Agriculture of Devon* (1794); C. Vancouver, *A General View of the Agriculture of Devon* (1808); M. Overton and W.E. Minchinton, 'The 1801 Crop Returns for Devon', *Devon and Cornwall Notes and Queries*, 32 (1973), pp. 197–203; VCH, *Somerset*, ii (1911); J. Billingsley, *A General View of the Agriculture of Somerset* (2nd edn, 1798); T. Davis, *A General View of the Agriculture of Wiltshire* (1794).

[9] W. Giddy, Tredea, to Addington, 20 April 1801, Devon County Record Office (subsequently DCRO), Sidmouth Papers (subsequently SP), D152M/Corr. 1801. PRO, Ministry of Agriculture and Fisheries (subsequently MAF), 10/284, 285.

[10] Collector of Customs, Padstow, harvest return, 31 October 1800, PRO, Board of Trade (subsequently BT), 6/139.

[11] Drowas to Hatton, 14 April 1800, PRO, HO 42/49. Fraser, *Cornwall*, p. 21.

[12] White, *History Gazeteer and Directory of Devon*, notes this decline for every town. D. and S. Lysons, *Devonshire*, 2 vols (1822), i, pp. cci–ccciv; W.G. Hoskins, *Industry, Trade and People in Exeter, 1688–1800* (Manchester, 1935), p. 81; Lieutenant-Colonel Harding, *The History of Tiverton*, 2 vols (Tiverton,

some effect on demand for textile workers, though the primary arena for the struggle against machines was the border region between Somerset and Wiltshire.[13] None the less the decline of the textile industry in our area ensured that even at Exeter, where the distributive trades expanded as the town developed as a major road centre and 'helped considerably to allay the first symptoms of economic distress', there were large numbers 'hardly one generation removed from the labouring class'. Modbury was 'filled entirely with poor decayed Manufacturers'.[14] Thus the population of many towns was doubly vulnerable to rising prices.

The government's policy in 1800–1 developed from the emergency measures of 1795. In essence the plan to overcome the subsistence crisis was three-dimensional. First, the deficiency of the 1800 harvest was to be partially remedied by importation. Secondly, steps were taken to reduce cereal consumption by the introduction of bread substitutes. Thirdly, the national food supply was to be equally distributed through the mechanism of the free internal provision market. The last aspect is crucial. What Thompson has called the 'triumph of the new ideology of political economy' evolved from a pragmatic appreciation of a political and economic situation, and Adam Smith's 'superb, self-validating essay in logic' was consulted to provide a relevant theoretical base. The Pitt ministry publicly adopted this stance during the extremely critical months of June and July 1795. The decision was upheld by parliament the following autumn, and the government rigidly adhered to it, with suitable declarations whenever popular actions threatened to destroy free trade.[15]

The 1800 harvest failed to remedy the shortages following the deficient 1799 harvest, and in September 1800 grain prices rocketed. In many provincial urban markets riotous crowds imposed maximum prices, disrupting supplies, and famine threatened.[16] The Duke of Portland, as Home Secretary, worked hard to control this situation, and ordered local authorities to overthrow price controls. Two of his letters, to the Town Clerk of Nottingham, and the Lord Lieutenant of Oxfordshire, the Duke of Marlborough, were widely published to disseminate government policy. The former was instructed

continued

1845), i, p. 148; Andrew Clephane to James Losh, 11 April 1801; R.M. Buddle-Atkinson and G.A. Jackson, *Brougham and his Early Friends: Letters to James Losh, 1798–1809*, 3 vols (privately printed, 1908), i, pp. 243–44. *Monthly Magazine*, 9 (1800) p. 515.

[13] The ability of wives to earn 3s. 6d. by spinning had gone by 1808. Vancouver, *General View of Devon*, p. 385; J.S. Taylor, 'Poverty in a West Devon Parish', *Reports of the Devonshire Association*, 101 (1968), pp. 174–75; K.C. Ponting, *The Woollen Industry of South-West England* (Bath, 1971); A. Randall; *Before the Luddites* (Cambridge, 1991).

[14] Hoskins, *Industry, Trade and People*, p. 127; W. Foot, Plymouth to Earl Fortescue, 23 May 1801, DCRO, Fortescue Lieutenancy Papers (subsequently FLP), D1262M/L53.

[15] Wells, *Wretched Faces*, esp. pt 3. Cf. Also J. Ehrman, *The British Government and Commercial Negotiations with Europe, 1783–1793* (Cambridge, 1962).

[16] See the mass of letters on the subject PRO, HO 42/51.

that whenever any reduction in the price of a Commodity has been effected by intimidations it has never been of any duration, and besides, by throwing things out of their natural and orderly courses, it almost necessarily happens that the evil, instead of being remedied, returns with an increased violence . . . whenever a scarcity of Provisions exists . . . the only means which can lead effectually to obviate it, and to prevent the Grain from rising to an excessive price, consist in holding out full security . . . to all Farmers and other lawful Dealers, who shall bring their Corn . . . to market and . . . to suppress . . . every attempt to impede by open acts of violence, or by intimidation, the regular business of the Markets.[17]

But at the time public opinion held that the scarcity was artificial. Portland's high-handedness, his arbitrary assertion of a real scarcity,[18] provoked a massive reaction, a broad-based crisis of confidence in the ministry, and a demand for a parliamentary inquiry.[19] Shaken, the government were only too happy to hide behind parliament which was hurriedly called for 11 November 1800.[20] A select committee thereafter announced its support for 'free trade', confirmed the reality of scarcity, and advocated the renewal of earlier policies. Bounties were again provided for imports, and the plan of conserving available stocks of cereals by greater use of substitutes was strengthened in conjunction with poor relief. On 22 December a new Parish Relief Act was passed to permit, but not to compel, parochial authorities to lay in stocks of all types of food to retail to needy parishioners at a loss. Up to one third of parish relief was to be given in cereal substitutes instead of cash. The most important aspect of policy overall was that the 'moral economy' was not only deemed unconstitutional, but economically counter-productive. The implication of the concepts behind 'moral economy' was that the scarcity was artificial. This notion could not be accepted when parliament insisted that the crisis could only be overcome if cereals were rationed (and price rationing was the only available form for a late eighteenth-century government), and other foods partially used in their stead.[21]

Several important factors decided many local authorities in the south west against the new Act, and made them reluctant to take stringent and costly measures to guarantee food supplies. First, the local harvest was at least average, and in Cornwall above average, though the potato crop failed.[22] Second, most

[17] Portland to George Coldham, and to Marlborough, 10 and 30 September 1800, PRO, HO 42/51; 43/12, fos 110–11.

[18] This point was emphasised in the letter to Marlborough.

[19] October 1800 witnessed the start of a national petitioning movement for the recall of parliament led by London. *The Times* and the provincial press give full details.

[20] Pitt believed parliamentary advocation of free trade more powerful than ministerial. Pitt to Addington, 9 October 1800, Lord Stanhope, *Life of Pitt*, 4 vols (1862), iii, pp. 244–45.

[21] Six Reports from a Commons Select Committee, and two from another in the Lords, announced this to the nation. The reports are printed in *Debrett's Parliamentary Debates*, 3rd series, 14. Parish Relief Act, 41 George III, cap, 12.

[22] The replies from the clergy, the tax and customs officers to government all agree on this. The harvest was most productive in the extreme west. Poorer yields were reported in north Somerset,

agricultural workers were provided with provisions at constant and low prices by their employers. Some rural workers in Somerset were similarly protected against the pressures of inflation by the Speenhamland system.[23] Third, the provision of parochial food supplies under the Act placed an immediate heavy burden on the rates, which the many thousands just above the poverty line could ill afford to pay.[24] But the greatest obstacle to the Act was the poor's hostility to bread substitutes. The vicar of Bideford's efforts on behalf of government earned him a stern rebuke accompanied by threats:

> Mr Parson this is to let you know you had better read no more about pinching our Bellis on shoe Lowance of Bread, you had better open your heart and shew more Generosity about the Poor and preach Charity instead.[25]

Magistrates for the Williton Division of Somerset candidly admitted that they

> found it much better to leave the Poor . . . to their own choice of food . . . from the general dislike we found the Poor to entertain against being compelled to take any part of their Relief in any other than the usual way.[26]

Moreover, those magistrates who favoured the Act complained that it gave them insufficient powers over recalcitrant overseers.[27] A combination of rate-conscious overseers and diet-conscious poor served to defeat the Act's intention of ensuring supplies throughout the coming year.

Precedent was therefore a greater determinant than the new Act when poor relief was extended. The system of supplying the poor with cheap grain was expanded in some parishes. Farmers at Newton Ferrers agreed to provide cheap barley to all parishioners,[28] and non-employees were supplied from the granaries of the Drake Estate Home Farm.[29] Elsewhere the rates were used to subsidise the price of locally produced grain and potatoes to the rural poor.[30] Identical

continued
but in our area the crops were average or above. PRO, Pitt Papers, ii 30/8/291, fos 46, 48, 63–64; HO 42/54; BT 6/139.

[23] Lord Rolle, Bicton, Devon, to Fortescue, 28 December 1800, DCRO, FLP, D1262M/L46; Vancouver, *General View of Devon*, pp. 361–63; Worgan, *General View of Cornwall*, p. 159; VCH, *Somerset*, ii, pp. 327, 329.

[24] Rolle to Fortescue, 28 December 1800, DCRO, FLP, D1262M/L46. Rolle advocated subscriptions among the affluent instead.

[25] Mayor of Bideford to Portland with enclosures, 8 January 1801, PRO, HO 42/61.

[26] Return, 8 April 1801, Somerset County Record Office (subsequently SCRO), Quarter Sessions Roll, Easter 1801, CQ/3/1/369.

[27] Rev. E. Giddy to Addington, 13 February 1801, DCRO, SP, D152M/Corr. 1801. Overseers continually frustrated Berkshire justices' attempts to order greater poor relief. M. Neuman, 'Speenhamland in Berkshire', in E.W. Martin (ed.), *Comparative Developments in Social Welfare* (1972), esp. pp. 107–18.

[28] *Exeter Flying Post*, 1 January 1801.

[29] Estate Account Book, DCRO, D346M/E16.

[30] Clayhidon Vestry Minute, 23 November 1800. Rev. R. Walker, and J. Inglett Fortescue, to

schemes operated in some densely populated Cornish parishes, but their accounts show that grain was purchased locally on a monthly basis.[31] Somerset's
Speenhamland parishes increased wage supplements considerably, and more
people received them.[32] In the towns extra relief was provided in cash from
the rates, and in subsidised bread from subscription funds. But only a small
minority of authorities in the centres of consumption acted to guarantee food
supplies. Plymouth Corporation led a subscription to purchase corn to sell to
the poor at low rates, but the scheme was only operational during the winter.[33]
Plymouth and Exeter participated in a government inspired scheme to use Scotch
herrings, but a host of difficulties during the first quarter of 1801 minimised
the impact of this source on the overall food supply.[34]

The relief operations undertaken by subscriptions and poor relief officials,
combined with capitalist market conditions, were of fundamental importance.
For while the south west depended on some supplementation of indigenous
produce, markets were still regional; after September 1800 regional prices
reflected the *relative* abundance of the south-western harvest. The lack of bulk
buying by local authorities over the winter failed to increase to any great extent
local demand and regional prices, though the rejection of the economy
programme led to no reduction in the normal consumption of bread corns.
While prices rose continuously during the winter, they remained under those
current in the eastern counties until April 1801; therefore the south-west regional
markets failed to attract their customary suppliers from East Anglia and the
south east. An Ivybridge man reported that, 'our Harvest has been abundant

continued

Earl Fortescue, 26 March and 4 April 1801, DCRO, D1061 A/PV, I; FLP, D1262M/L48, L59.

[31] Breage vestry decided to purchase on 31 October 1800. 'Respectable' ratepayers were free
to make bargains on behalf of the overseers in the first instance, but early in 1801 agents had to be
sent to Helson. Morwenstow parish purchased corn and potatoes locally. Cornwall County Record
Office (subsequently CCRO), Overseers' Accounts and Vestry Minutes, DD P18/8/1; P110/12/3;
P158/12/2, 3.

[32] Mells was typical. In December 1800 the number in receipt of payments increased from thirty-
five to eighty-seven. Simultaneously wage supplements were introduced in the smaller parishes of
Stoke St Mary and Staplegrove. At Milverton, a non-Speenhamland parish, expenditure on 'in
Necessity' payments doubled between October and December. SCRO, Overseers' Accounts, D/P/mb.
13/2/5; D/P/stoke S. ma. 13/2/2.3; D/P/stapg. 13/2/3; D/P/milv, 13/2/3.

[33] Information from files of local newspapers: *Exeter Flying Post, Sherborne Mercury, Bath Chronicle,
Bonner and Middleton's Bristol Journal, Felix Farley's Bristol Journal.*

[34] The papers of the committee elected at Exeter are extant. Although these administrators
continually invited orders from local authorities within a considerable radius of the city, sales were
sluggish. Many correspondents feared that consignments would be rotten on arrival. Others had
already ordered trial deliveries of Cornish pilchards. Rural authorities stressed the poor's disinclination. Only where powerful resident landlords actively assisted (Lord Borringdon of Plympton was
one of the few) was herring extensively used. Exeter City Record Office (subsequently ECRO),
Correspondence and Minutes of the Exeter Committee, Misc. Papers, box 10. Notices issued by
the mayor of Plymouth, chairman of the Plymouth Committee, Plymouth City Archive, W 646,
bundle 1.

both of Wheat & Barley & our Market lower than any other in the Kingdom; in consequence we are left to subsist ourselves'. The official returns prove his point.[35]

The south west's centres of consumption were forced to rely on indigenous produce, 'naturally' brought to market. Even 'the immense consumption at Plymouth, Stonehouse, & Dock' was 'virtually . . . supplied by the Growth of Devon'. Captain Rodd, stationed at Totnes with a detachment from the Cornish Militia, noted the daily supplies of corn from local farmers, ground and sent to Plymouth by the town's millers. The major centres were frequently placed 'in most critical situation' over the winter. The stocks of Plymouth millers and bakers were often under forty-eight hours' demand.[36]

The crisis point was reached in March 1801. Parkham labourers 'lost one and two Days work in going about to the Farmers to procure Corn'.[37] At Bideford 'the principal complaint is for want of corn and Potatoes'. In March only half the 120 bushels of wheat, and two fifths of the hundred bushels of barley consumed weekly, appeared in the markets. On 1 April there was insufficient for 'any private Family Miller or Mealman', and the mayor found on touring the local farmers that under one in twenty 'hath more Potatoes than for his own use, nor one in Ten . . . hath any more Barley than is necessary for the poor of their Parish'.[38] An investigation into stocks in the Hundreds of Ermington and Plympton immediately to the east of Plymouth revealed insufficient barley for the use of the nineteen constituent parishes, and a small 'overplus' of wheat which was 'insufficient for one week's consumption' of Plymouth. The magistrates concluded that 'the country . . . [is] certainly drained . . . nearly if not quite exhausted'.[39]

In these circumstances of absolute dearth there was very little scope for town workers to demand higher wages to counteract escalating prices. Some Cornish mine-owners supplied their men 'with Corn at very reduced prices with an enormous' loss, but these decisions were taken after the Cornish bench suggested the measure to control the major disturbances of 1796, during which the miners went on the offensive against the food suppliers rather than their employers.[40] However, there was one major exception; the Devonport dock workers were unionised. Each of the several trades elected a committee, from which

[35] A Totnes miller confirmed that low local prices 'rendered a supply from . . . the Eastern Counties . . . impracticable'. D. Yonge to R. Pole-Carew, 25 October 1800, CCRO, Carew MSS, CC/L/31; Welsford to Fortescue, 4 April 1801, PRO, HO 42/61.

[36] Rodd to Portland, 28 October 1800; Welsford to Fortescue, 4 April 1801, PRO, HO 42/52, 61; Colonel Bastard MP, Commanding Officer Devon Militia, to Addington, 4 May 1801, DCRO, SP, D152M/Corr. 1801.

[37] Deposition of John Bate, 15 April 1801, DCRO, FLP, D1262M/L52.

[38] J. Willcock to Fortescue, 1 and 15 April 1801, DCRO, FLP, D1262M/L52.

[39] Bastard to Addington, 3 April. Statement and table forwarded to Fortescue by T. Lane and W. Symons, 11 April 1801, DCRO, SP, D152M/Corr. 1801; FLP, D1262M/L53.

[40] Cornwall Easter Sessions notice, 7 April; *Exeter Flying Post*, 14 April 1796. Giddy to Addington, 20 April 1801, DCRO, SP, D152M/Corr. 1801.

delegates were deputed to a central committee. Similar organisations existed at the other royal yards, and 'communications of Events' were made between them. The workers were so powerful that Commissioner Franshawe, in charge at Devonport, warned that 'the whole navee workes in all the yards are liable to be Protracted by what may be done in the Case of an individual in either of them'. In March 1801 delegates from each central committee met in London to petition the Navy Board for pay increases. The Board met them on 1 April to tell them that whilst a permanent wage increase was out of the question, 'it was the desire of the Lords of the Admiralty that a Bounty should be . . . given them during the present high Price of Provisions in proportion to the number of their families'. The Board recorded 'that the Men appeared satisfied with this answer'. The strength of these workers was founded on their vital role in the war effort, and is clearly untypical, despite the delightful irony that a branch of the very government which initiated the Combination Acts 'maturely' negotiated with its own employees.[41]

The comparative weakness of other sectors of the working population was but a minor factor in determining popular reactions. Badly supplied markets and rocketing prices over the winter provoked great tension and speculation on the causes.[42] Many agreed that the farmers were withholding supplies, thereby stimulating prices. A handwritten bill, read by order of the author by the vicar of Branscombe to his congregation, complained of 'the Roages of Farmers' who were 'more like savages than any thing else to think you keep up such a extortionate prise of every thing, and constantly every day rising'.[43] At a meeting of 'the lower class' of Exonians on 23 March, 'Resolutions were produced read and approved of complaining of the great Scarcity of all kinds of provisions, particularly Bread, alledging it was owing to the Farmers not bringing their Corn to Market, & not from Scarcity'.[44] But this analysis was not merely the poor's prerogative; 'the Tradesmen immediately above them . . . seem to have imbibed those ideas'. Once rioting commenced an anonymous informant lamented that 'The worst symptoms . . . is the secret good wishes of the middle sort of people', who hoped 'that the mob may be the cats paw to help them to a reduction of prices'. Most importantly, the magistracy were in sympathy with the popular analysis. General Simcoe, the regional military commander, rather ominously reported that everybody praised Lord Chief Justice Kenyon.[45] In September 1800, twelve Devonshire landowners combined publicly to threaten

---

[41] Navy Board Minutes, 1 April. Franshawe to the Navy Board, 11 April, and to Fortescue, 27 April 1801, PRO, Admiralty (subsequently ADM), 106/1916, 2664; HO 42/61.

[42] For example, Plymouth wheat wholesale prices for the first week in each month from September 1800 to March 1801 were (in shillings): 101, 98, 110, 126, 150, 154, 162, PRO, MAF 10/284, 285.

[43] Rolle to Portland with enclosures, 22 December 1800, PRO, HO 42/55.

[44] R. Eales, Devon County Clerk of the Peace to Fortescue, 23 March 1801, DCRO, FLP, D1262M/L59.

[45] Letters to Portland from Simcoe, 27 March, and anon. (Weymouth), 12 April 1801, PRO, HO 42/61.

their tenants with the non-renewal of leases unless they marketed their produce.[46] Justice Montague of Kingsbridge believed that the farmers, aided and abetted by millers and dealers, were 'in a great measure . . . the cause of the existing distresses of the poor', and argued that the moral economic preceptor ought to be embodied within statutory law.[47] Lord Rolle's reaction to the first threat of disturbance was to address farmers on 'the Impolicy as well as Impropriety of . . . asking . . . extravagant Prices', an action imitated by the mayor of Bideford among many others.[48] The farmers were thus condemned by all. Simcoe concluded that 'the language of too many of all Classes' united in this consensus.[49]

The crisis which exploded in March did not uniformly affect the entire region. The town and mining centres of consumption were hit as supplies failed to reach their markets. Simcoe reported that:

> The general conversation of the Country Towns received a tone most hostile to the farmers: & it evidently appeared to me, that more industry was used to disseminate opinions of their Avarice, than to meet the Scarcity with the economy and patience that had been recommended by the Legislature.

Colonel A.J. Taylor, a magistrate, agreed that

> those who have the Management of the poor in the Towns have never done their duty by making proper provision for them, and have studied, to throw all the Odium of starving the people on the Farmers, every art is used by the Inhabitants to inflame the Manufacturers.[50]

Thus the pressure was primarily felt by the miner and the town worker who depended on the open market. Desperation drove them to action. During the first quarter of 1801 the town dweller's frustration became increasingly obvious. The 'common Men' of the Darmouth Volunteers told their officers 'that Government had been applied to long enough & Nothing done for them, therefore it was high time they should do something for themselves to prevent their Families from starving'.[51] The summons of the author of a Stratton handbill was explicit:

---

[46] The notice was published in the *Exeter Flying Post* on 17 September and reissued on 17 October 1800.

[47] Montague to Fortescue, 4 May 1801, DCRO, FLP, D1262M/L53.

[48] Rolle to Portland, 22 December 1800, PRO, HO 42/55; Willcock to Fortescue, 15 April 1801, DCRO, FLP, D1262M/L52.

[49] Simcoe to Fortescue, 28 March 1801, DCRO, FLP, D1262M/L48.

[50] Simcoe to Portland, 27 March, PRO, HO 42/61; Taylor to Simcoe, 1 May 1801, DCRO, FLP, D1262M/L53.

[51] H. Studdy, Commanding Officer Dartmouth Volunteers to Fortescue, 7 April 1801, DCRO, FLP, D1262M/L52. An earlier attempt involving leadership of crowds by Volunteer soldiers in the Exmouth district seems to have been nipped in the bud in December 1800; events are poorly documented but see esp. Captain Marker to Simcoe, 21 December, and Simcoe to Captain Townsend, and Home Office under-secretary King, 26 and 28 December 1800, PRO, HO 100/94, fos 309–13.

My fellow Sufferers and Country Men, now is the time to exert yourselves Men and true born English Men . . . now is the time to come forward and take Vengeance on your Oppressors, Assemble and emeadiatly march forward in Dreadful Array to the Habitations of the Griping Farmer, and Compell them to sell their Corn in the Market, at a fair and reasonable Price, and if any refuse and will not comply with our just demands, we must make them feel the Punishment due to their Oppression and Extortion.[52]

Crowd actions began at Exeter on 23 March, following a week during which crowds met on Southernhay. On the 22nd, a Sunday, 'several of Col. Wrights Volunteers were with them and promised them support'. Wright paraded his men that afternoon, and insisted that 'all those who approved of such meeting' hand in their arms that evening. Ten did so supported by 'a Mob of between 2 and 300, huzzaing them'. Confident that they would be poorly opposed, the crowd agreed to meet on the morrow morning, 'to proceed to different Farmers to inform them quietly that if they do not bring in their Corn to Market they will compel them'.[53] Two thousand accordingly assembled at 7 a.m. The dismissed Volunteers arrived in their regimentals. Papers listing maximum prices for all primary foodstuffs were drawn up, and 'between 7 & 800 of the mob filed off in divisions, towards Crediton, Tiverton, Cullompton'. The crowd returned later 'loaded with Corn' to announce that 'all the Farmers have promised to bring their Corn to Market on Friday' at the stipulated prices. The remainder of the crowd appear to have forced the city bakers to halve their prices.[54] Prices in Exeter's markets were now controlled, and the district's farmers under an obligation to supply it.

Within the following week most towns in Devon and southern Somerset witnessed similar phenomena with some sort of maximum price imposed on the markets. In Devon, Tiverton was affected on the 24th, Crediton and Honiton on the 25th, Dartmouth on the 27th, Totnes, Brixham, Ashburton, Bideford, Torrington, South Molton and Plymouth on the 30th, Modbury and Uffculm on 1 April, and Tavistock on the 2nd. In Somerset crowd action commenced simultaneously with an itinerant mob leaving Wellington on 23 March, and another Taunton on the 25th, Bridgwater on the 28th, and Holcomber and Chard on the 30th. Itinerant crowds were active during the following week in the Stogursey and Nether Stowey district to the west of Taunton while poorly documented incidents in the east of the county included price-fixing around Warminster on 6 April. Trouble in Cornwall started rather later, but rioting was reported from St Austell, St Just and Falmouth on 9 April, Redruth on the 10th, and about the same time from Liskeard and Penzance. On 28 March Simcoe 'concluded' that Devon and Somerset were 'in a complete State of Anarchy'. On the 30th he informed Addington that 'the law of the country was totally

---

[52] Handbill forwarded by Eales to Rolle, 25 April 1801, PRO, HO 42/61.

[53] Eales to Rolle, 22 March 1801, PRO, HO 42/61.

[54] Eales and Rolle, to Fortescue, 23 and 26 March, DCRO, FLP, D1262M/L59; *Bonner and Middleton's Bristol Journal,* 4 April 1801.

overthrown from the Paret to the Teign, and that the mischief was increasing'.[55] The chairman of the Cornish Sessions represented his entire county as being in riot and confusion, and his father a little later confessed that 'most parts of this Country have been disturbed'. The fact that several letters from Simcoe were erroneously filed by the Home Office with the Irish correspondence speaks for itself.[56] The prices from six of the eleven markets making returns for the week ending 11 April demonstrate that some sort of maximum price had been imposed.[57]

Whilst the distribution of disturbances was very wide, excessive violence was not a primary feature, although many reports related that the crowd 'went round to the farmers with a rope in one hand, and a paper in the other, by which the farmers were to engage to sell their corn at reduced prices'.[58] The crowd of course used numbers to threaten but invariably their first object as the Totnes People's Committee stated was 'to claim Humanity of the Farmers', and to obtain 'promises to prevent an approaching Famine . . . by bringing regularly to Market Bread Corn & in the proportion to the Quantity they posses'.[59] Violence seems to have occurred only when farmers refused. Thomas Hookaway of Sandford's experience were typical. The crowd surrounded his house, and demanded his signature, but

> on his hesitating to sign, a person came up to him & pulled out a Rope saying 'if you do not sign here's your Trussel and I'll truss you up' on which many present said 'well done Forward hang him up' & particularly one John Jones Jnr. said aloud 'hang him up hang him up'.

Hookaway signed.[60] Farmer Coneybeare was nearly throttled by a crowd in the street at Ashburton, and a 'farmer of Kingston was suspended' at Modbury. Most farmers capitulated and signed like Hookaway, though many like Christopher Savery of Modbury, 'considering it not to be binding'. Whilst only the interposition of the 'gentlemen' prevented a lynching at Chard, considering the temper of the people the fact that nobody sustained serious injury indicates strong social discipline.[61] Indeed the crowd in several instances was easily deterred. The men of Crediton withdrew with a volley of stones when the farmer identified the leader and threatened to 'apply to a magistrate', and

[55] Simcoe to Fortescue, 28 March, DCRO, FLP, D1262M/L59; and to Addington 30 March 1801, cited by G. Pellow, *The Life and Correspondence of Henry Addington, First Lord Sidmouth*, 3 vols (1847), i, pp. 362–63; *The Times*, 2 April; *Salisbury and Winchester Journal*, 13 April 1801.

[56] E. Giddy to Portland, 1 April; Simcoe to Portland, 28 March to 3 April, PRO, HO 42/61, 100/94. W. Giddy to Addington, 20 April, 1801, DCRO, SP, DI52M/Corr. 1801.

[57] PRO, MAF 10/285.

[58] *The Times*, 2 April; *Bonner and Middleton's Bristol Journal*, 25 April 1801.

[59] Totnes Committee of the People handbill, 3 April 1801, PRO, HO 42/61.

[60] Hookaway's deposition, 3 April 1801, PRO, HO 42/61.

[61] For these incidents see DCRO, FLP, D1262M/L50, L53, L54 and L59. The man strung up at Chard was a farmer who had refused to sign; anon., Yeovil, to Portland, 31 March 1801, PRO, HO 42/61.

a Plymouth baker, a member of the Volunteer cavalry, faced the crowd with a drawn sword, successfully 'intimidate[d] the nearest and prevented any mischief being done to his person or premises'.[62]

On 5 April Simcoe lamented to Portland 'the System of compromise all around me'. At the outset of the riots almost every corporate authority capitulated to the crowd's demands, and accepted the maximum. Devon Grand Jurors, who were actually empaneled when disturbances began at Exeter, were so incensed that 'neither the Mayor or any Justice took any Notice', that they deputed two of their number to consult Mr Justice Le Blanc, the Assize judge. He replied,

> that an assembly of persons requiring the price of Corn to be lowered & dispersing without committing any Act of violence had better not be noticed by the Magistrates by taking any of the persons into custody . . . & that their having acted illegally the preceding Day, could not be coupled with the merely assembling, to create any present illegality, for which the Mayor was authorized to disperse them.

This opinion strengthened the city authority's resolution not to oppose the crowd. Elsewhere the decision of the authorities against intervention was either expedient or pragmatic. The Totnes magistracy made no attempt to stop their townsfolk's ventures into the countryside, and a committee of aldermen 'appointed for pacifying the rioters' three days later accordingly supported the maximum price they had set. When miller Harrison refused to sign his agreement, the committee 'repeatedly and forcibly' represented

> that if he would not sign the paper . . . the Mob had declared their determination . . . [to] send to all the Mobs in the County . . . and pull down the Mills . . . and that they the Committee . . . would as long as they lived ascribe and impute to his obstinacy all the Blood that should be split, and all the Evils and Mischief that might happen in consequence.

Harrison signed 'to avoid the horrid Responsibility . . . charged by the Committee Men'.[63] According to reports made to Portland the mayor of Plymouth ordered a baker to abide by limits imposed '& some of the Upper Bench that evening congratulated themselves upon it as a good thing'. When the Cornish riots started the crowd 'so far carried their point as to induce the Magistrates' in the corporate towns 'to call the farmers together & recommend to them to fix a Maximum'. Identical bullying was reported from Somerset.[64]

[62] Deposition of farmer John Fromlett, Sandford, PRO, HO 42/62. John Harris, *A History of Plymouth*, 2 vols (1808, MS copy Plymouth City Library), ii, pp. 141–42.

[63] John Pulling, Totnes, to his brother William in London, 6 April; statement of G. Welsford on events of 1 April, PRO, HO 42/61, 62; T. Kitson to Fortescue, 20 May 1801, DCRO, FLP, D1262M/L53.

[64] E. Giddy to Addington, 20 April, DCRO, SP, D152M/Corr. 1801; *Bonner and Middleton's Bristol Journal*, 11 April 1801.

Although the region, especially Devon, was nominally well provided with regular troops, these were not initially employed.[65] The crowd's success was accelerated by the active support of the numerous town corps of Volunteers. The Volunteers had become 'the Farmers Bull Dogs' in 'vulgar' popular parlance, and those in Devon and Cornwall had already shown a disposition to rid themselves of this epithet during the winter. Several Volunteer corps threatened to deal with the farmers, and although Simcoe dismissed these developments as an ephemeral 'Little Cloud' which would 'pass away', others were not so sure. Their services would have to be bought by setting 'a maximum & other Terms', complained a Cornish magistrate in January 1801. Although there is no actual evidence of participation by Volunteers in Somerset and Cornwall during the March and April riots, law enforcers there clearly endorsed Montague's fear that the 'greater part of them are . . . not to be trusted under the present circumstances'. The Rev. E. Giddy stated his preference to Addington for regular as opposed to volunteer troops, because the former 'might enable us to carry our point'. A Taunton man argued that the town Volunteers were drawn from the same social strata as the rioters and would not have opposed their own neighbours. The crucial role of the Volunteers is well illustrated by events at Brixham. The populace assembled on 29 March, and agreed to tour farms on the morrow. Several Volunteers attended this meeting as they did at Exeter, and their commanding officer, John Underhay, also paraded his men and 'remonstrated . . . with them on the impropriety of going round to the Farmers'. His address was cut short by the arrival of the Sea Fencibles who told Underhay's Volunteers to stick to their resolutions. Underhay tried to maintain his initiative, conversed with several farmers and convened a vestry. Meanwhile Lieutenant Pridham rushed to Dartmouth and ascertained the prices fixed there. The Brixham farmers agreed to honour those prices but comparatively few farmers actually lived in the parish, and the crowd decided to visit adjacent parishes as planned. Underhay and his officers knew this for Pridham told a farmer on the 29th that he 'might as well settle it now . . . tomorrow we should be obliged to sign it'. Underhay kept out of the way on the 30th but the crowd containing many privates assembled at Captain Saunders's house and refused to leave without him. He and Lieutenant Pridham later asserted that they feared 'what might be the consequences unless some person was to go who might have some little influence on their Conduct'. Two borough constables went allegedly for the same purpose. Farmers who were visited testified that the officers

---

[65] There were relatively few of the regular cavalry, the most efficient force for this purpose. The total forces available were as follows. Devon: 1400 militia at Plymouth, and a permanent detachment of seventy cavalry at Devonport, 200 plus cavalry and 650 infantry at Exeter, 200 Militia at Topsham, with small detachments of Cornish Militia and regular cavalry in some South Devon towns. Cornwall: small detachments of regular cavalry at Falmouth, Padstow, St Austell and Truro; three troops of militia at Penzance and Lostwithiel. Somerset: 140 Infantry at Taunton. Based on Duke of York to Addington, February 1801, with report of army strength in Devon, DCRO, SP D152M/Corr. 1801; monthly summaries of returns to the War Office, and regimental returns PRO, WO 17/19, 887, 898, 919, 973, 2785.

led sections of the crowd and that Pridham, at least, was on horseback. Although Pridham 'behav'd . . . with impertinence' at one house, the officers were able to arrive at the farms before the main body and warn the farmers that they should sign immediately; 'hundreds were near your house who will not otherwise by pacified'.[66] Dozens from the Totnes and Newton Abbot Volunteers accompanied the crowd and the Dartmouth folk were led into the countryside by 'Tradesmen' Volunteers.[67] As one Axminster Volunteer said, in the event of his commander ordering 'him to fire' on a crowd attacking farmers, 'he knew exactly where to place the Ball'.[68]

Several factors thus combined to undermine the forces on which society relied for the maintenance of order and the undisputed right to private property. This permitted the crowd to seize and hold the initiative. The corn returns show that several markets were subjected to price controls for a considerable time. Fixed prices lasted at Barnstaple, Totnes, Kingsbridge and Launceston from 11 April until 9 May, and at St Austell from 11 April until 25 July, though wheat prices were raised on 9 May from 80 to 112s. The later price was still well under the county average.[69] Although Totnes miller Pulling exaggerated when he said that the unopposed 'rabble' in all towns had 'appointed' committees to supervise the markets,[70] several examples are documented. After three days rioting at Totnes a committee including aldermen, the vicar, the town clerk, an attorney and the commander of a detachment of troops, was established under the mayor's auspices to adopt 'measures . . . to prevent a continuance'. The crowd responded by electing a 'Committee of the People', who effectively administered the market, though they promised to 'protect Persons and Property from the least outrage' so long as maximum prices were maintained. Their orderliness was emphasised in a handbill which also decreed, 'N.B. The better to prevent Confusion Women are required not to attend the Corn Market'. Miller Harrison, who proved obdurate, was told by the People's Committeemen that 'he shall sign' the agreement, to the accompanying cheers of the crowd. The alderman who eventually obtained the signature promptly delivered the paper to Henry Hannaford 'clerk' to the Committee of the People. All agreed that Hannaford's Committee were the primary force behind the durability of the maximum, and that they continued 'compelling the Farmers to bring in

[66] Account based on deposition of N. Mossey and W. Snelling farmers at Stoke Gabriel, and P. Gillard, farmer at Brixham; letters to Fortescue from Sanders and Pridham, and Underhay explaining their conduct, 20 April and 30 May; Kitson to Fortescue, 25 April 1801, DCRO, FLP, D1262M/L61; PRO, HO 42/61, 62.

[67] Letters from Eales and Studdy to Fortescue, both 30 April; undated memo re participation of the Volunteers, DCRO, FLP, D1262M/L48, L52; Welsford to Roedean, Fortescue's secretary, 1 May 1801, PRO, HO 42/62.

[68] Deposition of J. Lidden, 20 September 1800, DCRO, Sessions Roll, Michaelmas 1800, 3/4B/1b.

[69] PRO, MAF 10/285.

[70] J. to W. Pulling, 6 April 1801, PRO, HO 42/61.

Wheat and sell it' at low prices throughout April.[71] Similar lengthy crowd organisation is documented for Newton Abbot and Modbury. At the former 'the mob stiled themselves . . . the Newton Regulators', ordered the town crier to announce fixed prices each market day and the constables to arrest recalcitrant farmers.[72] Weaver Nicholas Wakeman, the 'leader of the People' at Modbury, and three colleagues met nightly to discuss tactics. Wakeman 'told Andrews . . . a flour man . . . That he might carry flour to Plymouth, & need not smuggle it, he would assure him a free passage'. No wonder Wakeman was known as 'Buonoparte'.[73]

The most interesting example of the exercise of worker power in the vacuum created by the partial abdication of the magistracy developed at Devonport. On 31 March the people of the town imitated proceedings at Plymouth the preceding day, and fixed prices on market goods and on bread supplied by the bakers. Although the farmers obeyed 'and desired the assistance of the Constables to deliver out their potatoes . . . at Low prices', the bakers refused and windows were smashed. The magistracy, who had anticipated trouble, ordered the troops to charge, and three people, two women and a dockyard artisan, were arrested. Although the crowd were subdued, these incidents were but the start of a lengthy confrontation with the highly organised dockyard workers. Soon after the arrests, 'the Dock yard men . . . struck their work having compelled . . . the Storehouse Men . . . to shut up the Store houses', and 'came out of the yard in a body, whooping and huzzaing' to the magistrates, despite the fact that the authorities were 'supported by a Troop of the Queens Bays, the Picquets of the Wilts and East Devon, and the Artillery with four field pieces, loaded with Grape and Canister'. The Central Committee 'approached the magistrates and demanded the release of' the prisoners. The authorities, fearful that 'many hundreds would have fallen', agreed and the men's colleague was shouldered 'and carried . . . thro the town huzzaing and making shouts . . . in the face of the insulted Soldiery'.[74]

The Devonport JPs and the corporation of Plymouth both requested military patrols during the next few days and issued handbills against riots. Although 'A report very generally prevailed that the Dock Yard men intended to seize the Arms in the Dock Yard', the committee's first intention was to negotiate with the bakers and butchers. They issued their own handbill to state 'that our

[71] Committee of the People handbill, 3 April; Welsford to Roedean, n.d., and to Fortescue, 10 May; Town Clerk Totnes to Fortescue, 10 May; Kitson to Fortescue with a summary of Harrison's evidence, and draft reply, both 10 May 1801, PRO, HO 42/61; DCRO, FLP, D1262M/L59.

[72] A.J. Taylor to Fortescue, 1 May 1801, and memo re participation of Volunteers, n.d., DCRO, FLP, D1262M/L52, L53.

[73] Draft list of suspects and witnesses at Modbury, n.d., DCRO, FLP, D1262M/L53; anon., Modbury to Bastard, 15 April 1801, PRO, HO42/61.

[74] Franshawe to the Navy Board, 31 March and 11 April; St Aubyn and Williams, Devonport JPs to Portland, 1 April, and a letter from an eye-witness addressed 'My dearest Brother', with signature erased, 31 March, PRO, ADM 106/1916; HO 42/61. Another eye-witness report was printed by the *Courier,* 2 and 4 April 1801.

Intentions are NOT TO RIOT AND TUMULT'. A projected meeting with butchers' representatives on 3 April failed when only one butcher attended. This drew a stern rejoinder from the committee, addressed to the 'Butchers, Bakers, etc. of Dock and its Vicinity'. All food traders were advised to 'Step forward now and prove yourselves the Friends of Mankind . . . Suffer not your Conduct in future to be the continued Cause of human Misery'. If losses were incurred by selling at reduced prices, 'Complain not . . . you have more than a Compensation in hand, by Advantages you have taken when a Rise has took place'. The bakers agreed, and thirty-nine decided to pay no more than 63s. for a sack of flour. The saving was to accrue to the consumers.[75] But soon after this the forces of law and order, directed from London via the Lord Lieutenants, finally caught up with the rebellious south-west, and the reimposition of traditional sources of power began.

The Home Office primarily feared a repetition of events elsewhere in September 1800, when the supply to urban centres collapsed and greater disorders threatened. In the south west complaints about supplies to markets under controlled prices were heard almost immediately. Kingsbridge was well supplied by the farmers on the first market day after crowd action, but in the following three weeks 'no corn . . . of any consideration' was marketed.[76] After the mayor of Bideford prevailed on farmers to fix lower prices, the complaint of a 'want of a proper supply' was made, and available corn 'was with much difficulty delivered to the poorer sort . . . by the Peck to each person, and not nearly sufficient for them'. Emotive scenes followed:

> The General Cry of the Poor is we are Starving, we are Starving alive, many of them with Money in their hands saying they could not get a potatoe in the Market nor a Penny loaf in the Town was it to save their lives.[77]

Barriers had to be built at Falmouth to protect market stalls. But as Colonel Bastard appreciated, local farmers had to sell in local markets, even if it was to agents there, and the majority of the region's farmers had but small remaining stocks if any.[78] Whatever the dislocation to trade at the local level, long-distance trade, which was more easily disrupted, was now essential if the people were to be fed until harvest. Immediately a maximum was imposed at Totnes, one miller wrote to his partner in London to decide 'how we are going to make the most of the Flour we have in hand'. He though it best to 'ship 50 or 60 Sacks for London' and demanded current prices by return. At Plymouth 'all

[75] Committee handbills, 4 and 7 April; bakers' handbill 6 April; St Aubyn and Williams to Fortescue, 8 April, PRO, HO 42/61; ADM, 106/1916; mayor of Plymouth to Major-General England, 31 March 1801, Plymouth City Archives, W382/5/1–3.

[76] Montague to Fortescue, 4 May 1801, DCRO, FLP, D1262M/L53.

[77] J. Willcock to Fortescue, 15 April 1801, DCRO, FLP, D1262M/L52.

[78] The following section is largely based on this and similar correspondence in DCRO, FLP, D1262M; and Home Office papers in the PRO, HO 42/61 and HO 43/12.

the Corn Factors Agents, Merchants etc . . . countermanded their orders', and corn ships sailed for the east.[79] The bakers abandoned their price ceiling four days after imposing it, and the demand was met for several crucial days only by the arbitrary intervention of Bastard, who ordered the navy victualling agents to purchase corn 'which was not unshipped, as well as that which was actually reshipping'. Economically the implementation of the 'moral economy' was a disaster, except where sufficient stocks were available locally.

The complete cessation of long-distance supplies necessitate urgent action to impose order before famine replaced scarcity. The Home Office recognised that the apathy of the magistracy was the first hurdle, if order were to be restored through traditional channels. Portland told Mount Edgecumbe, the Lord Lieutenant of Cornwall, that his presence was needed to 'give confidence to the well disposed and animate the exertions of the Magistrates in the endeavours to restore tranquillity'. Lords Lieutenant Poulett and Fortescue were ordered to go down on 30 March, exactly a week after rioting commenced. They were to summon special meetings of the magistrates, explain the government's insistence on free trade and enforce it. All Volunteer Corps were to be held in 'readiness to assist the Civil Power'. Commanders were to report immediately any refusals on the part of individuals. The magistrates were to notify their intentions to alleviate distress but also their determination to protect dealers and farmers, and to prosecute anybody arrested for disturbing the peace. Enquiries were to be made into the riots, and 'where there is Evidence . . . the Offenders [were to] be brought before the Magistrates, and the most culpable committed'.[80]

The government believed that 'the possession of an adequate and commanding Military Force is unquestionably the first step to be taken to enable the Civil Power to resume its authority'. The Lords Lieutenant were to arrange this with Simcoe. He quartered infantry in each of 'the Towns of the largest size' with 'a body of cavalry' who would 'pursue . . . Rioters issuing out . . . & . . . follow the Mob into the Country'. This would 'form a Cordon for the Protection of the Farmers' and 'segregate the Peasantry from the Inhabitants of the Town'. The regulars at Exeter were distributed across south and east Devon, and south Somerset. The 29th and the 32nd Foot were drafted into Somerset from Winchester and Bristol. Over 700 Light Dragoons from the 15th Regiment were brought into the area to strengthen existing detachments and to provide Simcoe with a mobile force under his immediate command. Detachments of Artillery were sent to Plymouth. The South Devon Militia, commanded by Colonel Bastard, who together with other senior officers had arrived on the scene, was used to strengthen the military presence in Cornwall. The

---

[79] Some dealers expected rapid price rises from the exhaustion of stocks in the south west and made speculative purchases in the east just before the riots. Undated memo; Bastard to Addington, 4 May 1801, DCRO, FLP, D1262M/L52; SP, D152M/Corr. 1801; St Aubyn and Williams to Portland, 18 April 1801, PRO, HO 42/61.

[80] Draft, Portland to Fortescue and Poulett, 30 March 1801, PRO, HO 42/61.

depleted garrison at Bristol was in turn replenished by troops from the east. The total force in the Western District, south of Bridgwater and west of Sherborne numbered almost 8,000 men, of whom nearly 2,000 were cavalry or artillery.[81] The Commander-in-Chief, the Duke of York, refused any further augmentation on the grounds that these were sufficient 'if the Magistrates will only make use of them and allow them to Act'. Colonel Bastard was however told 'that whatever Acts of Power he may have found . . . necessary' in using troops irrespectively of local magistrates 'will be readily sanctioned and confirmed' by government. Although ministers were anxious that the established local authorities should direct military operations, in default commanding officers were empowered to act on their own initiative.[82]

The speedy suppression of the riots was the primary item on the agenda of County Meetings held for Somerset on 30 March, for Devon on 7 April, and for Cornwall on 14 April.[83] At Taunton action was taken to undo the damage occasioned by Judge Le Blanc's statement at Exeter. The 'Grand Jury and Magistrates' put six questions on riot control to the Recorder of Bristol and three other lawyers, and printed their answers in the form of a handbill. The lawyers stated that the magistrates ought to oppose the intimidation of farmers and that military assistance could be summoned to 'prevent the completion of such illegal Act [i.e. compelling price reductions] . . . without any reference to the Riot Act'. Similarly no recourse to the Riot Act was needed 'if the Mob disperse into small Parties, doing illegal Acts'. In that event the magistrate, 'as he cannot be in all places at once', could depute his powers to constables. Moreover, the troops were under the uniform civil obligation 'to maintain the public Peace' even 'in the Absence of Magistrates and Constables'. Although the lawyers thought that in such circumstances, 'The Prudence of their [the troops] Acting must depend on the Occasion . . . in Cases of great Necessity, we have no doubt that they ought so to Act'.[84] This legal opinion was published in the press, and had some success in convincing magistrates of the illegality attendant on the implementation of the 'moral economy'.[85] The announcements following the Devon and Cornwall meetings promised an extension of poor relief, together with measures to 'afford the fullest Protection of Property, and the free Supply of the Markets'. The Cornish bench agreed to prosecute rioters at the county's expense, and ordered the Clerk of the Peace to direct

[81] Monthly returns (abstract) to the War Office, PRO, WO 17/2785; memo, 'Force Actually in the Western District', 3 April 1801, DCRO, FLP, D1262M/L63.

[82] Simultaneously over 5000 troops were deployed against feared insurrections in the west midlands and Lancashire; Colonel Brownrigg, aide-de-camp to the Duke of York, to E.F. Hatton, and Portland to Fortescue, 3 and 12 April 1801, PRO, HO 42/61, 43/12, pp. 513–16.

[83] The Somerset meeting convened earlier because the Assizes were in progress. The Cornish Bench, assembled for the Sessions, discussed the riots under the chairmanship of the Rev. E. Giddy, before the arrival of the Lord Lieutenant.

[84] Printed copy, SCRO, DD/TB, C1534; handwritten copy, DCRO, FLP, D1262M/L63.

[85] When rioting commenced at Bristol on 4 April, the city JPs immediately published their decision to use troops if necessary, *Bath Chronicle*, 9 April; *Felix Farley's Bristol Journal*, 11 April 1801.

proceedings. The numbers of magistrates in attendance are recorded only for Devon; thirty-six met Fortescue and Simcoe at Exeter, at least four times as many as normally attended the County Sessions.[86]

On 5 April Fortescue was convinced that many Devon magistrates had 'anticipated . . . the general meeting', and had taken 'more vigourous measures . . . by swearing in as Constables all the principal Inhabitants of the Town & Country . . . [and] by publishing declarations to the effect of giving full Protection to the Freedom of the Markets'.[87] Although he had some grounds for this assertion,[88] Fortescue was wildly optimistic. Simcoe, who was then in Somerset, complained at the supineness of the magistracy. Simultaneously, horrified to learn that Poulett himself had temporised with a crowd at Chard, to the extent of permitting a maximum whose imposition was only nominally voluntary. While Simcoe despatched an urgent 'no compromise' note to stress the impolicy of neighbouring counties being under different 'systems', Poulett none the less chaired another meeting three days later at Ilminster where another seventy-four farmers and dealers agreed to maximum prices.[89] How Poulett reversed these decisions remains unclear, though at Chard the bakers had to stop baking for three days and the crowd was afterwards reported 'repentant'.[90] Thus the destruction of the 'moral economy' got off to a very fragmentary start.

The control of the Volunteers posed a most urgent problem.[91] Few magistrates had acted against suspect corps, though at Barnstaple the authorities disarmed the entire force, and at Plymouth Bastard confiscated the side arms of the infantry Volunteers. But neither Simcoe nor Fortescue relished the idea of stringent action against all Corps in the first instance. The latter adopted the idea suggested by the Honiton force, who published a declaration to assist the civil power. Both he and Simcoe were instrumental in modifying Portland's original demand for the disbanding of all corps where any members refused to act against rioters. Instead Fortescue ordered all corps to affirm their support of the magistracy. Many corps made suitable statements and by 5 April Fortescue felt assured of success. Four days later he issued the first of several orders for Volunteers to be put on permanent duty.[92] Yet the membership of many corps were not

[86] Resolutions of magistrates at Exeter Castle, handbill 8 April, PRO, HO 42/61; Cornwall County Resolutions, 14 April 1801, CCRO, Sessions Minute Book, QSM 7, fo. 99.

[87] Fortescue to Portland, 5 April 1801, PRO, HO 42/61.

[88] Details of repressive measures in letters to Fortescue from Simcoe, Eales, Recorder of Exeter, J.B. Cholwick, and J. Inglett Fortescue, 26 March to 5 April 1801, PRO, HO 42/61; DCRO, FLP, D1262M/L48, L49, L59.

[89] Simcoe to Poulett, 1 April, to Portland, 5 April, and to Fortescue, 15 April; anon., Yeovil to Portland, n.d.; Ilminster handbill, 4 April; Portland to Poulett, 7 April, and to Fortescue (draft), 23 April 1801, PRO, HO 42/61; 43/12, pp. 497–99; DCRO, FLP, D1262M/L52.

[90] Poulett to Portland, 8 April. Portland was satisfied that Somerset was freed from the maximum by 23 April 1801; draft to Fortescue, PRO, HO 42/61.

[91] The unreliability of the Volunteers convinced Simcoe of the necessity for the intervention of the Lords Lieutenant; Cholwick to Fortescue, 27 March 1801, DCRO, FLP, D1262M/L48.

[92] *Exeter Flying Post*, 9, 16 and 23 April; Fortescue to Portland, 5 April; list of corps put on permanent duty, 9 to 27 April 1801, PRO, HO 42/61; DCRO, FLP, D1262/L48, L52, L59.

unanimous. Most but not all of the Ippleden force signed their declaration. Several of the Dartmouth Volunteers, belatedly paraded on 27 April, refused. Privates at Kingsbridge considered themselves sworn only to serve the king and not to assist the magistrates; thirty-two of the fifty were dismissed on the parade ground. Their commander hopefully asserted 'that an open enemy is not half so much to be dreaded as a secret one'. Severe measures were restricted to the Brixham Volunteers, whose officers had led the crowd. Justices Taylor and Kitson were to arrange support from regular troops, before parading the whole corps, and breaking them. The three officers were arrested. All Volunteer regiments were informed of these proceedings.[93] Elsewhere leniency was the rule. Fortescue argued that the men who had left the Kingsbridge corps should be readmitted if they expressed 'a hearty contrition', and went to Barnstaple 'to revive the Spirit of Volunteering'.

Gradually magistrates throughout the region regained control. At Bideford the Volunteers attended the market with loaded arms whilst the price ceilings were removed. Colonel Orchard promised supplies would arrive 'at the Market Price, but not a bushel on any other Conditions'. Two Okehampton magistrates visited neighbouring farmers to promise their protection if the town market were supplied. The generous distribution of troops must have intimidated the populace of many towns: there are few reports of the actual use of troops, apart from Plymouth, but in Cornwall at least the situation was tense despite the army. The magistrates accompanied troops guarding markets. Giddy swore in '50 of the principal inhabitants' at Redruth, 'which fortunately having no Corporation is under the Care of the Justices of the County', but he was 'chagrined' to find that the cavalry contingent of a promised force of twenty-five horse and thirty-two foot was deficient. Giddy decided to keep the military hidden, presumably to avoid showing the weakness of his forces. Instead the justices

> frequently walked through the Market taking every opportunity of impressing on the minds of the people the folly as well as the illegality & danger of their [previous] proceedings, shewing them it was owing to this that they were deprived of their usual Supplies.

But Giddy felt his situation to be perilous. He was thankful that the shoppers avoided any confrontation: 'what gave us the Sincerest pleasure was "that no propositions were sent to us"'. Meanwhile, 'We could not help thinking that our houses, situate at a distance from a military situation & our persons, unsafe'. More troops were quickly drafted into Cornwall.[94] Several arrests were made by the troops in each county. Mount Edgecumbe reported that the miners had returned to work by 18 April, and others agreed that after a week's disturbances,

---

[93] Fortescue to Studdy and to Taylor (drafts), both 14 April, DCRO, FLP, D1262M/L59; *York Herald*, 2 May; *Bonner and Middleton's Bristol Journal*, 9 May 1801.

[94] Simcoe and W. Giddy to Addington, 9 and 20 April, DCRO, SP, D152M/Corr. 1801; Rev. E. Giddy, diary entries, 17, 23–25 April, CCRO, DD, DG 16; *Courier*, 20 April; *Bonner and Middleton's Bristol Journal*, 25 April 1801.

rioting had finished in Cornwall. With the exception of Devonport and some Torbay towns, Devon was free from danger about the same time, although Simcoe still complained 'at the apparent listlessness & want of Energy in the higher classes of People', and still sought 'a List of such magistrates & Gentry who will act as Peace Officers, & lend their influence to the Military in suppressing any future tumults'.[95]

The lengthy duration of the maximum in Torbay towns was partially due to magisterial apathy. Further violence was feared when supplies fell off. The people in Brixham advised 'the Farmers that they are to be visited again . . . as they are in a starving state'. The situation was complicated by the fleet anchored in Torbay. Captain Rodd reported that:

> Many of the Sailors wives . . . at Brixham . . . feel the pressure of the times . . . [and] having constant intercourse with their husbands in the Bay of course do not conceal from them their wants nor the difficulties of supplying them.

On 11 April A.J. Taylor was

> reliably informed by several persons . . . that great part of the Crews of the *St Joseph* and *Glory* had conspired with the Brixham Mob, to penetrate into the Interior . . . to regulate the prices of Provision. The Brixham men were to assemble on . . . Furze Hill, overlooking the Bay, and give three Cheers, on which signal the seamen were to seize all the Ships Boats and push for the shore.

Two troops of dragoons were rushed to the area, but if the plan existed, it was foiled by the weather. That night the wind suddenly changed and a gale drove the fleet from anchor, doing considerable damage. Two ships were aground in the morning. In the midst of this mayhem, it was suddenly discovered that the Torbay postmaster was a long-standing spy in the pay of France, who 'communicated to Paris all the orders which came by post' for naval officers, '& such letters from the fleets as he thought interesting'.[96]

If the weather frustrated a renewed offensive by the Torbay crowd, no such phenomenon could dilute the 'very feverish disposition' or stop the renewed aggression of the Devonport crowd and its dockyard leaders. On 11 April Devonport and Plymouth were on the verge of starvation, and three days later the justices 'permitted the Mob . . . to distribute a Load of Corn among their party'.[97] On 15 April it was learnt that a Devonport baker had sixty sacks of flour warehoused 'and the Mob . . . were pleased to say, that the flour was concealed there and that they would have it'. This was effected and the maximum was reimposed on butchers and bakers. Before military support arrived, the

[95] Simcoe to Fortescue, 15 April 1801, DCRO, FLP, D1262M/L52.

[96] Rodd to Portland, 5 April; Taylor to Fortescue, 12 April, PRO, HO 42/61. Thomas Grenville to former First Lord of the Admiralty, Earl Spencer, 23 April, BL, Althorp Papers, G. 43. The gale was reported in the *Courier*, 15 April 1801.

[97] Mayor of Plymouth, and Bastard, to Portland, 11 and 18 April 1801, PRO, HO 42/61.

constables arrested a waterman, Charles Jacob, active in window smashing. The crowd demanded his release, and broke into the court where he was being interrogated 'by means of large pieces of Wood which they made use of as Battering Rams . . . & the Constables running away rescued him'. Although Jacob was not employed in the Dockyard, he was instantly secreted there and escaped pursuit by the justices, now supported by troops. Two men active in the rescue were however arrested, though the crowd was able to smash the windows in magistrate St Aubyn's house before soldiers cleared the streets.

The release of these prisoners was the principal demand of the dockyard men the next day. Admiralty Solicitor Eastlake's description of developments is instructive:

> the affair commenced with the Blacksmiths . . . they began by cheering the other artificers some of whom answered & some did not . . . the Smiths then went round to the Artificers to induce them to strike, some joined them & some were found very unwilling to do so, particularly some Shipwrights . . . who secreted themselves and would not come forward; as also some of the Rope house; where 'tis said the Blacksmiths took the work out of the Hands of some, to make them join them. By these proceedings they at length collected about ⅔ or more of the People & proceeded to a Green . . . where some of their speakers harangued them . . . The cry at intervals was 'to work, to work', which was answered by 'to Gate'.

where according to special constable Elford 'a very large Mob, was assembled outside the Gates in order to receive and join with the yard men'. But the authorities were now determined to resist. A warrant for Jacob's arrest was issued and the yard gates remained locked under military guard. Troops drove the crowd away. Eventually a deputation of eight men 'came out to question the Magistrates'. Although the justices were prepared to parley, Colonel Bastard was not: he told the eight 'that the magistrates would hold no communication with traitors, and that the only answer they would receive would proceed from the artillery', drawn up near the gates. The artillery commander added 'that the Guns would fire the Moment they were unprotected' by the yard walls. This show of force completely intimidated the artisans; an hour and a half later they had all returned to work.[98]

Faced with the possibility of a bloody defeat at the hands of the troops, some artificers adopted more secretive tactics to avoid future confrontations with the military. At least two boatloads of men put out of the yard on 23 April and sailed up the Yealm, disembarking in the rural area to the east of Plymouth. They then toured farmers' houses to force them to sell corn at reduced prices 'or 500 would come to their Assistance'. The farmers complied, but these enterprizes stopped after the arrest of six men by a 'Gunboat'. Full-time criminals simultaneously exploited the situation. One Devonport burglar recruited six

---

[98] Letters to Portland from St Aubyn and Williams, 17 April, and Fortescue with enclosures, 25 April; Eastlake to C. Dicknell of the Admiralty Office, in answer to request for information, 18 April, PRO, HO 42/61; Bastard to Addington, 4 May 1801, DCRO, SP, D152M/Corr. 1801.

sailors from the *Carolina* gunboat and hired a boat to take them up the Yealm. The gang's exploits finished with a ferocious attack on farmer Honey's house near Plympton, stealing arms in the process, before retreating once the alarm was given.[99]

The suppression of the dockyard workers assumed primary importance, but in the first instance this was frustrated by Commissioner Franshawe, who refused to co-operate with the magistrates.[100] On 17 April Franshawe informed the justices that Jacob was in the yard, but stressed 'the expediency of avoiding the risque of commotion', and refused to assist with his arrest.[101] Basically the commissioner wanted to forget the affair, and resisted the suggestion that he should be given greater powers because of the strength of his men. Although the Devonport justices were told that the yard lay within their jurisdiction,[102] neither JP felt able to direct reprisals against the delinquents, and argued that this should be done by government. Eastlake agreed; any attempt by the magistracy would be 'no good'. However he considered it vital that

> those mistaken people should be undeceived ... told ... that they have not Rights or Privileges distinct from other subject that they have no pretence to arrogate to themselves the liberty of interfering with constituted authorities, of taking the lead upon the Occurences of the times; of keeping up a Government by Committees or within themselves, & of putting their whole body in motion, whenever it shall please them to enforce their demands, to the terror of the Country about them.

Bastard agreed 'that an appearance of Contempt backed indeed by force if necessary for the Dockyard Gentry.[103]

At this moment, south-western problems were but one element in the national crises obtaining in the aftermath of Pitt's resignation along with most of his cabinet. If other regions were gripped by food riots, these – including London – were more ominously affected by serious insurrectionary plotting of fifth

---

[99] Although this attack provoked great fears at the time (the parish added £100 to Honey's £50 reward), the culprits remained at large until the Devonport. J.P. Williams arrested one of a much hunted gang of burglars on 3 July. This man, James Hayes, aged eighteen, revealed some of his burglar accomplices, and admitted his participation in the Honey affair. A man jailed for robbery at Bodmin later provided further information and two men were executed at Exeter. Depositions of R. Honey and family; reward handbill, 23 April; Williams and Bastard, to Fortescue, 15 and 18 July 1801, PRO, HO 42/61; DCRO, FLP, D1262M/L55, L56; *Exeter Flying Post*, 25 March, 19 August and 2 September 1802.

[100] On 5 April Franshawe refused even to discuss magisterial suggestions to enrol dockyard officers as special constables; Williams and St Aubyn to Fortescue, 8 April 1801, PRO, HO 42/61.

[101] Copies of four letters between Franshawe, and St Aubyn and Williams, 17 April 1801, PRO, HO 42/61.

[102] Portland told the JPs that they should 'have committed the Commissioner had he refused to obey you'. Letters to St Aubyn and Williams from Fortescue, and Portland, 21 and 27 April 1801, DCRO, FLP, D1262M/L52; PRO, HO 43/13, fos 29–32. St Aubyn and Williams to Portland, 23 April 1801, PRO, HO 42/61.

[103] Eastlake to Dicknell, 18 April, PRO, HO 42/61; Bastard to Addington, 4 May 1801, DCRO, SP, D152M/Corr. 1801.

columnists in alliance with Irish nationalists and the French government. Home Secretary Portland, who remained in office, orchestrated a multi-dimensional counter-revolutionary campaign on several fronts. In this scenario, the situation of Devonport was of some significance. 'I do not care one Damn for all the Caulkers & Carpenters in all the Yards', volunteered Portland, when the subject was discussed between the Home Office and the Admiralty about 17 April. New statutory proposals were rejected for the purpose of short-term remedies. The Admiralty agreed to risk a strike in the interests of smashing union organisation and of demonstrating the error of the men's conception of their own indispensability. The Navy Board agreed to mass sackings. Proceedings were put under Fortescue's superintendence and the Board set out for Plymouth. This offensive was aided by the partial collapse of unity in the yard. On 18 April 'all the other Departments and particularly the Shipwrights, are execrating the Blacksmiths for having drawn them into such a scrape' with the Artillery. Moreover on the 23rd the central committee were split over their pay offer. 'There was great jealousy amongst the members. No date was set for the next meeting, and Fortescue believed the leaders and others prominent in the riots could be sacked without a strike.[104]

The Navy Board reached Plymouth on May Day, and spent the next three days collecting names. These moves drove a further wedge between the men and no resistance appeared possible. Sixty-eight men, including eleven of the twelve central committee, five of the eight deputed to negotiate with the justices on 16 April, and several of the trades committee men were sacked on 5 May. The blacksmiths and shipwrights lost seventeen and twenty-two respectively. Eleven labourers were also sacked, with six carpenters (three of whom were central committeemen), three caulkers and three sailmakers. The only blockmakers, joiners and painters sacked were their representatives on the central committee. This passed off quietly with 'the remainder . . . [at] their work'. The central committee sent 'circular letters . . . to the different yards', but nothing came of this. Meanwhile there were no fears 'that the Ins will pay any attention to the Outs'. On 14 May Bastard asserted that 'the name of a Dockyardman is now nothing more than the name of any other workmen'. The butchers responded by raising the price of meat and openly said 'that they shall do what they like now the Dockyard men are silenced'.[105]

The government were anxious to prosecute selected dockyard workers: Portland originally wanted to employ the Combination Acts against the entire

[104] For the national situation, see esp. R. Wells, *Insurrection: The British Experience, 1795–1803* (Gloucester, 1983), esp. chs 9–10; idem, *Wretched Faces*, pp. 144–60; idem, 'Britains Avoidance of Revolution in the 1790s Revisited', *Bulletin of the Society for the Study of Labour History*, 54 (1989), pp. 36–37. Portland to Fortescue, 23 April; J. Elford to J. Elliott, 18 April; Fortescue to Portland with enclosures, 23 and 26 April; Tyrwitt to Fortescue reporting the meeting at the Home Office, 18 April; Navy Board Minute, 17 April; Bastard to Addington, 30 April 1801, PRO, HO 42/61; ADM 106/2664; DCRO, FLP, D1262M/L58; SP, D152M/Corr. 1801.

[105] Fortescue to Portland with enclosures, 5, 6 and 7 May, PRO, HO 42/62; Bastard to Fortescue, 10 and 14 May 1801, DCRO, FLP, D1262M/L53.

central committee. This was frustrated by the crown's legal officers who advised that the artisans had only petitioned the Navy Board and, as the text 'cautiously avoided any particular expression of intimidation or . . . intention to strike', a prosecution would fail.[106] Portland was undeterred, and arranged for the Treasury Solicitor to hire Messrs Elford and Foot, the local legal firm, to draw up other charges. The justices were to assist. The government wanted capital charges and selected Prout, Moses and Browne, all dockyard workers,[107] for offences relating to the release of the prisoners on 31 March. However, the lengthy examinations of witnesses, and no doubt their interrogation by their neighbours, put all likely victims on guard. Several central committeemen including Browne, and others including Prout, absconded when St Aubyn very ostentatiously sent for troops prior to the issue of warrants. Indeed many inferences suggest that St Aubyn was an unwilling participant. First, he lived in the town and had his windows smashed on at least one occasion. Secondly, as lord of the manor he had benefited from the rapid growth of proletarian Devonport. In 1795 there were 135 ale-houses; in 1801, 247. He owned at least one brewery, and 'all Victuallers' were 'bound to the Lord of the Manor in all leases granted by him to buy their Beer' from his brewery. Many dockyard workers also ran ale-houses, but Fortescue wanted to employ sanctions against licence holders to attack the union.[108] Although both Prout and Browne were eventually tried with Moses, they were acquitted at the summer Assizes.

The government at least managed to get these men to court. Portland insisted that the most culpable participants in the riots should be prosecuted, and magistrates meeting at Truro and Exeter formally agreed to do so.[109] Two men, Samual Tout and Robert Westcott, were arrested near Bridgwater on 30 March, after a baker's shop was invaded by the crowd and his wife forced to sell bread at low prices. They were capitally charged, tried at the Assizes on 3 April, whilst the region was still disturbed, and sentenced to death. Together with seven thieves they were executed at Taunton on 15 April, a market day, 'instead of Ilminster by way of stronger example'. The authorities provided a strong military guard but were surprised when the 'populace shewed no signs of commotion'. Poulett assumed that the executions would 'have a good effect', and Portland was pleased that the penalty of 'certain and capital punishment' for rioters had been demonstrated.[110] But whatever the effect on the

---

[106] Navy Board Minute, 17 April; Attorney General and Solicitor General to Portland, 14 April 1801, PRO, ADM 106/2664; HO 49/4, fos 60–61.

[107] Only Brown was on the central committee, and he was dismissed with Prout on 5 May. Moses, against whom the evidence was weakest, was a shipwright and does not appear on the dismissed list.

[108] Treasury Solicitor White to W. Foot, *c.* 8 May; Bastard and Foot, to Fortescue, 10 and 21 May 1801; list of licenses issued, 1795–1801; copy of advert for brewery lease in Fortescue's hand, n.d., DCRO, FLP, D1262M/L53, L63.

[109] Draft, Portland to Fortescue and Poulett, 30 March; Devon Meeting handbill, 7 April PRO, HO 42/61; Cornwall Sessions minute, 14 April 1801, CCRO, QSM 7, fo. 99.

[110] Poulett to Portland and reply, 4 and 7 April, PRO, HO 42/61, 43/12, fos 497–99; Assi, 23/9;

riotous populace of Somerset, they certainly had a significant impact on the administration of justice across the south west.[111] In Somerset one John Budge, against whom a warrant for theft was issued after a riot at Wayford, was subsequently charged with a non-capital offence. Two women who stole capital amounts of flour at Holcombe were only charged with petty larceny with their cases heard at the Sessions.[112] In Cornwall, fifteen person were charged with offences committed during the riots, but none of them capital. Although all but two were found guilty, punishments ranged from fines of shillings to £5, and sentences of two and three months imprisonment.

In Devon, Fortescue's attempts to prosecute considerable numbers of rioters were frustrated by a number of factors. When he arrived in the county, only two arrests had been made. The Lord Lieutenant instantly indicated his ardour with a suggestion that one of them ought to be prosecuted for high treason. This exaggerated sense of duty was hardly calculated to win Fortescue the sympathy of his subordinate magistrates, many of whom were as convinced of the righteousness of the 'moral economy' as the intended victims. Fortescue's determination was counterbalanced by magisterial indifference. Totnes justices represented many who 'were glad to let off the offenders upon the Idea that there is plenty of Corn & that they were incited by Hunger'.[113] Many magistrates would favour the escape route followed by Mr Justice Carpenter, who was prepared to forego judicial proceedings against six canal workers who had threatened farmers, in return for the public acknowledgement of their offence. The offenders paid for the distribution of a cautionary handbill addressed 'TO THE LABOURING POOR', in which they admitted their 'great Crime', begged 'Pardon of the Country at large', thanked the farmers involved for their leniency and extolled the virtues of the free market.[114] In addition, just as threats had deterred magistrates from active opposition to riot, threats now determined them and potential witnesses against legal measures. Captain Studdy of Brixham noted that 'no man likes . . . to bear the Odium of Informer', together with the 'danger which may follow'.[115]

This process can be examine minutely at Totnes. Here Fortescue had a potential ally in miller Welsford, who refused to 'admit the Principle of . . . fixing a maximum on my Property' and insisted 'that some Person should be brought

continued

Bonner and Middleton's Bristol Journal and *Felix Farley's Bristol Journal*, both 18 April 1801. Local traditions that all nine were hung for riot soon appeared, *Taunton Courier*, 29 July 1829.

[111] Devon and Cornwall both had similar precedents with executions in 1795 and 1796.

[112] Budge was sentenced to a year's imprisonment on 4 April. The women were sentenced to be privately whipped, PRO, Assi, 25/1/3, Somerset Sessions Minute Book and Easter Sessions Roll 1801; SCRO, CQ2, 2/4(3), fo. 182; CQ3, 1/369.

[113] 'D.G.' to Bastard, 5 May 1801, DCRO, FLP, D1262M/L63.

[114] Carpenter to Fortescue with enclosed handbill, 25 April 1801, DCRO, FLP, D1262M/L61.

[115] Taylor to Fortescue, 12 April 1801, PRO, HO 42/61.

to justice for the purpose of establishing the point'.[116] Fortescue directed the Rev. Kitson to investigate offences outside the borough, and the Mayor those committed within: he warned Kitson 'not . . . to expect much . . . co-operation' from the Mayor. Kitson successfully approached farmer Palk of Little Hempston who 'expresses a wish to prosecute if he could be protected', and made a statement naming Tippett, Hannaford and Wheeler, 'three of the Committee of the People [who] acted very conspicuously' in forcing Palk's door, calling for a halter, and threatening 'that he and his Wife should be hung across the Door'.[117] When Kitson returned with a colleague, Palk's 'information fell greatly below our expectations. The Door . . . not broken upon . . . no halter ever heard of . . . no threatenings to do them personal injury'. Farcical proceedings followed the attempts to arrest Totnes rioters named by another farmer, Penny. He accompanied the constables to identify suspects. One of the accused immediately produced eight alibis which 'the Justices admitted to destroy the credibility of Penny's Oath'. Another suspect 'Halse Ley was permitted to go home guarded by a Borough Constable, a great Rioter, to put on his better Coat, and escaped by jumping out of his Chamber Window'. Although the county justices put the fear of God into the constable, Kitson wearily concluded that he had 'failed in my endeavours to send those to the Court of Justice who were properly pointed out to be made Examples in it'.[118]

The failure of the county magistrates meant that any prosecution now rested with the obstructive borough authority and the enthusiastic Welsford. The only overt act within the town was the intimidation of miller Harrison by the crowd, once again led by Hannaford. The town clerk airily told Fortescue that they knew nothing of this, and Welsford was ordered to provide the Mayor with details. Welsford's ardour abated. He received one threatening letter, which intimated that it was he who was informing the Lord Lieutenant, an intimation confirmed by the visit on 1 May of the Rev. Froude, a member of the official committee set up by the mayor. Froude told Welsford that if he did not stop proceedings, 'an Irritation against me [Welsford] might be excited, that would not perhaps ever be allayed'. Welsford feared that 'it wod. be impossible for me or my Family to live in', the town, and agreed to stop if Hannaford made 'the most ample submission to Mr Harrison'. Ten minutes later Hannaford appeared with a suitable promise. On 2 May the price agreement was destroyed in the market place 'before a great Number of Rioters & Farmers', and Hannaford was universally 'forgiven'.[119] Fortescue exploded. On receipt of Welsford's letters he dashed across from Plymouth to interview the miller, and was even more horrified to

[116] Torn undated letters from Welsford to Roedean, and Welsford to Fortescue, 4 May 1801, PRO, HO 42/62; DCRO, FLP, D1262M/L59.

[117] Palk's deposition, PRO, HO 42/61.

[118] Penney's deposition; Kitson to Fortescue, and Welsford to Roedean, both 1 May 1801, PRO, HO 42/61, 62.

[119] Welsford to Roedean, 1 and 2 May, and to Fortescue, 4 May; Town Clerk Totnes to Fortescue, 10 May, PRO, HO 42/62; *London Gazette*, 28 April 1801.

find the market still under some sort of maximum. A violent letter to the mayor, in which he threatened to lay all information before Portland for a decision 'as to the means it may be necessary to have recourse to for supplying the want of a Jurisdiction in . . . Totnes', only elicited the reply that the mayor had no evidence against Hannaford. Their stubbornness paid off. Kitson was also tired of the matter and, although he promised not to let the offenders escape, he argued that the climate ought to be allowed to cool. Fortescue went to the crown lawyers, but they advised that all cases ought to be dropped on the grounds of the impossibility of proof, the length of time since the offences and Welsford's position. Fortescue had to be content with redrafting a proposed acknowledge-ment of guilt from Halse Ley when he 'became visible again'. On the apprecia-tion of victory 'the sort of Triumph' manifested was so great that Kitson sent his clerk to see if these amounted to 'indecent exultations'.[120]

Eventually sufficient evidence was obtained against twenty-three Devonians. Supported by the Home Office, Fortescue relentlessly pursued the Volunteer officers who had led the Brixham crowd, only to see their acquittals at the 1802 Lent Assizes. Other prosecutions, all for non-capital offences, were successful. One official triumph was the conviction of six Modbury rioters, who received sentences of fines and short terms of imprisonment. But this had required the intervention of the Treasury Solicitor's agents. That department was also responsible for the conviction of two men from Exeter.[121] Prison sentences were also imposed on four Devonport offenders. The remaining case, the only one heard at the Sessions, ended with a Poughill man receiving six months for lead-ing a crowd which broke into a parish potato store.[122] In Devon the trials themselves did nothing to restore tranquillity. The acquittal rate suggests that jurors did not consider the peace of the county depended on making examples, and the absence of capital charges suggests that the authorities thought convic-tions would not materialise. However, the arrests and judicial enquiries certainly played some role in the return of tranquillity. The morale of the Exeter crowd was dampened by arrests and the Totnes rioters were 'completely frightened and humbled' by the investigation.

Although there can be no doubt that regular troops supported by reliable Volunteers played an effective part in stopping riots in the first instance, the primary cause of the restoration of order must be sought in the urgent measures taken to remedy the dearth. Portland's first object was to stop rioting, but the Lords Lieutenant were instructed to alleviate distress. The Parish Relief Act was belatedly implemented. Its adoption was ordered in every Devon parish,

---

[120] Fortescue to Kitson, 10 May, and replies 19 and 20 May; Fortescue to the mayor, and reply, 9 and 10 May; Welsford to Fortescue, 10 and 28 May, and reply *c.* 29 May; Welch and Harrison to Welsford, 23 May; Portland to Fortescue, 22 July 1801; draft amended statement, Halse Ley, n.d., PRO, HO 42/62; DCRO, FLP, D1262M/L53, L55, L59.

[121] White to Hatton, 26 May; Portland to Eales, 29 May 1801, PRO, HO 43/13, fo. 78; 49/4, fos 70–71, Assi 25/3/1.

[122] Devon Sessions Roll, Easter 1801, DCRO 3/4b/1b.

whose authorities were instructed 'to take the most immediate Means of procuring the necessary Importation of Corn and other Provisions'. Where necessary magistrates would 'give their personal aid' when 'Agreements' were made between overseers and factors. Relief was to be extended to all who could not afford to feed their families, though the receipt of this aid would not entail 'being . . . brought into the Description of Persons receiving Parochial Relief'.[123] The region required a substantial and immediate importation. The speediest mode was for its organisation by the local authorities.

These instructions were anticipated by many authorities, who obtained supplies to forestall disturbances. Fortescue was able to report that 'most' towns had agreed to get corn by 5 April. Exeter was quickly off the mark, with a subscription started on 25 March and over £3000 raised by 2 April. A committee supervised the distribution of bread and meal to constituent parishes.[124] The 'principal inhabitants' of Plymouth were longer 'coming to their senses'. Corporate funds were not used to launch a subscription until after the second series of disturbances.[125]

Parish records in all three counties prove that serious efforts were made during the last half of April in many places which had not previously implemented the Act. In many Somerset parishes Speenhamland payments were replaced by grants of food.[126] Bread substitutes were introduced in Cornish parishes.[127] By 24 April Eales had received favourable replies from all over Devon. Everybody agreed that these steps had 'sav'd the County from riot, distress & famine'. Although Mount Edgecumbe made no equal claim, he was satisfied that the Cornish judiciary were implementing the Act, and that this would stem the tide of discontent. Moreover, the gradual restoration of order coincided with an improvement in the national grain supply. This permitted large quantities to be released for the south west. The reopening of the Baltic ports and the arrival of imports from North America vastly increased the volume of grain on the national exchanges, especially London. Meanwhile, freed from the maximum, prices in West Country markets rose above those current in Sussex, East Anglia and London. Welsford was able to report an offer of Sussex grain well below Plymouth prices, and his ability to supply profitably his district.[128]

[123] Exeter Meeting handbill, 8 April. Fortescue also wrote personally to all JPs, 19 April 1801, PRO, HO 42/61.

[124] *Exeter Flying Post*, 26 March and 2 April; Fortescue to Portland, 5 April 1801, PRO, HO 42/61; Exeter Bread Committee Accounts, ECRO, Misc. Papers, box 10.

[125] *Exeter Flying Post*, 23 April; Bastard to Addington, 4 May, DCRO, SP, D152M/Corr. 1801; Plymouth Common Council Minute Book, 1 June 1801, Plymouth City Archives, W 61, fo. 110.

[126] Parish accounts for Charlton Adam, Staplegrove, North Perrot, Stawley, Shepton Beaumont, West Harptree, West Hatch and North Wootten, SCRO, DD, D/P/ile.b. 13/2/2; D/P/w.harp. 13/2/3; D/P/hat.w. 13/2/4; D/P/n.wo. 13/2/2; D/P/she.b. 13/2/1; D/P/staw. 13/2/3; D/P/per. 13/2/6; D/P/cha.a. 13/2/1.

[127] Parish records for St Clements Truro, St Cleer, Lanivet and Breage, CCRO, DD, P33/8/3; P33/12/1; P110/13/3; P32/12/1; P18/8/1.

[128] PRO, MAF 10/285; Welsford to Fortescue, 4 May 1801, DCRO, FLP, D1262M/L59.

In conclusion a major point which requires emphasis is that these were not *rural* riots. Nor were the majority of eighteenth-century food riots rural, as is often assumed or stated too categorically. For instance, Shelton in his work on hunger and *industrial* disorders, continuously refers to the food riots in the 1760s as 'agrarian', or 'rural', with the 'rural population' participating. Shelton concentrates too heavily on agricultural reorganisation in the first half of the eighteenth century. Although he recognises the existence of the various branches of the textile industry in both large and small provincial centres, he underates the activities of the textile workers in favour of agricultural labourers. Closer attention to the economic and social background of the affected areas, instead of a slavish application of such textbook concepts as the 'Agricultural Revolution', an analysis of the precise distribution of riot, the occupations of those tried, will reveal that as in the south west in 1801, the rioters of 1766 were predominantly from towns and mining regions.[129] Almost every person tried by the courts in the south west lived in an urban setting and depended on town markets. The occupations of six of the seven Modbury rioters are known, but in the indictment they are all described as labourers. Many lawyers who prepared legal documents simply entered 'labourer' to describe any person who was not a 'gentleman'. Most courts' order and minute books exhibit similar tendencies. While not invariably the case, this is an important point to be borne in mind in studies on riots, crowd behaviour and crime. It is possible that some recent authors, including Shelton and J.M. Beattie have overlooked this, though the point was made by Rudé.[130] The precise occupations of the Modbury rioters have been ascertained from depositions, letters and memoranda on the disturbances and perpetrators. For example, the Rev. Stackhouse, making his statement over a month after the event: 'Francis Hole, a Plush Weaver working with Robert Horsewell brought . . . a paper' for the vicar to sign. Local inhabitants, of course, often knew other locals they encountered in crowds and would identify them precisely from the basis of that knowledge; Hole's fellow rioters included two other textile workers, two shoemakers, and a retired sailor.[131]

Three members of the Totnes People's Committee are known; again two were shoemakers, the other a constable. A currier and a master cabinet-maker were named as crowd activists.[132] The Brixham Volunteer officers who led the crowd represented that class of town dweller somewhat above the rank of artisan, whose encouragement of the crowd was considered important. Pridham kept a shop,

[129] W.J. Shelton, *English Hunger and Industrial Disorders* (London, 1973). See, in particular, ch. 2, 'The Economic and Social Background of the Provincial Hunger Riots'; and ch. 4, 'The Provincial Rioters'.

[130] J.M. Beattie, 'The Pattern of Crime in England, 1660–1800', *Past and Present*, 62 (1974), pp. 47–95; G. Rudé, *The Crowd in History, 1730–1848* (New York, 1964), p. 14.

[131] Indictments, PRO, Assi 25/1/13; Memo on Modbury riots, and Stackpole's deposition, DCRO, FLP, D1262M/L50, L53.

[132] Miller Pulling provided his brother with these details to indicate that 'the Committee appointed by the rabble . . . are . . . dispicable'; J. to W. Pulling, 6 April 1801; depositions of Penney and Harrison, PRO, HO 42/61.

Collier was a schoolmaster and Saunders was a butcher.[133] Rural workers were not involved in the main disturbances. It is just possible that the two Sandford men who stood trial were agricultural labourers. They were named but not described by the farmers.[134] However, the census recorded more people 'in Manufactures' than 'in Agriculture'. The six rioters of rural Winkleigh may well have worked on the land, but their offence was to compel the overseer to sell them subsidised barley, although a vestry had previously ruled that 'they were Men of Ability had no Head Money and did not want it'. Their protest was not of the same type.[135] Similarly untypical were disturbances at Parkham. Here trouble followed the refusal of farmers to extend their system of supplying all the poor with corn at stable prices to sales of seed corn for labourers' allotments.[136] Rural labourers may well have been forced, as with Christopher Roach of Modbury, to join itinerant town crowds once they were in the countryside.[137]

Secondly, the pattern and type of riot were features of the social and economic structure of the region and were further influenced by the local consensus of opinion on the causes of the crisis. The same conditions and influences affected the return of tranquillity. Withholding farmers were held responsible for the scarcity in town marts; therefore those sectors of the population which depended on this source headed for the rural areas and conducted their negotiations with the culprits on farmhouse doorsteps. Because parts of Cornwall were unprovided with corn markets this type of approach was even more natural. The principal exception to this pattern occurs at metropolitan Plymouth and Devonport, the supply of which depended to a much greater degree on the middlemen activities of the dealers and greater bakers. Thus here we find demonstrations against these traders.

The principal reason for the duration, and perhaps the extent of mass action, must be sought in the reluctance of town authorities firstly to make adequate provisions for their poor and, secondly, to intervene immediately trouble commenced. Thirdly, the role of the Volunteers is clearly crucial. This shows that Professor Western correctly assessed the potency of the Volunteers as an 'anti-revolutionary' movement, but exaggerated their role as a police force.[138] The virtual abdication of the magistracy and the Volunteers put the smaller town

---

[133] Depositions of farmers Moysey and Gillard. Their indictments described them accurately, PRO, HO 42/61, Assi 25/1/13.

[134] Depositions of J. Fromlett and Hookaway; indictment, PRO, HO 42/62; Assi 25/1/13; committal documents, Devon Sessions Roll, Easter 1801, DCRO 3/4B/1b.

[135] Prosecutor's brief against five 'labourers' and one 'spinster', PRO, Treasury Solicitor, 11/914.

[136] Rev. R. Walker to Fortescue, 26 March 1801; PRO, HO 42/61; depositions of J. Bate and W. Heywood, DCRO, FLP, D1262M/L52.

[137] Deposition of S. Worth, yeoman, Modbury, DCRO, FLP, D1262M/L50.

[138] J.R. Western, 'The Volunteer Movement as an Anti-Revolutionary Force', *English Historical Review*, 81 (1956), especially p. 613. Cf. R. Wells, 'English Society and Revolutionary Politics in the 1790s: The Case for Insurrection', in M. Philp (ed.), *The French Revolution and British Popular Politics* (Cambridge, 1991), pp. 209–12.

crowd on a similar footing to the notorious miners. Every Cornish observer testified to the 'lawlessness' of the mining communities.[139] Three justices related how a posse of constables 'saved their lives only by flight and Concealment' after a whole community revolted to save one of their members from arrest. The miners were 'more in a state of independence, and less subject to the influence of superiors' than any other sector of the working population. Tightly-knit mining communities were capable of unified and concerted action. Any retribution by authority was difficult, 'as they find so safe and ready Asylum in the Mines: and therefore no Magistrate can attend in Person'.[140] The plebeian consumer could always expect his interests to be protected wherever large occupational groups existed, because these could oppose the authorities with some hope of success. In Devon the primary example of this concerns the men of Devonport, who spearheaded the popular revolt, despite the fact of their adoption of union tactics.[141]

The initial collapse of authority also permitted the crowd to demonstrate its powers of discipline and negotiation. At Totnes and Plymouth this reached surprising heights. Despite the violence the crowd showed considerable self control. A man who tried to filch a side of bacon from a Brixham pub 'was compelled by' the others 'to carry it back . . . with disgrace fastened to his back . . . and to make restitution'. Another fellow was ejected from Plymouth market by rioting women after he tried to steal a bag of potatoes.[142] Another aspect of the discipline and organisation shown concerns the reports of collusion between crowds. The Exeter crowd 'instructed' people from Exmouth on the prices to set. There are too many independent suggestions of some communications carried on between different towns through the medium of 'the numerous associations of Wool-combers' to ignore this possibility.[143] Unionism in the textile trades was strong; the well-organised tramping system possibly facilitated communication. Poulett alleged that Friendly Societies discussed tactics before rioting began in Somerset. Friendly societies were often no more than a cover for union lodges. They were very numerous in Devon.[144] Wellington wool-combers met on 26 September 1800 and drafted a set of resolutions, respecting food prices, and sent these for the adoption of colleagues at Cullompton and Tiverton.

---

[139] Fraser, *Cornwall*, pp. 20–21, 28.

[140] T. Steadman (ed.), *Memoir of the Rev. W. Steadman*, (1838), p. 148; Messrs Trevenen, Johns and Marshall, to Portland, n.d. (1796); Drowas to Hatton, 14 April 1801; similar statements were made about the role of miners in food riots throughout the eighteenth century. Cf. mayor of Bristol to the Duke of Newcastle, 21 May 1753, and 'E.F.' Coventry to Lord Holdernesse, 30 August 1756, PRO, HO 42/39, 49; State Papers Domestic, 36/122, fos 39–42; 36/135, fos 281–82.

[141] Chatham magistrates reported similar manifestations; they feared the 'unanimity of operation', of which the local shipwrights were capable; Chatham JPs to the War Office, 25 March 1795, PRO, WO 1/1084, fos 241–42.

[142] J. Underhay to Fortescue, 31 May, PRO, HO 42/62; *The Times*, 2 April 1801.

[143] Simcoe to Portland, 27 March 1801, PRO, HO 42/61.

[144] On unionism see A. Aspinal, *The Early English Trade Unions* (1949); and on the tramping system, E.J. Hobsbawm, *Labouring Men* (London, 1964), ch. 4.

Uffculm weavers convened before they joined the crowd and later put out a handbill to deny riotous intent. The crowd at Sheepwash agreed not to regroup on 2 April because a friendly society meeting was scheduled. The 'idolised' leader at Modbury, Wakeham, was strongly suspected of communicating with leaders at Exeter. Another magistrate obtained evidence that delegates were appointed to co-ordinate popular action across South Devon.[145] These details at least suggest the participation of men who were used to self-organisation, and this may provide one clue to the crowd's discipline. There is absolutely no doubt of this at Devonport.

Of all the forces which determined the nature of popular action the role of the magistracy was crucial. The critical role of the English justices of the peace was again amply proven. Their failure to act against riot is paralleled by their reluctance to prosecute, or at least to arraign suspects on capital charges. Magisterial indifference to the claims of the free market was one of the reasons for the survival of the 'moral economy' and for the length of the struggle between two opposing economic and social philosophies. Another mode by which the authorities maintained their support for the 'moral economy' was to order their constables to watch closely for market offences.[146] While the government was not a totally helpless spectator of events, the regional authorities were only propelled to act after the intervention of the Lords Lieutenant, one of whom soon indicated what he thought of *laissez-faire*. Portland's offensive ultimately rested on the courts and on enthusiastic magistrates. These were few. The indifferent had to be goaded by the Lords and direct orders from the Home Office.[147] In the end the government had to bring in its own legal department.[148] But with the exception of the two Somerset executions the courts cannot take much credit for the restoration of order, far less the victory of *laissez-faire*. The local press moreover failed to report proceedings at the Cornish Sessions and the Devon Lent Assize of 1802. The most cursory notice was taken of the main bulk of the Devon trials in the summer of 1801. The government was really only able to act forcibly when the situation was under its direct supervision. Despite their strength, the dockyard workers were more vulnerable than those they led. The government destroyed their power by attacking at its base, their employment. The law could not provide such a demonstration of power. The 'moral economy' survived these attacks. Although its implementation was a recipe for disaster, it appeared to be the only rational ideal to counter the economic

[145] Letters to Fortescue from Kennaway with enclosures, 9 September 1800; J. Inglett Fortescue, 4 May, and J. Marley with enclosure, 19 May; memo, n.d., re Modbury rioters, DCRO, FLP, D1262M/L44, L53, L58, L59; letters to Portland from Poulett, 30 March, Tucker, 9 April, and Bastard 18 April 1801, PRO, HO 42/61.

[146] Exeter City Sessions fined several people for minor offences after September 1800; ECRO, Sessions papers, 1794–1802, box 11.

[147] Portland wrote directly to several magistrates, including those at Devonport, who received more than one strongly worded missive, PRO, HO 43/12, 13.

[148] The depositions in the Home Office papers, many of which have been quoted, owe their existence to this step.

problems caused by shortages. It remained so until the nation's food supply stabilised with the return of peace and its equal internal distribution was finalised by the railway. Until these economic conditions arrived the crowd remained the major 'defence of the poor' because it 'united many different strata in a joint effort to resist worsening experiences'.[149] It is an ironical, but explicable, fact of social history that that joint effort was led by the best organised and most powerful industrial workers.

[149] The phrase is from R.B. Rose, 'Eighteenth-Century Price Riots, the French Revolution and the Jacobin Maximum', *International Review of Social History*, 6 (1959), p. 435. G. Rudé, *Wilkes and Liberty* (Oxford, 1962), p. 13, notes that food riots hardly figured in London's 'periodic rioting'. Shelton, *English Hunger and Industrial Disorder*, p.200, suggests that this was due to the power of unionism in London. The virility of unionism is accepted by M.D. George, *London Life in the Eighteenth Century* (Harmondsworth, 1966), p. 116, but London was the nation's major corn market and rarely poorly supplied whatever the price. When supplies were endangered in the 1760s the corporation acted speedily. In 1795 when the government directed the distribution of vital imports, the rest of the country was virtually forsaken in London's favour. But Londoners did demonstrate against excessive prices. The most famous is the attack on the King's coach in 1795. The riots in September 1800 took the form of street demonstrations against middlemen believed to be speculating, and in this respect were similar to earlier demonstrations against 'crimping houses' in 1794. Cf. J. Stevenson, 'The London "Crimp" Riots of 1794', *International Review of Social History*, 16 (1971).

3

'The Perfect Wage System?' Tributing in the Cornish Mines

John Rule

No group of nineteenth-century workers received more praise for their conduct, order and intelligence than did the Cornish miners. This regard was in marked contrast to the reputation of the eighteenth-century tinners for riot and disorder. In 1850 Wilkie Collins found them to be 'a cheerful, contented race', with the views of the working men 'so remarkably moderate and sensible' that he had not met elsewhere with so few grumblers. Samuel Laing thought the Cornish section of the 1842 report on child labour in the mines, 'by many degrees, the brightest picture we have ever met of the condition of any considerable proportion of the labouring class in England at the present day'. To a writer in the *Quarterly Review* in 1857, they were 'one of the most orderly and civilized societies in the world'.[1] To a surprising degree the credit for this was given to the methods of wage payment used in the mines, especially to the much publicised 'tribute' system.[2]

In their pioneering history of trade unionism, first published in 1894, the Webbs commented that trade unionism among the tin and copper miners was 'absolutely unknown'.[3] While they offered no explanation for this, for an earlier generation of observers it had been explained by the apparent effect of the tribute system in reducing industrial conflict to insignificant dimensions. An early nineteenth-century propagator of tributing, John Taylor, an experienced mine manager, who introduced the system into metal mines elsewhere in Britain, was quite certain of its benefits:

> The rate of wages ... regulates itself by the circumstances that ought to control it – the demand for labour. No one has heard of disagreements between the Cornish miners and their employers, no combinations or unions on the one side or the other exist; nor have turn-outs or strikes been contemplated or attempted.[4]

---

[1] Wilkie Collins, *Rambles beyond Railways* (2nd edition, 1852), p. 78; S. Laing, *National Distress: its Causes and Remedies* (1844), p. 41; *Quarterly Review*, 102 (1857), pp. 321–22.

[2] For a detailed description of the systems of wage payment in the Cornish mines see my unpublished thesis: 'The Labouring Miner in Cornwall, *c.* 1740–1870' (unpublished Ph.D. thesis, University of Warwick, 1971), pp. 34–72.

[3] S. and B. Webb, *History of Trade Unionism* (London, 1911), p. 421.

[4] Taylor's article is among several reprinted in R. Burt (ed.), *Cornish Mining: Essays on the Organization of the Cornish Mines and the Cornish Mining Economy* (Newton Abbot, 1969), pp. 38–39. The original publication was in *Transactions of the Geological Society*, 12 (1814), pp. 309–27.

Taylor's accounts were a main source for others' recommendation of the system. Charles Babbage was impressed enough by them to urge a more general extension of the principles of the tribute system to manufacturing as well as to mining, while John Stuart Mill was similarly approving. He wrote of the Cornish miners in 1845, that for, 'intelligence, independence, and good conduct, as well as prosperous circumstances, no labouring population in the island is understood to be comparable'. Later in his classic *The Principles of Political Economy*, he described the tribute system as being responsible for lifting the condition of the Cornish miner 'far above that of the generality of the labouring class'. A writer in 1834 thought it the perfect system to reconcile the conflicting interests of masters and men, letting normally difficult relationships adjust themselves in such a manner as to make strikes unknown among the Cornish miners. Giving evidence to a key select committee on trade union activities in 1834, a Birmingham steam engine manufacturer, who had experience of the county, advised that the tribute system, 'so perfectly prevented strikes that its extension would remove the necessity for any laws against combinations'.[5]

What was distinctive about the Cornish system? It paid by results, but hourly wages were generally rare in mining. In many industries piecework was used as a productivity incentive, but where underground labour was involved, the difficulty of supervising small gangs scattered over extensive workings made payment by results necessary, not as much to raise productivity but simply to stop output from falling below the norm.[6] In the Cornish mines underground work was divided into two categories: tribute work and tutwork. The former was used to pay the miners who excavated the actual ore; the latter the men who did the preparatory work of sinking shafts and driving levels. Tributers were paid a proportion of the value of the ore which they produced. Tutworkers were paid by the measure of the ground they excavated. There was little interest in the latter, but the peculiarities of tributing were the subject of numerous writings. What distinguished the tribute system from other methods of payment by results was that remuneration was not related simply to quantity, but also directly to quality: the wage eventually received by the miner was a proportion of the price the ore raised by him realised when sold by the mine. Observers were excited by what they persisted in seeing as a joint-venture in speculation by capital and labour. John Stuart Mill headed his section on the Cornish mines: 'Examples of the Association of Labourers with Capitalists'.[7]

Tributers undertook to work measured portions of the mine (known as 'pitches') for so much in the pound of the price which the ore they raised fetched when sold. Rates varied from a shilling or less to as much as fifteen shillings in

---

[5] Ibid., p. 48; J.S. Mill, *Principles of Political Economy* (1849), ed. W.J. Ashley (1917), p. 765; and idem, *The Claims of Labour* (1845) Toronto Edition of Collected Works, iv, (1967), p. 383; *Penny Magazine*, 27 December 1834, p. 500; BPP, SC, HC, 1824, v, 51 *Artisans and Machinery*, pp. 323–24.

[6] E.J. Hobsbawm, 'Custom, Wages and Workload in Nineteenth-Century Industry', in *Labouring Men* (London, 1965), p. 353.

[7] Mill, *Principles*, p. 765.

the pound, depending on the estimated prospects of the pitch in terms of both quantity and quality of ore. If it promised to produce a large amount of high quality ore, then the tributers would undertake it for a lower rate than if it did not promise to be very productive. The wage which the tributer received depended, therefore, not only on the amount and quality of ore which he produced but also on the current market price for tin or copper.

A further distinctive feature of the tribute system was the manner in which agreements were made with the miners. Pitches were contracted for periods of one month or two months. They were put up to the men at a form of auction known as the survey or setting. Prior to the auction, the pitches were inspected by the mine captains (managers), who were to put up the pitches, and by the men. Each side formed its own estimate of the value of various pitches, and the rates at which it would be possible to make good wages from working them. The captain put up the pitches in turn, describing their location and the number of men required. The miners, in groups known as pares, bid against each other, the group offering to work it for the lowest rate securing the pitch on offer; the contract becoming then known as the 'bargain'.

It has been suggested by a modern historian that, 'by forcing the miner to compete with his fellows at periodic settings of work for pitches offered to the lowest bidder, the system helped frustrate the growth of trade unionism in the mines and deprived the miner of the combined voice with which he could have demanded change'.[8] L.L. Price, in a lengthy description first published in 1888, referred to the 'divergent' interests of the men on setting day; and it is true that a situation in which labourers bid against each other to lower the price of their own labour was hardly a propitious one for the development of collective action.[9] The miners' preference for the system and their willingness 'to sacrifice a certain steady income, for the freedom and chance of great profit' can seem difficult to understand. An unwise attachment it may have been, but that does not mean that it was made unwillingly. A writer in 1849, who wondered that such a speculative system should be preferred at all by the miners, found that tributers would be on the verge of starvation before they would undertake tutwork, driving levels and sinking shafts in the dead ground: 'He was a tributer and tributers look with as great a contempt upon the tutman, as the tutmen do upon the surface labourers.'[10]

Status considerations certainly played a part, the tributers felt themselves to be the 'proper' miners. But the fundamental attraction was the possibility of great gain. The chance was offered of a sudden and substantial windfall. Although accurate estimation of the potential of a pitch was brought to a fine art by the captains and by the tributers, there were always times, given the geological

[8] Burt, *Cornish Mining*, p. 10.

[9] L.L. Price, '*West Barbary': or Notes on the System of Work and Wages in the Cornish Mines* (1891), cited in Burt, *Cornish Mining*, p. 115. Price's book was first published as an article in the *Journal of the Statistical Society*, 50 (1888), pp. 494–566.

[10] *Morning Chronicle*, 24 November 1849.

uncertainties of hard-rock mining, when the mineral content might prove to be in excess of expectations. The following case, reported in 1804, will serve as an example:

> within the last six or seven days two poor men [were] working in a part of the mine where the lode was very hard and poor, they sudainly [sic] cut into a bunch of rich copper ore, very soft and consequently easy to break. The poor fellows having by their contract 12s. out of the pound for their labour of all the ores they can break ... Their time expires at the end of the month, and if the lode continues so good as it is now in sight, I expect, they will get a hundred pounds each for themselves for two weeks' labour, and that same piece of ground will be taken next month for less than one shilling in the pound.[11]

The possibility of earnings of this size goes a long way towards explaining the working-miners' attachment to a system which often denied them a worthwhile wage, and sometimes allowed them less than a living one. The mineral content of the pitch could as well deteriorate as improve; false promise binding a man to a pitch which offered him little chance of good earnings.

The occasional worker's 'bonanza' did not affect the shareholders adversely, for, as John Taylor pointed out, they were likely to be rare enough. When they did occur they would 'animate all the others who increase their exertion in hopes of some similar discovery; they encourage competition, and frequently bring neglected parts of the mine into effective and profitable working'.[12] The discovery of a good lode could indeed have just this effect of intensifying competition and so lowering wages. In 1805, following a good discovery, a pitch was taken as 5d. in the pound. The captain's estimate had been a shilling but, 'there was no stopping them in the survey so eager were they to have that pitch'.[13]

Dr Burt has suggested that few miners could afford such speculation, and that most were the losers by it.[14] This was certainly the opinion of James Sims, whose account of the working practices in the Cornish mines was written in 1849:

> It may be urged that the present system gives every man a chance of having work; – granted; but it does not give to every one the means of purchasing the necessaries of life.[15]

The local poet John Harris, himself for many years a tributer, summed up the less attractive side of the system in his poem 'The Unsuccessful Miner':

---

[11] Courtney Library, Truro, Jenkin Papers, W. Jenkin to R. Hunt, 24 November 1804.

[12] Burt, *Cornish Mining*, p. 25.

[13] Jenkin to Dr Colewell, 25 February 1805.

[14] Burt, *Cornish Mining*, p. 10.

[15] James Sims, 'On the Economy of Mining in Cornwall', *The Mining Almanack for 1849*, reprinted in Burt, *Cornish Mining*, p. 10.

> A month had nearly ended,
> And he severe had wrought
> Day after day in darkness,
> And it was all for nought.
> The mineral vein had faded
> And now 'all hope was fled,
> Tomorrow should be pay day
> His children have no bread.[16]

The average earnings of tributers were higher than those of tutworkmen (in 1843, £3 11s. 7d. compared with £3 1s. 11d.),[17] but the earnings of the latter were much more consistent, although they depended to a certain extent on the hardness of the ground. A witness in 1864 thought that 'nine times out of ten' their wages would be between £3 and £3 3s. a month.[18]

A monthly advance known as 'subsist', was made to the tributers on the security of their expected wages, in order that they might survive in the long intervals between the receipt of their irregular earnings. It has been suggested that this practice gave the mine a financial hold over the men and lessened their ability to change their place of employment.[19] In fact the evidence suggests that, although there was considerable movement between mines at some times and in some districts, generally speaking there were advantages to be gained from becoming established at a mine. Established tributers were usually given preferential treatment by the captains; a tendency which led to the practice known as taking 'farthing pitches', that is working at a nominal tribute rate in order to get a footing in a mine with the option of renewing the pitch bargain on more favourable terms at the next setting.[20]

L.L. Price, in 1888, wrote of 'a district and industry, which seems to have escaped the disturbing influences of the industrial revolution'.[21] It was not, however, the divergent interests of the miners at the setting which seemed to him the most important contribution of the tribute system to promoting this state of affairs. He asked why there were no strikes, and why the relations between the miners and the mine owners seemed to adjust themselves so successfully. The real reason, he suggested, was because: 'the workman is in a sense his own employer'. He stressed this point: 'the comparative absence of strife is due, not to the elimination of the capitalist, but to the practical disappearance of the employer'.[22] Men who saw themselves as independent contractors, bargaining with the shareholders through the medium of the captains (who were sometimes alternatively called the 'agents'), might well have been slow to exhibit

---

[16] J. Harris, *Wayside Pictures, Hymns and Poems* (1874), p. 158.

[17] J.Y. Watson, *A Compendium of British Mining* (1843), p. 6.

[18] BPP, 1864, xxiv, pt 1, *Report of the Mine Commissioners; Minutes of Evidence*, p. 564.

[19] Burt, *Cornish Mining*, p. 11.

[20] *Morning Chronicle*, 24 November 1849.

[21] Burt, *Cornish Mining*, p. 122.

[22] Ibid., pp. 155–57.

the collective solidarity of a wage-earning working class. Since earnings were determined by individual bargaining and estimating skill, and by the fluctuating price of tin or copper, there was no need for any direct confrontation with the labourers in enforcing wage reductions in times of recession. Competition among the men would naturally achieve this end.

The 'practical disappearance of the employer' was not just the result of the adoption of the tribute system, it derived as well from the financial organisation of the industry, which was based on the so-called 'cost-book' system. To spread risk, mining enterprises were undertaken not by single owner-entrepreneurs but by a group of adventurers, who provided the working capital when called upon in proportion to their share holding. Day to day management was in the hands of the captains, men promoted from the ranks of the skilled miners. So far as Cornish mining was concerned, the representative capitalist was a financial investor, not a working entrepreneur. This was emphasised in a parliamentary report of 1842:

> The mine adventurers, the real employers, are not brought into contact in any way as masters with the working miners; so that the agents, men taken for the most part from their own ranks, are the only superiors with whom they have to do.[23]

The absence of a 'boss class' in direct daily contact with the workers might well be expected to have slowed the development of an articulate class consciousness. An experienced mine inspector, who remarked in 1855 that one excellence of the tribute system was that it prevented strikes, sensed that it did not provide the complete answer:

> it may be questioned whether this is not rather due to other causes than the excellence of the system of tribute and tutwork ... the system of labour and payment amongst the colliers in the north ... also shows excellence of plan and method, but still the colliers are as often ready to strike as if they were most unfairly dealt with.[24]

Trade unionism should not perhaps be expected to have been weak almost to the point of non-existence in a particular industry because of a single feature of its organisation. Its weakness was more likely to have been the product of a variety of factors which together formed an environment unpropitious for its early flourishing. Charles Barham thought that the tributer's hope of material and social betterment was an important factor: the hope that through fortunate contracting he might find himself, 'on a parity as to station, with the wealthier individuals near him, who have for the most part, at no remote period, occupied the lowest steps of the ladder on which he himself stands'.[25] H.S. Tremenheere agreed:

---

[23] BPP, SC, HC, 1842, xvi, *The Employment of Children in Mines*, p. 759.
[24] J.R. Leifchild, *Cornwall, its Mines and Miners* (1855), pp. 147, 155.
[25] BPP, 1842, xvi, p. 759.

They see around them numerous examples of individuals from their own ranks in every stage of progress towards independence and well-being; many possessing cottages and land, many placed in honourable and responsible situations in the mines, many who have risen to still higher points of social elevation.[26]

In the absence of a class comparable to the mill-owner of the northern industrial revolution, power and influence in the mining districts was wielded not so much by the adventurers as by the 'lords', the landowners under whose lands the mineral lodes ran. Men like Sir Francis Basset, Sir John St Aubyn and Sir Charles Lemon were tied to the working miners by all the strings of patronage and deference. This was a relationship more subtle and complex than the cash nexus, in which charity and ceremony were important components.

Being paid under the tribute system, and not seeing a class of employers visibly opposed to their interests, the miners continued to see the profiteering middleman, or grain-hoarding farmer as the enemy in hard times. They continued to express their discontent in the form of food rioting down to 1847. In addition in the Cornish mines, sickness and accident relief were paid from a mine club which was controlled solely by the mine, but to which miners' contributions were compulsory. The miners lacked the experience of the independent mutual funds, which played a clear role in the development of artisan trade unions. A letter from some miners in 1853 claimed that in many instances the dependence inherent in the prevailing system made it 'worse than parochial aid'.[27]

A factor more difficult to evaluate is the influence of Wesleyan Methodism, perhaps the strongest single cultural influence in the county. In Cornwall, the Methodists provided positive opposition to political and industrial radicalism by openly opposing it; and competitive opposition by monopolising local working-class talents and energies. A writer in 1865 remarked: 'We have few turbulent demagogues in Cornwall. A miner who has any rhetorical powers and strong lungs prefers the pulpit to the platform.'[28]

A writer in 1857 found it surprising that such a hot-blooded people should be 'comparatively indifferent' to political agitation: 'Leagues and unions, and Chartist gatherings have had small attraction for them, nor has any merely political cause found numerous and sanguine adherents in Cornwall.'[29] Much of the explanation, the writer thought, lay in the county's geographical position, which almost cut it off from 'the contagion of foreign zeal'. This isolation helps to explain the ignorance of the miners' struggle in the north, which both the Chartist missionaries in 1839 and the delegates of the Miners Association in 1844 found in Cornwall. It also helps to explain why the Cornish miners were able to be used as 'blacklegs' in several coalfield disputes. The tribute system

---

[26] BPP, 1841, xx, *Report of the Committee of Council on Education*, p. 94.
[27] See above, Chapter 2, pp. 17–51. *West Briton*, 26 August 1853.
[28] *Western Morning News*, 10 January 1865. See below, Chapter 9, pp. 169–235.
[29] *Quarterly Review* (1857), p. 312. See below, Chapter 9, pp. 169–235.

may have been of considerable importance in explaining the weakness of Cornish trade unionism but, with so many other factors playing a part, it can hardly be said that any significant lessening of the frequency of industrial conflict would have necessarily followed its introduction into other regions.

Contemporary writers and subsequent historians have tended to overstress the antiquity of the tribute system, seeing it as an inheritance from the 'free mining' of the middle ages.[30] To a degree it was: importantly so in the sense of the 'independence' which the tributer was widely acknowledged to possess. However, there is a danger of overlooking the way in which from the mid eighteenth century the tribute system further developed to meet the needs of an increasingly capitalised and yet highly speculative enterprise. The continued use of 'tinner', as synonymous with 'miner' through the eighteenth century and into the nineteenth, obscured the fact that the period of the industrial revolution was associated with a largely new product: copper. In 1787 an enumeration of copper mines gave 7196 adult male and 2684 women and child employees. Tin mining at that time probably employed around 2000. By 1851, despite considerable expansion and recovery in tin mining, within a total labour force, male and female, child and adult, of 36,284, adult male copper miners at 15,608 still outnumbered tin miners by 3000.[31] The copper boom brought new capital into mining and, though only to an extent, operated without some of the traditional constraints of the older industry. It was not brought within the jurisdiction of the Stannary Courts, which had administered tin mining since the middle ages, until 1836.

Those writers like Babbage and Mill who, as we have seen, praised the tribute system for producing exceptionally good industrial relations had never observed the system closely at first hand. Their accounts were based on a number of well-known descriptions. In fact there was not a complete absence of combination and conflict and in the industry;[32] and in its day to day operation, the system was far from 'perfect' from the point of view of labour management. R.M. Ballantyne, who did closely observe the industry before writing his novel *Deep Down* in 1869, provided a very full account of a setting at Botallack mine:

The men assembled in a cluster round the window ... while Mr Cornish read off as follows:
'John Thomas's pitch at back of the hundred and five ... By two men. To extend

---

[30] See, for example: E.P. Thompson, *The Making of the English Working Class* (1968), p. 68, 'the traditions of the free miner coloured responses into the nineteenth century'.

[31] Birmingham City Library, Boulton and Watt Papers, box 32; 1851 figures from general census.

[32] I am aware of seven strikes between 1793 and 1859, but none of them were long lasting and they were over local grievances at individual mines. The first long-running strike with an underlying union organisation, the Miners' Mutual Benefit Association, took place in the newly developing mining districts of East Cornwall and West Devon in 1866. *Cornwall Gazette*, 1, 8, 15 and 29 March 1866, note on strikes.

from the end of the tram-hole, four fathom west and from back of level five fathom above'.

John Thomas ... at once offered 'ten shillings' but the captain also knew the ground and the labour that would be required and his estimate was eight shillings a fact which was announced by Mr Cornish simply uttering the words: 'At eight shillings'.

'Rut her sown, s'pose', said John Thomas after a moment's consideration ... The pitch was therefore set to John Thomas ...

'Jim Hocking's pitch at back of the hundred and ten ...'

'Won't have nothing to do with her', said Jim Hocking ... resolving to try his chance in a more promising part of the mine.

'Will any one offer for this pitch?' inquired Mr Cornish. Eight and six shillings were immediately named by men who thought the pitch looked more promising than Jim did.

'Any one offer more for this pitch?' asked the manager taking up a pebble ... and casting it into the air. While that pebble was in flight, any one might offer for the pitch, but the instant it touched the ground the bargain was held to be concluded ...[33]

It will be noticed that John Thomas and Jim Hocking were given the opportunity to agree terms for continuing at their pitches for a further period; and that when the former accepted the captain's estimate matters were concluded. When the latter declined, then the pitch was auctioned. In theory in the former case a lower bid could have been offered and accepted. None was offered, nor did the management expect one to be. At most times there was a strong convention not to bid against the 'old pare'. At times when work was scarce, or in new areas, it broke down. The miners of the St Just region had a meeting in 1853 'respecting some bad customs among themselves', to reestablish the convention after a period of disregard. The captain at Boswidden Mine resolved to crush this combination, and his action in setting reserve prices precipitated one of the very few strikes in Cornish mining history.[34]

In general so confident were tributers of being allowed first refusal on reasonable terms that at times, as we have noted above, it was known for pitches to be worked for nothing:

To my surprise two of them were taken for nothing. The reason given was the expectation of being employed the following months and the hope of a better price next survey day.[35]

Some of the practices described below, viewed as fraud or stealing by management and by the courts, depended upon the assumption that tribute bargains were commonly renewable.

---

[33] R.M. Ballantyne, *Deep Down: A Tale of the Cornish Mines* (1869), pp. 267, 271–72.

[34] BPP, 1842, xvi, *Report of the Committee on Child Employment: Minutes*, p. 833, but the witnesses remarked that convention was better kept in some districts than others. *West Briton*, 25 March, 15 April, 22 April 1853.

[35] Jenkin Papers, 5 August 1816.

Throughout the period from the later eighteenth to the mid nineteenth centuries there were recurrent complaints of fraudulent practices by tributers. Pryce in 1778 complained that captains were sometimes bribed with drink and presents by 'takers upon tribute' whom they then allowed: 'to mix and manage the ores in such manner as will most conduce to their own advantage'.[36] Twenty years later a mine steward wrote of one mine: 'there was never a mine worse managed, nor was the process of Kitting ever carried to such a height.[37]

Kitting was the local name for fraudulent mixing of ores and complaints about it were made throughout the period. In 1832 a clause was inserted into an Act (2 & 3 Victoria, cap. 58), for the 'prosecution and punishment of frauds in mines by idle and dishonest workmen removing or concealing ore for the purpose of obtaining more wages than are of right due to them'. The clause, specific to Cornwall, defined this fraud as a felony and prescribed punishment as for simple larceny. Ore concealing was the simplest form, and all the ethnographic evidence points to it as widespread and as considered fair game if it could be got away with. If a tributer working at a low rate broke towards the end of a 'bargain' into good ore, he would have only a very limited time in which to raise it before his rate would be considerably reduced at the next setting. Accordingly, such ore was sometimes concealed or disguised in the hope that the captain's impression of the pitch's potential would not be revised and the pitch set again at a high rate. The concealed ore could then be presented along with the ore raised during the second period.

Another form rested upon cooperation between two 'pares' working on different tribute rates. They would mix their ores underground. If one had agreed thirteen shilling and the other five shillings, ores from the second would be presented by the former taker as having been raised from his pitch. Taking place underground, such practices were difficult to guard against. The Act of 1839 does not seem to have brought any increase in cases before the courts. When detected, 'kitting' miners were usually dealt with by dismissal and the attachment of a stigma which made it difficult for them to find work in other mines in the district. As a mine steward wrote in 1809:

> Altho' we might fail in bringing these men to a legal conviction, yet I hope the Agents in every copper mine in the County will faithfully unite in repelling those men from obtaining employment under them either as tributers or otherwise.[38]

Four tributers at East Pool were sentenced to six months at Quarter Sessions in 1835, having been convicted 'of a conspiracy to defraud the Adventurers of certain sums of money', but details are not reported. In a case before the Stannaries Court in 1847 a tribute pare, father and son, sued Wheal Budnick mine for recovery of wages of £11 7s. 3d., due as tribute for working in a pitch

---

[36] William Pryce, *Mineralogia Cornubiensis* (1778), p. 175–77.
[37] Jenkin Papers, 15 February 1791.
[38] Ibid., 16 September 1809.

set at ten shillings in the pound. It was claimed they had forfeited their earnings by breach of an article of the mine regulations directed against 'fraudulent and irregular working'. The captain in this case did not dispute the quality but the quantity of ore presented by the tributers. He had observed them to work only irregularly: too irregularly to have raised that amount in the time. He claimed they had presented ore raised by another tributer. Three miners were called as witnesses and, despite their evidence that the pare had done 'a pretty good month's work for two men', that they had been seen regularly at work and that they had worked in 'a miner like manner', the jury did not find the case proved. At no point was it suggested that the men stole the ore.[39]

But this was the accusation made by a captain against two 'poor men' in 1836. They were suing the mine for recovery of £39 2s. due to them as tribute on copper ore which had been set at eleven shillings in the pound. This case has much interest. The tributers had been working with only modest expectations when they 'broke into a good bunch'. The captain went down to their pitch and accused them of taking ore from beyond its defined limits. He turned them forcibly off the mine and refused them pay, alleging that they had 'forfeited their ore to the use of the adventurers'. The tributers established their case by producing witnesses to their having actually broken the ore within their pitch; and also by satisfying the court that 'in the course of mining, lodes are found varying in colour, size and quality'. What won their case was their lawyer's convincing of the jury that the captain, having set a pitch at a rate which made it much more profitable to the men than had been anticipated, sought to cover himself from employer dissatisfaction by turning off the men with a false accusation. In reporting the case, the local newspaper sympathised with the tributers, but changed its position somewhat the following week, claiming to have been made aware of evidence in support of the captain which would have caused the jury to find otherwise had it not been concealed 'from motives of compassion'.[40]

Cases of ore stealing only sometimes involved taking ore from beyond the bounds of a pitch, as in 1842 when two tributers were discovered by the captain, 'concealing themselves in a part of the mine which was not set to any one'. At other times it meant stealing from a pitch set to another tributer. In such a case the offending tributer could be charged with stealing ore, 'the property of the adventurers and the men working at tribute'. A case from 1847 can serve as an example. Two tributers were charged with stealing ore from a fellow tributer at United Hills Mine. The accused had taken a pitch at twelve shillings, the victim at eleven shillings, but had broken into better ore and was expected to take a next setting at eight or nine shillings. Experienced miners from United Hills testified that among the ore presented by the accused was some that was clearly from the good bunch into which the other tributer had broken. They were found guilty and sentenced to six months. It should be noticed that in

---

[39] *Cornwall Gazette*, 4 July 1835; 9 April 1847.
[40] Ibid., 8 April and 15 April 1836.

this, as in other cases where the charge was stealing from a fellow miner as well as from the adventurers, there seems to have been no reluctance to testify.[41]

Shortly before its sale to the smelters, raised ore was piled on the surface, a separate pile for each pitch. Sometimes, when a really good lode was discovered, the owners would hold it back from tribute and set it to directly waged miners, who were then described as working on 'owners' account'. Accordingly, as well as the piles raised by the tribute gangs, there could be piles belonging wholly to the owners. There was a temptation for tributers to wheel ore from such piles and to add it to their own: 'Oh that we should have been so foolish!', lamented one of two tributers convicted in 1835. They had been seen by several witnesses to remove ore from other piles and add it to their own. They had been charged with: 'feloniously mixing certain ores ... the property of the Adventurers with a view to fraud'. Piles belonging to fellow miners were also raided. When a miner missed some ore from his pile in 1833, he followed some footprints from it to another pile. Unfortunately for the two men accused, the footprints were unmistakeable: one of them had the only wooden leg in the mine. Supporting testimony was nevertheless needed. The tributer from whose pile the ore had been missed, examined the defendants' pile and 'knew prisoners worked where no such ore could have been raised'. He returned with the captain, who confirmed that it was ore of a richness which was found only in one shaft of the mine. Further investigation of the footsteps of the wooden-legged miner discovered four piles of the rich ore concealed under piles of attle (rubbish: oreless rock). An interesting witness in this case was a female surface worker who was employed breaking ores. She testified that the defendants had presented to her some of the richer ore for breaking. Faced with such evidence, the accused confessed and revealed where even more ore had been hidden. Once again it seems that in the cases where stealing from other tributers was involved, no difficulty in securing witnesses seems to have been found.[42]

In terms of punishment, ore stealing was dealt with differently from other forms of stealing from mines. Sentences ranging from three to six months, with sometimes a small fine, were usual. Yet when a miner stole a piece of iron worth 6d. from Dolcoath mine in 1778, he was sentenced:

> To be confined to hard labour in the Bridewell ... for a month and that he be then conveyed to Dolcoath mine and he there stript naked from the middle upwards and whipt till his body be bloody.[43]

This is not simply a case of eighteenth-century barbarism. Sentences including public whippings continued to be passed on miners who stole property other than ore through the early nineteenth century. For example, on two men for stealing a brass sieve in 1831 and on two other in 1835 for stealing eleven candles.

[41] Ibid., 18 March 1842; 9 April 1847.
[42] Ibid., 28 March 1835; 30 March 1833.
[43] CCRO, Quarter Sessions minutes, 17 July 1788.

On the other hand, no increase in severity of sentencing for ore stealing seems to have followed the passing of the specific Act in 1839, inviting them to be 'punished in the same manner as in the case of Simple Larceny'. Cases in the 1840s do not suggest any change in practice, but presumably the clause was intended to resolve some confusion. Two tributers in 1835 who took ore from piles and added it to their own are reported as charged with 'feloniously mixing certain ores ... the property of the Adventurers with a view to fraud': presenting it as their own for wages to which they were not entitled. Yet two years before two others had been charged with 'stealing' copper ore, 'the property of the adventurers and the men working at tribute'. They had done exactly the same thing. Both cases were heard at the Assize.[44]

Of more than a dozen descriptions of the tribute system published nationally in the early nineteenth century, while all commended it as offering freedom from industrial conflict and from trade unionism, only one chose to mention some of the imperfect practices indulged in by some of these 'model' workers. Yet, as we have seen, frauds and certain forms of stealing were inherent in the system. The *Quarterly Review* in 1827 did describe practices which have otherwise to be gleaned from few and scattered local sources.[45] How big was the iceberg of which a handful of court cases a year represented the tip? It is impossible to know. What is certain is that the derivative and bare accounts presented by nineteenth-century writers, even by those of the distinction of Mill or Babbage, were idealised economic models. They were not humanised descriptions of the social dimensions of a wage system whose peculiarities were of great importance in the lives of the thousands who made up a distinctive occupational community.

---

[44] *Cornwall Gazette*, 8 January 1831; 30 March 1833; 28 March, 10 April 1835; *West Briton*, 11 April 1835.
[45] See *Quarterly Review*, 72 (1827), pp. 85–86.

4

The Chartist Mission to Cornwall

John Rule

To some of the fifty-three delegates who assembled in London in February 1839 to form the first Chartist General Convention of the Industrious Classes, that body represented an alternative to the Westminster, a true 'People's Parliament'. But whatever it symbolised, the Convention had immediate practical matters to organise. Paramount among these was the collection of signatures for the national petition for the six points of the People's Charter. To this end it was determined in March to send 'missionaries' to parts of the country as yet unrepresented in the movement. Among them were the mining districts of west Cornwall, to whose unenlightened condition they had just been alerted. Two men, Robert Lowery, an experienced radical from the coal-mining area of the north east, and a Scotsman, Abram Duncan, were accordingly sent there:

> We, the delegates of the industrious classes assembled, having appointed you as mis-
> sionaries, do hereby instruct you to explain the People's Charter – to obtain signatures
> to the National Petition for Universal Suffrage – to collect subscriptions of Rent,
> and by every legal and constitutional means, to extend political information among
> the people, and in the prosecution of the above objects, we hereby charge you not
> to hold communication with any associated body, not to infringe the laws in any man-
> ner by word or deed.

They were cautioned to be 'an economical as possible' with their allocation of funds, and were then despatched into a county neither had previously visited nor had any personal contacts in. Their well-documented experiences, however, provide a chapter interesting not only in the general history of the Chartist movement, but also for the significant contribution which it makes to the controversial question of the role of Methodism in early nineteenth-century working-class politics.[1]

---

[1] For a succinct account of the Convention see E. Royle, *Chartism* (1980), pp. 22–25. *Northern Star*, 2 March 1839. The historiography of Methodism and its relation to radical politics revolves around the so-called 'Halévy Thesis', after the French author of the monumental *History of the English People in the Nineteenth Century* (published between 1913 and 1932), who argued that Methodism was significant in preventing a revolution in England. Interest was revived, with the hostile view of Methodism taken by E.P. Thompson in his classic *The Making of the English Working Class*, in 1963. For a recent overview which puts forward a thesis of its own see A.D. Gilbert, 'Religion and Political Stability in Early Industrial England', in P. O'Brien and R. Quinault, *The Industrial Revolution and British Society* (Cambridge, 1993), pp. 79–99.

The two missionaries travelled by ship from London to Falmouth (the railway was not to cross the Tamar for another twenty years), arriving there on the evening of 4 March. The town did not much impress them. They reported it full of 'drunken sailors and prostitutes', with a large number of shops which 'profited by their expenditure'.[2] The scene did not seem propitious for the opening meeting of their mission, so they contented themselves with circulating copies of the National Petition. Next day they set out for Truro where they proposed to hold the first meeting. Unable to book a hall, they decided to hold an open-air meeting in High Cross, and employed the town crier to announce it. Interest was certainly aroused, for a thousand people attended and it lasted for two and a half hours.[3] The interest of the local press was also aroused. The *West Briton* reported:

> They harangued the populace for a considerable time ... Their addresses evinced considerable talent, but were highly inflammatory. We hope the good sense of Cornishmen will prevent them from being tainted with notions so wild and visionary as those of the Chartists.[4]

The following day they went to Redruth, in the heart of the mining district. Here, despite a warning from a magistrate that they would be arrested if there was any disturbance, they held a well-attended meeting. Returning to Truro on the next day, they held a second meeting there, this time in the Town Hall. Resolutions adopting the Petition and in support of the National Convention were passed.[5] This outcome was perhaps not surprising, for a group of Chartists had already established themselves in the town. In his report of the meeting, Lowery wrote: 'We got a working man Mr Heath to take the chair, Mr Spurr and Mr Rowe moved and seconded the acceptance of the National Petition.' Neither elsewhere in his reports, nor in his autobiography does he make any further mention of these men. Duncan is similarly silent. Spurr in fact had presided over a named Chartist meeting in Truro five weeks before the arrival of the missionaries. He had had a very active career as a local radical and continued an active Chartist after his removal to London, where he was arrested on a sedition charge in 1840. For some reason the missionaries did not inform the Convention that they had met up with an existing group of committed Chartists.[6]

---

[2] *The Weekly Record of the Temperance Movement*, 11 October 1856, p. 234. Lowery's autobiography was serialised in this journal. It has been edited, by B. Harrison and P. Hollis, as *Robert Lowery, Radical and Chartist* (London, 1979). Letters from Lowery were sent directly to the *Northern Liberator*, a north-eastern based newspaper with which he had regional links. As well as in the Chartist Letterbooks in the British Library, there is some reporting of the mission in the *Northern Star*. Duncan also wrote a few letters to the *True Scotsman*.

[3] BL, MS Add. 34245, vol. A, fo. 120.

[4] *West Briton*, 5 March 1839.

[5] *Northern Liberator*, 16 March 1839. See below, Chapter 8, pp. 153–68.

[6] BL, MS Add. 34245, vol. A, fo. 120. For Spurr see below, Chapter 5, pp. 81–89, and PRO, HO, 40/54.

After this meeting the two men went back among the miners, holding meetings in the open air, despite snow, at the large village of Chacewater and at the town of Camborne. At the latter, the 'Whigs', they complained, had bribed the crier not to advertise the meeting, and they had to resort to having handbills printed and distributed around the mines.[7] At this point they seem to have conceived the idea of holding a grand, final meeting at nearby Gwennap Pit, a natural amphitheatre, which had been one of John Wesley's favourite preaching places on his many visits to the county. It was very much considered a 'holy place' by the local Methodists. The attempted implementation of this intent was later to provide one of the key moments of the mission.[7] The next day being a Sunday, they decided against holding a meeting, and went themselves to the local Wesleyan chapel. Lowery remarked on the custom of the women and men sitting on opposite sides of the aisle. The men, of course, sat hatless and Duncan noticed something which dimmed his hopes of success in the far south west:

> My Scotch friend, being a phrenologist, observed emphatically: The development of the women is splendid but did ye ever see such a set of bad heads as the men have?

He never did overcome his dislike of Cornishmen. At St Ives he complained that the 'working men' lifted their hats to him as they passed by: 'It could only be because I had a good coat on. I cannot bear such servility to the appearance of wealth.' The women, however, were another matter: 'Duncan says the Cornwall girls have almost tempted him to marry, would the Convention allow anything for a woman?'[8]

From Camborne they had moved west to Hayle and then onto St Ives and Penzance. From there they returned again to Falmouth, where this time, despite the attentions of small boys gratuitously armed with fireworks by the 'Whigs', they did hold a meeting.[9] Here they were heard by a local Quaker, who noted in his diary that both Lowery and Duncan were eloquent, 'but inflammatory, not to say seditious, shrewd designing scamps ... misguiding honest men with a blaze of enthusiasm'. He feared little, however, for although 'hearty cheers seemed to indicate that a flame was lit' he knew 'enough of Falmouth to feel pretty sure of its going out unless well fanned'.[10] Fanning the flame was a huge task. By now the missionaries had been more than two weeks in the county, and were due to return. They asked for an extension of their time: 'two months would be too little to agitate this county, the people being so scattered'.[11] From Falmouth they went on to neighbouring Penryn and again to Penzance. From

[7] BL, MS Add. 34245, vol. A, fo. 120.

[8] *Weekly Record*, 25 October 1856, p. 250; BL, MS Add. 34245, fo. 120.

[9] Ibid., fo. 148.

[10] Cited in A. Jenkin, 'The Cornish Chartists', *Journal of the Royal Institute of Cornwall*, 9 (1982), p. 57.

[11] BL, MS Add. 34245, vol. A, fo. 169.

there they visited the very end of the country, holding a meeting in the old tin-mining capital of St Just-in-Penwith. From there there was nowhere to go, except for the empty cliffs of Lands End, and they retraced their steps back up the county, through the village of Goldsithney and on to Camborne again. They then returned to St Ives, where, for reasons which will be explained below, they failed to attract a crowd. All that remained now was the planned final meeting at Gwennap Pit.[12]

From the foregoing narrative it can be seen that the missionaries concentrated their agitation on the mining districts, and further that they visited the larger settlements twice. This was a tactical decision. The scattered nature of the population among the mining villages and hamlets made it the best course to hold large central meetings, trusting that the spread of the news of the first meeting would bring the miners into the second in larger numbers.[13] Some of the reports they sent back to the movement's general secretary, William Lovett, conveyed a qualified optimism. Thus, on 12 March, Lovett read to the Convention a letter, 'giving a most cheering account of their reception in Cornwall' and of the effect of their agitation. Their mission had proved that nothing was wanting 'to rouse the community to a sense of their wrongs and obtain their co-operation, than a little trouble on the part of the Convention'.[13] Lowery also wrote:

> Our meetings are well attended, they come from curiosity, they are Radicals and do not know it, they are poor and oppressed and the moment they hear our expositions they adopt them.[14]

With the hindsight of historians, we could add, 'and then they go home and forget them!' For, despite Lowery's optimism, Chartism did not take root among the Cornish miners. From his letters and those of Duncan, we can see the real nature of the huge difficulties which faced them, which weighed more heavily in the scales than even the large crowds assembled for the moment. By the end of their first week in the county, they realised that they were addressing a labouring people to whom the great political awakening was yet to come. Duncan lamented bitterly that the Convention might as well have sent missionaries 'to the South Sea islands, to instruct the natives there in the principles of a free government, as to Cornwall'.[15] Lowery, typically was a little less dramatic in his assessment, but it was cautionary enough:

> The people here have never heard Politics, nor had any agitation on that question, when we enter a place we know no one, and if we ask if there are any Radicals they

[12] Ibid., fo. 178.
[13] *Northern Star*, 16 March 1839.
[14] BL, MS Add. 34245, vol. A, fo. 148.
[15] Cited Jenkin, 'Cornish Chartists', p. 58.

don't seem to know or when they answer in the affirmative it turns out the persons are mere Whigs or Anti-Corn Law men.

So unused to political agitation were the miners that they appeared, 'thunderstruck at anyone talking so boldly of authority they have thought unassailable'.[16] Some years later he recalled the response he had got from an old man at St Ives, when he had inquired if there were any radicals in that town:

'A' what, Master?' said he, with a vacant stare, 'Any Radicals or Chartists?', said I. I shall never forget the vacuity and bewilderment of his countenance. 'No', answered he, 'they catch nothing but pilchards and mackerel.'[17]

Lowery drew some comfort from his familiarity with the northern pitmen, pointing out that they too had been ignorant of politics until their great struggle with the coal-owners of 1831. Cornwall might yet become:

A rich mine of Radical ore which if skilful miners bring it forth may be fashioned into weapons that will do fearful execution on the host of misgovernment.[18]

Things were not to turn out that way. Instead, significant numbers of Cornish miners were to go to the north in the great coal strike of 1844 as strike-breakers.[19]

The missionaries encountered active opposition from a number of sources. 'The magistrates had condemned, the parsonocracy had preached, and the tyrant masters threatened', wrote Lowery.[20] Among the Chartist documents in the British Library is one which was not written by the missionaries themselves. Entitled 'Address of the Radical Reformers of the Western Division of the County of Cornwall, in Publick Meeting Assembled at Gwennap Pit to the General Convention of the Industrious Classes', its purpose was to appoint Lowery and Duncan as the Cornish delegates to the Convention. After describing their good work in the county, it went on to say that the Chartist cause would have been still further advanced:

had it not been for the interference and false intimidations held out by the Magistracy, Clergy and Employers, (who we feel proud to say are not the most intelligent men in our county). The Magistrates in many places have threatened to issue warrants for the apprehension of the missionaries. The Clergy who are always timid of any alterations in our glorious constitution as it fits to term it, employ themselves instead of

---

[16] BL, MS Add. 34245, vol. A, fos 120, 148.

[17] *Weekly Record*, 25 October, p. 250.

[18] *Northern Liberator*, 16 March 1839; BL, MS Add. 34245, vol. A, fo. 120.

[19] The coalmining unions sent delegates to Cornwall to dissuade the Cornish from 'blacklegging' but were unable to prevent many from going north. See *Northern Star*, 8 June, 17 and 31 August and 14 September 1844; and R. Fynes, *The Miners of Northumberland and Durham* (Sunderland, 1873), p. 91.

[20] *Northern Liberator*, 6 April 1839.

watching over their flocks in going to every cottage door, and declaring to the women if their husbands sign the National Petition, they would subject themselves to the penalty of transportation. The employers intimating to the men that worked under them, if they attended the meeting or signed the National Petition, they would directly discharge them.[21]

Their efforts were not always successful. The vicar at Falmouth forbade the town crier from announcing the meeting, but he was a sympathiser and went around to all the houses saying at each that he was not allowed to tell them about it.[22]

The mayor of Penzance was thrown into such consternation by the arrival of the missionaries, that he wrote straightaway to Lord John Russell at the Home Office, asking how to proceed:

> I write to your Lordship from a part of her Majesty's Dominions in which there is no clashing of interests between the agriculturalist and the manufacturer – in which the labouring classes are in constant employment, where absolute poverty is unknown, where loyalty is proverbial and contentment almost universal – But all this desirable order of things threatened to be overturned and society disjointed by a party of itinerant politicians who style themselves 'Chartists' and profess to be 'Missionary Delegates from the National Convention' and who held their first meeting in this town last evening – at which the most seditious inflammatory language was fearlessly made use of – Her Majesty the Queen was insulted, the Ministers were grossly abused, all the established institutions of the country ridiculed and the working classes were called upon to arm themselves and obtain by force redress from some alleged grievances and to sign a National Petition to be presented to Parliament insisting on many unconstitutional arrangements.[23]

The report is alarmist but, if they were preaching the use of force and using seditious language so overtly, the missionaries were certainly exceeding their instructions, and it is unlikely that they would have received only threats from the magistrates. One of Lowery's favourite oratorical methods may have contributed. If he noticed any gentry at the back of the crowd, he would look directly at them and in a loud voice announce, 'Fellow countrymen, I stand here to preach revolution', and would pause to enjoy their startled reaction before continuing, 'But mark my words and do not misconstrue them, Revolution simply means change, and the Revolution I advocate is a change from bad to good, from corrupt and extravagant government to a real representation, retrenchment and reform'.[24]

The mayor of Penzance's comment and the general prosperity of the county in 1839 was echoed by a Falmouth observer: 'Can't do much harm here, I think, People too well off to kick up a row.'[25] This was a sentiment shared by the vicar

[21] BL, MS Add., MS 34245, fo. 178.

[22] *Weekly Record*, 11 October 1856, p. 234.

[23] PRO, HO 40/41.

[24] *Weekly Record*, 25 October 1856, p. 250.

[25] Jenkin, 'Cornish Chartists', p. 57.

of Gwennap, who wrote to the Home Secretary, assuring him that 'a more complete mistake never was committed by the Chartists, than in supposing they could make converts here'. Any sensation their language had caused had soon died away and, despite large crowds, few converts had been made.[26] Neither was the Whig *West Briton* any more alarmed when it congratulated the mining population on 'the good sense they have shown in giving no encouragement to the Chartist Missionaries'.[27]

It is probable that had Lowery and Duncan been asked to nominate the group whose opposition they regarded as most significant, then, despite the efforts of gentry and clergy, they would have indicated the Methodists. Duncan, especially was emphatic on this:

> I don't think there can be much love of liberty here; its too full of Methodist Chapels, and they are too Priest ridden to like freedom.[28]

Lowery came to share this view, although as usual he was a little more reflective than his colleague:

> The working classes in general were a simple primitive people with strong religious feelings of an excitable temperament ... the Methodist style of preaching, however good to work upon their feelings, wanted some of the Presbyterian reasoning to cultivate their understandings.[29]

From the other side, Methodist counter-influence to Chartism was recognised and applauded: 'What', asked the *West Briton*, 'but our religious light is it that has kept our working classes at peace and free from Chartism?'[30]

The relationship of Methodism to the Chartist movement has often been discussed. The hostile attitude of the Wesleyan Methodist national leadership is undeniable, but so too is the sympathy of sects like Primitive Methodism to the movement in some parts of the country. The work of R.F. Wearmouth in this regard is now more than forty years old. More recently Epstein, for the framework-knitters of Nottinghamshire, and Colls and Jaffe, for the pitmen of the north-eastern coalfield, have indicated an input of leadership and organisational skills from Primitive Methodism into early trade unionism and Chartism.[31] So far as

[26] PRO, HO 40/41.

[27] *West Briton*, 5 April 1839.

[28] *Weekly Record*, 25 October 1856, p. 250.

[29] Ibid.

[30] *West Briton*, 14 February 1840.

[31] R.F. Wearmouth, *Some Working-Class Movements of the Nineteenth Century* (London, 1948); R. Collis, *The Pitmen of the Northern Coalfield: Work, Culture and Protest, 1790 to 1850* (Manchester, 1987); J.A. Jaffe, *The Struggle for Market Power: Industrial Relations in the British Coal Industry, 1800–1840* (Cambridge, 1991), pp. 120–48; J. Epstein, 'Some Organisational and Cultural Aspects of the Chartist Movement in Nottingham', in J. Epstein and D. Thompson (eds), *The Chartist Experience* (London, 1982), pp. 221–68. See also D. Hempton, *Methodism and Politics in British Society, 1750–1850* (London, 1984), pp. 211–16.

Cornwall is concerned, such an input is hard to find. E.J. Hobsbawm, in an influential survey article, concluded that it was probably wisest 'to put the lack of interest in and feebleness of Cornish Chartism down to factors unconnected with the religion of the Cornish', although Brian Harrison in a review of this essay pointed out that this was not the view of Lowery and Duncan.[32]

Analysis of the local relationship in the county must begin with an assessment of Methodism's overall influence and strength. Cornwall was the most Methodist of English counties. The religious Census of 1851 showed that the 49 per cent of the total population attended services on census day: 32 per cent Methodist and only 13.2 per cent Anglican. The parent body of the Wesleyans themselves accounted for 20.5 per cent, the revivalist sects of the Bible Christians and the Primitive Methodists for 6 per cent and 2 per cent respectively. In so far as historians have stressed the positive role of the last named in early radical movements, then it is clear that it was took weak in Cornwall to have had any significance. The percentages for the county as a whole disguise the fact that Methodism generally was much stronger in the western mining half, where three quarters of all the county's Wesleyans lived. They were numerically the significant body and their influence was strong.[33] Local Wesleyan leaders of the time, were not necessarily conservative. Men like Thomas Garland were liberal, even reformist, but while they might see manhood suffrage as a longer term goal, they believed it should await the general educational improvement of the working class. Garland described Chartism as one of the 'noxious weeds that spring from the ground where no care has been taken that it should produce healthful fruits'.[34]

The effect of Methodism on Cornish Chartism can be examined under three headings: 'Positive Opposition', 'Competitive Opposition' and 'Negative Effect', meaning by the last any effect which the dominant Methodist culture had on the miner's attitude of mind and outlook on life, which might to some degree have contributed to his observed political apathy.

The clearest example of 'Positive Opposition' in 1839 came over the intended final Chartist meeting at Gwennap Pit, a place to which local Methodistsusb were historically and sentimentally attached as the favoured preaching location of the great John Wesley himself. Although the *West Briton* reported that the meeting took place as planned, it is clear that there was confrontation. The *Cornwall Gazette* provided a more detailed account of what actually happened on the day, swallowing its usual Tory line to approve of Wesleyan doings:

[32] E.J. Hobsbawm, 'Methodism and the Threat of Revolution in Britain', in idem, *Labouring Men* (London, 1964), p. 30; B. Harrison, review in *Economic History Review*, 10 (1967), p. 179.
[33] T. Shaw, *History of Cornish Methodism* (Truro, 1967), p. 96; R. Currie, 'A Micro-Theory of Methodist Growth', *Proceedings of Wesleyan Historical Society*, 36 (1967), p. 72.
[34] T. Garland, *Memorials Literary and Religious* (1868), p. 398.

It will scarcely be credited that these fellows had the assurance to advertise their meeting to be held at the PIT at Gwennap, a place – as most of our readers know – consecrated by the ministrations of the venerable founder of Methodism, and still retained by his followers for periodical religious worship. The Methodists, however, knew better what was due to their own character, and to the memory of Wesley, than to suffer this profanation; the senior minister of the circuit very properly repaired to the spot with the parish constables, and kept the gates against all intrusion.[35]

Lowery's is interestingly different. He mentions the refusal of the Methodists to allow the use of the Pit, but suggests that, thanks to Duncan's oratorial skill, this did not work to the Chartist's disadvantage:

The Wesleyan Conference had been written to and had refused the use of the Pit, but all would not do. Although it commenced to rain long before the hour of meeting and continued to rain heavily, yet for four long hours did the thousands of people stand drenched to the skin, and urged the speaker to go on for they did not mind the wet. There was upwards of 15,000 people on the ground and not a place near to shelter them … Mr Duncan then came forward amid great cheering and addressed the people with great energy for an hour and a half. He denounced the aristocracy's plundering of the people, and with withering sarcasm he pointed out the hypocrisy of the bigots who would not let them have the Pit to meet in, though erected by the people's labour. (Here there was a cry of 'To the Pit!' and in three minutes though holding upwards of 6000 people it was filled – The Speaker refused to go) No they would show them they had the power, but would not use it …[36]

The meeting then continued to appoint Lowery and Duncan, the county's delegates to the Convention. In a letter to the Home Secretary, the vicar of Gwennap passed on approving mention of the Methodists' action: 'The leaders consulted with me and cooperated in the most effectual manner to prevent any outbreak, and also to discourage the intruders.'[37]

The element of 'Competitive Opposition' was also strong. Despite attracting large crowds, the missionaries realised that if a permanent basis for the movement was to be established, leaders would have to be forthcoming from among the miners themselves. 'The spirit is raised in the People', wrote Lowery to Lovett, 'But they want leaders to organise them'. It was through Methodist and Teetotal competition that he despaired of finding leaders: 'The Teetotallers and the Methodists have monopolised the speakers, and their leaders are against us.'[38] Duncan was even more specific:

They have been taught to believe that tee-totalism is the only cure for all the ills that the flesh is subject to; that all other reforms are idle – that it is a sin to attend to any

---

[35] M.S. Edwards, communication in *Journal of the Cornish Methodist Historical Association*, 2, May 1966, p. 109.

[36] *Northern Liberator*, 6 April 1839.

[37] PRO, HO 40/41.

[38] BL, MS Add. 34245, vol. A, fo. 148.

other … The Methodists have all Cornwall divided into districts. The tee-totallers keep their division of territory; in each of them they have from three to six speakers. They keep up an interchange of these agitators throughout the various districts. Between the religious and tee-total agitation, a considerable amount of enterprise and talent is absorbed. I could have no objection in young men devoting themselves to both; but it is a fact of which I have ample proof, that were any of these young men to give the mission the smallest countenance, they would never again be permitted to address a religious or tee-total meeting. Toryism and Pharisaical cant is omnipotent in every tee-total committee in Cornwall. These things have been obstructions and hindrance in our way.[39]

It was a view that was held within the county and, to many, a matter for congratulation. Looking back over the social history of the mining population almost three decades later, a local journalist remarked on the weakness of radical politics in the area: 'We have few turbulent demagogues in Cornwall. A miner who has any rhetorical powers and strong lungs prefers the pulpit to the platform.'[40]

Chartism's most immediate and direct competition came from the coincidence of the mission with the early heady days of teetotalism. James Teare had first visited the county in January 1838, when the impact was enormous. In the competition for signatures the National Petition was not in the same league as 'the pledge'. At Teare's first meeting at St Austell 150 people signified their renunciation of the 'demon drink'. Through 1838 and 1839 the progress of the total abstinence movement was sustained at a high level. By February 1839 the society at Ludgvan claimed a membership of 800 from a village population of 2500, while in May of the same year the 2500 members of St Ives added up to half of the town's population. During the week the Chartists visited Truro, a further 150 of its citizens signed the pledge.[41] At national level, Wesleyan Methodism was hostile to teetotalism as it was to Chartism, but it was not until 1841 that the Wesleyan Conference closed its chapels to teetotal meetings. Over the previous three years, however, the teetotal movement had built on the already strong temperance inclination of many Cornish Methodists in a county which by 1834 had by far the biggest membership per thousand of the British and Foreign Temperance Society of any county. To many Wesleyan miners, signing the pledge was an extension of their normal attitude towards strong drink, rather than a conversion from the ways of the devil. The local leaders of chapel society rapidly embraced the new movement. Examples proliferate in the teetotal press: at St Buryan in 1839 six of the eight class-leaders had joined; in the more populous Gwennap eighteen, while at Germoe, the local preachers were said to have taken up the cause in 'right good earnest'.[42] When there was an attempt at St Ives to

[39] B. Harrison, *Drink and the Victorians: The Temperance Question in England, 1815–1872* (London, 1971), p. 180.

[40] *Western Morning News*, 10 January 1865.

[41] H.L. Douch, *Old Cornish Inns* (Truro, 1967), pp. 108–9.

[42] On the close connection between Methodism and teetotalism see J.G. Rule, 'Methodism, Popular Beliefs and Village Culture in Cornwall, 1800–1850', in R.D. Storch (ed.), *Popular Culture and Custom in Nineteenth-Century England* (London, 1982), p. 51.

enforce the ban of 1841 on the use of chapels, the outcome was the secession of 250 chapel members from the parent body to form the Teetotal Wesleyan Methodists.[43] Tension between Chartism and teetotalism existed beyond Cornwall. Chartists found themselves unwelcome in the teetotal societies, leading to the establishment of a distinct Teetotal Chartist movement. As the *Chartist Circular* explained:

> The true mode of killing drunkenness, and the equally mischievous habit of moderate tippling, is the adoption of the Tee-total pledge. The Chartists, we have reason to believe, are generally in favour of testing the good to be derived from total abstinence. But many of them object to take the pledge from the present organizational societies in consequence of their exclusive or sectarian tendency. Many a man has said to the writer of this, 'I cannot join our Tee-total Society, for while its rules pretend to exclude all discussions on political matters I am constantly insulted and my Chartist principles derided.[44]

However, it was not only in respect of teetotalism that local independence was a characteristic of Cornish Methodism. No new national attempts at propriety, for example, could dampen the miners' extreme revivalism. Lowery and Duncan were to find this too for themselves when they returned to St Ives for a second meeting, having held what they judged a successful one there a week before. This time they could not get an audience. A revival had broken out. There were no people for a Chartist meeting, while the chapels were full night and day for three days, during which most of the people ceased work and the shops closed. Frustrated, the missionaries went themselves to the chapel to witness events. Lowery was familiar with such scenes of religious excitement, having observed similar happenings among the Primitive Methodists in the pit villages of Northumberland and Durham. He later offered an explanation for such outbreaks:

> The population possesses all the materials for such explosions, being full of warm religious feeling which overrules knowledge. Their daily language and the religious services they attend are replete with rapturous exclamations. Perhaps the mother is out on some errand, she has left the children to play with those of a neighbour until she returns. Bye and bye in imitation of their elders, they begin singing a hymn and uttering the expressions which they have heard at chapel. In the midst of this the mother returns. Her paternal feelings are delighted, and she exclaims, 'Bless the Lord!' She joins the hymn calls on her neighbours, who become similarly affected, and the enthusiasm spreads from house to house; then the chapel is sought, and the whole neighbourhood are infected.[45]

---

[43] M.S. Edwards, 'The Tee-Total Wesleyan Methodists', *Proceedings of the Wesleyan Historical Society*, 30, pts 3–4, September-December 1961, pp. 66–68.

[44] *Chartist Circular*, 1, no. 1.

[45] *Weekly Record*, 25 October 1856, p. 250.

As well as offering this plausible view of recurrent revivalism in a community with a strong chapel culture, Lowery recorded his disgust at the raw emotion of the scenes he witnessed in the chapel. Insight into the causation of revivalism and distaste at the phenomenon are well enough, but the essential fact remains: in competing with a revival for an audience, the Chartists were not simply losers, they were non-starters.

The underlying 'Negative Effect' of Methodism on the outlook of the Cornish miners is more difficult to evaluate. Clearly they had some tendency towards fatalism which was a not unexpected consequence of working at such a dangerous occupation. There is, however, a difference between a habitual fatalism and the passive acceptance of this world's trials which too much emphasis on the world to come can generate. The reporter on the mining districts to the parliamentary inquiry into child labour, in 1842, thought that:

> Nothing can indeed be more admirable than the cheerful confidence with which in the trust of a future life, the miner contemplates that termination, often an early one, of his labours.[46]

The system of wage payment at the mines even made it possible for an attitude of resignation to extend into this area. It is difficult in most circumstances for a labour force to see poor earnings as the work of God, but under the tribute system this was often the perception. The miners contracted in small groups to work a 'pitch' that is a defined part of the mine for the percentage of the value of the tin or copper ore which they raised from it. They offered to work at rates which they judged would give them good wages from the quality and quantity of ore they considered to be in the pitch. They had experience enough in making this estimation, but the best of judgements can err. Lodes can unexpectedly disappear, narrow or worsen in quality and it was common enough for miners to find that they had poor or even no wages at all to come at the end of a month's hard work. The opposite too could happen, lodes could improve in quality or quantity after the rate had been agreed and bring, on occasion, very good earning indeed. Under such a system, Methodist miners could see the hand of God, testing, punishing or rewarding. In 1846 a local evangelical journal carried an article entitled, 'The Cornish Miner: Or the Blessed Effects of Piety in Humble Life'. This portrayed a miner claimed to be representative. After a disastrous tribute agreement, the man and his family had been brought to the edge of destitution, yet:

> No rankling ill will to those whom Providence had placed in easier circumstances, arose in their minds. No hatred to their employers, or rebellious thoughts against the government of the country, for a moment found a place in their hearts. They laboured, they sorrowed, they suffered; but they patiently endured.[47]

---

[46] BPP, 1842, xvi, p. 759. See also above, Chapter 3, pp. 53–65.
[47] *Cornish Banner* (1846), p. 22.

The writer was anxious that readers unfamiliar with the Cornish miners should accept this case as typical:

> We are fully persuaded, that we have brought into notice ... that which contributes very greatly to give a character to the mining population of Cornwall. Great numbers of them are truly converted to God, and walk in the light of his countenance; and to the same extent that they are influenced by this holy religion, are they made sober, industrious, and patient in their temporal calling. Philosophy may extend its researches and give us beautiful pictures of moral life. Philanthropy may search out cases of suffering, and labour after means of relief. But while we rejoice in the operations of each, we cannot forget that this religion is the remedy which God has provided for the ruin of a world; and that it is the only agent on which we can certainly rely for teaching, guiding, raising and saving, fallen men.[48]

Max Weber described a 'theodicy of suffering' in which the effect of religious teaching is to turn the experience of deprivation and suffering from finding expression in social discontent into a vehicle of personal redemption. It was something of the kind that John Longmaid, one of the few known Chartists active in the county around the time of the mission, had in mind when he wrote to the *Northern Star* in 1841:

> The Wesleyans ... are the people's bitterest enemies. They preach up peace and content-ment as the only true test of their being in the right road to heavenly bliss.[49]

It should be as evident to historians, as it was to Lowery and Duncan, that the role of Methodism cannot be ignored in any discussion of the proclivities and responses of the Cornish mining community. Hobsbawm, however, pointed to other factors which, he suggests, contributed more to the weakness of Cornish Chartism. He described the county as having an industrial and social structure which was 'in many respects archaic'. 'Archaic' is perhaps a matter of a decep-tive continuity. The organisation of the mining industry represented, in fact, a high degree of specialised adaptation to the productive needs of a high (and increasing) level of capital investment in what remained a risky enterprise. It is correct to point out that 'the feeling that workers as a class opposed employers as a class developed slow and late'. But this was less the direct result of the tribute system than of the fact that, to spread risk, the mines were financed under the 'cost book system' with a plurality of absent shareholders. The clas-sic owner/entrepreneur of the industrial revolution did not figure in the Cornish experience. There was no equivalent of the factory-master and no direct one of the coal-owner. Hobsbawm further suggests that being paid under the tribute system, and not seeing a class of employers opposed to them, the miners continued to see the grain-hoarding middleman, or profiteering farmer, as the enemy when high food prices brought hunger. Accordingly they continued to

---

[48] Ibid., p. 24.
[49] Jenkin, 'Cornish Chartists', p. 64.

express their discontent in the traditional form of the food riot down to 1847.[50] Abraham Duncan learned of one such incident (presumably the food riot of 1831) at Penzance, but failed to put the right interpretation on it:

> The men of Cornwall relied now as they ever had done more upon physical then moral force; instancing two examples of their determination on former occasions. The one when a vessel was laden with corn in scarce times, for transportation; upon which the miners and fishermen rose, released the cargo sold it for the real value and paid the receipts to the owners.[51]

Food rioting, however, revealed the miners' conservatism and commitment to a prior political economy, rather than their potential for political radicalism.

There are other reasons too which contribute to explaining the observed political apathy of the miners, including the geographical remoteness of west Cornwall. The writer has surveyed these elsewhere in considering whether there was a 'configuration of quietism'.[52] Close study, however, of the Chartist Mission of 1839, suggests that it is not possible to offer an adequate explanation if the religious culture of the mining community is not taken into account.

Chartism in Cornwall did not end in 1839. Groups of Chartists continued to attract notice from time to time in the local press and activities were reported occasionally in the *Northern Star* through the 1840s. Camborne, Falmouth, Helston, Hayle, Falmouth, Truro and Penzance all experienced some level of activity. Groups of tradesmen in these towns ensured a persistent, but small, radical presence. Dorothy Thompson has stressed the importance of such artisans to the movement, but the real failure of 1839 was that it built no bridge to the 20,000 miners.[53] At a tee-total meeting in the large mining parish of Gwennap in 1840, a visiting speaker told a crowded meeting that he had had 'opportunities of knowing' that the Chartists were habitual takers of intoxicating liquors, and that but for this they would not have been led into violent acts. At the end of the meeting, forty-eight persons signed the pledge.[54]

---

[50] Hobsbawm, 'Methodism and the Threat of Revolution' p. 30.

[51] *Northern Star*, 13 April 1839. See above, Chapter 2, pp. 17–51.

[52] J.G. Rule, 'A "Configuration of Quietism"? Attitudes towards Trade Unionism and Chartism among the Cornish Miners', *Tijdschift voor sociale geschiedenis*, 18 (1992), *Regional Implantation of Labour Movements in Britain and the Netherlands*, pp. 248–62.

[53] See Jenkin, 'Cornish Chartists'; Dorothy Thompson, *The Chartists: Popular Politics in the Industrial Revolution* (Aldershot, 1984), p. 203. The places mentioned are listed in her appendix of Chartist locations, except for Hayle for which there is evidence in PRO, HO, 40/41.

[54] *Cornwall Gazette*, 20 March 1840.

5

Richard Spurr of Truro:
Small-Town Radical

John Rule

Richard Spurr was a carpenter or cabinet-maker who occupied premises in Pyder Street. Like many of the small tradesmen of the town, he most probably belonged to a branch of the Methodist Church. Possibly he was a Bible Christian.[1] Truro was a settlement which had prospered with the mining industry and, although not the assize town, it was unquestionably the financial capital of the county and the centre of most of the commercial transactions connected with the mining industry. But although drawing its wealth from mining, Truro was not itself inhabited by miners. The nearest mining settlements, Kenwyn and Kea, were outside the town. Trouble from the miners came in the form of disturbing visitations on pay nights, or when food was short. The lower orders within the town itself consisted of operatives like Spurr himself, small tradesmen like his butcher associate William Rowe, shoemakers, apprentices, storemen working for forage merchants, and casual labourers of various kinds. If we are to look for radical activity it is among such people as these that we must look.

The local press first reported Richard Spurr's political activities in March 1838. The mayor had called a public meeting on the 19th for the purpose of 'considering the propriety of presenting an address to Lord Melbourne declaratory of its approbation of the general policy of the Administration, and of confidence in their future policy'. Spurr addressed this meeting at considerable length on matters 'not at all relevant to the object of the meeting', concluding by proposing an amendment to an amendment, which had been proposed by a liberal named Concanen, calling for the abolition of slavery in the West Indies. Spurr wished to add 'something about the liberation of white slaves being also insured'. Sadly, the *West Briton* thought it unnecessary to print his speech, only recording the fragment about 'white slaves' to indicate its radical nature.[2]

On the 8 May in that same year, Spurr played his part in a day of some excitement in Truro: the day of the so-called Church Rate Riot. Spurr was among five persons charged with inciting the riot. The disturbances were unquestionably organised by the defendants. That is to say that they adopted a course of action explicitly designed to stir up the populace of the town. The five were:

---

[1] The only one of four men imprisoned with Spurr following the riot over Church Rates in 1838, whose religion was precisely identified was a member of this Methodist sect.

[2] *West Briton*, 23 March 1838.

Richard Barrett, draper, Jacob Corin Edwards, ironmonger, Samuel Randall, pipe-maker, William Ball, watchmaker, and Spurr himself. Barrett, Edwards and Randall were dissenters. Edwards was in fact a preacher of the Bryanite Connexion. They had refused to pay church rates for two years past. Consequently, an officer was sent to make a distress on their goods. It was here that what seems to have been a well-organised attempt to gain popular support began. Randall insisted on the officer taking a Bible, and the other defendants gave some other articles, all of which were taken to the saleroom of William Oke, an auctioneer, and a time for the sale of the seized property was announced. A handbill then appeared in the town signed by the three men:

> This is to inform the public, that the summonses, which have been so frequently served on us during the past month (21 in number), have this day been carried into execution, by the distraining of our property to a very considerable amount, so as to form a complete bazaar of plunder. The prosecution against us is instigated by Mr John Ferris, currier and tanner, and Mr. William Warren, attorney, the impartial church wardens for this town, no doubt through the instigation of a party who covet their neighbour's goods and anything that is his. The mock sale will take place at Mr Oke's Pyder Street (he being once a rigid dissenter, now a churchman; what he will be time will tell), on Tuesday 8th May instant, at ten o'clock precisely, probably that the church party may have a better opportunity of dividing it among themselves, as has been generally practised towards the society of friends for three centuries past; but we give this information for the satisfaction of our friends, and to assure those persons who may be disposed to become possessed of those goods, we shall notice their part also in this religious persecution, by handing down their names as family memorials in connexion with this religious crusade against us, inflicted because we deem it right to be dissenters.
>
> The articles are very appropriate viz:
>
> One Bible, three japan waiters, containing good likenesses of the Rev. John Wesley, and three ditto of Mr Samuel Drew, and one with a church in the centre, and several others with interesting representations, together with a general assortment of linen drapery, household furniture etc.
>
> We shall be in attendance for the purpose of informing strangers of the particulars and articles of sale.

On the same day Richard Barrett inserted the following advertisement in the *West Briton*:

> Taken by the constable of Truro, this day from Richard Barrett, London House, to support Holy Mother Church, and to provide sacramental wine for the ladies and gentlemen of this town, the following goods to pay £1.0s.10d. demanded for what the churchwardens, Mr Ferris and Mr Warren, called church rate.

It was on the morning of the sale that the two men later to become locally notorious as Chartists, Spurr and William Rowe, began to become involved. Rowe blew a bugle at 10 a.m., playing a call known as the 'General Assembly' to summon people to the sale. Promptly at ten, Edwards, Barrett and Randall entered the saleroom with a crowd at their heels. Among the crowd, Ball, Spurr, and Rowe were especially noticed. Spurr, claimed one witness, although another claimed it was Ball, cried out, 'Oke, how can you sell people's goods to support a d——d bloody church?'. The crowd began hissing and hooting, and to cry out, 'Put up the Bible'. Oke said that it was not intended to be sold. He told Miners, the constable, to show the Bible. Miners accused, 'You know Randall, you forced me to take the Bible'; an assertion which was not contradicted. At 10 a.m., Oke commenced the sale by putting up a hat which was knocked down amidst uproar, a waiter was then knocked down, and when Oke asked for the money, he was told that it had already been passed to him via William Rowe, who claimed: 'I believe Oke have got the money'. There followed complete uproar. Rowe called out: 'Oke adjourn for six months, you will never carry out the sale'. At this point Oke's window was broken and several of his shop fittings smashed, and he announced an adjournment to 2.30 p.m. Barrett now denied he had the power to adjourn, to which Oke replied that he would accept the responsibility. What happened next is best described in Oke's own words:

> There was a sort of groan, I can hardly describe it for I was in such terror – the crowd rushed upon me and broke the counter to pieces before me; and I being a little higher than the people, threw myself towards the kitchen door. They then layed hold of me and tore my coat in pieces.

The crowd tried to hold him, but aided by friends he managed his escape to the kitchen.

Just before two in the afternoon, Barrett and Edwards came to the shop and broke their way in with a crowd of people. Oke escaped, but does not seem to have lacked the courage to return and recommence the sale, although by now there were upwards of 600 persons in the street. He knocked down all of Barrett's goods from an upstairs window, through which a stone was immediately thrown. At this moment the mayor arrived with the town constables, cleared the shop and nailed it up. The crowd did not yet go home, however, for all evening they paraded the town behind a band of music, and when they came opposite Oke's shop they stoned it.

The five men were to be found guilty, but the trial was not held until the Lent Assize of 1839, leaving some eleven months intervening for Spurr to continue to build up his growing reputation as the town's most outspoken radical.[3] On 22 June 1838, the mayor called a public meeting to consider the best means of celebrating Her Majesty's coronation. Here at least, he must have thought, was a subject for a fair degree of consensus. He was wrong. Proposing a beef distribution to the poor, he announced that two bullocks had already

---

[3] The fullest accounts of the riot can be found in the report of the trial of the rioters at the Lent Assize of 1839. The *West Briton* provided a full account of the proceeding in a supplement to its issue of 5 April 1839.

been earmarked for the purpose. William Rowe with strong support from the floor, pointed out that two would hardly be sufficient. Ten at least would be needed. At this point Spurr intervened. The *West Briton* continues the account:

> he said as he had anticipated certain resolutions would be proposed to which he should have objected, he had prepared an amendment. But since he had heard what had fallen from the chair, he would now propose his amendment as a resolution, first premising it by a few observations.

By now Spurr was notorious and the mayor interrupted:

Mayor	Before you go on, I must tell, Mr Spurr that if you mean to begin any political harangue I will not listen to it.
Mr Spurr	It is not a political harangue – but it is a matter connected with the subject.
Mayor	If you continue yourself to the subject we will listen but not else.'

Spurr, after reminding the mayor that he ought to be impartial, read his resolution, which was simply the best way of testifying loyalty to the Queen was by 'everyman attending to his business'. This was greeted with a loud hiss, and Spurr amplified his resolution by explaining that any money expended in celebration would come out of the pockets of the labourers. He continued in similar vein until interrupted by the mayor, who to the accompaniment of loud cheers threatened to close the meeting if Spurr did not choose to confine himself to the business of the meeting: 'There is no need of such nonsensical harangues that you are now always bringing forward. Whenever the people are gathered together; they are doomed to listen to such nonsense as this ...' The meeting then proceeded in a more orderly manner and the first propositions were agreed to.[4]

When Spurr's political activities were next reported, the meeting was occasioned by a matter more serious than celebrating the coronation of the Queen. For some time complaints of hooliganism and drunken crime had increased in Truro, and it had been proposed to form a police force to maintain order in the city. A meeting was called for the purpose of opposing this intention, and a motion to this effect was put by a Mr Tealor and seconded by Mr Concanen. The motion was passed and Spurr then ascended the platform and proposed a vote of thanks to those who had called the meeting for their resistance to 'so oppressive a scheme'. This meeting held in December 1838, not surprisingly did nothing to stop the force being formed and, in January 1839, five subalterns and an inspector commenced their duties.[5]

The 8 May 1838, the day of the Truro riots, was also one of the most significant dates in the nineteenth-century history of the British working class. On that day was published the People's Charter. Drawn up by the Newlyn-born William

---

[4] Ibid., 22 June 1838.
[5] Ibid., 21 December 1838, and 1 February 1839.

Lovett, then secretary of the London Working Men's Association, it set out the principles of reform on which Chartism, the first really national labour movement, was to be based. The principles were equal representation (200 electoral districts of equal size); universal adult male suffrage; annual parliaments; no property qualification for members of parliament; vote by ballot, and payment of members.[6]

It was some months before the Charter began to provide a fresh impetus for radicalism in a town so distant from the main centres of political activity as Truro. But on 1 February 1839 the *West Briton* was reporting local Chartist activities for the first time. To established radicals, like Spurr, the clear formulation of principles in the Charter gave a new core to radicalism, and it is not surprising to find him taking the lead in establishing a local Chartist group. The first meeting was held at the Truro Institute. The room was half full and there were only three persons on the platform: Spurr, a Mr Longmaid, and one other whom the paper does not name. There were loud calls for Mr Tealor to take the chair. Tealor was the man who had called the meeting to protest against the police force, but it became apparent that acceptance of the clear principles of the Charter was to separate Spurr and a few others from men who had made common cause with them on past issues. Tealor asked Spurr the purpose of the meeting. Spurr outlined the principles of the Charter, and said the purpose of the meeting was to adopt the national petition for the Charter, a petition already signed by 'two million Britons determined to be free'. Tealor declined the chair. He felt such power should not be conferred upon the multitude until they had been fitted for them by previous education. He was hissed until he resumed his seat. Spurr stood up and was soon in full stride denouncing Tealor, the 'sham Whigs', the Tories, the Poor Law Bill and the 'blue devil' police force of Truro. Tealor attempted to support the Poor Law bill, but the meeting would not hear him, and passed on to conclude by adopting resolutions put to it by Spurr and Longmaid.[7]

The emergence of Chartism clearly had the effect locally of throwing into sharp relief the different political groupings in the town. Around Spurr had collected a small group of radicals who had accepted the principles of the Charter. Among them were certainly William Rowe the butcher prominent in the Church Rate riot, and Longmaid, who had shared the platform with Spurr at the first Chartist meeting, and who was to chair a meeting addressed by the Chartist missionaries when they came to Cornwall later in 1839. Spurr was clearly the group's leader and its most articulate speaker. The first meeting had shown that one man, Tealor, from whom they had hoped for support, neither believed in immediate universal suffrage, nor shared their opposition to the new Poor Law. A further split was revealed by a public meeting called on 15 February

---

[6] Two recent summary accounts of the Chartist Movement of value as introductions to the interested reader are, F.C. Mather, *Chartism*, Historical Association Pamphlet 61 (revised 1972), and J.T. Ward, *Chartism* (London, 1973).

[7] *West Briton*, 1 February 1839.

1839 to adopt a petition for the repeal of the Corn Laws. The petition was proposed by a Mr Stokes and, after he had spoken, Spurr stood up to give one of his longest and most emphatically radical of speeches. He agreed with Stokes, but he wished to go a good deal further. Besides the Corn Law delegates there was also sitting in London the People's Parliament, who aimed at getting them not just a cheap loaf, but a little bit of beef with it. He would put the Corn Law reformers to the test to see how far their support for the working man really went. Would they support this amendment?

> That in order to avert the ruin with which our country is threatened, it is not only necessary that the Corn Laws, should be immediately and unconditionally repealed, but that the exclusive mode of electing the House of Commons should be changed ... so that the productive millions may be fairly represented, that being the best way of repealing those odious, oppressive and starving imposts ... There were two ways of getting rid of a thing – by lopping off the branches by degrees, and by tearing up the roots. He was for tearing up the roots. They might be continually agitating the country – first to get rid of the Corn Laws, and then of some other law equally objectionable. But give the people their rights – they asked for no more and they would accept nothing less. The time was when the people were told they had nothing to do with the laws but to obey them; but in 1839 the people entertained a different opinion – they now thought that they had a right to a voice in the making of them. The people were oppressed but they would make themselves heard ...

He continued until the mayor interrupted by telling him to keep to the question:

Mr Spurr   I am proving to you that the best of getting these Corn Laws repealed is by enfranchising the people.

Mayor   That we cannot listen to. (*uproar*)

Spurr continued saying he would keep as close as possible to the question but before he did that he would say that Cornishmen should not want a working man to support their claims. As to the question, he was opposed to petitioning the House of Commons, because it would amount to a trial before an unjust judge and a packed jury. The Corn Laws had existed for the last twenty-five years, and he swore 'by the God who made him and by the Redeemer who he hoped would save him' that he would sign no petition but the National Petition of the Chartists for parliamentary reform.

Stokes tried to patch the rent by pointing out that over the country Chartists had signed the petition for the repeal of the Corn Laws, quoting the famous radical poet Ebenezer Elliot who had signed on the grounds that he was not prepared to starve while waiting for the Charter. Stokes thought there must be many present who would be happy to sign both petitions. Spurr was adamant: 'I will have no compromise ... The Cornish motto is "one and all", and let us all go together on this occasion. Let us either have our rights, or let us be content till we can get them'. This the mayor thought 'rather too rash'. Mr Heath, described as an operative, stood up to say, 'I cordially, willingly and gladly second neighbour Spurr's resolution'. (Heath joins Spurr, Longmaid and Rowe to provide our fourth named Chartist in the town.) Concanen, one of the town's best-known moderate reformers, begged the agitators not to wreck 'a rational cause' by their intemperance. He would not go side by side with such men as Feargus O'Conner, Mr Stephens, and Mr Oaster, whose conduct would go to make the home of everyman unsafe. He called upon the meeting not to be misled by men whose proceedings could only result 'in the destruction of property, the disjointing of society, and the endangering of life'. Spurr described Concanen's speech as 'humbug' and refused all demands to withdraw his amendment – 'I will never withdraw it. I stand up for the working classes of this country, and I will have it put'. The eventual outcome of the meeting was that the proposal for petitioning for the repeal of the Corn Laws was carried by an overwhelming majority, and greeted with hearty and long-continued applause. The *West Briton* headed its report: 'Defeat of the Chartists'.[8]

This account has been given at some length because it is the fullest account we have from which to see something of the nature of Spurr's oratory, and because it shows how uncompromising his radicalism had by now become. In the spring of 1839 the Chartist National Convention sent two missionaries, Abraham Duncan and Robert Lowery, to see support for the Charter in Cornwall. They held meetings in the towns and addressed open-air meetings in the mining districts. At their Truro meeting, the chair was taken by Heath, the operative who had supported Spurr at the Corn Law meeting; and Spurr, seconded by Rowe, proposed the adoption of the National Petition.[9]

This meeting was held in mid March and was Spurr's last public meeting for a while. On 1 April the Lent Assizes began, and the bound-over defendants on the Church Rate riot charges were tried. Spurr, with the others, received sentence of a month's imprisonment.[10] When their sentences had run their course, the five were released to demonstrations of enthusiastic support from the populace. They were drawn into Truro in a chaise and four preceded by flags and music, and followed by a body of Chartists and others. After parading the streets they went to the Institute, where a dinner was held. Probably the mass support was for the opposition to church rates rather than for the principles of the Charter, for at the dinner the most significant speaker was Edwards, the Bible Christian preacher, who spoke of the law under which he had been sentenced as 'a pagan law fraught with Popish bigotry'.[11]

[8] Ibid., 22 February 1939.

[9] Ibid., 15 March 1839. A full account of the Chartist Mission to Cornwall is given in my 'The Labouring Miners of Cornwall' (unpublished Ph.D. thesis, University of Warwick, 1971). A printed summary is provided by my 'Methodism and Chartism among the Cornish Miners', *Bulletin of Society for Study of Labour History*, 22 (1971), pp. 8–10; see also, above, Chapter 4.

[10] *West Briton*, Supplement to 5 April 1839.

[11] *Royal Cornwall Gazette*, 3 May and 10 May 1839.

Spurr's time in Truro was now drawing to an end. His business had suffered badly. Presumably a month in gaol had not helped, but his political activities had almost certainly lost him the patronage of wealthy customers. In June 1839 he pleaded want of work for many weeks when charged with not having paid his shop rates since 1835. This clearly contributed to his decision to leave Truro for London, although, on the mayor of Truro's own admission, so closely was he being watched by the police (the very force whose institution he had so vehemently opposed), that circumstances were combining to make life in Truro difficult for him. Out of work, on the verge of being prosecuted for rates he was in no position to pay, and bothered by the close attentions of police, he went to London and ended his career as a small-town radical.[12]

It was not, however, Spurr's career as a radical, but only the small town period of it which ended. In London he quickly established himself in the Chartist movement, becoming involved with the more extreme 'physical force' wing of the movement, and has been described by one authority as an advocate of insurrection, and opponent of the moderate William Lovett. In January 1840 while addressing a meeting he was arrested with other Chartists, and charged with sedition. Reading of his arrest in the papers, the Mayor of Truro took it upon himself to inform the Home Office of Spurr's earlier activities in Truro. He described him as 'a most violent declaimer at public meetings', 'a suspicious and dangerous person', and further claimed that he had not ceased to trouble his native town, for he was sending Chartist literature for his wife to distribute. With his leadership lacking, however, there seemed to have been no regular Chartist meetings in Truro after his departure.[13] The further details of Spurr's London activities are for the historian of London Chartism to uncover, but it would appear that for reasons either of a change of heart, or simply for tactical reasons, he was expressing a more moderate line by the end of 1841 when he joined hands with William Lovett and actively supported his National Association for the peaceful securing of the aims of the Charter.[14]

In small towns all over the country there must have been men like Richard Spurr, radical shoemakers, tailors, artisans of all kinds, who, unable in share in the more strongly supported radicalism of the industrial areas and some of the decaying older centres of industry, kept the condition of the working classes, and the great radical issues of the period from being entirely neglected in towns where many would have been happy to ignore them. The number of meetings reported in the columns of the *West Briton*, remind us that at least one Cornish

---

[12] 28 June 1839 and PRO, HO, 40/54, mayor of Truro, ' Respecting an individual named Richard Spurr, a speaker at Chartist Meetings', 21 January 1840.

[13] M. Hovell, *The Chartist Movement* (Manchester, 1918), p. 209; PRO, HO 40/54. For an account of Spurr's arrest see R.C. Gammage, *History of the Chartist Movement* (London, 1894), p. 172.

[14] Hovell, *The Chartist Movement*; see also the list of supporters footnoted by William Lovett in his autobiography, *Life and Struggles in Pursuit of Bread, Knowledge and Freedom etc.* (London, 1967), p. 214.

town experienced in the eighteen-thirties the regular cut and thrust of political debate on national issues. Without Spurr and his small group of supporters the debates would have been more ordered, certainly more sedate, but they would have been much narrower in range. They would have been more comfortable, but less vivid, and less real.

6

Resistance to the New Poor Law in the Rural South

Roger Wells

Early in 1838, the Chartist Bronterre O'Brien, reviewing 'The progress of that skulking pestilence', the Poor Law Amendment Act, castigated

> the apathy which prevails, in respect of that measure, in most parts of the country ... It is disgraceful, as well as lamentable, and the disgrace attaches, more or less, to every class of Englishman. It is disgraceful to the upper and middle orders, because it implies ... a barbarous insensibility to the wants and sufferings of those from whom they derive all their enjoyments; and it is almost equally disgraceful to the working and less affluent classes, because it implies, on their part, either a cowardly acquiescence in wrong, or a reckless disregard of the evil consequences which menace their order.

O'Brien pointedly exempted 'the men of the North' from this devastating charge. If Southerners (and others) had mobilised against the Act as had Yorkshiremen and Lancastrians the 'Starvation Act would have been, long since, a dead letter'. Until recently, O'Brien's contemporary criticism has been largely reflected in historical perceptions of southern social protest in the first half of the nineteenth century. That topic has inevitably been dominated by the Swing insurrection of 1830. Dr Reay's fascinating study of the Battle of Bosenden Wood in Kent in 1838, in which a small rising led by a millenarian figure collapsed after an unequal shoot-out with an army detachment, may technically usurp Swing's status as the last *rural* labourers' revolt in an historical panorama going back to medieval times. But Reay insists that ultimately Bosenden was 'against the removal of the crutch of the Old Poor Law', and he makes no suggestion that this localised eruption succeeded in modifying the operation of the New Poor Law.[1] Heroic and effective resistance in the form of the anti-Poor Law movement is perceived as principally a northern phenomenon, by its specialist historians, one of whom interprets Bosenden as the last gasp of southern opposition which was simply 'ruthlessly suppressed'. Dr Knott argues that southern protesters were driven 'underground', but does not challenge his predecessor Professor Edsall's dismissal, that 'for all practical purposes these disturbances

---

[1] *Northern Star*, 14 April 1838; B. Reay, *The Last Rising of the Agricultural Labourers* (Oxford, 1990), passim; quote from p. 140.

might as well never happened ... The new law in rural southern England became very quickly a matter of routine'. 'The rural poor reacted belatedly and ineffectually', chimes Dr Digby.[2]

These conclusions are strange on a number of counts, not least because the hated Bill of 1834 was primarily designated to eradicate the omnipresent poverty problem in rural southern communities. Agrarian capitalists exploited the Elizabethan Poor Law, which assumed a centrality in social and economic life, and few agricultural labourers escaped its clutches. At Oving (Sussex) the parish-run gravel pit functioned approximately to an employment exchange:

> a farmer used to go to the pit, and order a man to come to him and if it was wet in the morning sent the man in the afternoon to the pit again ... the masters ... always knew where to find men at half an hour's notice, and the consequence was, that they would not keep them employed longer than they wanted them.[3]

Totally inadequate wages – notably for family men with children – were supplemented weekly from the rates, and further payments made 'in need' to cover the costs of rents, fuel and clothes. Farmers laid off most of their men at slack times of the year, precipitating the unemployed on to medium-term total dependency on public funds. The downland parish of Willingdon was typical with fifty-three of the seventy-nine labourers unemployed in midwinter 1834–35. The degree of labourer dependency on the old Poor Law was irrefutably proved by Poor Law Commission's famous *Report* of 1834 and reiterated by its officers like W.H.T. Hawley, who wrote of the Weald that

> every abuse which has accompanied the career of Pauperism ... may be traced through the parochial annals of this district which present an unblushing Account of Labour-Rates, Billetings – payment of Rents, cheap Labour at the Expense of Ratepayers in the putting out of parish Children, employment of parish paupers and...that pernicious system ... giving Relief in aid of Wages.[4]

Rural craftsmen were not immune from this subjugation. Bad weather and low demand for labour forced many artisans and tradesmen to seek parochial relief; employment for some was found in the maintenance of workhouses and other parish property, and Burwash vestry stipulated that 'all Tradespeople applying

---

[2] J. Knott, *Popular Opposition to the 1834 Poor Law* (1986), especially pp. 70–71, 74–75, 82; N.C. Edsall, *The Anti-Poor Law Movement, 1834–44* (Manchester, 1971), pp. 27–31, 40–41; A. Digby, 'The Rural Poor Law', in D. Fraser (ed.), *The New Poor Law in the Nineteenth Century* (1976), pp. 151–52. But cf. J. Lowerson, 'The Aftermath of Swing: Anti-Poor Law Movements and Rural Trades Unions in the South-East of England', in A. Charlesworth (ed.), *Rural Social Change and Conflicts since 1500* (Hull, 1983), pp. 55–82; and Lowerson, 'Anti-Poor Law Movements and Rural Trade Unionism in the South East, 1835', in Charlesworth (ed.), *An Atlas of Rural Protest in Britain, 1548–1900* (1983) pp. 155–58.

[3] BPP, SC, HC, 'Agricultural Depression', 465 (1837), xvii, Q. 14561, evidence of farmer William Field, Rumboldswick.

[4] Hawley to the Poor Law Commission, 9 February and 15 August 1835, PRO, MH 12/12854; 13138.

for work are to draw a Ticket for their Master'. Others at Midhurst, including brickmakers, sawyers, joiners, papermakers, fishermen and a 'hog-butcher', were put to degrading parish work alongside agricultural labourers on the roads.[5]

Inevitably, Poor Law administration became a forum for struggle, much of it on class lines. The propagandist – and polemical – 1834 *Report* selectively analysed this conflict. It emphasised workers' assumptions that they had an indisputable right to relief, which encouraged idleness and insolence to employer and parish officer alike; and it claimed that the Bench, on appeal, regularly reversed parochial relief decisions made in the cause of economy, and so as to discriminate against workshy and subordinate claimants. In reality, magistrates were not invariably soft touches, but commonly 'treat ... complaints' from appellants 'with indifference ... hautiness and severe reproof'. Vestry oligarchs were not invariably self-interested small farmers and petty entrepreneurs who allegedly used their control of Poor Law administration to channel the rates into the pockets of their own employees and customers. Robertsbridge vestrymen 'never call a man Tom, Dick etc. but you damned rascal ... at every word'; 'Every parish' with its 'own peculiar system' was 'directed more strictly and executed with more or less Severity', according to a Wealden cleric. The 'greatest merits' of Poor Law officers, especially salaried ones, turned on 'browbeating the Applicants for relief': no wonder 'paupers' designated them 'their Enemies'.[6] But if the Poor Law Commissioners' presentation of their findings was essentially unbalanced, they correctly identified considerable vested interests which had developed across time and were embedded in the old system's machinery in the 1830s. The radical ideology which nurtured the most stringent clauses of the Poor Law Amendment Act, especially the commitment to abolish all non-medical outdoor relief to able-bodied males, literally threatened the socio-economic equilibrium of the rural south.[7]

The Act's supporters claimed that it would terminate exploitation of the social security system by employers; employees would be forced to subsist exclusively on their earnings to escape incarceration in punitive workhouses, but this revolution would be eased by automatic, upward pressure on wage levels. Utilitarian

[5] Petition from Bramber, *Sussex Weekly Advertiser*, 25 January 1822. Vestry minutes, Midhurst 1818, and Burwash 5 March 1831, West Sussex County Record Office (subsequently WSCRO), Par. 138/12/3. East Sussex County Record Office (subsequently ESCRO), Par. 284/12/1. R. Weale, Midhurst, to the Duke of Richmond, 10 April 1834, WSCRO, Goodwood Papers (subsequently Goodwood) 669. For a more extended review of this evidence, see R. Wells, 'Social Protest, Class, Conflict and Consciousness in the English Countryside, 1700–1880', in M. Reed and Wells (eds), *Class, Conflict and Protest in the English Countryside, 1700–1880* (1990), especially pp. 131–47.

[6] *Kent Herald*, 25 November Rev. Collingwood, Battle, to Home Secretary Melbourne, n.d. (November 1830), PRO, HO 52/10, fos 448–52. Inigo Thomas JP, Willingdon, to Edwin Chadwick, 25 September 1834, PRO, MH 12/12854. Draft, return to PLC questionnaire, from Wealden Squire, George Courthope, n.d. [1833], ESCRO, Sussex Archaeological Collection, CO/C/230.

[7] It must be emphasised that the 1834 *Report*, 'was not much concerned about [out] relief to the non-able-bodied, the aged, and the infirm'; the Commissioners' prime target, before and after that, remained the various modes of outdoor relief to able-bodied men. Karel Williams, *From Pauperism to Poverty* (1981), esp. pp. 52–53.

ideology also promised huge rate reductions for rural capitalists; it extended moral regeneration through the restoration of healthy independence for their workforce. 'The Honest Industrious Labourer' would be rewarded, made '*much better off* than the idle or the Drunkard ... who would scarcely exert himself for his Family', to be designedly discriminated against by the new system.[8] For such a radical proposal, the Bill enjoyed a relatively easy passage through parliament. Few southern MPs, with the notable exception of T.L. Hodges of West Kent, opposed the measure. The Bill's failure to divide parliamentarians on party lines was reflected in the regional press. Prior to the foundation of the ultra-radical *Brighton Patriot* in February 1835, only the maverick Whig *Kent Herald* remained obdurately opposed to the entire edifice. Whig and Tory newspapers extolled the Act's virtues and explained its ideological premises. Criticism was largely muted and partial, as exemplified by the Tory *Brighton Gazette's* hostility to a centralised bureaucracy and its defence of the magistracy against the Poor Law Commission's claim of inept intervention in relief administration. The liberal *Sussex Advertiser* devoted many columns to support the Act prior to implementation, and thereafter converted materials supplied by an assistant commissioner into news items. Certain southern magistrates, notably William Day of Sussex, were leading advocates of fundamental Poor Law reform; their propagandist role was fortified by the Commission's secretary Chadwick's circular letter, enclosing copies of the Act to all JPs and requesting their support late in 1834.[9]

The universally hostile reception accorded to the Act and all its works demonstrates the signal failure of this propaganda. Four important factors – two of which were the direct product of the activity of the assistant commissioners before the Act actually became law – aggravated the suspicion, fear and enmity generated by the knowledge of imminent change. First, in the autumn of 1834, farmers seized on the pretext of further falls in the price of agricultural produce to cut wages; those who resisted – on humanitarian grounds – were commonly bludgeoned into compliance at heated vestry meetings.

Secondly, this fortuitous negation of the promise of the new law's architects provided fertile ground for the exploitation of the issue by radical activists anxious to sustain claims of Whig treachery and politicise the masses in favour of the democratic reform not achieved through the 1832 Reform Act. In West Sussex 'fellows with placards in their hats' were encountered 'hawking about at a cheap rate the new Poor Bill'; in November 1834 'discussions are very common on the subject at the Beer shops'.[10]

[8] John Ellman, Glynde, to Richmond, 16 June 1835, enclosing his printed address to Sussex agricultural labourers, published 18 May 1835, WSCRO, Goodwood 1574.

[9] *Kent Herald*, 11 April and 21 November 1833; *Brighton Gazette*, 3 October 1833, 16 January, 13 March, 15 May and 23 October 1834; *Sussex Advertiser*, 19 and 26 January and 16 February 1835; Hawley to the PLC, 1 December 1835, PRO, MH 12/12931. A. Brundage, *The Making of the New Poor Law, 1832–39* (1978), pp. 30–31, 75, ch. 3, passim.

[10] BPP, 1837, xvii, QQ. 604–9, 11256–57; *Brighton Gazette*, 6 November; John Woods, Chidgrove, to Richmond, 28 October 1834, WSCRO, Goodwood 1477.

Thirdly, the assistant commissioners strove to extend the transition period and to reduce the impact of the new legislation, by forcefully encouraging the implementation of the principles of the Act in the parishes over the winter of 1834–35, before the Unions were even designated, let alone operative. Hawley, disgusted by the non-provision of work for the unemployed of Willingdon, ordered the parish officers to rent land and cultivate it in such a fashion as 'to effect a separation of the men of different characters'; piece rates were to govern payment, but earnings must remain lower than those of 'independent labourers', and were (with other relief) to be withheld from the ill-behaved and insubordinate. Payments with respect to children under automatic scales were to cease, in favour of specific investigation of the real requirements of individual claimants. The overseers were told that the objects of this 'first essay' were not profits, but intimidation, namely getting 'rid of some of your worst and most idle characters'.[11] Hawley insisted that Battle relief administrators should ensure that claimants had legitimately expended all their peak harvest earnings before receiving unemployment benefit; his intervention generated a street protest by 'starving' claimants and a formal protest from the parish officers to the Poor Law Commission.[12] As Hawley himself testified, many 'overseers are afraid in single parishes to take upon themselves the originating … reformation'. The results were the disparity and confusion registered by Inigo Thomas JP: some parishes experimented with 'gradual and minute alterations' while others were 'plungeing at once into bolder and harsher measures'. Some, like Barcombe, did nothing. No work was organised for the ninety men unemployed in November 1834, who were – according to Hawley – 'when not absolutely in a state of idleness, are employed in pilfering and highway Robbery', ironically a claim with some justification.[13] If disparity meant that these grievances were not experienced universally, too many from the ranks of claimants, ratepayers and authorities got a nasty foretaste of the reality of utilitarian values, without the protective shield of the law or the strategic support of the Poor Law Commission and government.[14]

Fourthly, assistant commissioners arrived in the south late in 1834 to explain the new machinery to ratepayers, and to assess socio-political geography prior

[11] Hawley to the PLC, 9 February, enclosing copy Hawley to overseer Denman, Willingdon, 7 February 1835, PRO, MH 12/12854.

[12] Solicitor C. Burney, Robertsbridge, to the PLC, 30 November; Battle overseers and churchwardens, and Hawley, to the PLC, 4 and 5 December 1834, PRO, MH 12/12747; 32/38.

[13] In the late 1830s Barcombe hosted the Heasman gang, whose eventually notorious activities commenced at this moment. R. Wells, 'Popular Protest and Social Crime: The Evidence of Criminal Gangs in Southern England, 1790–1860', in B. Stapleton (ed.), *Conflict and Community in Southern England* (Gloucester, 1991), pp. 149–55. Hawley to the PLC, 25 November 1834 and 9 February 1835; Thomas to Chadwick, 25 September 1834, PRO, MH 12/12854; 32/38.

[14] Cf. William Day's advocacy that poor relief reform 'under the sanction of the law' was vastly preferable; 'however it may be murmured at, the odium is removed from the obnoxious vestryman or the individual magistrate'. W. Day, *An Inquiry into the Poor Laws and Surplus Labour* (2nd edn, 1833), pp. 68–69.

to the formation of the new unions. This public relations exercise was badly handled from the start, partly because the Poor Law Commission insisted that invitations to meetings should be confined to the more affluent inhabitants; 'knowing the prejudices which guide the Majority of' ratepayers, the assistant commissioners were 'to avoid' genuinely public meetings. At Uckfield, Hawley approached the 'Owners of Property and influential Ratepayers ... to render the meeting as select and little thronged as possible'. This strategy failed on two counts; where private meetings convened successfully, secrecy served merely to antagonise the excluded and to aggravate their suspicions. Where knowledge of the assistant commissioners' furtive invitations was leaked, large numbers commonly turned up to demand admittance. Hawley's clandestine approaches to overseers at Lewes were promptly communicated to the press; subsequent stormy conventions in each component parish formally recorded the outspoken opposition of massive majorities.[15] The Commission's officers were relentlessly confronted by hostile assemblies of their own making; tempers flared, and the commissioners' increasingly arrogant and autocratic public response increased alienation, notably of those whose support was crucial. Assistant commissioner Pilkington told the Rev. Edward Eadle to 'Hold your tongue', whereupon the meeting dissolved in uproar. A Fareham objector who voiced the widespread disgust at the separation of families consigned to the workhouse was rudely informed that a public forum was 'a most improper time and an unsuitable occasion for declamatory addresses and appeals to the passions'. The entire operation served principally as a vehicle for opposition; only one supporter of the Amendment Act emerged at meetings at Arundel and Shoreham, while seventy-three opponents at Sittingbourne petitioned against. Most Wadhurst ratepayers eschewed consultations with Hawley, and the minority who did turn up 'appeared ... hostile to the new law, and did not disguise the distaste to a Union' with other parishes. Lamberhurst ratepayers delivered an 'unqualified censure', and their Burwash counterparts testified to their 'highly unpalatable' perceptions of the Act to Hawley's face. The assistant commissioners were left in no doubt that the lesser ratepayers were universally opposed, and that they were supported by many greater contributors to the rates, notably in the towns.[16]

The assistant commissioners took residual comfort in the mechanics of the patriarchal rural system, for their sole consolation lay in the 'resident gentry' who mostly comprehended the Act's objectives and were 'highly favourable'. The Act enhanced landlord power. A combination of plural votes based on property values, the vulnerability of tenants to landowners' directives over the use of the vote, and the magistracy's *ex-officio* status on the new Boards of Guardians proved crucial when the assistant commissioners commenced implementation in the spring of

[15] Hawley to the PLC, 18 and 23 January, and 1 February, PRO, MH 12/13015; 13157; 32/38; *Sussex Advertiser*, 26 January, 2 and 9 February 1835.

[16] Hawley to the PLC, 15 August, PRO, 12/13138; *Hampshire Telegraph*, 4 May; *Sussex Advertiser*, 20 April and 6 July; *Brighton Patriot*, 4 August 1835; BPP, 1837, xvii, QQ. 17005–17033.

1835. Nevertheless, the opposition maintained its momentum despite the gentry. A number of parishes, especially but not exclusively those not within the grasp of major landowners, refused to elect guardians. Orchestrated defiance provided a forum for the articulation of other grievances – Northiam tried to make elections conditional on a resolution of a local tithe dispute – but such demonstrations exposed obstructive communities to the full electoral policing powers of the Poor Law Commission, which were also deployed to impede the election of outspoken opponents of the law, including Charles Brooker of Alfriston.[17] However, in many towns, the elections fuelled party conflict, and obstruction through non-election where psephological conditions were most favourable evaporated in the struggle for supremacy between Whig and Tory. Indeed, in some urban locations, the new neo-democratic arm of local government facilitated a determined political thrust by radicals. At Lewes, 'a complete political Hornet's nest', according to Hawley, aspirant 'greasy interested artisans' plunged the town into chaos 'in the full enjoyment of their fancy for elections'; here, opponents also concluded that participation was the key to defeat government and 're-establish all the abuses' of the 'Old System'. Hawley was horrified when certain guardians, including some from predominantly rural unions, leaked pre-implementation planning decisions. The Boards' 'proceedings', he opined, 'ought to be sacred', and thus began the assistant commissioners' protracted struggle to guarantee confidentiality and preserve the guardians from the prying eyes of the press. But this initial secrecy early in 1835 did nothing to alleviate fears; on the contrary it stimulated rumours of conspiratorial progress and fuelled exaggerations of the reformed system's objectives.[18]

The assistant commissioners, supported by the bulk of the gentry, forged ahead in this pregnant atmosphere to implement the Act piecemeal across the south from the spring of 1835. Some support in key areas was lost, and tension increased, when the commissioners brushed aside the nervousness exuded by timid, newly-consolidated Boards of guardians. Pilkington's autocratic reaction wrecked his relationship with the virtually handpicked Board at Westhampnett, at the centre of the domain of one of the Act's ministerial architects, the Duke of Richmond. Fierce argument over implementation led to undiplomatic statements by several supporters, including the vicar of Piecombe who opined that 'till now the poor had lived too much like gentlefolks', and one of his congregation whose odious reference to Irish peasant diets earned him the nickname 'Old Buttermilk'.[19]

[17] Hawley to Nicholls, 9 April and to the PLC, 11 January, 30 March, 12 June and 15 August; Brooker to the PLC, 17 and 19 March, PRO, MH 12/12747; 12854; 13136; 13157; 32/38; *Sussex Advertiser*, 6 April, 19 October and 7 December 1835; *Brighton Patriot*, 31 July and 7 August 1838. For Brooker, see below, p. 113, and 'Southern Chartism', below, Chapter 7, pp. 127–51.

[18] Hawley to Nicholls, 18 July, 7 and 11 August 1835, and 7 February 1836, and to the PLC, 15 July, PRO, MH 12/13015; 32/38; *Sussex Advertiser*, 16 February and 3 August 1835.

[19] R. Raper, Chichester, 1 and 20 May, and R. Prime, Walburton, to Richmond, 16 May, WSCRO, Goodwood 1573; *Brighton Patriot*, 7 July 1835.

Riotous popular resistance was galvanised by formal, initial starts at implementation. These were relatively minor affrays when compared with the most recent precedents during the Swing explosion five years earlier. Events at Rodmersham in Kent were typical. Opposition hardened when cash allowances were partially replaced – as an interim measure – by vouchers exchangeable for provisions in local shops. A crowd of protesters, 150 strong, several with blackened faces and bludgeons, sporting hats 'inscribed with "No Tickets"', surrounded the vestry room where the newly-appointed relieving officer distributed the vouchers. Most of the recipients were women; as they emerged they were hauled before a coterie of protesters, headed by John Murton – known variously as 'the Judge' or 'the Major' – and 'asked whether they were satisfied'? Some clearly were, and hid their tickets, only to be searched in the 'most indecent and unbecoming manner'. Vouchers were confiscated, and the claimants ordered back to demand hard cash. Fisticuffs commenced on the intervention of a couple of farmers, and further violence flared when the crowd tried to overturn a horse-chaise full of London policemen, hastily despatched to the disturbed districts. A posse of troops ended this altercation, and made over twenty arrests. These prisoners' escort was attacked in the streets by stone-throwers on arrival at Canterbury, but they were safely locked up in the gaol, which soon held over forty defendants awaiting trial after Kentish disturbances.[20]

Relieving officers were pitched into the thick of disputes elsewhere too, typified by events at Ringmer. On 22 May relieving officer Webb arrived for the first time; he was to pay the unemployed put to work by parishes in cash and vouchers, and replace cash allowances to the children of those in work with parcels of flour. This put both sets of claimants on a par, the unemployed arguing that 'they had worked for money and would have it', the others furious because most had no ovens and depended on the baker: they all chanted 'Money or blood for supper'. Anger that the relieving officer represented a non-parochial body, and was domiciled at Barcombe, led to assertions that Webb 'had no business' at Ringmer as claimants 'did not want any body out of the parish'. Cornered by the crowd, Webb capitulated, hastily accepting cash from the parish officers to pay according to claimants' demands. The crowd celebrated their victory by readopting the Swing ceremony of carting the relieving officer across the parish boundary. Parallel incidents engulfed Willingdon about the same time, with relieving officers similarly expelled from Ewhurst, Mountfield and Sedlescomb when the Battle Union commenced operations in July.[21]

---

[20] Rev. Dr Poore, Sittingbourne, to Home Secretary Russell, 3,5,6,7 and 9 May; J.M. Tylder, to Poore, 7 May, PRO, HO 52/26, fos 130–32, 135–39, 144–48, 152–53; *Kentish Chronicle*, 12 May and 9 June; *Kent Herald*, 28 May and 4 June 1835. See also D. Hopker, *Money or Blood* (privately printed, Broadstairs, 1988).

[21] Justices Shiffner, Partington and Richardson, Lewes, to Melbourne with various depositions, 29 May, PRO, HO 52/26, fos 188–92; *Sussex Advertiser*, 8 June; Hawley to Nicholls, and to the PLC, 26 and 29 July, PRO, MH 12/12747; 32/38; I. Thomas, Uckfield, to Richmond, 23 July 1835, WSCRO, Goodwood 1575.

The incarceration of claimants in workhouses, and the separation of families, comprised the other major, specific cause of disturbances. Social tensions in the Horsham Union rose as employment fell off and the guardians prepared to implement the Act in the autumn. Transitional changes in outdoor relief appear to have caused no trouble, but issue was taken with the decision to designate specific workhouses, miles apart, to house different categories of pauper. This represented a severe aggravation of the emotive issue of the separation of families within one workhouse, for it erected additional difficulties for husbands to see wives, and for both to see their children. Moreover, Shipley, the workhouse designated for children under an ex-prison officer, was hopelessly dilapidated and had inadequate furnishings. On 16 December the Board was subjected to a mass lobby by rowdy contingents from component parishes; workers who refused to take a day off to picket were dragged from their work. This militancy delayed the transfers of inmates; appeals for special constables went unheeded – an identical response to an identical appeal in the Swing era – and the Bench, four of whom had assiduously attended all the Board's deliberations, summoned aid in the form of London policemen and the army. On 21 December children from Horsham were transferred to Shipley workhouse in the middle of the night, but the removal of others from Warnham was stopped by the reassembled masses. They were finally removed on Christmas Eve by a military escort which drew swords while passing through Horsham. The four elderly ladies at Shipley were also moved under military escort to their new abode at Warnham. The amateur soldiers comprising Lord Surrey's West Sussex Yeomanry, responsible for these operations, were disparagingly dubbed the 'Workhouse Guards'.[22]

A simple incident count of the 'major' anti-Poor Law disturbances fails to do justice to the scale of even overt protest.[23] The record is hopelessly defective respecting events like that at Feltham, deep in Richmond's domain, which was remembered for years as a 'very partial ... rising', and used to pressure one of its leaders into emigration. Disturbances at Eastbourne in April 1835 led to the postponement of the separation of families in the workhouse; further trouble flared when a renewed attempt was made in November. New issues – including inedible bread at Hastings, rotten bacon at Willingdon and the termination of

[22] Horsham Board of Guardians, minutes, 12, 16 and 23 December 1835, 20 January and 22 June 1836, WSCRO, WG 6/1/1. H. Stedman, Horsham, to Melbourne, 18 December, PRO, HO 52/27, fos 193–94. Summary convictions, Horsham, 19 December; indictments and depositions against Warnham rioters, 16 December 1835, Epiphany 1836 Sessions Roll, WSCRO, QR/W779. Sergeant D'Oyley to Richmond, 21 January and 28 February 1836, WSCRO, Goodwood 1870. *Brighton Patriot*, 22 September, 29 December 1835 and 31 May 1836; *Sussex Advertiser*, 18 January 1836.

[23] Among the incidents escaping Lowerson's mapping, 'The Aftermath of Swing', p. 83, are riots at Cuckfield and Peashurst, January 1836, Chiddingstone, February 1836, and Fishbourne, March 1836. Riotous portents accompanied implementation subsequently in Hampshire, as revealed by the Yeomanry being put on permanent duty. Hawley to Nicholls, 9 January, and 25 September; assistant-commissioner Tufnell, Kent, to Lefevre 11, 14 and 16 February, PRO, MH 32/38; 69; *Sussex Advertiser*, 28 March and 2 May 1836.

publicly-funded boarding out for widowers' children at West Firle – erupted in localities which remained tense, and might rekindle what one JP described as 'the "Labourers' war"' at any moment. The Cuckfield Board of guardians were permanently apprehensive over which of their meetings would provoke a concerted mass lobby by claimants from every component parish. Collective protests were in fact common: at Maresfield several men ordered into the workhouse turned up, ate their dinners and left; Chailey claimants riotously refused to work; and at Midhurst 'a sort of combination among the paupers' cannily put up the women – with implied impunity – to continuously harass relieving officers, leaving the authorities to ruminate that the resultant 'intimidation' was a more effective form of protest than the violent category.[24]

However, these events demonstrated that protesters who took to the streets, who attacked relieving officers and who shattered vestry room and workhouse windows exposed themselves to legal retribution. Hawley positively welcomed news of the initial series of riots at Sittingbourne: a handful 'of these ebullitions of feeling *well* and *firmly* put down', he asserted, 'will do our Cause the greatest good'. He was confident that the 'prompt ... punishment' intended for the leaders of the Willingdon protest would 'check the Spirit of Opposition' in his region. Over forty protesters were prosecuted at an emergency meeting of the Kent Sessions, and most were sentenced to up to two years' hard labour. Similar sentences were imposed on the dozen or so people arrested during the Sussex disturbances. The magistracy clearly believed that the judicial response was essentially temperate; as one chairman told a dockful of defendants, forcing an officer to hand over cash against his will could be legally construed as robbery, punishable by transportation. Other offenders were treated with greater sympathy; Sussex Assize and Quarter Sessions judges were prepared virtually to let off certain protesters by binding them over to keep the peace – much to Hawley's chagrin. His complaint did not override the fact that the Bench invariably seized the opportunity to support the Act; suggestions that protesters' acts were tantamount to 'High Treason' were contrived, judicial, rhetorical flourishes, but there was no real ambiguity over the threat to adopt a severe approach in the event of further troubles. As the 'general peace' of Sussex was at stake, county rates were used to finance prosecutions, and Boards of guardians also demonstrated their mettle with parallel allocations of funds. If leniency preserved the Bench from damaging and dangerous accusations of severity, protesters entrapped in this retribution felt no moral guilt. They were remonstrating on behalf of the majority, their own class, domiciled in the countryside. They believed

[24] *Brighton Patriot*, 21 April and 26 May; *Sussex Advertiser*, 1 June. Captain Lyon, Rogate, to Sir Charles Paget, and Paget to Richmond, both 28 June; Pilkington to Richmond, 1 September 1835; copy, D'Oyley to Home Office under-secretary Phillipps, 20 January 1836, WSCRO, Goodwood 1574, 1577 and 1870. Hawley to the PLC, 25 November 1835, and to Nicholls, 9 January 1836; W. Day, Maresfield, to Edwin Chadwick, 11 May 1835, PRO, MH 12/13015; 13157; 32/38. Deposition against Robert Poole, labourer, Bolney, November 1835, ESCRO, QR/E833; BPP, SC, HC, 'Agricultural Distress', third report, 465 (1836), viii, pt 2, QQ. 13162–67.

that the Act removed fundamental rights and threatened the fabric of the family. Moreover, the odds were demonstrably stacked against them. H.D. Goring, the pugilistically-inclined JP who literally exchanged punches with inmates who resisted transfer from Steyning workhouse, actually left the Bench for the witness-box to give evidence against defendants. In the dock, James Blaber exclaimed that the 'words' of the village worthies who gave evidence against him, 'will be taken before mine'. 'I expect it's no use what I have to say' echoed a joint-defendant, John Trigwell, who eloquently proved the unfairness of it all: flour was no use to him, as his family, like others in Ringmer, had no oven, and people depended on the baker. The Bench were unimpressed and refused to 'suffer an offence of this kind to pass off' unpunished. The trials, and the sentences, were forcible illustrations of the dangers attendant on open protest in the rural regions.[25]

Attempts to orchestrate and to capitalise on the anti-Poor Law protests by an apparently newly-formed trade union of agricultural labourers the 'United Brothers of Industry', also resulted in failure in 1835. The union's origins are obscure,[26] but they were a rural reflection of the very marked national upsurge of trade union organisation in the early 1830s, and also represented a response to farmers' attempts to seize on more reductions in the prices for agricultural produce to beat down wages even further.[27] The union's prime concern was to head off wage cuts; this assumed a greater urgency and moment with the implementation of the Poor Law Amendment Act, and necessitated mobilisation for wage increases as opposed to action against cuts. The issues of the Robbery Bill's imposition overshadowed that of wages, however, notably at a series of public meetings held between April and July. While these aimed to accelerate recruitment, they tended to become populist anti-Amendment Act conventions, which diluted the propagation of trade unionist principles. A juxtaposition of the issues was apparent at the first mass meeting at Jevington on 26 April, when many attended from fifteen parishes incorporated in the new Eastbourne Union, 'to consider how to prevent being robbed of their children and wives'. Speakers

---

[25] *Sussex Advertiser*, 25 May, 1, 8 and 15 June, 6 July and 10 August; *Brighton Patriot*, 26 May and 15 September; *Kentish Chronicle*, 9 June; *Kent Herald*, 11 June, I. Thomas to Fox Maule, 21 May; Justices Shiffner, Partington and Richardson, Lewes, to Melbourne, with enclosures, 29 May; Goring to Russell, 13 September, PRO, HO 52/27, fos 180, 188–92, 203–4. Hawley to Nicholls, 10 May and 7 August, and to PLC, 14 May, PRO, MH 32/38; Horsham Board of Guardians minutes, 30 December 1835, WSCRO, G.6/1/1; Undated note, Lewes JPs, ESCRO, QR/E830.

[26] There are suggestions of associations, adopting radical political and trade unionist principles, in some localities, as at Brede, which predated the Swing insurrection, and possibly eked out a continuous existence ever since. See Wells, 'Social Protest', pp. 188–93; and idem, 'Tolpuddle in the Context of English Agrarian Labour History, 1780–1850', in J. Rule (ed.), *British Trade Unionism, 1750–1850: The Formative Years* (London, 1988), pp. 119–23.

[27] Notably in West Sussex, which resulted in strikes in late 1834. *Brighton Gazette*, 6 November; *Poor Man's Guardian*, 15 November; letters to Richmond from J. Woods, Chalgrove, 28 October, J.B. Freeland, Chichester, 5 and 6 November, and Frankland Lewis, London, 7 November 1834, WSCRO, Goodwood 1477; BPP, SC, HC, 'Poor Law Amendment Act', first and eleventh reports, 422 (1837–38), xvii-xviii, QQ. 604–9, 11256–57, evidence of farmers Foard and Lawrence.

were preoccupied in condemnation of claims made in the 1834 Poor Law Report, and relentlessly reiterated by New Poor Law supporters, that agricultural labourers 'prefer a small sum in idleness to a larger one in wages'; the workshy were vehemently castigated. Trade union demands for the right to work achieved a lesser profile, and even then were subordinated to the anti-Poor Law case: that unemployment – attributed to 'Tenants who chose to grow crops of weeds instead of corn' – should not be used as a vehicle to force people 'into the union Prison houses'. This meeting formally condemned the separation of families – both within central workhouses and by distribution round designated, segregated workhouses – and elected two representatives from each parish to lobby the next meeting of the Board of guardians. A meeting summoned by the United Brothers at Rye, on 16 May, extended an invitation to 'all Brothers of the different Unions', and 'PARTICULARLY REQUESTED' the attendance of 'ALL AGRICULTURAL LABOURERS' to hear delegates from 'the London, Manchester and Birmingham [Trade] Unions on the "Poor Laws Amendment Act"'.[28] On 24 July the Brothers – by then reeling under an exotic combination of lock-outs and semi-coordinated strike action – mobilised its forces to coincide with a meeting of the Battle Board of guardians. Yet another mass lobby backed a formal petition:

> That your Servants and Labourers view with much alarm the fearful infringements which this Bill is calculated to make upon their rights and Liberties; that your Servants and Labourers have always been willing to work for their Bread; and to use their utmost exertions to maintain their families; and that your Petitioners are determined not to let the law of God be torn asunder by the Laws of Man, which will be the case if the present system is acted upon; Your petitioners therefore humbly request that relief may be given them as heretofore and that your Petitioners may not have their wives and families taken from them when they are thrown out of employment or overtaken with sickness or casual Misfortune: but that they may live as they have hitherto done in their own humble cottages and in the Bosom of their Families.

Neither the noble tone nor the Christian sentiments of this protest should obscure the fact that it constituted no more than an impassioned plea for the maintenance of the Old Poor Law, with the preservation of outdoor relief, allowances-in-aid-of wages and the rest, in unadulterated purity. The guardians' response was emphatically negative; the Board 'will not hold communication with persons who are assembled illegally and for the evident purpose of endeavouring to intimidate them in the performance of their Duties'.[29]

---

[28] *Sussex Advertiser*, 4 May; *Kent Herald*, 7 May; *Brighton Patriot*, 12 and 19 May; United Brothers handbill, 8 May, PRO, HO 52/26, fo. 168; John Storr, Eastbourne, to Richmond, 7 and 10 May 1835, WSCRO, 1573.

[29] Chairman T.C. Bellingham, Battle, to Russell, 25 July enclosing Board minutes, 24 July, PRO, HO 52/27, fos 212–213A; guardian's clerk Ticehurst, and Hawley, to PLC, 24 and 29 July 1835, PRO, MH 12/12747.

All the well-publicised mass meetings were held in the presence of posses of coastguards, special constables and army detachments. Professional London policemen – who had some success in detecting Swing leaders five years previously – were also drafted in at the request of the regional magistracy. Nevertheless, the union made quite spectacular progress against these odds, to which must be added threats of the sack from many employers; by mid May 'Lodges are formed from Seaford to Dover, and many are formed inland', as the union spread out from its coastal centres and 'greatly agitated' Kent and Sussex. The press, both Tory and Whig, inflamed the fears of farmers and gentry by emphasising the secrecy of the union; claims of balaclava-sporting 'itinerant orators', furtively addressing knots of labourers, were added to ominous allegations of incendiarism and accusations that the rank and file were bound by esoteric oaths.[30] The latter represented a transparent attempt to invoke the memory, *in terrorem*, of the transportation of the celebrated Tolpuddle Martyrs, whose legal offence was not membership of a trade union but to take secret oaths as part of their initiation. In fact, the United Brothers did enjoin members against revealing union business to non-members, and further preserved confidentiality through the imposition of pass-words at branch meetings; neither was illegal, and indeed both were common, current trade union practices. The union specifically denounced all forms of violence, provided expulsion penalties on members who broke this rule and extended sanctions to such as even verbally abused their employers.[31]

In fact, there is little evidence of violence prior to the lock-out of union members, initially orchestrated in the Rye area by the East Sussex Whig MP, Curteis. His supporters were subjected to intimidatory visits from itinerant pickets who tried to forcibly stop non-union labour working for farmers effecting the lock-out. Further violence against Curteis's leading lieutenants, including farmer Samuel Selmes and the vicar of Icklesham, took the form of nocturnal raids during which both men's houses were peppered with buckshot. Fighting between unionised and non-union labourers also accompanied the spread of the union to new territories, as at Bodlestreet Green. Repression also forced essentially localised and premature strike action, long before the harvest, the period correctly identified by the leadership as the only season when a strike would be speedily effective; by then recruitment should have been well advanced and

---

[30] Eg. *Brighton Gazette*, 19 March; cf. *Kent Herald*, 7 May, which contrasts vividly with the temperate report of T.P. Durant, 25 July, who spied on a recruitment meeting at Heathfield, enclosed by W. Day to Richmond, 27 July. See also I. Thomas to Richmond, 2 July, WSCRO, Goodwood 1575. D. Deune, Lydd, to Russell, 14 May; Curteis to Phillipps, 6 May, PRO, HO 52/26, fos 134, 167–167A; Hawley to Nicholls, 19 March, PRO, MH 32/38; *Brighton Patriot*, 19 May and 2 June 1835.

[31] See especially the defensive pamphlet written by John Goddard, a major activist, *An Answer to an Address from the Rev. C. James Curate of Playden to the Labouring Classes who have Become or are Invited to Become Members of the Friendly Society of Agricultural Labourers* (Battle, 1835). The union rules were partly printed in the *Brighton Patriot*, 2 June. Incendiarism was specifically denounced at a United Brothers meeting at Pevensey on 22 May, ibid., 26 May 1835.

funds increasing. The failure of negotiations in the interim period would add a moral imperative to solid groundwork.[32]

The union faced a long uphill battle from the moment it launched the recruitment campaign. It was not without friends: several leaders, including John Goddard, had been members of the Grand National Consolidated Trade Union, and thus had a broader perspective of the labour movement. Financial support came from other unions: collections were held at union lodges of bricklayers, plasterers, stonemasons and sawyers in Brighton, for example; and further contributions were made by radical groupings when the cause of the agricultural workers was expounded at regular meetings in pubs including the Globe and the Bricklayer's Arms. But these were insufficient to salvage the United Brothers' finances, already depleted when a divisional treasurer decamped with his funds, thereby exposing the union to well-publicised accusations of fraud from its opponents. This publicity engineered rank and file suspicion of the leaders; Thomas Maule was openly challenged over funds in his possession in a heated exchange at a rally, which released further complaints at his autocratic conduct.

Agrarian workers' poverty prevented many from payment of the two shilling entrance fee; the union was reduced to admitting many recruits free, and also had to waive fourpenny weekly subscriptions for some. Employers exploited both the social intimacy of village communities and the overflowing labour market to intimidate their plebeian neighbours. Magisterial opposition was also publicised. The New Romney Bench flooded the region with posters warning the 'LABOURING POPULATION AND OTHERS AGAINST MEETING IN LARGE BODIES'. In some locations only those who habitually resisted the dictates of rural deference actually joined, which gave a little credence to repeated allegations that the membership comprised the 'worst characters'. Publicans who permitted union meetings at their establishments were blatantly threatened by the magistracy: the future East Sussex Tory MP George Darby openly 'sent to a publican to say an Application would be made to take away his license' if he persisted in hosting meetings; and several licensees were exposed to harsh interrogation by the Bench at the annual Brewster Sessions in August. The presence of London policemen sowed apprehension and distrust, as revealed by repetitive denunciations of 'police spies' by speakers at union rallies. But, in spite of extravagant claims about the efficacy of these policemen made by assistant poor-law commissioner Tufnell, the union was principally defeated by the lock-out, as anticipated by the anguished immediate reaction of the Brothers in a published address 'to the Farmers'. The union appealed for negotiations 'to establish ... a better understanding', but feelings of weakness were apparent in their denunciation

---

[32] Ibid., 24 March, 26 May and 14 July; *Brighton Gazette*, 19 March; Curteis to Phillips, 29 April and 1 May; Goddard to Selmes, 29 April, PRO, HO 52/26, fos 122–28; *Kentish Chronicle*, 12 May; *Sussex Advertiser*, 20 July; I. Thomas and C.H. Frewer to Richmond, 2 July 1835, and 21 November 1836, WSCRO, Goodwood 1575, 1870; Hawley to Nicholls, 7 May, and to PLC, 19 May and 24 June 1835, PRO, MH 12/12747; 32/38.

of 'the shackles of Slavery' tightened by the farmers' 'unjust, uncharitable, impolitic, rash and inconsistent infringement of the rights of Man'.

Union funds were totally inadequate to defray the pecuniary cost of supporting locked-out members; within two weeks those who had not capitulated and resigned, were reputedly 'plunged into want and misery'. After a month Hawley reported that the union was 'gradually expiring', and on 24 June that it had 'nearly disappeared' in the Rye area, its strongest centre. Authority was convinced that its westward thrust would evaporate if 'the farmers will ... act properly, and discharge every labourer who joins'. Although some residual fears of a strike were articulated in the autumn, the last mass meetings were reported at Pulborough early in July; the union failed in their stated objective to lobby the Battle Guardians for a second time on 31 July. As an effective organisation the United Brothers were dead shortly before the harvest period, leaving Curteis to crow repeatedly about his central role in that defeat at social, political and agricultural meetings in East Sussex during the remainder of the year. Curteis's political career had a shaky constituency basis, and his actions were transparently designed to shore up his support; as the *Brighton Patriot* caustically noted, Curteis contrived 'to obtain the votes of the farmers ... well knowing that the agricultural labourers have no votes'. Moreover, the Poor Law Amendment Act was a peculiarly appropriate tool in the hands of agrarian capitalists. Remaining outdoor relief was withheld from union members in several parishes. It was never extended to either locked-out or striking unionists, who were immediately exposed to the reality of incarceration in workhouses. The early use of the discriminatory and punitive machinery of the Act played a role in smashing the union, thereby enhancing the new law's standing among thousands of previously antagonistic farmers. The point was not lost on the Poor Law Commission, who needed every iota of favourable propaganda; their first and greatly publicised annual report in December emphasised the fact. The entire episode served only to prove the special vulnerability of the agricultural workforce. Unionism, like riot, exposed men – and as the United Brothers admitted 'their Wives and Families' – to suppression either under the criminal law or by the repressive new social security system.[33]

Precedents for these failures of overt, public, rural protest, stretched back through Swing to the later eighteenth century. The operation of the Old Poor Law, however central to the labourers' existence, generated considerable conflict over perceptions of injustice; efforts to redress grievances by open-handed methods were largely unsuccessful. By the mid 1830s the alternatives, hinging

---

[33] *Poor Man's Guardian*, 22 August; *Brighton Patriot*, 19 and 26 May, 2 June, 14 and 21 July, 8 December 1835 and 7 August 1838; *Sussex Advertiser*, 31 August and 7 December 1835. Deune to Russell, 9 and 14 May; Goddard to Selmes, 29 April; Curteis to Russell, 1 May; posters, United Brothers, and New Romney Bench, 29 April, and 9 May, PRO, HO 52/26, fos 122–28, 143, 150–51, 167–167A. Hawley to Nicholls, 18 May, 2, 24 and 29 June, and 17 July, and to PLC, 23 May and 15 August 1835; Tufnell to Lefevre, 14 February 1836, PRO, MH 12/13138; 32/38; 69. R. Tredcroft, Horsham, and Darby, Uckfield, to Richmond, 17 June and 25 July; Durant's report, 25 July 1835, WSCRO, Goodwood 1574. Goddard, *An Answer to an Address*.

on covert, secret protest – 'malicious damage' to crops, fences, gates, and farming implements, animal maiming and above all incendiarism – were firmly entrenched in the countryside.[34] An upsurge in this form of activity accompanied collective, open resistance to the new law, intensifying once direct protest collapsed. At Alfriston eight sheep were killed, but only one carcass taken; seed barley was dumped in a pond and scattered over the fields in an orgy of 'wanton' destruction, which extended to kitchen gardens and included threats of further 'vengeance' chalked on barn doors. Sheep were also victimised in Kent, as at Ash where twelve had their throats cut and were left to bleed to death; John Ellman's show sheep had crowbars rammed through their heads on the South Downs. Landowners contributed to substantial subscription funds at Hailsham and Lewes to finance detection and prosecution. But this mode of protest continued almost unabated through the rest of the 1830s and beyond; the largest single attack on sheep comprised the twenty slaughtered in the fields overnight at Haslemere (Surrey) in March 1839. Cows were also maimed, and those belonging to farmers at Newtimber and Arundel were turned into growing corn. Horses' tongues were cut out at Buxted, ducks poisoned by arsenic at Southover, and prize cockerels crucified on barndoors with pitchforks at Warnham. Animal maiming, a 'truly un-English offence' according to the radical *Champion* reporting a 'great ... increase' in March 1840, which attained such magnitude at Angmering that farmers created a fund to reimburse victims. Less lethal modes of protest included the decimation of milk yields at Poynings by tying cows together by their tails, numerous incidents involving the trampling of growing crops and the destruction of agricultural machinery and farmyard fixtures. At Maresfield – a notorious trouble spot – even a nurseryman's award-winning dahlias were not sacrosanct.[35]

Arson was much more damaging for victims and frightening to the entire landed interest. As early as May 1835 Inigo Thomas JP insisted that 'the most serious object of our attention now is the repeated recurrence of incendiarism', and a colleague echoed his concern over the relationship between the repression of the United Brothers and arson.[36] Repeated suggestions that 'the press ... observed a *discreet* silence, through fear of aggravating the evil by publicity' were made, implying that the total of about forty recorded fires during the first year of the Poor Law Amendment Act's operation represents a considerable underestimate. Radical newspapers correctly and repeatedly attributed the escalation of incendiarism to a combination of repression and poverty, producing

---

[34] R.A.E. Wells, 'The Development of the English Rural Proletariat and Social Protest, 1700–1850'; idem, 'Social Conflict and Protest in the English Countryside in the Early Nineteenth Century: A Rejoinder', reprinted in Reed and Wells, *Class, Conflict and Protest.*

[35] *Sussex Advertiser,* 30 March, 13 and 20 April, 18 and 25 May, 1 and 15 June 1835, 22 August 1836, 8 April 1839 and 6 April 1840; *Brighton Patriot,* 16 May 1837; *Sussex Agricultural Express,* 5 January 1839; *Brighton Gazette,* 7 January 1841; *The Champion,* 29 March 1840. Cf. J.E. Archer, 'Rural Protest in Norfolk and Suffolk, 1830–70', in A. Charlesworth (ed.), *Rural Social Change,* pp. 84–85.

[36] Thomas to Fox Maule, 21 May PRO, HO 52/26, fo. 180. W. Day to Richmond, 27 July 1835, WSCRO, Goodwood 1575.

a 'sullen discontent', aggravated by the harshness of the new law.[37] Specific arson campaigns included four burnings at Midhurst in September 1835 when the Act came on stream; victims were also newly-elected guardians, including their chairman. Nobody would let a house to the new relieving officer at Rogate, 'knowing that [it] would be burnt down'. The most spectacular case, fifteen stacks destroyed in Lord Templemore's extensive rick yard near Sevenoaks on 5 September 1835, was celebrated on its anniversary in 1836 by the firing of his clover stack; his losses totalled over £2600. By the late 1830s arson campaigns were almost wintertime institutions, as revealed by the fear and anticipations of the landed interest at East Grinstead after a fire on 11 November 1838; the winter months would be occupied in long, cold and wet, nocturnal watches.

The problem acquired such proportions that the Poor Law commission decided to monitor the situation from 1837. Arsonists did not exclusively select those directly involved in Poor Law administration. For example, the destruction of a Hurst Green factory producing agricultural machinery, in October 1837, reinvoked a major grievance from the Swing epoch; but continuity was represented, and typified, by the firing of guardian Dirk's stacks at Leominster (Sussex) in October 1841 following a huge rumpus over relief issues. Lord Templemore was the local 'architect' of the Sevenoaks Union; like Ellman at West Firle, he was irrevocably associated with the new system since its inception. Against such figures, covert protest – 'the spirit of incendiarism', or 'secret mischiefs' to use one Kent farmer's expressions – reached epidemic proportions, which led one visiting estate owner to state that the Weald over the 1835–36 winter 'was in quite as bad a state as his neighbourhood in Ireland'. Moreover, many agricultural labourers clearly, if clandestinely, supported agrarian terrorism. Few responded positively to the numerous massive rewards offered for evidence producing convictions of incendiaries. Some reports acknowledged that the parsimony of insurance companies meant that plebeian fire-fighters went unpaid for their labour, unreimbursed for damage to clothing, giving them a pecuniary aversion to assisting firemen. There are too many reports of workers' 'ill-concealed pleasure' and even open delight when witnessing fires to ignore: as guardian Gates of Clinton's barn burned, at 'every fall of a beam increasing the body of flame ... the people set up a shout of exultation'. This type of event further exemplifies Dr Archer's significant observation: that while arson was committed covertly, it facilitated open protest, at least by less cautious villagers.[38]

---

[37] *Poor Man's Guardian*, 8 November 1834; *Brighton Patriot*, 19 May 1835, 1 November 1836 and 24 October 1837.

[38] *Kent Herald*, 1 April; *Brighton Gazette*, 28 October 1841; *Brighton Patriot*, 4 August and 29 September 1835, 24 October 1837 and 13 November 1838. Earl of Chichester, Goodwood, to Phillips, 3 October, PRO, HO 52/27, fos 219–20; Tufnell, and Hawley to the PLC, 5 September 1836 and 21 October 1837, PRO, MH 32/39; 68. Letters to Richmond from Paget, 28 June 1835, Templemore, 7 September 1835, Ellman, 16 September 1835, H. Hollist, Midhurst, 1 October 1835, and Frewer, 21 November 1836, WSCRO, Goodwood 1574; 1577–78; 1870. *The Champion*, 22 March, 1840. J. Archer, '*By a Flash and a Scare': Arson, Animal Maiming and Poaching in East Anglia, 1815–70* (Oxford, 1990), especially pp. 102–6.

The Act's implementation was achieved against this background: but protest, once rioting declined and the United Brothers were dead, was not restricted to covert forms, manifesting itself within the new system, and nowhere more fervently than in the reformed punitive workhouse itself. Attempts to tighten up workhouse discipline – especially by making inmates work – comprised part of the assistant commissioners' campaign to lay the ground and extend the transition period before the Unions started to function formally. These were reflected in a marked increase in the convictions of inmates for various forms of insubordination over the 1834–35 winter; scores of inmates – often collectively – simply refused to execute tasks allotted to them and some, like Ann Clapon at Framfield, extended their protest by demanding extra rations.[39] Thereafter, a number of individuals caught up in the system directly and repeatedly challenged the rules which underpinned utilitarian ideology and enforced 'less eligibility'. Henry Stapeley, a jobbing labourer, spent the Christmas of 1835 in Ardingly workhouse; he and two others got permission to walk the five miles to Arlington workhouse to see their wives. Once there, they refused to leave, brushed aside the entreaties of the parish constable, and stayed put for the New Year. They were still at Arlington when an outraged Board of guardians convened on 4 January. They directed arrests, and the three appeared before no less than nine magistrates on the 5th. Stapeley emerged as the spokesman: it was Christmas, his pregnant wife and toddler were both sick; he was not allowed to see them on a weekly basis. 'I will submit to the laws of God in this instance ... I cannot to the law of man'; and he announced his intention to return to Arlington as soon as possible. He received a stinging rebuke from their worships, who also told the Arlington governor to have Stapeley arrested instantly on any repetition. He was repeatedly admonished by the Board of guardians, to whom he invariably gave a 'damn good tongue banging'. He came before the Bench on several further occasions, swore 'never to recognise the Poor Law Amendment Bill' and refused to wear workhouse dress, or to work unless adequately fed and allowed to live with his family. He denounced one magistrate as a 'two-faced fellow' from the dock, and repeatedly celebrated his release from Lewes Gaol by heading straight for Arlington. Stapeley's courage certainly won the adulation of his peers; each court appearance drew a considerable audience of agricultural labourers who vociferously articulated their support for Stapeley in his heated exchanges with the Bench. After two years the Bench was 'tired of hearing his name'; he responded by 'quoting several texts of scripture illustrative of the tyranny and injustice of parting him from his wife'.[40] Shoemaker James Dunster, a twenty-nine year-old family man, allegedly

[39] E.g. summary convictions returned to Sussex Epiphany and Easter Quarter Sessions, 1835, especially Herstmonceux offences committed on 23 January, by Stephen Tickbon, Edward Birchett, Traytor Page and James Martin, and 26 January by Thomas and Stephen Marchant, Samuel Hayward and John Brissenden, ESCRO, QR/E. 826; 828. Hawley to Richmond, 12 January 1838, WSCRO, Goodwood 1872.

[40] *Sussex Advertiser,* 1 December 1836; *Brighton Patriot,* 19 January, 2 February, 8 and 22 March 1836, 7 and 14 February, and 4 April 1837.

an 'extremely bad character and [of a] most violent disposition, and when excited works himself into a frenzy', was more certainly the emergent leader of an inmates' movement to challenge the rules of Battle workhouse.[41] He lionised his first incarceration by threatening 'any one who was the cause of parting me and my wife'; for that, and denouncing the governor as 'a moving reptile', he got twenty-one days in jail. He celebrated his return to Battle by demanding that his meal portions were weighed in his presence. The governor admitted that his charges had 'no means of knowing ... that the food is properly weighed', but denied inmates 'the right ... to demand it'. Dunster advanced his argument by marching into the kitchen and taking a carving knife to the governor. Like Stapeley, Dunster transformed the dock into a platform for the anti-Poor Law movement; the 'densely crowded' committal hearing lasted for six hours.[42]

All these issues were reevoked by hundreds of protests by lesser rebels. Robert Poole of Bolney repeatedly applied for 'relief or work', and demanded a small capital sum to commence operation as a hawker of fish. When finally presented with a workhouse order he objected to the designated Hurst house in preference for Cuckfield, and tore up the warrant on the litigious pretext that his age was not entered. Poole's weekly contrivances transformed relief days into a public farce; claiming starvation, he ostentatiously lifted three pounds of cheese, challenged the relieving officer – whom he threatened to knock 'Arse over Head' – to prosecute him and postured as a riot leader. Revolts against dismal workhouse dietary were also common. Hellingly inmates demonstrated in the streets with their bread portions, one of which was impaled on a turnpike gate to maximise publicity; two inmates at Eastbourne convicted of stealing turnips dramatically advanced hunger in mitigation, exhibiting 'a very small modicum of bread' and an ounce of unappetising cheese in proof to the Bench; and five inmates from Chailey scored a spectacular success when a prison doctor declared they were unfit to serve their sentence on the treadmill. The installation of handmills to provide hard labour proved a repeated bone of contention; they were smashed at Hailsham, while Eastbourne inmates struck against them on the grounds that they were too undernourished to do this work. Many protests were indistinguishable from insubordination, notably those involving juveniles, like the boys and girls who locked the East Grinstead governor in his own punishment room and their counterparts at Ticehurst who made unfounded accusations against the schoolmaster who was clearly unable to control his charges.[43] Poor Law administration developed a quasi-juridicial sub-system from this constant

---

[41] Governor Lomas related that 'it struck me how very polite he was to the people in the house and how different he was to me'; Dunster reiterated his threat 'to stab any man, whether gentle or simple, that attempted to apply the rules of the workhouse', to the Bench on his first appearance.

[42] Tufnell to Chadwick, 19 and 22 August, PRO, MH 12/12747; *Brighton Patriot*, 22 August, 5 and 19 September 1837.

[43] Deposition of Relieving Officer Cooper, Cuckfield Union, and others, November 1835, ESCRO, QR/E833; *Brighton Patriot*, 23 February and 29 March 1836, 7 February 1837, 27 February, 20 March and 8 May 1838; Ticehurst Union Board minutes, 29 April, 6 May and 30 July 1841, ESCRO G10/1a/1,2.

conflict. Workhouse governors obtained autonomy of limited punitive powers over inmates, while some also imposed unofficial punishments by reducing food portions. Boards of guardians inflicted heavier penalties, for example at Horsham imposing a bread and water diet for a week for 'Disorderly Conduct and ... damaging property'. They generated a system of 'informal convictions' which were totted up.[44] At Hastings punishment lists were posted on notice-boards inside and outside the workhouse. Boards also assessed the cases of recidivists with a view to orthodox criminal prosecution. Several Benches added encouragement. Brighton magistrates advised they should deal with habitually troublesome workhouse inmates. They recommended arraignment on more serious charges, thus exposing miscreants to lengthier prison sentences than the twenty-one day maximum for insubordination under the Poor Law Amendment Act. Sergeant D'Oyly, a chairman of Sussex Sessions, turned court cases into a public relations exercise: the evidence would 'open the eyes of all parties to the manner in which things were being conducted under the New Poor Law Bill'.[45]

The Poor Law Commission's bureaucracy remained ambivalent on this issue of publicity. Assistant commissioner Hawley's devotion to the privacy of Union boardroom discussions led him to ensure that Boards did not convene on market days, so that outvoted Guardians would not rush, flushed with adrenalin, to make 'intemperate ex parte declamations' in crowded inns; he steadfastly adhered to his exclusion of newspaper reporters from boardrooms. When the Lewes Union flew 'in the teeth of the strongest remonstrances I could make' against the admission of reporters, Hawley's rage even got the better of his customary lucidity when communicating with his superiors in London. He insisted that 'that dangerous engine "The Press" will become a complete dictator to the meetings' of Guardians, some of whom would seize the opportunity to curry favour with their constituents through speechifying, while others would be reduced to silence; all Guardians would be exposed to interrogation outside the boardroom, and possibly to vengeance. In this instance the Poor Law Commission backed Hawley and the Lewes decision was reversed, but elements of the press campaigned for admission, or at least 'authorised' details of proceedings, fed on leaks and applauded when the Greenwich Board finally challenged the Commission successfully in 1838. D'Oyley's opinion was by no means universal in official circles. The magistracy publicly castigated the Hailsham Board for prosecuting Stapeley at Lewes Petty Sessions, where journalists had ample courtroom provision, instead of Hailsham where he 'could have been sent quietly off to prison without bothering the public ... about the matter'. However, those who followed Hawley in wishing to maintain the privacy of boardroom proceedings were entrapped by the publicity accruing to the

---

[44] A legal perversion strangely reminiscent of one of the younger Pitt's cabinet colleague's coinage of 'acquitted felons' for those found not guilty of political crimes in the 1790s. See G.A. Williams, *Artisans and Sansculottes* (1968), ch. 6.

[45] *Brighton Patriot*, 24 January and 19 September 1837, 31 July and 4 December 1838; Horsham Union Board Minutes, 5 October 1836, WSCRO, WG 6/1/1.

enforcement of the criminal clauses of the Amendment Act. Secrecy was an inherently contradictory strategy and never more than a short-term possibility.[46]

Criminal proceedings ensured that the southern anti-Poor Law movement had a continuous flow of authenticated evidence, in addition to leaks from hostile and ci-devant guardians and personal information from those on the receiving end of the new system. It all constituted grist to the mill of the radical *Brighton Patriot*, which campaigned relentlessly against the Act and all its works from February 1835 until its demise in August 1839. The *Patriot* is rarely recognised by historians, who prefer the *Northern Star*. The latter was not established until late 1837 and cut its teeth on the vociferous northern anti-Poor Law movement, thereby enabling it to become the premier Chartist paper. The *Patriot* was, in fact, a most effective precursor of the *Star*, and its radical and polemical content earned it a primary position in the estimation of the grand old man of early nineteenth-century radicalism, William Cobbett. The *Patriot* portrayed the Act as a vast, nepotistic edifice, creating a huge pool of patronage for Whig ministers of the crown and their provincial minions. Elections to guardianships were exposed as farces controlled by aristocratic tyrants, notably the Duke of Richmond. The plural voting system was decried as a vehicle for upper-class domination of a quasi-democratic institution, as was the *ex-officio* guardian status of JPs who represented nobody but themselves and their order, arrogantly lording it over lesser, elected personnel, whose property qualifications were nevertheless also derided. So too was the failure to extend voting rights to the working class. These faults were subjoined to jobbery in the award of Union contracts, the *Patriot* endearing itself to village shopkeepers who lost lucrative parochial business on the creation of Unions. The *Patriot* confronted utilitarian ideology: the Act would not increase agrarian wages, as claimed, but facilitate reductions especially for unmarried men. The heralded savings in relief costs would be swallowed up to finance the centralised bureaucracy and the exorbitant salaries of creatures like Hawley. When poor rates fell despite these prognostications, savings were attributed to being 'pinched out of the bellies of poor women and children'. Every facet of the Act was mercilessly attacked: the notorious bastardy clauses increased infanticide; and internal migration schemes comprised a wicked contrivance to use surplus agricultural labour as 'white factory slaves' to inflate the already bloated profits of 'cotton tyrants'. Workhouse orders, hand mills, separation of families and harsh ex-military governors were all denounced; workhouse diets were neatly contrasted with the 'groaning tables' laden with multiple dishes for guardians on audit days: the latter were 'embezzling through the mouth, and pilfering through the stomach'. Column upon column of empirical evidence was published in support of these contentions. But even this list is incomplete; and moreover hardly does justice to the paper's tone, typified by

---

[46] Hawley to Nicholls, 9 and 12 January 1836, and to the PLC, 9 October 1837; PLC to Hawley, 12 January 1836, PRO, MH 12/13015, 32/38, 39; *Maidstone Gazette*, 1 January; *Kent Herald*, 13 June and 8 August 1839; *Brighton Patriot*, 9 February 1836.

an attack in 1837 on Lord Chancellor Brougham, the Act's main apologist in the Lords. Brougham was the

> Nero of the House of Lords ... none but a man having a heart like the mother-killing Nero could have invented a Bill that covers the land with child murders and incendiary fires – that separates the man from the wife ... that tears children from the embraces of their parents – that sends thousands [through financed emigration] to perish in the swamps of Canada ... that starves the widow, and sends the aged in sorrow to their graves. A Bill which has covered the country with huge bastile prisons, for the incarceration of every man, woman and child, who may ... be reduced to poverty.[47]

The *Patriot* quickly became a painful thorn in the side of the assistant commissioners, and their complaints were echoed by the gentry and other Amendment Act supporters. Hawley described it as 'one of the most rascally publications in England', as its contents were 'doing more harm than I can describe'. As early as May 1835, he despatched a copy for the edification of Somerset House; the Act's approvers had no comparative antidotal 'engine'. Hawley took refuge in hopes that the *Patriot's* stridency would expose it to libel action at least, which he unsuccessfully attempted to engineer in 1836. Many southern gentry expressed fears of the radical press in the 1830s; the 'poison of some popular periodical publications' was 'instill'd into' Wealden agricultural labourers, said Inigo Thomas in 1834; repeated reports confirmed that 'at beer shops newspapers are read which could not be procured by the poor at their own houses'. The *Patriot's* own claim that 'not a few' of the 'Labourers of Sussex ... read this paper' was substantiated by John Ellman in February 1836: it was 'read eagerly in every pot house and is doing *immense mischief*', not just in plebeian circles, but on 'the feelings of really *well disposed men*' from higher ranks of rural society. The influence of the radical press in the countryside revealed itself in many ways; one squire took an additional copy of the Tory *Brighton Gazette* for free circulation in his village to counteract 'mischievous "cheap papers" that deluge the country', and the Uckfield guardians finally authorised their workhouse governor to inspect and censor 'all Newspapers ... delivered ... for the paupers'. One West Sussex enthusiast for a professional rural police supported his argument by claiming 'An increase of information amongst the Peasantry'.[48]

The *Patriot's* campaign against the Poor Law proved to those on the receiving end that they were not isolated, and also exposed them to democratic ideology. The paper gave some coherence to the southern anti-Poor Law movement. Some paupers contributed directly, including an inmate of Hellingly workhouse

---

[47] *Brighton Patriot*, 24 February 1835 to 13 August 1839, passim.

[48] Hawley to Nicholls, 3 May and 18 July 1835, and 9 March 1836; Thomas to Chadwick, 20 November 1834, PRO, MH 12/12854, 32/38. *Kent Herald*, 11 April 1833; *Brighton Gazette*, 28 March 1833. T. Broadwood, near Horsham, enclosing unsigned memorandum, 30 July 1835, and Ellman to Richmond, 15 February 1836, WSCRO, Goodwood 1575, 1870. *Brighton Patriot*, 22 September 1835. Uckfield Union Board minute, 19 March 1842, ESCRO, G11/1a/2.

(Stapeley?); and James Dunster's legal defence – which was principally orchestrated to expose the realities of workhouse life under the new regime – was financially backed by Brighton radicals who were also significant supporters of the *Patriot.* The paper also provided a forum for middle-class opponents, amongst whom pride of place must go to Charles Brooker, shopkeeper and dissenting lay-minister of Alfriston – a Sussex village with a radical presence since 1792. Brooker's initial support for the Act's objectives was transformed into a fundamental aversion by the 'unscriptural and un-christian' separation of man and wife; he was further soured by the illegal chicanery used to keep him off the Board of Guardians. Brooker achieved a considerable reputation, becoming 'a sort of minor Stephens in the Eastbourne Union' in assistant commissioner Tufnell's estimation,[49] through a series of major contributions to the *Patriot.* Pamphlets based on these followed. Brooker's progress is best illustrated by his opposition to the United Brothers in 1835, his personal political disinterest emphasised in 1838, and his eventual emergence as a Chartist parliamentary candidate in 1841; in 1838 he celebrated his conversion by stating that 'religion ought to be mixed with politics as sugar was with tea'. His determination to rid the statute book of the Robbery Bill, and his experiences of the political implications of this mission, led him to conclude that manhood suffrage was the vital prerequisite for success.[50]

The Act generated fierce extra-parliamentary manoeuverings in the south. Petitions against the Act came from some rural locations in 1835 and 1836, and opposition was orchestrated in a handful of places, for example at Cowfold, where a committee was formed to monitor implementation and to authenticate evidence. The Cowfold organisers recognised that they would have to brave 'the frowns of aristocracy'; in the main, the grandees intimidated rural opponents. It was a retired farmer, domiciled at Chichester, Richard Cousins, who used his old friends in neighbouring Westhampnett to supply information about the creation of that model union under the dictorial sway of the Duke of Richmond, which was used to such devastating effect once passed on to William Cobbett. The opponents' evidence from Westhampnett examined by the 1837 parliamentary committee was also collated from the urban sanctuary of

---

[49] The Rev. J.R. Stephens, a major leader of the northern anti-Poor Law movement who achieved national notoriety through his advocacy of 'physical force' politics – which Brooker did not in fact support – to repeal the Act. See J.T. Ward, 'Revolutionary Tory: The Life of J.R. Stephens of Ashton-under-Lyne', *Transactions of the Lancashire and Cheshire Antiquarian Society,* 68 (1958).

[50] Edsall, *The Anti-Poor Law Movement,* p. 194 n. 2, claim that Brooker's publications were 'very mediocre stuff' compared with the Act's supporters' propaganda cannot be substantiated. *Sussex Weekly Advertiser,* 26 November 1792; *Brighton Patriot,* 24 April, 31 July, 7 August, 25 September and 10 October 1838, 28 May and 25 June 1839. Tufnell to Lefevre, 28 April 1839, PRO, MH 32/70. C. Brooker, *An Address to Englishmen* (Brighton, 1839); idem, *An Appeal to the British Nation* (Brighton, 1840); idem, *The Rejoinder* (Brighton, 1842); idem, *The Murder Den and its Means of Destruction* (Brighton, 1842). David Jones, *Chartism and the Chartists* (Harmondsworth, 1975), p. 91. For a parochially based portrait of Brooker, see Wells, 'Criminal Gangs', pp. 139–49; and below, 'Southern Chartism', below, Chapter 7, pp. 127–51.

Chichester: clothing-dealer James Gray secured details from Westhampnett residents, including parochial officers, and then protected his sources 'otherwise the persons who gave me the information would perhaps get ill-will, and be damaged in consequence'.

Chichester was also representative of larger towns where poor relief was administered on a municipal basis, under local Acts, and where townsmen fought hard to preserve this expression of corporate identity. Gray also chaired the Chichester Guardians – a pre-1834 body – which resisted moves to end Chichester's autonomy in this respect by incorporation in Richmond's Westhampnett empire.[51] Opposition to the Robbery Bill in Brighton, identically autonomous, materialised as early as May 1834; their case was fortified by claims that well-practised strict management had already achieved the economies promised by the Act, which by that token was deemed an irrelevance. But Brighton's successful fight against subjection to the Poor Law Commission was principally due to the magnitude of potential political problems. Protest from smaller urban centres on parallel grounds of established efficiency, however unanimous, as at Ashford in Kent, was brushed aside. Even towns like Horsham, with a long radical tradition and a vociferous radical presence, making the election of awkward guardians inevitable, were incorporated under Somerset House; the assistant commissioners calculated that urban representatives would be outnumbered by a tractable majority from the rural parishes in the new union. At Lewes, where the geography of the adjacent big landed estates and the power of their owners conspired to preclude this psephologically-inspired creation, Hawley delayed the formation of one of the smallest Unions for a year in hopes that the reductions in expenditure revealed by the Act's operation in neighbouring rural Unions would transform the attitude of a significant sector of the initially unified opposition. This strategem failed. As late as 1841, 736 of Lewes's 893 parliamentary electors petitioned against the Amendment Act. This dramatically illustrated the emergence of urban communities as the major residual source of hostility to the new system, which would have been more powerful if neighbouring Brighton had an identical vested interest in the Act's demise.[52]

Southern towns, including Lewes, Chichester, Rye and Horsham, repeatedly petitioned against the Act between 1835 and 1837, thereby posing problems for Whig parliamentary representatives of boroughs. R.H. Hurst, MP for Horsham, was fiercely denounced for refusing to present his constituents' petition to the Commons, and Whig support at Lewes began to crumble despite the less inept response of MPs to pressure. Thomas Kemp, MP for Lewes at

[51] *Brighton Patriot*, 29 March, 17 May and 6 December 1836; *Kent Herald*, 28 May, 4 and 11 June 1835. Hawley to Richmond, 15 and 25 March 1836, WSCRO, Goodwood 1872; Hawley to Nicholls, 24 June 1835, PRO, MH 32/38. BPP, SC, HC, *Poor Law Amendment Act*, 1837, xvii, especially QQ. 11530, 11532, 14365–69, 14764: see also QQ. 11461–529, 11538–43, 12632–48.

[52] *Brighton Gazette*, 8 and 22 May 1834, and 11 February 1841. Hawley to the PLC, 18 November 1834 and 8 February 1835, and to Nicholls, 3, 14 and 29 March 1836, PRO, MH 32/38.

least delivered the petition, but the Bundle of Sticks, a political club containing middle- and working-class Whig supporters collapsed into pro and anti-Poor Law factions. Kemp tried to head the matter off by supporting demands for a thorough parliamentary investigation of the workings of the Act and the introduction of a Bill to end *ex officio* guardian status for magistrates, while his colleague Sir Charles Blunt played to the tune of his most radical supporters through advocacy of the ballot and triennial parliaments.[53] Kemp's resignation, early in 1837, precipitated a crisis: neither the Whig nor the Tory candidate at the by-election supported repeal, but the Tory Fitzroy demanded a thorough revision of the Act, including an end to the separation of families and greater use of outdoor relief notably for those temporarily unemployed during the winter months. Fitzroy won and his victory proved to be but the start of the erosion of the Whig supremacy in southern constituencies, which accelerated with the general election in mid 1837 on the King's death.[54]

Professor Brundage's claim that the Act was not an issue in this election is wide of the mark. Certainly, the Act was not a party issue as such. The Tory, Darby, who took the Whig Curteis's East Sussex seat, had announced his conversion to support the Act at the Lewes Cattle Show in 1835. The *Brighton Patriot*'s scathing note that the Act was the only issue on which the 'aristocratic factions' of Whig and Tory united, was not totally devoid of truth. However, Whig and Tory opponents of the law, in the persons of Hodges and Disraeli, won seats for West Kent and Maidstone respectively. Where radicals stood against both parties, hostility to the Act was a potential vote winner. It was also an emblem of radicalism, which enabled candidates to denounce their opponents' unity on a major issue of the day. Respectable votes were won by Cobbett's son at Chichester and by Salomans at Bramber. But radicals stood in only a handful of southern constituencies and this prevented the testing of an earlier strategy of the Act's opponents: to vote only for candidates who declared for total repeal. Some sitting MPs – notably H.D. Goring at Bramber – forced on to the defensive, went on to qualify their support for the Act. Even where elections comprised a straight fight between the major parties, popular clamour at the hustings repeatedly forced candidates to address themselves to the topic, often clearly against their will. Curteis eschewed the subject in one speech but was called to order by a massive and hostile crowd determined to hear his sentiments. The weak and transparent response – that agitating the issue would split the Whig vote – at least had the advantage of accuracy. Tories advocated some reform, while their opposition to the splitting of couples in workhouses took the pressure off them and harvested votes. As the *Patriot* noted, many MPs were compelled to criticise details of the Act, though its confidence that the election released so

---

[53] *Brighton Patriot*, 8 and 29 March, 26 April, 14 and 21 June, 6 and 13 December 1836, 21 and 28 February, 11 April and 15 June 1837.

[54] Ibid., 25 April 1837.

much hostility to the Act that no government could survive, unless it was drastically pruned, proved very wide of the mark.[55]

The struggle against the New Poor Law materialised in a political environment greatly changed by the workings of the reformed parliamentary system. The Reform Bill was initially perceived as a process for the redress of all grievances. The passing of the Robbery Bill shattered this understandable brand of naivity, for post-1832 parliaments were no more responsive to proletarian demands than their predecessors. If further proof were needed, the 'indifference and … contempt' of most MPs for workers was revealed by 'their cold and formal receptions' of petitions against the Poor Law. The inability to engineer even effective modification of the Act through the representations to the select committees of 1837–38, coupled with the failure drastically to change the political complexion of the Commons at the start of the new reign, were significant in the south because they provoked shifts in existing political alliances. Moreover, the Act's implementation exposed millions to political decisions which impinged on their lives in a way no previous policy had. The struggle over the Poor Law – notably the conduct of the Whigs, including backbenchers representing southern constituencies – was one major cause behind the emergence of a distinct working class movement in the south. Out of the split in the Lewes Bundle of Sticks evolved a 'really independent party'; 'Who gave you the iniquitous Poor Law Bill,' exclaimed an advocate of ditching middle-class leaders. Parallel progressions are detectable in other places, including Horsham, Tonbridge and Brighton, all of which hosted elements of the early nineteenth-century labour movement. If southern radicalism did not have the stimulus of the Factory Movement, trade unionism, especially among skilled artisan groups, was pronounced in the major towns, many of the smaller of which had union lodges. Trade unionism and political radicalism were no more distinct or exclusive movements in the south than their counterparts in London and the north. This was revealed by the formation of many Working Men's Associations in the south from 1836, which readily contributed to the huge effort made by Poor Law opponents to mobilise mass support over the winter of 1837–38 behind Fielden's parliamentary moves to repeal the Act. Fielden's failure in March 1838, coupled with a sharp deterioration in plebeian living standards as the economy lurched into another depression, injected energy into the southern labour movement.[56]

Historians have overlooked both the depth of popular antipathy to the new law and, above all, its duration in the south. Both were revealed by the array of anti-Poor Law songs – staple lyrics in Wealden beershops. The governor of Newhaven workhouse was 'assailed with abusive language' every time he passed through the streets, and his Battle colleague was 'afraid to go out by daylight'.

[55] Brundage, *Making of the New Poor Law*, pp. 164–65; *Sussex Advertiser*, 7 and 14 December 1835; *Brighton Patriot*, 24 July 1835, 13 December 1836, 11, 18 and 25 July, 1 August and 7 November 1837.

[56] *Brighton Patriot*, 15 March 1836, 12 December 1837, 6 and 13 March, 10, 17 and 24 April, 23 and 30 October 1838; Tufnell to Nicholls, 12 October 1837, PRO, MH 32/69. *Kent Herald*, 24 January 1839. *Sussex Agricultural Express*, 23 March 1839.

It was necessary to provide an all-night guard to prevent nocturnal damage to Horsham's new central workhouse while under construction in 1839. In December 1840 'many men are found abusing the new Poor Law and all acting under it, with the most violent and unmitigated rancour'. Rancour took its toll, on guardians who resigned, for example, over the 'cruelty and injustice of the system', while many others resisted pressure to stand for election. Moreover, the repeated failures of the campaigns against the law penetrated very deeply. In Hampshire, the Rev. Butler's collation of evidence to present to a parliamentary committee caused an excited furore 'among the agricultural labourers'; 'Mr Butler is the man for us, he is going to do everything for us; I have seen the *Sun* newspaper'. The resultant disappointment at the impotency of men in locally elevated stations can be imagined. The start of a rural, plebeian political transformation in the countryside was exposed by an anti-Poor Law petition of 1838. This advanced the 'rights of labourers who cause the earth to produce ... to extend to something more than POTATOES AND RAGS' and went on to castigate taxation levels which further drained 'their pitiful earnings to be lavished upon thousands of idle and profligate hangers on of the state'.[57]

In December 1838 assistant commissioner Tufnell, writing from Kent, insisted that the proven utility of the Amendment Act had swept away most non-working class hostility. George Darby's attempts to amend the Act through the substitution of a labour for the workhouse test failed to generate support from the rural electorate. Tufnell represented residual non-worker opposition as confined to

> small farmers who used to get their labour paid for by the rates, a few small shopkeepers who profited by the old abuses; and a few well-intentioned and benevolent but unreasoning people, who know nothing of the practical operation of the Act.

This swing in public opinion was decisive. It enabled the High Sheriff of Sussex to flatly reject Charles Brooker's association's request for a formal county meeting to orchestrate a further round of petitioning in May 1838, leaving him to fulminate against the 'insult to the poor and needy, the labouring class, and the small traders', whose opinions could be ignored because most had no vote. When an intrepid opponent of the new law was shouted down by the farmers and gentry assembled at a Hailsham agricultural social in December 1836, the *Brighton Patriot* said that this 'insult' extended to 'every agricultural labourer' in the country, and warned 'that such feelings rankle in every labourer's mind'. There can be no doubt that the operation of the Amendment Act enhanced working-class consciousness in the southern countryside, as the reduction of

---

[57] *Brighton Patriot*, 2 March and 19 September 1837, 13 March and 7 August 1838. Clerk, Newhaven Union, to the PLC, 23 August 1837, ESCRO, G7/8/1. *Sussex Agricultural Express*, 20 March 1839; *Sussex Advertiser*, 7 December 1840. BPP, 1837, xvii, QQ. 7977, 8095, 8225, 8802, 9503. Horsham Union Board minute, 8 May 1839, WSCRO, WG 6/1/3.

middle- and upper-class opponents, to a rump of do-gooders in Tufnell's parlance, forced rural proletarians to look to themselves. A poster advertising a meeting at Brede addressed itself principally to the working class:

> Consider, ye, who dislike the New Poor Law, and who do not dare to come foreward, that you are perfidiously betraying your wives and families, your liberty and your religion, into the hands of the very men you are afraid of.

Brooker's recognition of the new class base for the embryonic mass movement he hoped to lead in the spring of 1838 came in the form of his denial of opponents' claims that he 'wanted to set the man against the master'. But the anticipation of a proletarian impetus was revealed by his own association's monthly penny subscription. By the late 1830s opposition to the Poor Law was a *de facto* dimension of the war between labour and agrarian capital.[58]

The development of southern Chartism, from these anti-Poor Law mobilisations, precisely paralleled the much better-known and documented evolution of northern Chartism. Many plebeian activists in the political groupings in southern urban centres were recent migrants from rural villages. They had first-hand knowledge of the agrarian poverty problem. If colleagues with non-rustic backgrounds required persuasion, reference to the Swing explosion, the riots and burnings against the Poor Law and the smashing of rural unionism, as revealed by the celebrated Tolpuddle case and the experiences of the United Brothers, would suffice. All this revealed distress and discontent on a scale not dissimilar to the depressed northern industrial districts, and hence the potential to turn southern rural proletarians into a solid phalanx in support of the Chartists. Those at Brighton formed a 'visiting committee' to orchestrate rural campaigns, backed by propaganda composed specially for agricultural labourers. Lewes Chartists advertised their inaugural meeting in the villages and were gratified by the presence of many farmworkers. Activists from both centres hoped to found 'Chartist Associations', and several rural branches materialised. Through this mechanism delegates to the 1839 Chartist Convention – including Bronterre O'Brien – addressed labourers in the villages. Feargus O'Connor's visits to Brighton took in other smaller centres, including Dorking. Chartist speakers inevitably exploited the Poor Law, but those of O'Brien's calibre were eminently capable of broadening the analysis of the farmworkers' predicament. Every facet of agrarian capitalism was attacked, and the futility of every form of protest revealed except political reform on the principles of the Six Points:

---

[58] Tufnell to PLC, 2 December; Clerk, Battle Union, to Chadwick, with enclosure, 2 November 1838, PRO, MH 12/747; 32/70. *Brighton Patriot*, 20 December 1836, 8 May and 4 December 1838. On rural working class-consciousness, see Wells, 'Social Protest', pp. 181–98; and idem, 'Rural Rebels in Southern England in the 1830s', in E. Emsley and J. Walvin (eds), *Artisans, Peasants and Proletarians, 1760–1860* (London, 1985).

the landed aristocracy, aided by the middle men ... had brought the poor man, by that hell-born bill, the New Poor Law, to a state of starvation by reducing wages to that point that no man could exist upon his labour ... a Poor Law Guardian in that neighbourhood ... had the cruelty to ask a man to work for four shillings a week in ... harvest.

The Poor Law's centrality was revealed in other ways: Chartists convening on Ham Common in August 1839 erected the hustings in the shadow of the new workhouse, which caused no 'detriment to the enthusiasm ... but quite the reverse'. As Brooker rode across the South Downs to address the newly-formed 'Polegate Universal Suffrage Association' he

> had most unexpectedly a paper put into my hand ... signed by 58 of the male poor persons in the Hellingly Union Workhouse ... requesting me to have their names placed in the [People's] petition'[59]

The New Poor Law was primarily responsible for the invigoration of southern radicalism and proved the vehicle for an important intensification of rural politicisation. This facilitated the penetration of the countryside by a major, popular political movement and suggests that the implementation of the Act achieved an unparalleled significance in the history of the southern labour movement. This hardly accords with the view of those historians already mentioned who have seen opposition to the Act as little more than a hopeless kneejerk. But it does not confound the associated interpretation that protest made little difference to the operation of the Act. Those like Sheffield Grace, a Wealden landowner, who claimed – in the same breath as he marvelled at rate reductions in excess of 40 per cent – that 'the deserving poor are obviously and unquestionably better off', were living in cloud-cuckoo land; so too was the Duke of Richmond, who believed that farmworkers accepted that the new system achieved the Act's aim by operating in favour of the hard-working, forelock-tugging proletarian and that it justly penalised the socially irreverent and workshy. At most the Act split working-class communities at village level, between the 'really honest and industrious' and another

> class of labourers, who clinging to the expectation of temporary parochial assistance are still to be found [in October 1837] in an apparent state of idleness and

[59] T.M. Kemnitz, 'Chartism in Brighton' (unpublished D.Phil. thesis, University of Sussex, 1969), pp. 31, 173–74. *Brighton Patriot*, 4, 11 and 25 December 1838, 8, 15 and 22 January, 26 March, 9, 23 and 30 April, 7 May, 4 June and 13 August 1839; *The Champion*, 25 August 1839; *Northern Star*, 14 April 1838; *Sussex Advertiser*, 29 April 1839; *Sussex Agricultural Express*, 23 and 30 March, 27 April and 25 May 1839; *Kent Herald*, 28 March 1839; *Maidstone Gazette*, 22 January, 2 and 16 April 1839; *Hampshire Telegraph*, 27 May 1839; *Southern Star*, 1 March 1840. Letters to Richmond from Sir C.M. Burrell, 24 December, and J.B. Freeland, 22 May, 10 and 11 August 1839, WSCRO, Goodwood 1601. Chartist Convention sub-committee minute, 23 February and 14 April 1839; W. Dale, Dorking, to Chartist Convention, 21 March 1839, BL, MS Add. 34245A, fos 61–62, 78, 143–44, 244–45.

destitution ... those who prefer accepting the liberal but irregular remuneration derived from ... work ... and others.[60]

Even those in stable work were affected directly by the Act, notably when officials took legal action to force contributions for the support of aged parents and other close relatives. In 1837, a relieving officer confirmed that

> I see their faces altered; I see that they have got no clothes, and they have apparently got into a more wretched state visibly; I have seen a difference even in the faces of the people ... I was hurt in my feelings to hear the pitiful cries of the poor.

The clergy insisted that they were exposed to unprecedented appeals for aid; recipients acknowledged that they 'would have been nearly starved but for charity'. Ironically, one of the most outspoken clerical opponents was that scourge of the United Brothers, the Rev. Carnegie of Seaford but, as a major East Sussex landowner said, most of those clergymen who were not openly hostile were covert opponents. One cannot realistically speak of working-class acquiescence; detectable acceptance was attributed solely to the poor being 'completely stunned'. The clerk to the Uckfield guardians confirmed the 'undefined Terror which the New system has created'.[61]

Terror worked both ways: protest in both its riotous and trade unionist forms left the propertied in no doubt of the depth of proletarian hostility. Once incendiarism established itself as the most durable mode of resistance it exposed all concerned in Poor Law administration to potentially huge losses. Guardians speedily perceived this; and less quickly recognised that the abolition of outdoor relief to able-bodied men and their families was ruinously expensive if the legal corollary – incarceration of the entire family in the workhouse – was strictly enforced. Subsidiary problems, for example that those put temporarily in the workhouse were in danger of losing their homes, and thereby might become a long-term applicant, revealed the limits of the Amendment Act's strategy. Other practical difficulties, which the guardians technically could contain, notably the inadequacy of workhouse accommodation for all those temporarily thrown out of work by prolonged, inclement winter weather, were also experienced. A combination of terror ('apprehensions by the more timid

---

[60] Grace to Richmond, 14 September 1839, WSCRO, Goodwood 1602. Hawley to the PLC, 31 October 1837, PRO, MH 32/39. Kent estate steward John Nearne confirmed that farmworkers were 'distressed and in bad condition', and claimed that 'we select the best characters, and do all we can to find them work, and they are grateful ... Those that are out of employment are dissatisfied'. 'The best men are contented with it, but not the worthless', chimed Sussex farmer Hudson. Ellman opined that 'we have made friends of our best labourers and put the others at defiance, and that is as the thing should be'. BPP, SC, HC, *State of Agriculture*, 464, 1837, v, QQ. 1478, 1480–81, 3498; BPP, SC, HC, *Agricultural Distress*, 189 (1836), viii, Q.4529.

[61] BPP, SC, HC *Poor Law Amendment Act*, 1837, xvii, QQ. 2652, 2657, 2720, 5106, 5120, 5680. Liverpool to Nicholls, 26 May 1836; Uckfield Union clerk to the PLC, 1 June; Hawley to Nicholls, 4 July 1835, PRO, MH 12/13157, 32/38. *Sussex Advertiser*, 7 November 1836; *Sussex Agricultural Express*, 19 January 1839.

and mistrustful' Guardians was Hawley's euphemism), cost consciousness and practical problems underpinned the prolonged struggles between Union Boards attempting to modify the Act in practice, and a Poor Law Commission determined to enforce the Act in all its ideological purity. Every Kent Union fiercely resisted the introduction of the Commission's model workhouse dietaries in 1836, Tufnell explaining that 'Guardians are always violently opposed to lowering the pauper dietary especially as it excites great clamour in the neighbourhood on the score of "starving the poor"'. A Kent farmer 'found fault with the dietary, and gave 10 pots of beer to the inmates', while an assistant overseer at Tunbridge supplied oranges. At Tufnell's instigation both men were prosecuted; if this demonstrated the powers of Somerset House, it also encouraged Unions clandestinely to improve diets. The Ticehurst Union openly flouted the Commission with the provision of Christmas dinners for inmates in 1838. In Kent a gargantuan struggle developed between Tufnell and Boards who wanted to return to the old practices of clothing youths who received yearly work contracts and paying premiums to their employers. As Boards – and their officers – found their feet, other sleights of hand circumvented the Act. The Eastbourne Union denominated any claimant aged over sixty as 'old' and thereby ineligible for the workhouse test, despite the fact that 'many men in regular employ ... do a good days work at 70'. Union medical officers – commonly with covert authority from their Boards – drove coaches and horses through the Act by certifying the temporarily unemployed as ill, and also 'obtained a cheap popularity' by ordering relieving officers to provide generously for the sick. Nor were workhouse masters invariably the inhuman variety depicted in Victorian novels: sixty-three-year-old John Garton, a 'diseased' inmate at Petworth reserved a semblance of independence as he still hawked 'almonds and chestnuts for sale'.[62]

Many guardians resolutely refused to concede that outdoor relief to able-bodied males was a thing of the past; they exploited the Poor Law Commission's short-term authorisation of outdoor relief as an interim measure and, there-after, perceived its continuance 'as part and parcel of the new Law, rather than a temporary concession'. Guardians 'loudly and violently protested against' the Commission's use of formal outdoor prohibition orders, especially 'on the untenable plea of the inability of the Farmers to advance ... wages', and achieved some spectacular breaches of the order, including the Lewes Union's payment to 500 claimants in March 1838. Even where majorities resisted such wholesale evasion, individual guardians fought to except every claimant's case and the assistant commissioners had to take refuge in ensuring that excepted claimants were forced to work. Another device, common under the Old Poor Law, to take one or two children only from large families into the workhouse, was

[62] Tufnell to the PLC, 24 February 1836, and to Nicholls, 12 October 1837; Hawley to Nicholls, 20 April 1836, and quarterly report, 1 January 1838, PRO, MH 32/38–39, 69. Ticehurst Union minutes, December 1838; Uckfield Union minute, 11 June 1842, ESCRO, G10/1a/1; G11/1a/2. Mrs Gilbert, Eastbourne to Richmond, 19 September 1839, WSCRO, Goodwood 1602. *Sussex Advertiser*, 2 March 1840.

also repeatedly invoked long after the Commission's temporary authorisation had expired. This was the cause of a perennial struggle between the Horsham Union and the Commission; the Board, including the Whig MP who regularly attended, and supported by the vicar, argued that otherwise 'unnecessary' first institutionalisation of families would terminate 'independence of mind'. Midhurst threatened to follow. Hawley, who was driven to desperate demands for strongly-worded missives from Somerset House, fought a losing battle. Many of these disputes made the press; the Havant Board published its correspondence with the Commission in a transparent attempt to identify it as the source of inhumane rigidity and to exonerate the guardians. These struggles produced a crop of spectacular results. The Battle Board, tired of repetitive 'strong doctrinal letters' from the Commission, ignored them; when threatened with Somerset House's last resort – making guardians personally liable for unauthorised expenditure – several guardians, including the chairman, resigned. The decision to erect a new workhouse was also a casualty of this dispute. Most Unions were liable to backslide, some more than others. Hawley insisted that 'constant watchfulness' was crucial, calculating that seven out of his twenty-five in 1838 contained a 'disaffected' majority who concertedly tried to put the clock back. This minority of perennially difficult Boards became a majority in periods of aggravated economic difficulties; as the winter of 1836–37 approached, Tufnell was

> almost wearied to death in this difficult season. But I believe three fourths of my troubles never came under your [Somerset House's] notice. On Tuesday I have to send an express 80 miles, and the next day was obliged to travel 80 miles in another direction out of my intended course. Uckfield Union sent for me, and was vacillating in spite of its former poor law triumphs. However after some hours talk, I believe I have confirmed them in keeping strictly to our rules. Now however East Grinstead and Ticehurst are in a flame.[63]

Logistically, given the scale of the poverty problem, these struggles between the Poor Law Commission and the Unions, could have escalated and crippled the system. The real initiative for preventing that collapse did not originate with Somerset House, its assistant commissioners or the Unions, but with the parishes. For the latter retained one critical relevant function: road repair. On 14 February 1839 the Salehurst vestry convened to consider

---

[63] Hawley to Nicholls, 4 July 1835, to the PLC, 20 April 1836, and quarterly report, 1 January 1838; Tufnell to Nicholls, 13 November 1836, and to the PLC, 7 July 1838; Battle Union clerk to PLC, 11 July 1838, 10 and 20 January 1839; auditor's report 17 December 1838, and Board minute, 22 February 1839; S. Love, Shoreham Castle, Kent, to Tufnell, 19 January 1839, PRO, MH 12/12747; 32/38–9, 69–70. *Brighton Patriot*, 20 March 1838; *Sussex Advertiser*, 20 January 1839; *Kent Herald*, 13 December 1838; *Hampshire Telegraph*, 17 December 1839.

the best method of Employing or Relieving At the *Parish Expence* such labourers As Are not in the service of Any Private Individual And whose families would be Destitute without *Parochial Assistance* of some kind ... [my emphasis]

They devised an extensive road improvement scheme, voted considerable funds to finance it, and repeated the exercise throughout the 1840s. The Ashford (Kent) vestry, also meeting in 1839, noted 'much dissatisfaction' at the Amendment Act, and agreed to an unprecedented second highway levy to soak up the unemployed: the press commented that 'surely no reasonable man can require a stronger proof of the ineffectiveness of the New Poor Law than that it should require such a subterfuge ... to assist its working!' The new law simply did not work. Eastbourne farmers typically 'turned off their ... servants in winter to be maintained out of the Highway rates', just as they had sacked workers prior to 1834; 300 acre farms in the Horsham Union had but one permanent employee. Petworth hired a stone quarry for road materials which also provided jobs for the unemployed at any time of the year. South Bersted waywardens paid on a scale governed by the size of families, and when food prices rose in 1837 even used the highway rate to finance flour doles to employed farmworkers. Many guardians – like Michael Botting of West Grinstead – personally inspired these parochial decisions; several Boards formally recommended the measure to vestrymen in component parishes, and many relieving officers' books were peppered with entries against claimants' names 'recommended to the waywardens'. A parochial official from Romney Marsh blandly told a Union auditor that any expenditure disallowed by him would simply be financed from the highway or the church rate. By 1840 Chadwick himself recognised the complicity of auditors whose operations were 'more often a security for malversation than against it'. The assistant commissioners were soon advocating the takeover of the roads by the Unions. 'The Highways rate', insisted Hawley, 'is ... indirectly and unfairly converted into a poor rate'. 'The shifts and shufflings of these people to defeat the ... Law are abominable', he fumed, 'and I fear in this instance uncontrollable'. An Isle of Thanet farmer agreed that 'in fact the highways have become the workhouse'.[64]

To these evasions of the law, we must add private and voluntary parochial rates, and interventions by the gentry who tailored their improvement schemes

[64] Salehurst vestry minutes, 14 February 1839, 15 January 1841, 20 April 1843 and 14 February 1845, ESCRO, Par. 477/12/1; Horsham Union minutes, 5, 12, 16 and 23 December 1835; T. Stave, Eastbourne, to Richmond, 9 January 1839, WSCRO, WG 6/1/1; Goodwood 1606. W.W. Phillips, Southbersted, to Hawley, 20 January 1837; Hawley to Nicholls, 18 November 1836, and to the PLC, 5 May 1838; Tufnell to Nicholls, 23 January 1838, to Lefevre, 12 February 1838, and to Chadwick, 6 May 1838; Ticehurst Union clerk to the PLC, and draft reply, 27 and 29 January 1838, PRO, MH 12/13139; 32/38–39. *Kent Herald*, 7 February 1839. BPP, SC, HC, *Agricultural Distress*, 465, 1836, viii, Q.9523; BPP, SC, HC, *Poor Law Amendment Act*, 1837, xviii, QQ.1105, 1110, 1889, 1899. J.V. Moseley, 'Poor Law Administration in England and Wales 1834 to 1850 with Special Reference to the Problem of Able-Bodied Pauperism' (unpublished Ph.D. thesis, University of London, 1975), especially pp. 33–35, 78–80, 102, 151–52, 220–28.

to provide jobs for the unemployed. The Poor Law Commission maintained the tradition of perverting its own evidence established in the original enquiry of 1832–34; its annual reports from 1835 turned on 'specially selected items' from assistant commissioners' communications but a 'full examination of their correspondence ... gives a very different impression' from the published accounts suggesting a relatively smooth implementation. According to Dr Moseley 'the absence of any strong movement against the Poor Law in the 1840s may be explained in the essential ineffectiveness of the assistant commissioners' in enforcing the law.[65] They were defeated by a combination of guardians and parochial officials, whose own resolves were an ever-fluctuating mixture of humanitarian principles, a lack of conviction in utilitarian ideology, cost consciousness and, finally, fear. The Act's opponents could not claim that their protests were – as it turned out – a total triumph, because at best their success was qualified. People were incarcerated in the bastilles, and subjected to the 'starvation system'; cuts in benefits were imposed on the old, the sick and the infirm; and the system remained available for discriminatory, punitive infliction on individuals. But even the most stalwart administrators of the Act, however elevated, were permanently looking over their shoulders. Guardians insisted on formal inquests on workhouse inmates 'to satisfy the feelings of the public'. The Earl of Liverpool, as chairman of one Board, insisted on receiving full medical details prior to the amputation of an orphan boy's arm 'to put out of all doubt that this poor, friendless boy has received every attentive consideration' as

> it is well known how jealously the public watches the proceedings of the Poor Law Amendment no circumstances may possibly occur to impeach any of its proceedings in the Uckfield union.

Eloquent as this testimony is to opposition in the broadest sense it should not be forgotten that relief for the vast majority of those with a legitimate claim on the state remained; and, by and large, it remained outside the workhouse. When the Croydon Board insisted on all outdoor claimants presenting themselves for inspection in 1839, over a thousand turned up.

> Widows and orphans, the aged, the lame, and the blind, in short all who, by favour or the interference of friends, could obtain the smallest relief, and such an accumulation of poverty and misery combined could hardly have equalled – the sight was heart-sickening in the highest degree.

The scale of human misery and personal disaster was too great for the free market or unrestrained capitalism; it was beyond the resources actually tappable

[65] *Brighton Patriot*, 20 October 1835 and 16 February 1836. Moseley, 'Poor Law Administration', pp. 34, 109–10.

by utilitarian philosophy, but resistance helped to ensure that ideologues went no further down the road towards institutionalised solutions to the problem.[66]

This combination of mass mobilisations, followed by multifarious protests, however localised, and whatever the subtle intermixtures of overt and covert, was sustained in the rural south throughout the late 1830s and into the 1840s. Bosenden Wood was but one highly visible manifestation, however unusual. It was the prolonged resistance across a much longer period which in reality constituted *the* last labourers' revolt in the rural south, namely opposition to the Robbery Bill, its works, its main supporters and principal personnel.

[66] Hawley, quarterly report, 1 January 1838, PRO, 32/39; Liverpool to Dr Prince, 28 October 1837, ESCRO, G11/1a/1; *Sussex Agricultural Express*, 20 April 1839.

7

Southern Chartism

Roger Wells

Chartism, the first genuinely working-class mass political movement, has attracted numerous general, regional, and local histories. The overwhelming proportion of these works concentrate on Chartism's strongholds in London, provincial urban centres, and the theatres of industrialism – including those in Scotland and Wales. Yet despite these regional characteristics, the common assumption is that Chartism was a national movement. This assumption is implicit in works including J.T. Ward's *Chartism*, while Dorothy Thompson, the author of the most recent notionally national overview, suggests that countryside Chartism has been underestimated.[1]

But such statements and assumptions can be no substitute for analysis, particularly in view of a number of considerations. First, farmworkers were the largest single sector of the working-class population. Secondly, their numbers and those of their skilled neighbours in the rural service industries were expanding in the 1830s. Thirdly, this demographic expansion was generating greater population densities, notably in the country's premier arable regions in the east and the south. If Chartism did not penetrate, let alone embrace, the huge numbers in these vast tracts of countryside, its national characterisation looks decidely odd.

A study of Chartism in parts of East Anglia finds that the presence created in many of the towns was essentially weak, while efforts to enrol farmworkers, through the creation of village radical associations, met with at best very limited, and more especially, ephemeral success in 1838–39.[2] Chartist experiences in the south are largely uncharted. One study of the partly industrial and partly agricultural countries of Somerset and Wiltshire focuses almost exclusively on the manufacturing districts.[3] The movement's history in the counties of Dorset, Hampshire, Sussex, and the non-metropolitan parts of Surrey and Kent, is restricted to a local study, namely Brighton, which remains unpublished.[4]

---

[1] J.T. Ward, *Chartism* (London, 1973); D. Thompson, *The Chartists* (Aldershot, 1984), esp. pp. 173–79.

[2] A.F.J. Brown, *Chartism in Essex and Suffolk* (Chelmsford, 1982); cf. H. Fearn, 'Chartism in Suffolk', in A. Briggs (ed.), *Chartist Studies* (London, 1959).

[3] R.B. Pugh, 'Chartism in Somerset and Wiltshire', in Briggs, *Chartist Studies*.

[4] T.M. Kenmitz, 'Chartism in Brighton' (unpublished D.Phil. thesis, University of Sussex, 1969).

Historians of the emergence of the British labour movement traditionally ignore both southern market and other towns, and the vast tracts of countryside, with the brief – almost embarrassing – but apparently exceptional and isolated episode of Tolpuddle. Those participating in the Swing explosion of 1830, which engulfed the entire region examined here, according to its principal historians, articulated sentiments commensurate with 'the usual luggage of the pre-political poor', rather than the democratic ideology of simultaneous protesters in industrial, urban and metropolitan England.[5] I have argued, elsewhere, against these orthodoxies of rural historiography.[6] Radical nuclei were formed in numerous southern towns in the 1790s. If their histories are more irretrievable than those in the better documented centres of the democratic movement during the war years and beyond, circumstantial evidence suggests some continuity through to the 1830s – at least in some towns, including Maidstone, Horsham, Brighton, Lewes, Chichester, Portsmouth, Southampton and Winchester. Rural radicalism is even more elusive, though there are exceptions – notably in Hampshire. However, there is excellent evidence of the leading participation of plebeian democrats in several epicentres of Swing, while the lengthy duration of the Reform Bill crisis served principally to enhance the political atmosphere in town and country. The formation of political unions in the towns was followed by the creation of rural satellites in some country districts, including those centred in Horsham and Winchester. In certain districts, agrarian trade unionism began to take root. The Tolpuddle exemplar was in fact part of an ambitious programme by organisations and members of unions, closely involved with the Grand National Consolidated Trade Union, to embrace the largest sector of the English proletariat, namely landworkers.[7]

Moreover, the Poor Law Amendment Act, which principally targetted the rural workforce's dependency on outdoor relief under the ancient poor law system, had a major and traumatic impact throughout the southern countryside, arguably more so than in any other region. There is considerable evidence that the Act's implementation in 1834–36 greatly accelerated the development of rural working-class consciousness.[8]

From the 1790s through to the 1830s, there were important parallels between political developments in southern England and other parts of the country, prior to the Chartist period. If Edward Thompson's famous thesis respecting the 'making of the English working class' – so critical to the study of the

[5] E.J. Hobsbawm and G. Rudé, *Captain Swing* (Harmondsworth, 1973), pp. 41–43.

[6] R. Wells, 'Resistance to the New Poor Law in Southern England', above, Chapter 6, pp. 91–125; idem, 'Rural Rebels in Southern England in the 1830s', in C. Emsley and J. Walvin (eds), *Artisans, Peasants and Proletarians, 1760–1860* (London, 1985); idem, 'Tolpuddle in the Context of English Agrarian Labour History, 1780–1850', in J.G. Rule (ed.), *British Trade Unionism, 1750–1850: The Formative Years* (London, 1988); idem, 'Social Protest, Class, Conflict and Consciousness in the English Countryside, 1700–1880', in M. Reed and R. Wells (eds), *Class, Conflict and Protest in the English Countryside, 1700–1880* (London, 1990).

[7] Wells, 'Tolpuddle', esp. pp. 120–24; idem, 'Rural Rebels', pp. 140–43.

[8] Wells, 'Social Protest', pp. 187–95; and above. Chapter 6, pp. 91–125.

emergence of the labour movement in industrial and bigger urban theatres – can by a slight advance of the time scale to 1834–36, be made to embrace, rather than exclude, farmworkers, then the impact of Chartism in both town and country in the predominantly rural south demands analysis not eschewal. Chartism's initial performance in the key early years, 1838–39, and its subsequent achievements between 1840 and the mid 1850s, are established as the best periodisation for the movement's public presence. Although the Chartist Land Plan was by no means secret (with, for example, regular notices of cash instalments received from hundreds of places published in the *Northern Star*), individual shareholders could quietly make their payments without drawing attention to themselves. This was in stark contrast to more active forms of support, such as attending rallies, participating in branch meetings, or actually campaigning. The contrast between public activity and what could be described as Southern Chartism's private, almost secretive, presence in the 1840s is of some significance.

Ironically, the first Chartist initiative in the south aimed to subsume a new farmworkers' union in eastern Dorset, Tolpuddle country. All but one of the martyrs were now back in England, and George Loveless was among the campaigners who had succeeded in creating new union branches in many villages in a triangle formed by Shaftesbury, Bridport and Wimbourne. 'Orderly' mass meetings were held in some parishes over the summer of 1838, in addition to the rallies convening on Blandford race course, and Bear Down, on 24 August and 20 October respectively. Loveless also published an address emphasising that if 'the Farming Labourers and Working Men in Dorsetshire . . . act peaceably and avoid all secrecy in your Association', they – unlike the victims of 1833–34 – would stay within the law. But, in addition to demands for 'fair . . . wages', and anticipations of strike action to secure them, this movement voiced political aspirations. Loveless's propaganda included demands for the vote. Further political literature derived from the London Working Man's Association (WMA), and was one component of a problematic exercise orchestrated principally by non-local Chartists, to transform the 'very extensive' union into a populist, political organisation.[9]

The climax to this political initiative came with the mass rally, held on Charlton Down, outside Blandford Forum, on Wednesday 14 November. The main speakers were Robert Hartwell, the London-based secretary to the Dorchester Labourers' Fund, Henry Vincent, and two leading members of the Bath WMA, W.P. Roberts and Anthony Phillips. The Blandford district was placarded with bills: 'The People's Charter', 'Vote by Ballot', 'Annual Parliaments'. Some of the audience had travelled over twenty miles, but only a quarter of the five to six thousand present were landworkers, the probable product of local farmers threatening their labourers with dismissal for attending. The majority present

---

[9] A'Court to the PLC, 6, 7, 8, 10 and 26 August, 4 October, 9 and 17 November (enclosing MS copy of handbill, printed in London, G. Loveless, 'Grinstead, late of Tolpuddle') 1838, PRO, MH 32/4.

comprised shopkeepers, and craftsmen, masters as well as journeymen. In some senses this was Dorset's sole Chartist rally, at precisely the moment when the movement took off nationally, a fact symbolised by Loveless's election as county delegate to the planned Convention.[10] But the bulk of the speeches concerned low agrarian wages, depressed further by the effects of the New Poor Law, which conversely inflated farmers' living standards – a situation which may only have been remedied through a harvest time strike. No speaker appears to have discussed the relevance of political reform on democratic principles to the achievement of trade unionist objectives.[11]

Ominously, this rally convened under the watchful gaze of several magistrates accompanied by scores of mounted farmers. They made no attempt to intervene, and the rally was quickly followed by dozens of small meetings in villages where talk focused on a strike for higher pay whenever called by the leadership, while Hartwell simultaneously campaigned to turn union branches into 'political Unions' on 'the Working Men's Association' model. Farmers, notably those in the Blandford district, offered their men a stark choice – wage increases for those who resigned from the association, the sack for those who refused. The resultant lock out revealed the additional powers devolving on the farmers through their dominance on the Boards of Guardians, notably the unusually Chadwickian Board for Blandford itself,[12] whose sole response was to hire additional workhouse accommodation for the flood of relief applicants refused 'all' outdoor relief. This severely tested the most stalwart labourers, the more so when Hartwell was forced to admit that the relevant rule, projecting weekly seven shilling strike or unemployment pay, had been 'expunged'. Although pecuniary aid came from unaffected workers, and 'charitable assistance' from 'shopkeepers', even the most committed members were soon 'heartily tired', and as Vincent reasoned 'we cannot expect men to starve for us'. Sensing total victory, the 'tyrannical' Blandford farmers even forced men taken back to sign an instrument binding themselves 'not to belong to any Club Society or Association without the Consent of the Master', and undertaking to be backed by 'two bondsmen'.[13]

---

[10] In the event his attendance was 'utterly impossible', owing to his inability to pay somebody to work on the Essex smallholding, provided by trade unionist campaigners for the Martyrs on their return. Loveless to Lovett, 13 April 1838, BL, MS Add 34245A, fo. 240.

[11] A'Court to the PLC, 9 and 22 November 1838, PRO, MH 34/4. *Dorset County Chronicle*, 15 November 1838; *Sherborne Journal*, 22 November 1838; *The Operative*, 25 November 1838; Reports, and Vincent to Lovett, Birmingham Reference Library, Lovett Collections (subsequently BRL, LC) ii, fos 281, 285, 291; K.D. Bawm, 'Social Protest, Popular Disturbance and Public Order in Dorset, 1790–1838' (unpublished Ph.D. thesis, University of Reading, 1984), pp. 217–18.

[12] In March 1838, at the time of the first parliamentary scrutiny of the workings of the new system, the Blandford Board formally addressed the PLC praising it as 'an essential benefit offering a source from which they [the guardians] may seek an explanation of all doubtful points of law, and a means of affording advice on every measure of importance'; minutes, 28 March 1838, PRO, MH 12/2724.

[13] Frampton and Lord Digby to Russell, 22 and 23 November 1838, PRO, HO 40/36, fos 209–14;

By this time, December 1838, Brighton had not unexpectedly established itself as the epicentre of southern Chartism. The radical *Brighton Patriot* devoted its entire front page on 6 June to the People's Petition on publication. If the Brighton Radical Association (BRA) had only discussed reforming itself on the lines of the London WMA over the summer, it nonetheless sent a delegation to the Palace Yard rally in London on 17 September. Londoners were assured that 'the Radicals of Brighton . . . only wait the general radical movement of the towns . . . to evince our determination', but even O'Connor's speech in Brighton the following week did not precipitate much activity. The most likely explanation for apparent delays derived from the posture middle-class radicals in Brighton and other southern towns were starting to take. These varied. Working-class radicals at Horsham were warned against expecting customary middle-class support and appear to have done little. At Lewes, the 'Bundle of Sticks Club', which embraced politically motivated middle- and working-class men, split not only over the Charter itself, but also over the chairman's refusal to discuss the issue, and his assertion that the club's *raison d'être* was exclusively local: to keep the Tories at bay and Lewes a Whig constituency. Members, 'principally of the working classes', abandoned 'shallow-pated' middle-class allies, and formed the Lewes Patriotic Society. The BRA purged itself of members prepared to vote only for Whig candidates, and supporters of the new Anti-Corn Law League, but retained significant middle-class allegiance. On 22 November local activists John Good and John Allen were elected delegates to the forthcoming Convention.[14]

Towards the end of the 1838–39 winter, Chartism had made only a limited impact elsewhere in the south. The Croydon Radical Association was formed in January 1839 but the membership preferred regular engagement in relatively lively metropolitan Chartism. The old Political Union at Newport on the Isle of Wight had reconvened in November; in January, it formally adopted the Charter. This month also witnessed an unprecedentedly large political meeting in Winchester, at which the Charter was adopted, and a relatively sophisticated appeal issued against the potentially diversionary impact of Anti-Corn Law activists in the district. At this time, the radical nucleus at Tonbridge in Kent secured the oratorical aid of Henry Hetherington and Robert Hartwell from the London WMA. A public meeting comprising a 'large proportion of . . . agricultural labourers', with a significant number of urban 'tradesmen', discussed the 'principles of the Charter'. Although 407 signatures were eventually despatched from Tonbridge, projected meetings for other Kent towns, including Chatham, Sheerness, Dartford, Cranbrook, Tenterden, and Canterbury, did not materialise. While it was said that the inhabitants of Kentish parliamentary boroughs were

---

continued
Dorset County Chronicle, 22 November 1838. Hartwell, London, to the Blandford Board of Guardians, 7 December 1838, PRO, MH 12/2724; A' Court to Lefevre, 3 January 1839, PRO, MH 32/4. *The Operative*, 6 January 1839. Vincent to Lovett, 16 November 1838, BRL, LC. ii, fo. 291.

[14] BRL, LC, iii, fo. 241, 250; *Brighton Patriot*, 6 and 27 June, 7 August, 25 September, 29 October, 6, 20 and 27 November 1838; annotated notice of election; J. Harris, Brighton, to Lovett, 14 April 1839, BL, MS Add. 34245A, fos 13–14, 244–25; T.M. Kenmitz, 'Chartism', pp. 121–39, 376.

incapable of seeing beyond rival offers from 'the two dominant factions' at election time, another explanation derived from Canterbury, where a 'few . . . individuals . . . mostly working men' felt adequate to arranging political meetings but lacked 'the confidence or the ability to undertake addressing them'. Indeed one resident overcame his feeling of isolation from the movement by giving a friend journeying to London on business a proxy signature for the petition and a pound by way of subscription. It was the conclusion of Tonbridge activists that their county – which they stressed was principally agricultural – was 'rather dark respecting political matters'.[15] Another explanation probably lay in the very recent crushing of the Bosenden Wood rebels.

Rural Sussex was not in quite the same situation, because Chartists in both Lewes and Brighton perceived themselves responsible for taking the movement to their hinterlands, to address 'their fellow labourers . . . the agriculturalists . . . to solicit their aid'. Several leaders at Brighton are known to have been migrants from the southeastern countryside, and their 'Visiting Committee's' self-appointed mission included the extension of 'democratic principles' to the 'agricultural labourers'. Initially, in December 1838, the Brightonians held open meetings in a number of villages within easy walking distance, including Hove, Southwick, and Patcham, but 'no public meetings were held' once they ventured further afield, to Rottingdean, Poynings, Clayton, Newtimber and Hurstpierpoint. This speedy recourse to secrecy followed intimidatory action from farmers, ranging from withdrawal of traditional Yuletide gifts of meat, to sacking their men for attendance at Chartist meetings. Various devices were swiftly devised against licencees who allowed meetings on their premises. Alternatively, some landowners advocated wage increases, and at least one unilaterally imposed limits on the rents farmers charged for tied cottages. Lewes activists simply spoke of the 'manifold difficulties' they encountered in the villages, an eloquent expression of which was the collection of only 1017 signatures from their entire district by January 1839, though their derisory sum towards the National Rent was doubtlessly also a reflection of poverty.[16]

It was broadly believed by Chartists operative outside the movement's main centres that 'meetings . . . got up by persons residing and known on the spot' could not achieve comparability with speakers of national repute: 'Henry Vincent . . . could draw 10,000, where a local orator would not draw 10'. This message reached the 1839 Convention from several sources, including Tonbridge campaigners, and was powerfully reaffirmed by Brighton's representatives on that body. Both Brighton delegates – including John Osborne who replaced

[15] *Brighton Patriot*, 26 November 1838; *The Operative*, 30 December 1838, 3, 10 and 24 February 1839; Letters to Lovett from Claris, n.d., R. Hawes, Canterbury, and L. Snelling, Tonbridge, 21 and 28 February, and E. Stallwood, Croydon, 15 April 1839, BL, MS Add. 34245A, fos 12, 55–56, 78, 248; *Maidstone Gazette*, 22 January 1839; *Kent Herald*, 7 and 14 February, 1839. BRL, LC, ii, fo. 301.
[16] *Brighton Patriot*, 4, 11, 18 and 25 December 1838, 8 January and 5 February 1839; *The Operative*, 2 and 16 December 1838, and 6 January 1839; *Sussex Agricultural Express*, 12 January 1839; Sir C.M. Burrell to the Duke of Richmond, 21 December 1838, WSCRO, Goodwood 1584. BRL, LC, ii, fo. 282; *Sherborne Journal*, 20 December 1838.

Allen – emphasised that Chartism had an enormous potential constituency in the countryside, with the farmworkers' 'deep rooted sense' of their 'own rights as men', despite their 'intolerable condition of privation and wretchedness', underpinning a numerical occupational grouping far in excess of the handloom weavers. Good and Osborne were able to draw on their experiences with the 'Visiting Committee's' activities to argue that special attention, including the use of available funds, should finance appropriate lecture tours. However, these proposals drew a stern warning from O'Connor, who arged that:

> A deputy conversant with a manufacturing auditory would find himself at sea when addressing an agricultural population from whom all exciting language should be withheld, and who have only to be addressed on their interests, their hatred of the Poor Law – in plain matter of fact statement of pounds, shillings and pence.

Osborne's perceptions were more incisive. From experience he:

> Found that the agricultural population was ready to join the People's Charter cause . . . The people from the towns were generally too glib [in] applying harsh names to the inhabitants of the country – such as bumpkins, clodhoppers, etc.

The Convention appointed a 'Missionary Committee' which recommended funded lecture tours, though bitter argument raged over which regions should benefit. The Londoner, John Cleave, who had campaigned in both Brighton and Lewes, exclaimed with pardonable exaggeration, that southern Sussex was already 'the arena of more extensive agitation than any other locality'. Places as populous as Carlisle were equally remote from the Chartist mainsteam and were now threatened with isolation through exclusion from the currently proposed initiative. Bronterre O'Brien, who was clearly seeking power bases and was already committed to speak in Brighton, in the event was appointed the official 'missionary to the Southern Counties'.[17]

Between 25 March and 5 April O'Brien addressed meetings at Cuckfield, Brighton, Chichester, Portsmouth, Southport, Gosport and Newport; by 8 April he was back in his Convention seat. Of these venues, only the first was non-urban, and this engagement derived from the fact that he was met there on his route from London by a welcoming party from Brighton. As only Brighton and Newport had constituted Chartist bodies at this juncture, Bronterre's principal function was to stimulate people in the towns to organise 'themselves into permanent associations to cooperate with the National Convention'. These new associations were however enjoined to embrace those domiciled in their countryside hinterlands, the Brighton model being advanced as the means

---

[17] Letter from Cirencester, Gloucestershire, cited C. Godfrey, *Chartist Lives: The Anatomy of a Working-Class Movement* (New York, 1987), p. 196; *The Operative*, 27 January, 3 and 24 March 1839; *Brighton Patriot*, 26 February 1839. Convention sub-committee minute, 23 February 1839, BL, MS Add. 34245A, fos 61–62.

whereby 'it would be easy to organise the whole of the agricultural population'. O'Brien's tour succeeded in stimulating the creation of formal organisations at Southampton, Gosport, Portsea, Portsmouth, and Chichester. But he made no concession to either the hostility from official quarters in these towns, nor that of the 'rural despots' whose naked power would have to be confronted in the neighbouring countryside. At Chichester, where the Duke of Richmond had enormous influence, in addition to his absolute power in the huge, adjacent Goodwood Estate, and despite the fact that the city was placarded against him, O'Brien's marathon harangue lumped together:

> All landlords, capitalists, and farmers, as wilfull robbers, traitors, and murderers of the people . . . they deserved to be driven with fire and the sword out of every community on the earth . . . the farmer was to blame for conspiring with the aristocrats and fundholders to deprive the people of their rights, and for being ready to turn out with a prancing yeomanry cavalry, placing at their head some pauper grinding Duke of Richmond (tremendous cheering) to bayonet and trample under foot the very men from whom he wrung his opulence (renewed plaudits).

Interestingly, a 'large body' of farmworkers attended this meeting 'to defend the Chartists, in the event of an attack' from orchestrated gangs, rumours of which also reflected the city's reputation for boisterous parliamentary contests.[18]

O'Brien's intention to return to the south, to take the campaign to the 'agricultural population' of East Sussex and Kent, did not happen. He was replaced by the Lancstrian Richard Marsden, who was the Convention's only speaker – apart from O'Brien's Cuckfield engagement – to address assemblies in the villages. How many meetings transpired in the vicinities of Hastings and Lewes is unclear, but he directly experienced the strength of opposition forces in the countryside. At Ringmer, where a spy recorded details on the orders of a local Whig magistrate, Henry Blackman, Marsden:

> Attributed the thinness of the meeting to the contrivances of their oppressors, that he knew the men dare not attend, that they could not exercise their own thoughts for the loss of their work wd. be the consequence.

Blackman had privately instructed 'the principal occupiers . . . to keep back the men', and his intelligence concluded that mostly 'worthless fellows' had turned out, with some women and children, reducing Marsden to raising cheers through rhetorical flourishes confirming that southern labourers would never fight their mobilised northern counterparts.[19]

---

[18] *Brighton Patriot*, 2, 9, 16 and 30 April 1839; *The Operative*, 7 and 14 April 1839; J.B. Freeland, Richmond's agent, Chichester, to the Duke, 29 March 1839, WSCRO, Goodwood 1502; A.J. Linden, Gosport, to O'Brien, 30 April 1839, BL, MS Add. 34245A, fos 200, 345–46; BRL, LC, ii, fo. 354.

[19] Harris to Lovett, 14 April 1839, BL, MS Add. 34245A, fos 244–45; Blackman to Richmond, 25, 26, 29 and 30 April; Richmond to Russell, with enclosures, 1 May 1839; WSCRO, Goodwood 1601; PRO, HO 40/24 (2), fos 178–81, 186–93; *Brighton Patriot*, 30 April 1839.

Marsden also experienced difficulties in the towns. At Lewes dissent followed his refusal to condemn physical force, while tiny numbers formally enrolled following meetings at Rye and Hastings. That scheduled at Eastbourne had to be aborted.[20] The final tour by Convention speakers in the south, by the Mancunians Richardson and Dean, addressed meetings in Lewes, Brighton, Chichester, Portsmouth, Southampton and Newport, by now all organised centres, in the week commencing 21 May 1839. Whatever the logistics here, it effectively cemented the isolation of Kent, which must have been particularly frustrating to the newly-constituted Canterbury Radical Association, which had – in addition to collecting signatures for the Petition – created a fund to defray the Convention's missionaries' expenses. No doubt equal irritation was experienced at Tunbridge Wells, Tonbridge and Sittingbourne, which made National Rent payments. The modesty of Kentish Chartism during the movement's first phase was symbolised by both the sixteen shillings and sixpence Rent subscribed at Tunbridge Wells, together with the fact that 'The Carrier brings this gratis as his contribution to the same object'.[21]

A brief comparison between the experiences of Chartism in four southern towns during 1838–9 is also revealing. Although Horsham, a parliamentary borough, had a long history of political radicalism extending back to the 1790s, and was a district centre in the early 1830s, Chartism appears to have taken no root in the borough. The one attempt, a meeting arranged by the Brighton 'Visiting Committee' on 2 May 1839, was productive only of a display of physical violence, literally led by the sons of local grandees. There are no further references to the movement in the town. Political activities seem to have been restricted to recurrent campaigns against church rates and customary competition over parliamentary representation.[22]

Chichester's radical pedigree also went back to the 1790s. It resurfaced in both municipal and parliamentary politics in the early nineteenth century. One activist, the butcher James Gray, tried to turn the local Swing rising into democratic politicking in 1830, campaigned vigorously against the New Poor Law – from which the city was exempt – and despatched the sheets of signatures for 'annex[ation] to the National Petition'. Chartism took root following O'Brien's visit. The farmworkers mobilised again with their 'bludgeons' when Richardson and Dean's meeting was threatened by 'hired . . . ruffians' on 23 May 1839. The solid core of about 130, who were still meeting fortnightly in

[20] *Brighton Patriot*, 14 May 1839; Blackman to Richmond 30 April 1839, PRO, HO 40/24 (2), fos 186–89; *Sussex Agricultural Express*, 27 April, 4 and 11 May 1839; *Sussex Advertiser*, 29 April and 29 July 1839.

[21] *Brighton Patriot*, 21 May 1839; Anon., Tunbridge Wells, to Lovett, 28 April 1839, BL, MS Add. 34245A, fo. 325; *Kent Herald*, 7 and 14 March, 4 and 11 April, 30 May and 27 June 1839; Kent's experience is among those confirming Gammage, Chartism's first historian's stricture, that nearly all the Convention's missions eschewed the 'more unenlightened parts' in favour of fairly firmly established centres. R.C. Gammage, *History of the Chartist Movement* (1894), p. 107.

[22] *Sussex Agricultural Express*, 4 May 1839; *Sussex Advertiser*, 6 May 1839; *Brighton Patriot*, 7 May 1839.

August, comprised 'chiefly . . . agricultural labourers', with a leaven of city-based artisans and the odd shopkeeper. However, the sources – including the cessation of evidence relayed to Richmond by a city agent – are almost silent on any subsequent Chartist activity.[23]

On the other hand, Chartism's role in Dorking, not a parliamentary constituency and with only minor incidents comprising its record of contribution to populist militancy,[24] was enduring. A WMA was formed early in 1839, and a continuous organisation was maintained through most of the 1840s, in part through the unremitting enthusiasm of its first secetary, an ex-Londoner, the 'almost unskooled' William Dale. Despite threats from employers to workers, and from gentry to tradesmen, speakers from the Convention were obtained through a personal appeal to Lovett. In May 1839 – after relating how many interested people missed this occasion and had 'a great Thirst for another Public Meeting' – Dorking received an address from Feargus O'Connor. Notices obtained by way of London concerning ulterior motives were duly posted and contributions made to the National Rent. Thereafter the group functioned relatively unintrusively and, as shown below, were strong supporters of the Land Plan.[25]

By early 1839 Chartist support in Brighton was sufficiently strong to warrant imitation of the London system of 'district' organisation. Regular meetings were held at three public houses, the Brewer's Arms, the Globe and the Royal Oak. The Brewer's, tenanted by William Reeves, a local Chartist leader in his own right and one of the 'Visiting Committee's' speakers, was the largest establishment, where commonly boisterous meetings of up to five or even six hundred were held. Women Chartists also held tea parties. The police reported favourably on Reeves' management, as he was fastidious over closing times, on one occasion even stopping Richardson in full oratorical flow. The considerable confidence exuded by Brighton Chartists in 1839 is reflected in a number of ways. They discussed a range of issues. Debate over ulterior measures led to decisions to withdraw savings bank deposits, engage in selective dealing and to abstain from exciseable items; the latter saw an upsurge in the consumption of herbal teas and tobacco, though the sources are strangely quiet on alcohol.

---

[23] *Brighton Patriot,* 28 May 1939; *Hampshire Telegraph,* 27 May 1839; *Brighton Guardian,* 29 May 1839; Freeland to Richmond, 10 July, 10, 13 and 14 August 1839, WSCRO, Goodwood 1607; Gray to Collins and Hartwell, 2 May 1839, BL, MS Add. 34245A, fos 373–5; Wells, 'Social Protest', p. 183.

[24] The record, which is almost certainly defective, reveals minor food rioting, wage and poor relief protests during the wartime famines, and a more full-blooded, if ephemeral, mobilisation of the entire district during the Swing rising; Madame D'Arblay, diary entries, 3 and 22 March 1800, J. Hemlow et al. (eds), *The Journals and Letters of Fanny Burney (Madame D'Arblay),* 4 vols (Oxford, 1973), iv, pp. 401, 407; R. Wells, *Wretched Faces: Famine in Wartime England, 1793–1801* (Gloucester, 1988), p. 426. Crawford, Dorking, to Peel, 19 November 1830, PRO, HO 52/10, fos 204–5.

[25] Dale to Lovett, and to Hartwell, 21 March and 8 May 1839, BL, MS Add. 34245A, fos 143–45, 422; *Sussex Agricultural Express,* 23 March and 6 April 1839; *Brighton Patriot,* 2, 9, and 23 April, and 30 July 1839.

Confidence was also mirrored by delegate Osborne's militant speeches in support of Benbow's National Holiday strategy at the Convention in July. Osborne 'knew that cessation from labour would be the first step towards revolution, but that would not deter him' and went on to advocate arming for self-defensive purposes. Simultaneously, soldiers stationed at the barracks were taking Chartist literature, including the *Northern Liberator*, and 'eloping' to attend meetings. Finally, despite O'Connor's popularity in the town, O'Brien created a strong personal following in Brighton through repeated visits. The climax came in a three-hour address in mid August, when, having supported proposals for the strike and for arming, he focused on landownership. He reiterated orthodox arguments against the amalgamation of small farms into huge capitalist enterprises,[26] and castigated landowners for demolishing farmworkers' cottages. This drove the occupants into towns where they competed for work and housing with the indigenous population, while driving rents up and wages down to inflate 'money-mongers' profits. The answer lay in land nationalisation directed by a democratic parliament.[27]

Magisterial responses to the first phase of Chartism were essentially moderate. In south-east Dorset, the judiciary – including Tolpuddle veterans – supported the lock-out, but Prime Minister Melbourne specifically warned against Home Office involvement in any prosecution. The Duke of Wellington, Lord Lieutenant of Hampshire, where there was no reported attempt to politicise the villages, dutifully passed panicky reports of a possible rising from authorities at Southampton – which he studiously refused to endorse – to Whitehall.[28] The Sussex Bench was the most troubled by Chartism. Once Henry Blackman's spies revealed village Chartism's essential weaknesses, his worship quickly manifested the customary confidence of an experienced and resourceful magistrate.[29] Lord Lieutenant Richmond may have briefly feared that Chartism would penetrate Goodwood from its Chichester base, but he deftly countered

---

[26] A line of argument particularly attractive to the many Brightonians who were migrants from the Weald, a stronghold of small farmers, but where the equilibrium of many little proprietors was currently threatened: M. Reed, 'The Peasantry of Nineteenth-Century England: A Neglected Class?', *History Workshop Journal*, 18 (1984); idem, '"Gnawing It Out". A New Look at Economic Relations in Nineteenth-Century Rural England', *Rural History*, 1 (1990).

[27] *Brighton Patriot*, 4 June and 23 July 1839; *The Champion*, 14 July 1839; Justice Seymour, Brighton, to Russell, 25 July 1839, PRO, HO 40/24 (2), fos 204–5; T. Parsinnen, 'Association, Convention and Anti-Parliament in British Radical Politics, 1771–1848', *English Historical Review*, 88 (1973); *Sussex Advertiser*, 29 July and 19 August 1839; *Brighton Guardian*, 25 August 1839; *The Champion*, 25 August 1839.

[28] Melbourne to Russell, 1 December 1838, L.C. Saunders (ed.), *Lord Melbourne's Papers* (1889), p. 386; Mayor of Southampton to Wellington, and reply, 18 and 20 December; Wellington to Normanby, 24 December 1839, Southampton University Library, Wellington Papers, 4/1/10/57, 63, 66.

[29] Blackman to Richmond, 26 and 29 April 1839, WSCRO, Goodwood 1599; for Blackman's skilful demolition of the resourceful Barcombe gang shortly afterwards, see R. Wells, 'Popular Protest and Social Crime: The Evidence of Criminal Gangs in Southern England, 1790–1860', in B. Stapleton (ed.), *Conflict and Community in Southern England* (Gloucester, 1992), pp. 139–49.

exaggerated reports emanating from a Shoreham customs officer by offering him a magistracy to increase his authority in the port. Another grandee, the Earl of Chichester, domiciled within three miles of Brighton, was invariably calm. In 1839 he was not 'much afraid of any mischief at Brighton' owing to the town's 'intelligent police, watchful magistrates, & a numerous resident Gentry'.Chartism's mass following in the north was not present in the south, where 'Numbers alone are evidently against a revolutionary movement, or there would have been 10 times as many at the chartist's meetings'. The Earl's sole apprehension turned on the local reaction to a successful rising north of the Trent.[30]

While Chichester's analytical clarity impresses, Seymour, the seventy-year-old senior magistrate responsible for Brighton from day-to-day, who desperately wanted to retire, was more apprehensive. Serious trouble could occur if five hundred committed Chartists, backed by railway navvies, mobilised. His worries intensified over the summer of 1839 with Osborne's 'inflammatory Language at the Convention', growing local support for arming, and the engineered run on the savings banks. If Seymour successfully insisted that Brighton should invariably have a strong army presence, he was chagrined that a salutory lesson for the south's most volatile Chartist centre did not come in the form of Osborne's prosecution for sedition. On the eve of his annual tour of his Scottish estates in mid October 1839, Richmond did not evaluate 'any danger' in Sussex. The Duke's unprecedented step of appointing Chichester as acting Lord Lieutenant constituted Richmond's only modification of the structure of authority, a mild form of recognition of southern Chartism's strongest theatre. The region's establishment newspapers remained largely silent on the subject, barring odd occasions facilitating ridicule and contempt. One of the few substantial press analyses, which appeared in the *Sussex Advertiser* in July 1839, drew a similarly stark contrast between the northern and southern movements and acidly observed that despite the 'inflammatory resolutions' regularly passed at the Brewer's Arms, Brighton Chartists were too cautious 'to hazard a rencontre with our well-trained police'.[31]

Tracing southern Chartist activity from 1840 until the demise of the Land Plan in 1851 is beset by evidential problems. They principally derive from the quality of the radical press. The superb *Brighton Patriot* folded in August 1839. With the exception of the brief existence of O'Brien's *Southern Star* from January to July 1840, and apart from occasional detail from later 1841 to the end of 1843 emerging from the *British Satesman* and the *English Chartist Circular*, the *Northern*

[30] Letters to Richmond from Earl of Chichester, 5 April, F.F. Hastings, Shoreham, 28 May, Rusbridger, 9 and 17 August and Freeland, 10 August: Home Office to Hastings, 11 January and to ?, May 1839, WSCRO, 1600–2, 1863.

[31] Seymour to the Home Office, 13 March: letters to Richmond from Seymour, 7 June, 18 July and 2 August, and Chichester, 1 and 14 August 1839, WSCRO, Goodwood 1600, 1606; *Sussex Advertiser*, 29 July 1839; Richmond to Russell, 14 October 1839, PRO, HO 40/24 (2), fos 210–13.

Star is the principal source of evidence. The *Star*'s 1844 move to London made little difference, as it depended for local intelligence on correspondents whose characteristics ranged from the inert to the prolix. Much material that did arrive was too late for publication schedules, or consumed disproportionate amounts of editorial time to extract 'two lines' of usable copy from pages of text.[32] Moreover, as Chartism posed little threat to public order in any part of the region in either 1842, the year of the 'General Strike', or in the potentially revolutionary crisis of 1847–48, local authorities had few occasions to correspond either with each other or Whitehall.

A number of factors contributed to the continued virility of Chartism in Brighton. First, the numbers involved preserved the divisional structure copied from London. Secondly, ideological debate flourished, notably after the 1840 foundation of the Socialist Society. Thirdly, and perhaps paradoxically, the same divisions which occurred nationally were reflected in the town, with polarisations generating commitment to entrenched positions. Fourthly, and most importantly, the new parliamentary borough proved psephologically unpredictable, with Whig, Tory and Radical victories in the 1830s maintaining a high political temperature into the 1840s, which was exploited by the Chartists who 'attended all meetings and converted them to their own ends'. An early example involved the February 1840 address on Victoria's nuptials, when only the forcible clearance of the Town Hall (with troops in reserve) stopped a Chartist amendment for a free pardon 'to all the state prisoners . . . in order that all classes . . . may be enabled to rejoice on this auspicious event'. The establishment press made extraordinary claims – even denying the local existence of trade unionism – to counter Brighton's reputation as a radical proletarian stronghold. The Tory *Gazette*'s assertion that the tactical defeat over the wedding address constituted the 'death-blow to Chartism' in the borough was ludicrous.[33]

In February 1840 enfranchised Chartists founded the 'Radical Electors Association', which pledged to consult their comrades on voting tactics, including abstention. It was claimed that the Chartist vote was adequate to deciding the political complexion of the borough's MPs. The admitted incapacity to elect a Chartist representative did not stop the decision to fight the seat. 'After several ineffectual attempts' to attract a nationally-known figure, Charles Brooker, of nearby Alfriston, was chosen. Brooker, a Congregationalist minister, prosperous tanner, wholesaler and shopkeeper, had achieved an important local reputation through his vigorous, if eventually unsuccessful, campaign to create a southern anti-Poor Law movement on the northern model.[34] As he explained:

[32] *Northern Star*, 7 August, 4 September and 4 December 1841, and 3 September 1842; cf. *The Operative*, 23 December 1838, 'We do not want speeches'.

[33] *Sussex Advertiser*, 16 February 1840; *Southern Star*, 16 February and 8 March 1840; *Northern Star*, 16 February 1842; *Brighton Gazette*, 7 January 1841; Harris to Lovett, 14 April 1839, BL, MS Add. 34245A, fos 244–45.

[34] For further information on Brooker, see Wells, 'Southern Resistance to the New Poor Law', above.

His adoption of Universal Suffrage arose from the working of the Poor Law; . . . he saw through . . . that law, that class legislation would no longer do . . . [nor] for the rich to make laws for the poor.[35]

The 1841 general election gave Brooker both his first experience of parliamentary electioneering and also a highly relevant local issue on which to campaign. One of the casualties of Melbourne's collapsed Whig government was a Bill to subject places previously exempt under local Acts (including Brighton) to the New Poor Law and all its components, which most notably meant the loss of municipal control of social-security matters to the despised Poor Law Commission. The sitting Tory MP, Sir Adolphus Dalrymple, asserted that the Bill's expected reappearance comprised 'the principal subject of anxiety' to the Brighton electorate, while his Whig colleague Captain Pechell's vote against the measure facilitated his claim that he had kept the Commission out of Brighton. The radical candidate, the local banker Wigney, correctly asserted that the reformed Poor Laws were 'as much a Tory as a Whig measure', but pledged himself to vote only against such proposed alternations as were 'cruel to the poor Man'. His less ambiguous radical credentials were support for the ballot, shorter but not annual parliaments and limited extensions to the franchise. He was returned with Pechell. Brooker received a derisory nineteen votes. If there was acrimony over the 'conflicting mode of action among the Chartist electors', the figures torpedoed previous Chartist claims of significant middle-class support. In contrast to 1837, when the electorate had returned the radical, Faithfull, in 1841 voters had the chance of supporting radical *and* Chartist. As many clearly voted Whig and Radical, subsequent Chartist jibes that 'many of the middle class professed to be' democrats, 'but only made use of the working class for their own purposes', rang true. Impressive Chartist discipline at the hustings, however, created a favourable reputation which was subsequently and frequently acknowledged by Brighton MPs.[36]

Wigney's bankruptcy precipitated a spring 1842 by-election. Brooker stood again to 'forcibly show the moral determination of the people to overturn the monstrous system'. The voters produced a massive victory for the Tory over the Whig candidate by 1277 to 640, while a paltry sixteen votes accrued to Brooker. This was despite Fergus O'Connor's support on the hustings, which very ironically did not guarantee much coverage of Brooker's campaign even in the Chartist press. Indeed, the *Northern Star* coldly dismissed 'the election correspondence' from Brighton as of '[in]sufficient public interest to compensate for the space it would occupy'.[37]

Brighton's Chartist districts uniformly became National Charter Association branches in 1840 and a relatively large number of membership cards were

---

[35] *Southern Star*, 2 and 23 February 1840.

[36] *Brighton Gazette*, 17 and 31 March, 14 April, 5, 12 and 19 May 1842; *Northern Star*, 26 March and 9 April 1842; *English Chartist Circular*, 2, 59.

[37] *Northern Star*, 10 April 1837.

bought.[38] While O'Brien privately confided in 1840 that he never visited the town without being called upon to settle internecine disputes, and the hostile press occasionally sniped at the alleged inevitability of constant division in 'democratical' bodies, one of Brighton's Convention delegates admitted that his constituents 'had no differences or division; if any occurred they took care to settle them and not make them public'.[39] However, public disputes occurred early in 1841, when Woodward – then a Convention delegate – agreed with Lovett's new tactical arguments hinging on improved mass education. Woodward recanted but had to suffer the indignity of seeking re-election, while his association published a ringing denunciation 'of the everlasting cant about the ignorance and immorality of the working man', now seemingly confirmed by Chartist elements. Much more serious divisions developed over the Complete Suffrage Union. O'Brien had created a power base in Brighton and his pro-CSU stance, and the publication of his notorious 'Vindication', precipitated five consecutive nights of debate, during which O'Connorite and O'Brienite factions tore down rival posters and then exchanged blows. Solid polarisation, 'with the filth of personal spleen and irritable vindictiveness', coupled with selective trading, characterised the second half of 1842. The year ended ignominiously with the veteran Brighton radical, the septuagenarian William Flower, swapping insults with O'Brien himself at a public meeting, which 'broke up, each party grumbling at the others like . . . bears'.[40]

The issue of the Chartist prisoners, especially those sentenced to death for their part in the Monmouth Rising, stimulated southern participation in the widespread petitioning for clemency. Some even emerged from places without known Chartist links, including villages, but confidence that the 'numbers for a free pardon augurs well for the promotion of Chartist principles' was misplaced.[41] Southampton Chartists honestly admitted in September 1840:

> That thousands of the men of the South are sincerely attached to the principles . . . but they are, unfortunately, deterred from making any public demonstrations through fear of the vengeance of their tyrants, both Tory and Liberal, which abound in this degraded part of the country.[42]

Southampton was among the existing groups in several southern locations which formally affiliated to the NCA. Among the others were Bridport,

---

[38] J. Epstein, *The Lion of Freedom: Feargus O'Connor and the Chartist Movement, 1832–1842* (London, 1982), pp. 230–33.

[39] A. Plummer, *Bronterre: A Political Biography of Bronterre O'Brien, 1804–1864* (London, 1971), pp. 156–57; *Northern Star*, 23 April 1842.

[40] *Northern Star*, 24 April and 1 May 1841, 23 and 30 April, 25 June, 2 and 16 July, 27 August, 22 and 29 October, 5 and 19 November 24 and 31 December 1842, and 28 January 1843; *British Statesman*, 23 July, 6 August, 17 September and 8 October 1842. *Brighton Gazette*, 8 December 1842.

[41] *Southern Star*, 19 and 26 January, 2, 9 and 23 February and 1 March 1840. BRL, LC, iv, fo. 174.

[42] *Northern Star*, 19 September 1840.

Winchester, Portsmouth, Newport, Dorking, Tonbridge and Canterbury. NCA branches were also established in towns without a previous record of Chartist organisation. On the Isle of Wight men from Newport were instrumental in the creation of branches at Ventnor and Ryde. Other new branches appear to have formed after meetings addressed by London-based speakers, including those at Rochester and Sheerness. Kingston-upon-Thames came into the same category, with uniformed policemen ostentatiously watching the actual formation. But the record is hopelessly defective. Cash collection suggest significant pools of support in Sittingbourne and Maidstone. While the Newport branch proudly reported its anniversary dinners, its missionary activity on the island and the harrassment of the borough MPs in the 1841 election, the existence of the NCA's branch at Shaftesbury seems to be recorded only by the handover of non-forwarded subscriptions to the relatively huge tune of twenty pounds, in response to urgent demands for funds from the executive at the very end of 1841. One of the rare breaks in the blanket obfuscation of the movement in much of the press was a sarcastic report of a Kent open-air meeting, which was rained off, after the 'fresh-imported orator' juxtaposed 'Chartism and Socialism' while 'indulging in the old cry of the *levelling* system'.[43]

The southern campaign for the second petition received the scanty press coverage – including in the *Northern Star* – that its lacklustre calibre warranted. Ironically, the *Kent Herald*, given to occasional lurches to the left of the Whigs, printed the entire text, together with the comment that 'a very great part of the [county] population are unacquainted' with 'the precise nature' of the document. This publicity occurred during a parliamentary recess, when the provincial press was often short of copy. The *Herald's* promise to 'occasionally return to the subject' was not honoured, except with respect to the petition's eventual presentation to parliament.[44] Equally ironically, in 1842 and in contrast to 1838–39, a Kentish campaign was undertaken over the new year period, starting with Dr M'Douall's limited lecture tour, with engagements at Chatham, Strood, and Canterbury. Canterbury was identified as the epicentre and the Londoner, Edmund Stallwood, lectured there twice at the end of January. Supporters agreed to arrange further venues through fellow Chartists 'to agitate the leading towns', but this paper initiative came to little. Stallwood and M'Douall – in their capacity as Convention delegates in April – gave essentially pessimistic appreciations of the Kentish situation, not least as funds to finance lecture tours were unavailable. Identical remarks were made about non-metropolitan Surrey. Convention delegates were unable to recover their costs from subscriptions in the two counties. However, Dale at Dorking and Snelling at Tonbridge

[43] Ibid., 28 November 1840, 3 April, 12 and 19 June, 28 August, 9 October, 20 and 27 November and 18 December 1841, 1, 8 and 29 January, 12 March, 23 April, 25 June, 9 July, 12 and 26 November and 18 December 1842; *Southern Star*, 21 June 1840; *Brighton Gazette*, 15 June 1842.

[44] *Kent Herald*, 20 January, 28 April and 12 May 1842.

proved equal to public speeches, followed by collections of signatures, but their sterling activities were understandably restricted to their home towns.[45]

Chartists from Brighton visited and corresponded with a number of their counterparts in other towns, among them Chichester, Hastings, Lewes and Southampton. Signatures were certainly collected in these centres, and by inference elsewhere in Sussex, Hampshire and indeed Dorset. As the latter county shared the representative at the Convention for Devon and Cornwall, and he 'was not acquainted' with his easternmost constituents, no specific intelligence about Dorset was received. Only Brighton's delegate, Woodward, was able to put an optimistic gloss on a part of their achievement, namely that ten thousand signatures were collected in 1842, an increase of a quarter on 1839. Although circulation of the 1842 petition was not confined to the towns of Brighton and Lewes, it was categorically stated that Brighton Chartists:

> Had spent many pounds in agitating the villages round; yet, such was the opposition, that they were fearful whether greater evil than good was the result . . . Woodward then detailed many instances of dreadful revenge taken against parties in these country districts who dared take any part in the agitations.[46]

While the evidential problems discussed above impede any analysis of southern Chartism after 1842, there can be little doubt that apart from the Land Plan, with which we deal below, the movement's achievements were modest. Gammage's lecture tour to Brighton, Lewes, Tunbridge Wells and Southampton in late 1842 was ignored by almost the entire non-Chartist press. His next visit to the south, in the spring of 1843, included speaking engagements in Winchester on three successive nights, and further meetings at Southampton and on the Isle of Wight. The visit achieved the briefest of mentions in the liberal *Hampshire Independent*. But this report was partially aimed at Southampton's Tory authorities, who were lambasted for 'screening . . . from just punishments' the 'ruffians . . . of a hired mob' who had attacked a Chartist meeting in 1842. The *Independent*'s one-line report said that Gammage's Ryde meeting 'passed off quietly', and when called to account for such cursory and value-laden reportage, the editor responded by simply noting that outdoor and indoor political meetings of all hues leant themselves to disturbance, and that reportage of order was 'a matter of credit to the parties concerned'.[47] The scanty evidence, including irregular acknowledgements of monies received on different accounts, and the fortunes of the Land Plan, suggest that organised Chartism survived at the most modest level in most, though not necessarily all, those towns where it established roots in 1838–39. The organisation at Hastings must have been at best tenuous, for as late as February 1848 it was formally reconstituted as an

---

[45] *Northern Star*, 21 December 1841, 1 and 29 January, 5 February, 11 March, 2 and 23 April, 21 May and 25 June 1842.

[46] Ibid., 5 and 19 February and 23 April 1842.

[47] Ibid., 12 and 19 November, 1842; *Hampshire Independent*, 4, 11 and 18 March 1843.

NCA branch, which, significantly, met at a private house. There was little real expansion. A new branch was created at Crayford, not yet in metropolitan Kent, following the construction of a major new block-printing works, staffed by skilled men brought from London. Outside those locations with known Chartist organisations there were doubtless individual proselytes, or groups of them. This was symbolised by the Faversham activist's thanks, published in the *Northern Star*, for old copies of the newspaper sent by friends, which he 'distributed . . . to break up new ground'.[48]

Brighton Chartists retained some vigour throughout this period, reflected in the continuation of 'weekly meetings', but the fact that these were now held at only one venue – the Cap of Liberty and subsequently the Artichoke – suggests some decline in membership. Although the question of representation at the conventions was discussed, and there is some ambiguity over delegates. 1844 seems to have been the last Convention with any southern representation, prior to the 1847 Lowlands conference on the Land Plan. The O'Connorite-O'Brienite division lasted until at least late 1844, almost certainly longer, and it may have been reinforced by the McDouall-O'Connor dispute in 1845. Debates on major national issues were held, and single-issue campaigns were occasionally mounted, for example in 1846 against the Irish Coercion Bill. Brighton's non-incorporated status certainly militated against regular Chartist intervention in local politics in the calmer 1843–6 period, as the High Constable repeatedly and successfully rejected demands for public meetings at the Town Hall. Convivial meetings included celebrating the veteran Flower's seventy-fifth birthday in the same year – 'tripping the light fantastic toe' *ad infinitum* – and 'Democratic Suppers' on Henry Hunt's birthday.[49]

The launch of the Third National Petition proved to be a relatively low-key affair in the south, even in Brighton where between six and seven hundred turned out in January 1847 to hear Ernest Jones, joined on the platform by Captain Pechell MP. The almost customary itinerary, Portsmouth, Southampton, Winchester, Newport and Brighton, with the addition of Maidstone, was taken by nationally-known speakers, McGrath and Clark, at about the same time. Brighton was uncontested by a Chartist in the 1847 general election, but the significance here of Brooker's premature death in 1843 is unclear. Shortly before Henry Vincent fought the Ipswich constituency, he addressed Brightonians, but none of the town's three newspapers sent a reporter. One scorned:

> The absurdity of expecting the newspapers to devote time and space to the preparation and publication of a report of the sentiments uttered by every itinerant spouter who pays the town a visit.[50]

[48] *Northern Star*, 1845–47, passim, but esp. 29 June 1844 and 11 January 1845.

[49] *Northern Star*, 7 September 1844, 1 March, 26 April and 1 November 1845, 3 and 31 January, 25 April and 17 November 1846, and 12 February 1848.

[50] *Brighton Gazette*, 21 January and 22 July 1847; *Northern Star*, 23 January, 6 and 13 February 1847.

1848 – the Year of Revolutions – was more remarkable for nervous southern officialdom than any major Chartist activity. W.W. Attree, who was Recorder at both Hastings and Rye, outlined the laws against 'tumultuous assemblies' at inordinate length for the edification of grand jurymen in both jurisdictions. A number of towns sent congratulatory missives extolling the government's handling of recurrent crises in London and the north. Some urban authorities, including Worthing and Hastings, rather ridiculously used their powers to enrol special constables. The readoption of earlier contingency public order plans in Brighton was more understandable, as was the appointment in April of specials in Gravesend, Chatham, Rochester and Sheerness. Croydon – also uncomfortably close to London – resorted to posses of specials between 8 and 11 April and again on 12 June. Chartist public meetings at Brighton and Maidstone went ahead, only to experience fierce divisions between Chartists and middle-class reformers, particularly in Maidstone where the New Reform Movement was well supported. Neither town seems to have experienced even the threat of violence. Other Chartist events were equally innocuous, including the dinner at Tunbridge Wells in honour of the French Revolution, the protest meetings at Strood and Portsmouth against the government's handling of the massive London demonstration of 10 April, the celebratory send-off accorded to a Southampton man who gained a holding under the Land Plan, the numerous collections for the new round of defence funds, and votes of confidence in O'Connor as the Land Plan came under parliamentary scrutiny.[51]

After 1848 the Chartist movement in the south appears to have collapsed more speedily than elsewhere. Brighton retained some capacity for radical, popular politics, which covered a wide spectrum, ranging from a Chartist takeover, backed by the socialists, of the Working Men's Institute, to meetings specifically addressing issues of the day, including Ernest Jones on the Polish and Hungarian refugees in 1851. In 1849 and 1851 Chartist petitions, replete with the six points, were presented to the Commons by the long-serving borough MP, the now knighted George Pechell. However, as late as 1857, a meeting dissolved into 'uproar', with people 'pelting each other with gravel and dirt', when another radical parliamentary candidate for the town, William Coningham, claimed that 'the . . . Charter, and other political cries have died out'. But this, like a multitude of other political gatherings earlier in the 1850s, were characterised by little of 'the enthusiasm . . . once manifested at the meetings of the Brighton Chartists'.[52]

---

[51] *Brighton Gazette*, 16 March, 6 and 20 April and 25 June 1848; *Maidstone Gazette*, 11 and 18 April, 2, 23 and 30 May 1848, and 2 January 1849; *Northern Star*, 1848, passim, esp. 1 and 22 April and 17 June; letters to the Home Office from Mayor of Hastings, 9 April, and Justices' Clerk, Worthing, 19 July 1848, PRO, HO 45/2410B.
[52] *Brighton Gazette*, 3 May 1849, 11 July 1850, 27 March, 3 April and 31 July 1851, 26 February 1852, and 19 March 1857.

The clear urban bias in the public face of southern Chartism is not reflected by support for the Land Plan in the same region. Despite its incompleteness, the register of almost twenty (of the nearly eighty) thousand subscribers to the scheme reveals features of southern Chartism available in no other source.[53] The names of 170 Brighton subscribers are known. The largest categories, labourers, 16.5 per cent, is followed by cordwainers with 14.75 per cent, and carpenters at 7.5 per cent. Skilled working men, including tailors, bricklayers, plasterers, and watchmakers, comprise a significant proportion of the remainder, which – in addition to the 5 per cent giving no trade, including women – also contains a handful of petty entrepreneurs, including a brewer, one corn, one coal and one timber merchant, and five greengrocers. Various permutations in the membership pertain to other southern towns. At Southampton, where the names and addresses of seventy-eight subscribers are recorded, 19 per cent were labourers, while the fourteen tailors, the next largest occupational grouping, stood at 18 per cent. Shoemakers and carpenters were well represented, with a total of nine sailors (12 per cent). The register for Portsmouth, including subscribers domiciled in Gosport and Southsea, contains thirty-two names. A relatively large contingent (19 per cent) described themselves as 'servants' and almost all the remainder belonged to the skilled trades. There were only two labourers; of the southern towns, Portsmouth is exceptional in that labourers did not constitute the largest single category of Land Plan subscribers.

Luckily, one of the more interesting small southern town pockets of Chartism, at Dorking, is embraced by the twenty-eight names appearing on the register. Labourers, with eight, were the largest category, but the remainder – barring a 'youth' – were all skilled, and numerically dominated by six shoemakers and five tailors. There was a similar rough balance between the numbers of labourers (eleven) and shoemakers (twelve), who between them constituted exactly half the number of subscribers at Maidstone. In the Medway towns – Chatham, Rochester, and Gillingham – labourers again comprised the largest group, with eighteen out of the total of 137. They were nearly equalled by what appears to have been a local favourite, subscribing for children, of whom there were sixteen. The latter number was equalled by those recording 'no trade', a proportion of whom were again women, most of them subscribers' wives. Here, among the customary skilled trades, were some eight shipwrights, and two fishermen. Two fishermen were amongst those listed as shareholders from Sittingbourne, but the total of thirty-nine members here also reveals the largest occupational percentage in any covered southern urban location, with 50 per cent brickmakers.

The most fascinating details derive from essentially rural membership. Two regions are documented by this source. First, fifteen villages within a nine-mile radius of Maidstone contained sixty-one members who paid their instalments

---

[53] PRO, BT 41/474–76. For a discussion of localised support from this source see M. Chase, 'The Chartist Land Plan and the Local Historian', *Local Historian*, 18 (1988). My thanks are owing to Dr Chase for discussing many aspects of the topic with me.

through the town branch. Of these people, almost exactly one half were labourers, presumably principally farm-workers, though one shepherd is listed. The only craftspeople of numerical significance were the seven shoemakers. A similar numerical dominance of labourers is also found in the old trade unionist, and subsequently Chartist, epicentre, of Blandford in Dorset. The twenty-five villages within a ten-mile radius, contained 132 members, of whom just over half were labourers. Three farmers, two dairymen and four gardeners, also held shares. Only shoemakers, with twelve representatives, figured significantly as a specific, skilled occupational group. There were also seventy-seven members domiciled in the town of Blandford. Here labourers, comprising well under 10 per cent of the total, had a relatively small presence compared to elsewhere. A very wide range of skilled trades were represented, though all of them proportionally small, with well below 10 per cent made up of women and others classified as 'no trade'. The Blandford branch was run by its secretary, J. Saunders, who was originally from London. The inadequate evidence suggests that the shareholders in the villages were recruited after Saunders campaigned in Blandford's hinterland.[54]

The register records some snippets of evidence which are almost impossible to interpret, like the six subscribers, including a New Poor Law relieving officer, domiciled in four Dorset towns (Sherborne, Dorchester, Bere Regis and Swanage) and a village (Verword). In Hampshire, apparently isolated subscribers lived in the small towns of Christchurch and Romsey, with others in the relatively remote village of Newton Valence, and two villages – Eling and Fareham – which were in the vicinities of urban centres, Portsmouth and Southampton respectively. In Sussex, individual labourers subscribed in the town of Arundel and the village of Warnham, while an East Grinstead currier appears equally isolated. Lewes had a local branch of the Land Company, but the register records only seven subscribers who appear to have paid through Brighton, together with a sole member in each of four villages near Lewes. In Kent there were two gardeners subscribing at Margate and three labourers and one carrier who were members at Cranbrook. Under-registration may have operated in one, or both of two ways. The membership of entire Land Plan branches may have been unregistered, or only a proportion of subscribing members may have been listed. Chartists claimed that there were over two hundred subscribers in Brighton, and 160 were said to pay through Maidstone, yet these are somewhat larger totals than appear listed on the register.[55] Some Chartist centres, notably Chichester and Shaftesbury, respectively not known and known to have had branches of the Land Plan, are both unrepresented on the register.

The 1847 Land Plan Conference had four delegates representing towns in the south, partly owing to somewhat odd geographical apportionments. Dorking came under Surrey, whose other branches were all metropolitan, except Croydon.

---

[54] *Northern Star*, 7 August and 4 September 1847.

[55] BPP, *Second Report of the Select Committee of the House of Commons on the National Land Company* (1847–48), xiii, QQ. 1799–1802; *Maidstone Gazette*, 23 May 1848.

Brighton was lumped together with Lewes, Southampton, Winchester, Newport, Blandford and Salisbury, and Saunders of Blandford was the delegate. The Kent branches at Rochester, Maidstone, Tunbridge Wells, Sittingbourne and Sevenoaks (and metropolitan Woolwich), were represented by Charles Willis of Strood, but he also acted for Essex, Suffolk and one Hertfordshire branch. Gosport elected its own delegate, 'tinman' William Westlake, who said that the scheme brought him into the Chartist movement. Here the Plan proved divisive, for none of the original 1838 ten-man WMA committee are recorded as subscribers. Another activist, J. Malcolm, publicly opposed the Land Plan, as diversionary.[56] Saunders was certainly justified in his claim that the Plan had kept southern Chartism 'alive'. But it achieved a low public profile, even when launched through lecture tours by McGrath and other national figures, because reports were limited principally to the Chartist press. Both this and succeeding campaigns restimulated existing members and brought in recruits,[57] but in the localities and on a week-to-week basis, the Plan proceeded quietly, almost furtively, since the regular but bland cursory notices of monies received through branches, announced in the *Northern Star*, were the main publicity. Very few public celebrations were arranged. One of the largest and last, the tea and ball held near Cobbett's old village of Botley in August 1847, was ignored by the local press. The Winchester celebrants met their Southampton counterparts at the latter's committee rooms, and then made the short road journey in all manner of decorated vehicles. Further contingents, from branches in the Portsmouth conurbation, arrived by train, late, after the start of the buffet supper.[58]

The vast bulk of this evidence suggests that with the clear exception of Brighton, joined perhaps to a lesser extent by Southampton and Portsmouth, Chartism in southern towns was essentially weak through the national movement's principal period, 1838–48. At no time, even in its Brightonian epicentre and in 1838–9, did the movement ever receive anything remotely describable as mass support. In even the most persistent local pockets of activity, small but committed minorities struggled to maintain a presence. Local leaders were no doubt correct in their frequent assertions that much more support was there, be it essentially covert, with democratic advocates too exposed to risk middle- and upper-class ostracism – including dismissal of the directly employed and the non-patronisation of the self employed – to give any direct succour. The magistrates responsible for populous Croydon told the licensee of one inn that the holding of Chartist meetings was illegal and went on to 'intimidate . . . many of the publicans'. Constable Herbert was sacked from the Southampton police for signing the Charter, while Chief Constable Pasco of Chichester brazenly debated

[56] J. Moore, Secretary, Gosport WMA, to the Convention, n.d. (May 1839), BL, MS Add. 34245B, fos 21–22; *Northern Star*, 11 December 1847.

[57] *Northern Star*, 25 January, 1 February, 4 May, 2 June, 14 July and esp. 6 December 1845, 24 and 31 October 1846, 6 and 13 February and 31 July 1847.

[58] Ibid., 31 July, 14 and 21 August, 4 September, 6 November and 11 December 1847.

points of order with the itinerant orator Richardson. Pasco was implicated in the 'industrious' dissemination of a 'report . . . that every person who signed [the Charter] is expected to support the cause with Arms in his Hands', while in a unique instance of unity, Anglican and nonconformist pulpits in Chichester were 'employed to preach down the Cause'.[59]

There is strong evidence that Chartism in its public, campaigning stages, including the attempts to create local branches and to maximise support for the petitions to parliament, was effectively stopped from real penetration of the southern countryside. In both its urban and rural offensives, but especially the latter, southern Chartism seems to have been ineffective, notably in the non-realisation of the national leadership hopes of embracing the men of the south in general, and the overwhelmingly largest component, farmworkers, in particular. This appears to have been the case wherever attempts were made in the countryside, with agricultural labourers as the prime objective.[60] The weaknesses of urban Chartism also compromised the movement's capacity to mobilise support in the towns' rural hinterlands. When four Maidstone Chartists went on a Sunday in 1848 to read the *Northern Star* to farmworkers at Coxheath, home to several Land Plan subscribers, they were shadowed by a posse of six constables led by a magistrate. Such surveillance would have been impossible if a dozen or more such sorties had taken place simultaneously.[61] Paradoxically, the diffusion of countryside supporters, notably in the Blandford district of Dorset and the Maidstone region of Kent, and to a lesser extent the villages around Tonbridge and Tunbridge Wells, suggests that Land Plan subscribers in other rural districts were not registered. It also implies that there were Chartist supporters – though not necessarily Land Plan subscribers – in most country parishes. The numbers of subscribers in the modest market towns of Blandford and Dorking additionally suggest that there were Chartist coteries in every southern town, whose support was rarely if ever vocal. For example, the evidence of the Chartist presence in the Kent town of Cranbrook comprises the three labourers and one carrier who subscribed to the Land Company, and Cranbook's representative at the April 1842 Birmingham conference of the Complete Suffrage Association.[62]

The *apparent* failure of Chartism to establish and *reveal* itself in some highly politicised places is remarkable. But there is no evidence of rural Chartism in the Test and Stoke valleys in Hampshire, where strong popular radicalism is relatively well-documented in the early 1830s. Identical observations apply to the villages in the vicinity of Horsham which hosted Political Unions in 1832–33.

---

[59] *The Operative*, 14 April 1839; *Brighton Gazette*, 29 May 1839. J. Beaumont and three others, Croydon, and C. Cox, Southampton, to the Convention, 8 and 30 May; J. Gray, Chichester, to Collins and Hartwell, 2 May 1839, BL, MSS Add. 34245A, fos 74–75, 419; 34245B, fo. 27.

[60] David Jones, *Chartism and the Chartists* (London, 1975), p. 25; Thompson, *Chartists*; Brown, *Chartism*, pp. 50–56; Fearn, 'Chartism', pp. 161–62, and esp. p. 172; Pugh, 'Chartism', p. 216.

[61] *Maidstone Gazette*, 23 May 1848.

[62] *Report of Proceedings* (1842), BRL, LC, iv, fo. 247.

We must reiterate the most surprising apparent failure of the movement to establish itself in the borough. However, the hard evidence of Chartism in the town and hinterland of Blandford suggests that politicised working folk here, and particularly farm workers, had to reexperience all the dangers of open support for radical causes that their counterparts in other towns and villages felt in 1838–39. These experiences reinforced the lessons of the very recent past.

The defeat of Swing, the subsequent containment of rural democratic campaigning during and just after the passage of the Reform Bill, followed by the defeats of agrarian trade unionism in 1833–35, the final phase of open militancy against the Poor Law Amendment Act and, at least in Kent, the bloody events at Bosenden Wood, seriously compromised countryside campaigning by the Chartists before it effectively commenced. Its opponents had learned how to crush all forms of overt plebeian militancy, though of course the gentry and larger farmers were never able to suppress covert actions, incendiarism, multifarious malicious damage and animal-maiming. Although by this period many incidents of this calibre were expressions of multifarious social protest,[63] there is no evidence that countryside Chartists, disgruntled at the movement's frustration, were the authors of any instances. Reviewing 'Agriculture and Incendiarism' in January 1845 – following Thomas Campbell Foster's famous commentaries on the subject in *The Time*[64] – the *Northern Star* asserted that arson was 'growing into a system' in response to the central facets of what some historians dub the 'agricultural revolution', and the many deprivations of farmworkers. The *English Chartist Circular* put a similar construction on the thirty fires within a six-mile radius of the Dorset town of Beaminster in 1842.[65] The Chartist press was not, of course, going to suggest that supporters had turned to rural terrorism, even in the unlikely event of its having evidence to this effect. No indicted incendiary could suppose that his democratic principles had any advantage for his defence or plea in mitigation. Interestingly, as far as is known, prosecution witnesses made no assertions from the witness-box of defendants' politics. Suspicions, or perhaps mere innuendo, that the Chartists were incendiaries were articulated privately, including by the manager of an insurance company forced to reimburse a victim at Titchfield, Hampshire, where 'there are several . . . Chartists . . . in the Parish'.[66] Across the Wiltshire Border at Steeple Ashton, five of farmer Miles' wheat ricks were fired, very shortly after he sacked all his labourers who had attended a WMA meeting.[67]

[63] Wells, 'Social Protest', especially pp. 168–73, 200–1.

[64] D. Jones, 'Thomas Campbell Foster and the Rural Labourer: Incendiarism in East Anglia in the 1840s', *Social History*, 1 (January 1976).

[65] *Northern Star*, 25 January 1845; *English Chartist Circular*, 2, 73.

[66] D. Compigne, Hants and Dorset Fire Office, to Normanby, 4 May 1840; cf. Chairman of Penrith Petty Sessions to Russell, 24 December 1839, who asserted that three fires resulted 'from the exhortations to violence constantly held out by travelling leaders of the Chartists'. PRO, HO 64/9, fos 125–26; 64/10, fo. 142.

[67] *Sussex Agricultural Express*, 25 May 1839; cf. *Sherborne Journal*, 29 November 1838.

The evidence relevant to the question of Chartism's national status is then essentially ambiguous. Ostensibly, some centres of pre-Chartist radicalism, notably Horsham, remain outside the new movement, while the importance of others, including Brighton, remains consistent. Permutations include the hard *evidence* of Blandford's participation in Chartism, but not in the earlier movements. Yet the town's proximity to Tolpuddle strongly suggests that people from Blandford were involved in the labour movement in the early 1830s. The evidence for Chartism in the villages is equally ambiguous. A fair number of known subscribers to the Land Plan were domiciled in villages which are not mentioned in any source pertaining to the early nineteenth-century labour movement, a fact which suggests – though it can never prove – that there were nuclei of popular radicals in many, if not most, southern villages. Chartism's early days qualifies conceptualisation of Bosenden Wood as the last labourers' revolt. One suspects that rural worker's political radicalism remained covert, but this does not invalidate historical perceptions of Chartism as a national movement. Most of the principal features when examined from a notionally British perspective are detectable in its southern English manifestations, including the recurrent divisions over ideological issues, even socialism, strategies – among them physical force – and personalities. We should add, furthermore, the oscillations in enthusiasms across a decade or more and the especially cancerous impact of the collapse of the Land Plan. On balance, and despite the ambiguities, southern evidence, from both town and village, supports rather than detracts from the national characterisation of Chartism.

8

Social Crime in the Rural South in the Eighteenth and Early Nineteenth Centuries

John Rule

For the law they entertain respect in all cases, except those few in which the upright-ness of their judgement is unhappily perverted by ancient and ignorant prejudice.
(on Cornish miners, 1841)[1]

Social historians have begun to explore the nature and incidence of crime in eighteenth- and nineteenth-century Britain. Problems of measurement and defini-tion have been explored. Superficially crime is a form of deviant behaviour which should be easy to define. If an action is in breach of the criminal law then in the legal sense at least it is a crime. In fact few forms of human behaviour are more complex than the criminal. The legal definition of what constitutes criminal action changes over time, within any society, and can differ at the same moment from one society to another. As historians we can only understand changes in the nature and patterns of criminal behaviour if we are aware of changes in the criminal law itself. More especially is this so if we are concerned with those historical periods when a privileged minority had a near monopoly of law making and law enforcement. In such periods law can become ideology – an instrument of class power. In eighteenth-century England the law-makers were a powerful propertied minority, and the interests of the unpropertied major-ity were not reflected in the massive property-protecting additions to the statute book. Furthermore, the new laws of the landed classes who formed the govern-ment often cut directly across the customary practices of the governed.[2]

Several years ago the writer was one of a group of historians who produced a book on eighteenth-century crime which was fortunate in attracting a wide range of reviews. Some reviewers thought that the work displayed a tendency to glamorise and excuse criminals as protesters. Even George Rudé, in a friendly

---

[1] BPP, *Report of Committee of Council on Education*, 1841, xx, p. 95.

[2] See D. Hay et al. (eds), *Albion's Fatal Tree* (1975); J. Cockburn (ed.), *Crime in England, 1500–1800* (1977); V.A.C. Gatrell and T.B. Hadden, 'Criminal Statistics and their Interpretation', in E.A. Wrigley (ed.), *Nineteenth-Century Society* (Cambridge, 1973), pp. 336–96. On the role of law as ideology see D. Hay, 'Property, Authority and the Crimal Law', in *Albion's Fatal Tree*, pp. 17–63. On the vast increase in statutes protecting property with the death penalty see L. Radzinowicz, *A History of English Criminal Law and its Administration from 1750*, i, *The Movement for Reform* (London, 1948), p. 4. Professor Radzinowicz has counted an increase of 190 in the number of capital offences in the 160 years separating the Restoration from the death of George III.

and welcoming review, while recognising that there is 'a fairly close relationship between social protest and certain types of (mainly rural) crime', thought we were inclined to be 'overgenerous in giving the common-or-garden criminal the benefit of the doubt'.[3] In introducing the volume in question the editors were at pains to stress that there were dangers inherent in any other than a careful and qualified use of the categorisation 'social crime'. This essay argues that such a descriptive category is an essential one, if defined with care, in making sense of a range of popular attitudes and actions in the period under question.[4]

In eighteenth-century England many legal crimes were not regarded by the poor as crimes at all, and it is in this context that it is useful to think of 'social crime'. To make such a distinction between social and other crime is only one possible way of categorising criminal actions. Several other divisions may for certain purposes better serve to assist understanding. One, for example, would be to divide crime into casual and professional. It obviously has uses to be able to separate those for whom crime is a whole or even partial way of life from those who act in a moment of desperation, are driven by want into an atypical action or give in just once to temptation. However, it is not always easy to place one criminal in this category and another in that. The mid nineteenth-century criminologists certainly began to insist on the existence of a 'criminal class', but eighteenth-century writers did not tend to make this explicit separation, and neither do eighteenth-century historians find it easy to do so. Henry Fielding in his famous investigation of 1751 did not attempt to distinguish clearly the criminal poor from the poor in general, and did not see the problem of crime as one distinct from that of the general problems presented by 'the lower orders'. In the autobiography of Francis Place (written in 1825) we can see the process by which among London tradesmen a 'culture of respectability' was gradually drawing away from a violent and more squalid culture of poverty, and in so doing defining a respectable artisan class. But it was a *process*; the poorer artisans held the underworld at arm's-length away; at no time in the eighteen century should we expect to find it possible to draw a rigid line between a respectable and a criminal poor. Professor Rudé claimed respectability for many of his Gordon rioters by showing that they not only claimed a trade but in fact had served their time at such. Yet Peter Linebaugh has indicated that this test would work in the same proportion for felons executed at Tyburn. If we bear in mind the vast expansion of property-protecting law in the eighteenth century, transforming for example 'customs of the trade' into the embezzlement of materials and the gathering of firewood into a rural felony, then we can see the substance behind Edward Thompson's remark: 'Crime in the sense

---

[3] G. Rudé, review of *Albion's Fatal Tree* in *Times Literary Supplement*, 30 January 1976, p. 105.

[4] The views expressed are my own and would not necessarily be fully accepted by the other contributors to *Albion's Fatal Tree*.

of being on the wrong side of the law was, for vast numbers of undifferentiated working people, normal.'[5]

Nevertheless, there still seems to be much value in thinking of a category of crime as 'social crime'. Several historians have used the term, but it is by no means certain that they have all meant the same thing. Some view it as synonymous with protest crime; others as involving a wide grouping of collective as opposed to individual crime. Edward Thompson and others have expressed reservations about the validity of the distinction:

> There are 'good' criminals, who are premature revolutionaries or reformers, forerunners of popular movements – all kinds of rioters, smugglers, poachers, primitive rebels in industry. This appears as 'social crime'. And there then are those who commit crime without qualification: thieves, robbers, highwaymen, forgers, arsonists and murderers.[6]

It is recognised that there is a real difference at each pole; the community and its culture were more ready to turn out and assist a smuggler, poacher or food rioter than to inform on him, whereas they would like as not join the hue and cry in pursuit of a thief. But it is suggested that a close examination of the eighteenth-century evidence makes it less possible to sustain such a division:

> At petty and quarter sessions the JPs sentenced for poaching, for assaults for wood theft . . . and for the theft of chickens. At assizes the judges sentenced coiners, rioters, sheep-stealers, and servant girls who had run off with their mistresses' silk and silver spoons. Research has not yet confirmed that they were sentencing different kinds of people, from different sub-cultures.[7]

E.P. Thompson's point is that there is a distinction but that it must be used only with reservations (and with great caution in the handling of evidence). Otherwise it not only obscures more than it reveals, but also suggests wrong social meanings. However it is in the rural districts where the narrower horizons of village life sharpened the definitions of what was and what was not 'crime' that the distinction has most validity. It is in this context of rural crime, largely in the south of England, that this essay will attempt a usable definition of social crime.[8]

---

[5] Henry Fielding, *Causes of the Late Increase in Robbers* (1751); *The Autobiography of Francis Place*, ed. M. Thale (Cambridge, 1972); Conference Report on crime in *Bulletin of the Society for the Study of Labour History*, 25 (1972), summaries of papers by P. Linebaugh and E.P. Thompson.

[6] Editors' introduction to *Albion's Fatal Tree*, p. 14.

[7] E.P. Thompson in *Bulletin of the Society for the Study of Labour History*, 25 (1972), p. 10.

[8] With very few exceptions the examples used to support my argument have been drawn from the southern counties. I have concentrated on the rural districts but do not wish to imply that the concept could not be applicable in an urban context. See the paper by R. Samuel in *Bulletin of the Society for the Study of Labour History*, 25 (1972), p. 7.

Deviant Behaviour: Negative Sanctions Operative

The accompanying diagram suggests a way in which the problem can be approached. This gives three categories of action:
1. Criminal action which is legitimised by popular opinion.
2. Criminal action which is both illegal and not legitimised by popular opinion.
3. Action which though not illegal is not acceptable to community mores.

It is action in the first category which may be regarded as social crime. There is an obvious problem in determining the reference group by which such actions are regarded as acceptable. In the cases which will be discussed, the reference group for the most part transcends social class to an extent and corresponds to something much larger than particular deviant sub-cultures. In poaching the line is most obviously drawn between those who under the Game Laws had the right to take game and those who did not, but in smuggling and wrecking whole communities seem to have supported, openly or tacitly, illegal activities. However, despite varying degrees of marginal or occasional involvement by the better off, the basis of the reference group in all cases is simply the lower orders, 'the people'.[9]

Activities such as smuggling, poaching and wrecking will serve as examples of one of two categories of social crime (some reference for comparative purposes will also be made to illicit whiskey distilling in Ireland). The other category of social crime is of criminal actions committed as acts of explicit protest which represent collective grievances, but which are not in themselves regarded as legitimate actions in all circumstances and by whomsoever committed. The pulling down of fences following unpopular enclosures, rick-burning, cattle-maiming, and machine-breaking are protest actions brought into being on specific occasions. Although smuggling and illicit distillng may be seen as protests against oppressive excise laws, and poaching as a protest against the tyranny of the

---

[9] Diagram based on T. Morris, *The Criminal Area* (London, 1967), p. 32.

Game Laws, they differ, along with wrecking, from explicit protest crimes in that they are continuing activities which are pursued as ways of getting or supplementing a living; in some cases they can even be regarded as 'professional' activities. Crimes such as arson and cattle-maiming were often used against individuals with the broad support of the populace. David Jones has provided a detailed examination of rural incendiarism in East Anglia in the 1840s, describing it, along with 'poaching, maiming, the stealing of farm animals, machine breaking, the sending of threatening letters, and organised opposition to low wages, high prices and unpopular aspects of the Poor Law', as a traditional form of popular protest. Of course it was not confined to East Anglia. In many parts of England from time to time villagers could watch with satisfaction the burning down of barns of farmers against whom grievances were widely held. Thus the buildings of a Kent farmer were fired in 1844 because he had been the first in the district to cut wages and had been urging his neighbours to follow suit. In Gloucestershire in 1824 a barn was burned down because a farmer had been employing cheap Irish labour. Arson was only one possible form of protest crime. In Cornwall in 1801 a mob of 300 came to the home of the Reverend Dr Flamank armed with guns, axes, saws and weapons of every description. They shut off all the entrances and stopped all the travellers for half a mile around. They totally demolished his salmon weir, cut off the timber from his mill wheels, split the axle trees and pulled down the dams. 'They defied their King and the laws of their country and went off exulting in the depredations they had committed by huzzaing, firing of guns etc.' Clearly there was widespread resentment at the use the reverend gentleman was making of the river, depriving others downstream of its use to them. A. Peacock has claimed that in East Anglia after the failure of the Labourers' Revolt, sheep maiming and stealing reached levels and assumed forms which make them properly regarded as part of a guerilla war of protest against the farms.[10]

It is no easy task for the historian to establish the actual extent and character of rural crime and determine when crime becomes protest, but there can be little doubt that much rural felony in the eighteenth and early nineteenth centuries comes within a broad definition of social crime, in that the object was a particular target of community grievance and the action had broad-based community support. In such cases the actions were accepted and popularly justified precisely because they articulated widely-felt grievances, but they were committed against specific persons at specific times for specific reasons. Arson, sheep-stealing, cattle-maiming and various forms of property destruction were not in themselves 'legitimate' activities.

---

[10] D. Jones, 'Thomas Campbell Foster and the Rural Labourer: Incendiarism in East Anglia in the 1840s', *Social History*, 1 (1976), p. 5; *West Briton* (Truro), 5 July 1844; 'A Gravedigger's Diary', in J.W. Robertson Scott (ed.), *The Countryman Book* (1948), p. 160; *Sherborne Mercury*, 30 November 1801; A. Peacock, 'Village Radicalism in East Anglia', in J.P.D. Dunbabin (ed.), *Rural Discontent in Nineteenth-Century Britain* (London, 1974), pp. 27–61.

On the other hand, smuggling, wrecking, poaching and related activities were not held to be crimes in the popular view, no matter by whom committed or in what circumstances. As George Crabbe put it:

> the smuggler cries
> What guilt is his who pays for what he buys?
> The poacher questions with perverted mind,
> Were not the gifts of heaven for all design'd?[11]

Here is a belief in a natural legitimacy strengthened by the feeling that custom sanctions what the law disbars. To whom should property cast up by the sea belong? What kind of law would prevent a man from making whiskey at the price and to the taste preferred by his customers? This kind of social crime is distinguishable not just from actions whose explicit purpose is protest, but also from the social banditry examined by Eric Hobsbawm. In the case of the latter the popular acceptance rests on the man and not on the action itself. Armed robbery and kidnapping cannot in themselves be always acceptable. They are justified by the fact of their being committed by certain persons against certain persons or institutions. It is for this reason that elaborate mythologies of the Robin Hood kind grow up: they are intended to put their hero in the right, irrespective of the crimes committed. The bandit is seen as the victim of oppression and a justified rebel against authority.[12]

We can develop further our definition of social crime in this category by investigating how far our chosen examples meet the criteria thus far advanced. Were smuggling, poaching and wrecking regarded as legitimate activities by those who engaged in them? There seems little doubt that they were. The duke of Richmond, a sworn opponent of smuggling in Sussex, complained in 1749: 'The common people of this country have no notion that smuggling is a crime.' Another contemporary remarked that 'the common people of England in general fancy there is nothing in the crime of smuggling'. Poaching was similarly regarded. A writer on the Game Laws in 1821 pointed out that every magistrate knew that it was the defence of the poacher that: 'it is very hard he should be punished for taking what he had as great a right to as any other man'. The Game Laws of the period reserved the right to hunt the wild creatures of the woods to very few persons. The qualification was £100 a year from a freehold estate. One writer has pointed out that this would have amounted to only 800 persons in the whole of Staffordshire in the mid eighteenth century. Thus it was not only the poor, but many of the farmers as well who were excluded:

> Ye sov'reigns of Manors in Verse
> (Dull Prose would dishonour your name)
> The Muse shall your triumph rehearse

---

[11] George Crabbe, 'Tales of the Hall, Book XXI, Smugglers and Poachers' (1819) in A.J. and R.M. Carlyle, *The Poetical Works of George Crabbe* (1914), p. 487.

[12] E.J. Hobsbawm, *Bandits* (Harmondsworth, 1972).

> High sounding the Laws of the Game
> The farmer your sport shall supply
> Your beagles his fences shall break
> But 'touch not and taste not', you cry,
> The Law with its talons awake
> On Hundred a Year gives the right
> To challenge all Nature your own;
> Till short of the sum but a mite,
> And your ninety-nine pounds are as none.

This made the farmer too a disliker of the Game Laws and, if he did not indulge so often in poaching as the labourer, he and his kind formed the common juries described in 1790 as a 'professed enemy to all the Game Laws'. But any disinclination of juries did not prove too much of a problem for the landed gentry. Their law was changed to bring most poaching offences within the range of summary jurisdiction, and as magistrates they dealt with poachers from comfortable seats in their own houses.[13]

Eighteenth-century beliefs continued into the nineteenth century. A Bedfordshire justice told a select committee in 1826: 'The general opinion is that game is not private property. They say God has made the game of the land free and left it free.' A witness from Cambridge reported: 'They attach the idea of property to poultry, they do not to game.' Wreckers believed it was their right to take what they wanted from wrecked or stranded vessels. The Cornish miners were said to have inherited from their ancestors an opinion that: 'they have a right to such spoils as the ocean may place within their reach, many of the more enlightened inhabitants secure whatever they can seize without any remorse; and conclude without any hesitation, that nothing but injustice, supported by power and sanctioned by law, can wrench it from their hands'. But it was not only the Cornish. According to the magistrates of Glamorgan in 1837, wrecking had been carried out on their coast 'almost uninterruptedly from time immemorial' and was regarded by the common people as a right. In Denbighshire in 1824 the feeling that stealing from wrecks was 'no great moral offence' was said to be prevalent. The inhabitants of the Wirral peninsula of Cheshire thought themselves entitled to the effects of passengers and sailors. When a Lloyds agent tried to stop them plundering a wreck in 1838, the wreckers replied: 'We are not taking anything. I suppose every man has a right to take what is here, one as much as another.' From the southern counties the investigation of 1839 gathered instances of wrecking from Cornwall, Devon, Dorset, the Isle of Wight, Sussex and Kent.[14]

It was clearly a hopeless law which tried to make the Irish pay 9s. to 10s. a gallon for 'parliament whiskey' when their social life was hinged to cheap drink;

[13] C. Winslow, 'Sussex Smugglers', in *Albion's Fatal Tree*, pp. 148–49; D. Hay, 'Poaching and the Game Laws on Cannock Chase', ibid., pp. 207–11.

[14] BPP, SC, HC, *Criminal Convictions*, 1826–27, vi, p. 7; ibid., *Minutes of Evidence*, p. 22; J.G. Rule, 'Wrecking and Coastal Plunder', in *Albion's Fatal Tree*, pp. 176–77.

they knew how to make poteen and were not notably law-abiding. As Professor K.H. Connel, who wrote with such authority and insight on the subject, pointed out, 'Poteen making provides a striking example of the proverbial reluctance of the Irish to accept the laws' definition of an offence'. The industry clearly depended upon the widespread sympathy felt for the illicit distiller. This reluctance to accept the law's definition of a crime was not confined to poteen making, or for that matter to Ireland.[15]

It would further emphasise the value of regarding some actions as social crime if it could be shown that most of those who engaged in them would not have engaged in activities which they regarded as criminal. Adam Smith described a smuggler as a person who would have been 'in every respect an excellent citizen had not the laws of his country made that a crime which nature never meant to be so'. Edward Gibbon Wakefield told a Commons committee that some men transported for a smuggling offence were 'exceedingly ignorant, but, except that they were smugglers, they were valuable men in any place'. Smugglers spoke of their trade much as others might speak of theirs, and surviving autobiographies provide us not with material for the study of 'deviant careers', but with matter of fact descriptions of entry into an occupation. Jack Rattenbury of Beer in Devon, self-styled Rob Roy of the West, was once called to give evidence on a Bill to improve the harbour at Beer. At Westminster he gave his profession as 'sometimes fishing, sometimes piloting, and sometimes smuggling'. Captain Harry Carter of Prussia Cove in Cornwall describes how he never went to school but worked on his father's farm from an early age, then became a child worker at the mines and when he became seventeen 'went with my two oldest brothers a fishing and smuggling'. A witness from Christchurch asked in 1846 if the people there regarded smuggling as either a crime or a sin, firmly replied, 'Not in the least'.[16]

A Sussex witness in 1828 testified that many people who would feel no scruple in taking game would feel a scruple in taking poultry. Perhaps the matter was most clearly put by a farm labourer in 1845:

> There is a difference between poaching and stealing. I should not steal myself . . . Many people would be friends with a poacher, but would not like to be very great friends with a man convicted of felony.[17]

This is not to deny that night poachers would sometimes take a hen or, much more rarely, a sheep. Nor is it to deny that villains of the deepest dye were involved in the smuggling trade. But it remains true that most persons who engaged in

---

[15] K.H. Connell, 'Illicit Distillation', in his *Irish Peasant Studies* (Oxford, 1968), p. 28.

[16] Adam Smith, *Wealth of Nations* (1904), ii, p. 429; BPP, SC, HC, 1831, vii, p. 100, Q. 1421; J. Rattenbury, *Memoirs of a Smuggler* (Sidmouth, 1837; repr. Newcastle, 1964), p. 42; J.B. Cornish (ed.), *The Autobiography of a Cornish Smuggler* (1894; repr. Truro, 1968), p. 3; BPP, SC, HC, *Game Laws*, 1846, ix, pt 1, p. 166, Q. 3179.

[17] BPP, SC, HC, *Criminal Commitments*, 1828, vi, p. 34; quoted in J.J. Tobias, *Nineteenth-Century Crime: Prevention and Punishment* (Newton Abbot, 1972), p. 18.

these activities did not regard themselves as criminals and would have with-held from activities which they did so regard. Jack Rattenbury, imprisoned in Exeter gaol, complained of being 'most unpleasantly associated' with persons who were to take their trial for 'every description of crime'. When these 'criminals' tried to effect an escape by knocking out a warder, Rattenbury and his fellow smugglers prevented their breaking out.[18]

We can further point our definition of social crime by emphasising in what ways it is not distinguishable from other forms of crime. It is not a distinction between 'professional' and 'casual' crime. Degrees of professionalism varied, but wrecking, smuggling and poaching, like illicit distilling, were largely engaged in as a means of getting or supplementing a living. This distinguishes them from the 'protest' category of social crime. Wrecking, despite some lengends to the contrary, was not in the fullest sense a professional crime. Wrecks were unplanned but the property taken was not only used in wreckers' own homes but was frequently sold, sometimes through well-organised disposal networks involving marine store dealers. Smuggling was a way of earning a living from the entrepreneur at the top to the wage-earning carrier on land. These latter were so well paid in Sussex for their work in landing and clearing a cargo that the guinea a week paid had the effect of raising local farm wages in competi-tion.[19] The suburbs of Christchurch in 1846 were said to contain a population 'entirely supported by smuggling'. It seems that very large entrepreneurs were not characteristic of the English smuggling scene until after 1760, but at any time considerable sums were necessarily involved in purchasing or hiring a boat, paying for its crew, providing the large numbers of men and horses needed to transport the landed cargo, and making the initial purchase of the tea, brandy or tobacco. Disposal networks had to be highly organised and developed. Such an accepted part of rural life did the 'fair trade' become that it was possible for sharp operators to capitalise on this very acceptance and defraud trusting rural populations. At Gravesend in 1741 a man pretending to be a customs officer seized goods from country people on the pretence that they had been smug-gled; and in Plymouth in 1765 some men pretending to be smugglers with cargoes of tea and brandy to dispose of, but to be in want of funds to pay for the freight, bilked several farmers of cash. It was possible for one or two boatmen to get together and if they had a suitable craft arrange to run a cargo. If known and trusted they might even get credit from the continental suppliers, but that could not have been too often extended in such a risky trade. More usually syndicates put up the money. Some individuals became very wealthy and profits could be made in the distribution as well as in the running of cargoes. Sometimes extra profits seem to have been available. In 1773 a smuggler named Rushton, operat-ing in the Poole district, was employing many people in the area around

---

[18] Rattenbury, *Memoirs*, p. 42.

[19] Arthur Young, *Report on the Agriculture of Sussex* (1797), quoted in William Marshall, *Review and Abstracts of the County Reports of the Board of Agriculture from the Several Agricultural Departments of England*, v, *Southern and Peninsular Departments* (1818; reprinted Newton Abbot, 1969), p. 471.

Wimborne in collecting elder leaves. These were left to wither in barns and lofts and then wet in water in which sheep's dung had been steeped in order to colour them before being dried and mixed with smuggled tea. But this practice can hardly have been typical of a trade which depended for the success of its very widespread operations on the fact that its goods compared not only in price but also in quality with the duty-paid articles. Smuggling may have employed many different levels of operator, but as a whole it added up to big business with a large labour force and was supplier to a large section of the population of much-wanted commodities.[20]

Poaching was not such a large-scale activity. Single poachers or loose groupings of village men were responsible for a large share of poaching activity. But it should not be imagined that they operated only to fill their pots, or hoped simply to make an odd sale here or there to private individuals. There was a flourishing black market in game, as might be expected since there was no proper legal trade. Many village poachers worked for the money they could get for hares or pheasants through this organised, undercover marketing. There also existed large gangs, often from the towns, who descended in force upon estates to carry away as much in a night as they could.[21]

Professor Connell has doubted that outside of legend there were very many large fortunes made from whiskey distilling. The typical producer remained small scale, but supply networks had to be organised, and cooperation was needed in order to ensure safe transit of large amounts of poteen. It did not require a large amount of capital to set up a still. Early in the nineteenth century a good copper one could have been built for six to eight guineas and a tin one for two guineas less. More important for success was the choice of a good site, concealed, near water, where the process of first brewing then distilling the liquor could be carried out. Concealment was necessary not just from the revenue men but also from the populace, who esteemed the pot ale at the intermediate stage between brewing and distilling as stronger than porter and were not above 'discovering' it. To many, illicit distilling was a necessary way of supplementing their living. Considered as a whole: 'poteen making was no amusing trifle in Irish life: when craftsmanship in Ireland was ill-regarded, her pot-stilled whiskey at its best was unexcelled; it was amongst the most widely distributed of Irish manufactures; few industries gave so much employment'. In the two years 1833 and 1834, 16,000 stills were seized, and in the following forty years seizures on average were between two and three thousand a year.[22]

Social crime was not necessarily 'nice' crime. There is no distinction implied here between violent and non-violent crime. Violence, intimidation and corruption were all part of the smuggling trade. An atmosphere of romance and

---

[20] BPP, SC, HC, *Game Laws*, 1846, ix, pt 1, p. 272, Q. 4959; *Sherborne Mercury*, 23 June 1741 and 14 October 1765; *Hampshire Chronicle*, 28 June 1773.

[21] Hay, in *Albion's Fatal Tree*, pp. 203–6; and evidence of several witnesses BPP, SC, HC, *Game Laws*, 1846, ix, pt 1, *Minutes of Evidence*, p. 46, Q. 843; p. 127, Q. 2481.

[22] Connell, *Irish Peasant Studies*, pp. 10–28, 49.

derring-do has tended to obscure the reality of smuggling. We must forget the quiet slipping with muffled oars into dark and secret creeks. That was not the way, at least in the eighteenth century, that many smugglers operated. They did not always avoid the revenue men with stealth; they as often outfaced them with force:

> From Sussex we hear that the smugglers have grown so daring that a gang of 55 with their arms slung and their horses loaded with tea, at noon day rode through several towns in defiance of the Custom's House officers who durst not offer to molest them.[23]

That was in 1742 in a period during which one historian has recently written of a 'guerilla war' being waged in Sussex by the smugglers against the authorities. But such open defiance was not confined to the 1740s or to Sussex. The customs officer from Fowey in Cornwall faced a desperate situation in 1766:

> we are in danger of our lives by happening to meet with them; for whether we attack them or not, they seldom fail to attack us when their number and strength is so much superior.

He had twice recently met with gangs of tinners each with a horse load of brandy who because they worked in the mines some distance away had no fear of being recognised. He and his men had been badly beaten in one confrontation:

> It is now two months since we having dared to venture out after them, we having been informed by very good authority that they carry firearms, and have given out threats that if ever they meet with us again they will kill us.[24]

Around 1780 smugglers were said to be capable of assembling from 500 to 1000 men on extraordinary occasions and even on ordinary occasions to be assembled in greater numbers than anything which could be brought to oppose them. These gangs sometimes carried firearms but more usually bludgeons or loaded whips. After landing the cargo they subdivided into smaller but still formidable groups to distribute it. It was no unusual thing to see groups of ten to twenty horsemen bringing the cargo through the streets of London in broad daylight without fear of obstruction. In 1783 'armies of smugglers' were said to be riding 'with impunity' through the counties upon the sea coast.[25]

There are many examples of smuggling gangs not only resisting and routing excise officers, but of actually seeking confrontations with them. There were often successful attempts to rescue taken comrades and recover the cargoes taken with them. The best-known example of this is the attack on the customs warehouse at Poole by the notorious Hawkhurst gang in 1747. This gang operated in the

---

[23] *Sherborne Mercury*, 15 June 1742.

[24] PRO, WO 1/989, fo. 333.

[25] A.L. Cross (ed.), *Eighteenth-Century Documents Relating to the Royal Forests, the Sherriffs and Smuggling* (New York, 1928), pp. 240, 290.

border area of Hampshire and West Sussex. Outraged by the capture at sea of a load of tea whose landing they had been awaiting, they marched from Sussex to Poole in a gang of between thirty and sixty strong. They broke open the warehouse and secured the tea. The following day they returned in triumph, breakfasting on the way in Fordingbridge where hundreds of people came out to watch the triumphal cavalcade, the whole being seen by the populace at large as a 'gallant expedition'.[26]

What happened at Fordingbridge serves to link us with another aspect of smuggling violence. One of the gang recognised among the crowd a man named Chater with whom he had once worked. He shook his hand and threw him a bag of tea. Sadly for Chater this drew the attention of the authorities to him and he was taken up by the customs. Several months later with an officer named Galley he set out for Sussex for examination. On the way they were intercepted by the smugglers and, to cut a gruesome story short, were brutally tortured and murdered. Violence of this kind raises questions. Galley was a customs officer but Chater was not. Were the populace in the coastal districts acquiescent to smuggling only from fear? Chater was not the only informer harshly dealt with. Many were. A Hampshire blacksmith who stole some tea from a gang might have expected rough justice, but it was the fact that he was foolish enough to cry out that he recognised them when they came for the reckoning which explains why he was stabbed and thrashed and left for dead.[27]

The activities of the Hawkhurst gang certainly terrorised whole areas of Sussex and Hampshire. Their violence was extreme and it is only against them that we have a recorded instance of a citizens' vigilante band being formed. Violence may have been used more as a deterrent against locally *deviant* behaviour such as informing for money. It does not therefore follow that popular support rested on fear. Fear does not explain why a Cornish jury acquitted some smugglers who had fought off the customs on the grounds that sticks were not offensive weapons! Nor the testifying of a character witness called by a sheep-stealer that he had known the man some time and although he had been in gaol, it had not been for a felony, but only for smuggling. Nor would it explain the hostile crowd reaction to informers. At Hastings in 1748 some informers were pursued into the country by an angry mob, while at Chatham two informers besieged in a house were surrounded by an angry mob yelling: 'Informers, they ought to be hanged! It is no sin to kill them.' Fear does not explain the action of a London crowd who on hearing that some strangers being conducted through the streets were smugglers, speedily effected their rescue. The populace was so heavily involved in the trade, as customers even if not as principals, that it was not surprising for a parliamentary committee to find 'the generality of

---

[26] This section is based on the account by Winslow in *Albion's Fatal Tree*, pp. 119–66.
[27] *Sherborne Mercury*, 5 January 1784.

the people on the coasts' better friends to the smugglers than they were to the customs officers.[28]

Poaching activities often ended in armed affrays between poachers and gamekepers, with the murder and wounding of the latter being frequently a matter for report in the local press. The Ellenburgh Act of 1803 which made it a capital offence to be caught poaching armed had a worsening effect. It was in the nature of the poacher's trade that he carried a gun; if he could be capitally sentenced for merely carrying it, then the likelihood that he would use it to avoid arrest was strong. Keepers and their assistants could be intimidated by the size of armed poaching gangs just as the customs officers were by smuggling gangs: 'If you go back as far as 1819 we used to have fights with armed people with blackened faces and watch words and all ready to draw up in a line; they were regularly marshalled . . .', recollected one Norfolk keeper.[29]

Even if wreckers were not guilty in fact as they were in legend of deliberately luring ships onto rocks by displaying false lights, they sometimes used violence towards those who attempted to prevent their plundering; sometimes even towards the survivors of shipwrecks. There are recorded instances of sailors being forcibly robbed of their effects and even stripped of their clothing. Numbers were usually on the side of the wreckers. An agitated report from Cornwall in 1700 concluded: 'The number of the rioters was so great and their threatenings so high, and their proceedings so outrageous that the ordinary ministers of justice durst not attempt to suppress them.' In 1722 the Cornish wreckers overpowered thirty-five armed men placed on a wreck to protect it. From time to time such confrontations produced fatalities.[30]

In Ireland in the early nineteenth century poteen was made by gangs who were armed and able to confront the military. In 1815 in County Mayo a party of excise officers assisted by more than thirty soldiers were involved in a day-long battle with armed distillers. In the 1820s the traffic in poteen was ensured by force as well as by cunning. Gangs of around a dozen distillers would get together to escort their produce to market with firearms and loaded whips.[31]

Finally, the distinction between social and other crime is not one between serious and non-serious crime. In important respects some social crime had to be taken especially seriously by the authorities. Smuggling meant not only a heavy loss in revenue, but the very fact that it involved the participation of whole areas of the country made it at times seem a threat to the very nature of government. 'Smuggling traders in these parts are grown to such a head that they bid defiance to all Law and Government', came a complaint from Dorset in 1717. Sixty years later it was feared that the extent to which it was carried on had

---

[28] C.G. Harper, *Smugglers* (1909; reprinted Newcastle, 1966), p. 99; *West Briton*, 7 August 1835 and 14 August 1818; Winslow, in *Albion's Fatal Tree*, pp. 144–45 and 147; *Sherborne Mercury*, 1 December 1741.

[29] BPP, SC, HC, *Game Laws*, 1846, ix, pt 1, p. 27, Q. 544.

[30] J.G. Rule, 'Wrecking', in *Albion's Fatal Tree*, pp. 174–76.

[31] Connel, *Irish Peasant Studies*, p. 11.

acquired a vigour and consistency subversive both of law and government.[32]

In 1783 a writer regarded the loss of revenue as only one of the problems the trade posed for government:

> From the first landing of the goods to the final disposing of them, it exhibits such a source of violence, and every species of iniquity, as calls aloud for the interposition of Government, not only as an object of revenue, but as it substantially affects the morals of the people, and even the police of the kingdom. The frauds, forgeries and perjuries which accompany the circulation of smuggled goods to London and through the country, can be believed only by those whose business it is to be acquainted with them.[33]

It was not that government had to fear open rebellion from the large gangs of smugglers, although there were times when it was not too sure about even that: a Sussex officer in 1720 urgently requested troops to be sent for 'in a short time they will rise in a rebellion, the number of them is not less than 200, every man of them for the Pretender'. The real concern for the authority of government lay in the simple fact that large areas lived to an extent under a different law: the smugglers' law. The subversion of authority in the following treatment of a crown officer is obvious: tea and brandy were recovered by an armed gang at Wimbledon in 1743 after they had been taken by the customs. On checking the gang found that some brandy had been kept back by the officers: 'for which fraud they were heartily drubbed and obliged on their knees to ask pardon, and promise never to offend in the like manner any more'. The duke of Richmond clearly saw the implication of the unchecked activities of the Hawkenhurst gang:

> for this is not only murders of the deepest dye attended with the most shocking circumstances of cruelty but also committed by whole gangs of villains in open defiance of the laws and all government whatsoever. So though it may not be treason in law, I am sure it is so in common sense.[34]

Poaching has been described as an 'act of defiance and rebellion against constituted authority', although some poachers took game to live and others to sell. The Hammonds described the growing brutality of the Game Laws as the chief illustration of the extent to which poverty was driving the rural labourers to press upon law and order. In the three years between 1827 and 1830 one in seven of all criminal convictions were under the Game Laws, and the number of persons convicted was 8502.[35]

Wrecking was of less concern to government, although depredations on friendly foreign vessels were embarrassing enough. The pressure of merchants

[32] E. Carson, *The Ancient and Rightful Customs* (London, 1972), pp. 63–64; Cross, *Documents on Smuggling*, p. 239.

[33] Ibid., p. 308.

[34] ESCRO, Sayer Papers, 266; *Sherborne Mercury*, 3 May 1743; Winslow in *Albion's Fatal Tree*, p. 138.

[35] J.L. and B. Hammond, *The Village Labourer* (London, 1978), p. 140; Tobias, *Nineteenth-Century Crime*, p. 19.

and insurers was real enough too, but of its nature wrecking was an *ad hoc* offence. The opportunities for plunder were fortuitous and it did not therefore bring about the existence of large permanent gangs. It was more of a crowd activity than an organised threat to law and order.

It has been argued in this essay that it is useful to regard certain activities against the law in the eighteenth and early nineteenth-centuries as *social crimes*, but that this is a categorisation which must be used with caution and an awareness of its limitations. It has further been argued that the two main forms of social crime can be distinguished: crimes which draw their collective legitimation from their explicit protest and nature; and actions which although against the law were not regarded as criminal by the large numbers who participated in them whether their purpose was to make a protest or not. It has not been suggested that crimes in the second category cannot be viewed as crimes of protest to a certain degree. Smuggling and poaching lie within the traditions of resistance carried on by the poor to the laws and institutions of their rulers. But there is an area of distinction. A man might poach as an individual; he might poach as a member of a gang; he might be seeking meat for his own pot; he might want the shillings afforded by the black market in game; he might be consciously acting in defiance of the landed gentry; he might enjoy the excitement of the sport; or he might, like the grandfather of Joseph Ashby, be working off a personal grudge in poaching the lands of the person who foreclosed his mortgage. No matter, poaching is not a crime. In the case of arson or the killing or maiming of animals, the question of whose cattle or whose barn and for what reasons lies at the heart of the matter. A bad labourer, perhaps of violent disposition and quarrelsome in nature, who was dismissed by a well-regarded employer for reasons held justifiable by his fellows is no social criminal if he revenged himself by burning a barn. It is not possible to say with exactitude how much crime of the arson category can be regarded as social crime in the sense of being a popularly, supported protest action. The trend of recent work suggests that it has been seriously underestimated. The interactions of crime and protest in rural communities are at last beginning to receive from historians the attention which they have long merited.[36]

Postscript

George Rudé in *Protest and Punishment: The Story of the Social and Political Protesters Transported to Australia, 1788–1868* (Oxford, 1978) defined actions against the law connected with forms of collective protest such as trade unionism, machine-breaking, food rioting or radical politics as 'protest crimes' and regarded activities such as poaching and smuggling along with incendiarism and similar acts as 'marginal protest crimes' (pp. 3–4 and ch. 6). In practice it is not as easy

[36] M.K. Ashby, *Joseph Ashby of Tysoe* (London, 1974), pp. 3–4.

as he implies to distinguish between protest crime and crime as protest (p. 2). The problem seems to have been approached from the wrong end. The most important characteristic of 'social crimes' lies in positive popular sanction, not in the often present element of protest. Poaching and smuggling are 'social crimes' because they are not in any circumstances popularly regarded as criminal. I neglected persons convicted of manifest protest crimes such as trade unionists, machine-breakers or food rioters because they seemed to present little difficulty, but to have been self-evidently 'social criminals'. I agree with Rudé that the protest elements in 'marginal' actions such as incendiarism have to be carefully distinguished before such actions can be safely regarded as 'social' or 'protest' crime, but do not agree that it is useful to seek distinctions in motivation for the actions of smugglers or poachers. One is uneasy when rigid definition of protest makes ordinary criminals of Irish women who committed arson in order to join transported relatives or lovers (pp. 5, 147).

John Beattie in his magisterial study of the criminal justice system, *Crime and the Courts in England, 1660–1800.* (Oxford 1986), recognises the value of social crime as examined by myself and others. However, he considers that social crimes are best investigated in detailed case studies, because, 'what is required to make them intelligible is the detailed reconstruction of the social, economic and political circumstances in which they occurred' (pp. 6–7). The historian attempting to study crime on the wider canvas and over the longer period will, he argues, be more concerned with 'mainstream' crime. I am happy with that, although I do not know that it avoids problems of definition of the kind I examine in my subsequent paper on sheep-stealing (see below, pp. 237–53). John Archer acknowledged that 'Rule . . . more than anyone else has attempted to impose order on this subject'. He stresses the variety of motivations which underlay crime in rural East Anglia but, being especially concerned with the crimes of arson, animal maiming and poaching, he is much concerned with the relationship of protest and crime, and inclined to look favourably on the concept of 'social crime' as developed by myself. His first chapter, 'An Introduction to Rural Protest' is an important consideration of the definitional problem, and takes matters in this regard further than I did. See John E. Archer, *'By a Flash and a Scare', Arson, Animal Maiming, and Poaching in East Anglia, 1815–1870* (Oxford, 1990, pp. 1–24. Roger Wells admires my 'sensitive' discussion of social crime, but stresses the role of criminal gangs in the totality of criminal actions in rural crime. See R.A.E. Wells. 'Popular Protest and Social Crime: The Evidence of Criminal Gangs in Rural Southern England 1790–1860', in B. Stapleton (ed.), *Conflict and Community in Southern England* (Stroud, 1992), pp. 135–82. Clearly other historians like Clive Emsley, while acknowledging it to be of some value, find 'social crime' a concept of limited value to the general understanding of crime. (Emsley) I do not really quarrel with that. My argument was that it was, nevertheless, essential both for any full understanding of crime in the eighteenth and early nineteenth centuries and for a proper appreciation of the social, class and power relations of that time.

9

Crime and Protest in a Country Parish: Burwash, 1790–1850

Roger Wells

'Are there within your division any persons who have no visible or known means of obtaining their livelihood honestly, and who are believed to live by habitual depredation or illegal means? Will you state the numbers and supposed habits of such persons?' So ran typically-loaded questions from Edwin Chadwick in the mid 1830s, designed to elicit replies from the magistracy, supportive of utilitarian proposals for the professionalisation of the British police. The survey's author in fact believed in the existence of a *criminal class*, responsible for what he perceived as an escalating problem of crime. Respondents failed to sustain Chadwick's prejudice, primarily because their worships had inadequate concrete intelligence. In their critical role the amateur judiciary encountered those accused of crimes in summary hearings, where the magistrates dealt with the matter; or in committal proceedings, when the accused was either released principally owing to inadequate evidence, or was sent for trial at the Quarter Sessions or the Assizes. Magistrates conducted the former, and as many Assize Grand Jurors were also justices who collectively reviewed cases to determine whether suspects should be indicted and then tried, at least some members of the Bench were directly involved at every level in the criminal process. While particularly active and assiduous magistrates doubtlessly had considerable information about crimes and suspects which was legally inadmissible,[1] in addition to the formal paperwork they both composed and scrutinised, and therefore were knowledgeable, they were not necessarily well-equipped to answer authoritatively, let alone scientifically, Chadwick's enquiries. A proportion of alleged offenders might be recidivists, but many either had no criminal record, or documentation was unavailable, particularly where suspects had been convicted in other jurisdictions. Chadwick elicited numerous opinions as opposed to the hard empirical evidence he sought.[2]

---

[1] One magistrate committed his intelligence to paper respecting a Wiveslfield man he had just sent for trial to the Quarter Sessions: 'The Prisoner is an Old Offender and has been publickly Whip'd by order of this Court for similar offences and the last no longer ago than last Easter . . . He is the Terror of the Neighbourhood and if convicted it is hoped the Court will order him for Transportation there being no other Apparent way of preserving the Property of his Neighbours from him.' Note, no signature, but justice Shelley, September 1790, ESCRO, QR/E645.

[2] BPP, *First Report of the Commisioners on the Constabulary Force of England and Wales*, 169 (1839), xix, vol. xix, p. 7. Cf. Francis Place's earlier London-based identification in his 1822, *Illustrations of*

Undaunted the Constabulary Commissioners approached the handful of professional police forces established in towns, including the Metropolitan Police set up in 1829. Representatives were asked to *speculate*, on the basis of their observations, about 'the average duration of the career of common thieves or habitual depredators before their permanent removal from the field . . . by transportation, death, or other means?' Their opinions suggested that the supposedly 'habitual' criminal remained unconvicted for an average of six years during which they got away scot-free with scores, even hundreds of crimes, before being caught. This impressionistic material also propounded that 'in point of sensual gratification, the condition of the habitual depredator is, during his career, much higher than that of the honest labourer, living on wages', to reinforce the concept of a criminal class.[3]

But such information was urban; and not least as the criminal rookeries of the towns were notorious, long before the fascinating details were supplied in the later forties by Mayhew and others, the notion of a criminal class was plausible. As for rural England, Chadwick's report offered a variant. Here

> the most prominent body of delinquents . . . are vagrants, and these vagrants appear to consist of two classes; first, the habitual depredators, house-breakers, horse-stealers, and common thieves; secondly, of vagrants . . . who seek alms as mendicants. Besides these classes who travel from fair to fair, and from town to town, in quest of dishonest gains, there are numerous classes who make incursions from the provincial towns upon the adjacent rural districts.

Although this assertion did not, in fact, demarcate a criminal class resident in the countryside, more widely entertained notions of a such a class were certainly applied to rural districts, notably that more 'open' villages, those at the greatest remove from the controls of squire and clergymen, hosted such groups.[4]

Those historians who somewhat uncritically adopted contemporary notions of a criminal class,[5] have not been supported by more recent specialists. Clive Emsley's judicious review of contemporary and historical writing – located roughly in the mid-nineteenth century – concluded that 'most thefts, and most crimes of violence' could neither be attributed to 'professional criminals', nor to 'a group which can in any meaningful sense, be described as a class'.[6] Indeed, some historians, notably those on the left, attribute such concepts as biased judgements aimed to increase acceptance of professional policing in early

---

continued

the Proofs of the Principle of Population, cited B. Harrison, 'Two Roads to Social Reform: Francis Place and the "Drunken Committee" of 1834', *Historical Journal*, 9 (1968), p. 288.

[3] BPP, 169 (1839), xix, pp. 7, 11.

[4] Ibid., p. 13. For a classic statement on 'open' village crime, protest and politics, see D. Mills, *Lord and Peasant in Nineteenth-Century Britain* (London, 1980), esp. pp. 128–35.

[5] Notably J.J. Tobias, *Crime and Industrial Society in the Nineteenth Century* (Harmondsworth, 1967), esp. ch. 4, and K. Chesney, *The Victorian Underworld* (Harmondsworth, 1972 edition).

[6] C. Emsley, *Crime and Society in England, 1750–1900* (London, 1987), ch. 6 and esp. pp. 135–36.

Victorian Britain.[7] While further studies have confirmed some linkage between vagrancy and crime,[8] and established that organised crime by gangs warranted later Georgian and early Victorian fears and exhibited features illustrative of 'professional criminals',[9] these identifications do not invalidate another historian's observation, namely that of the 'grim cycle' into which most working-class communities were locked *throughout* the nineteenth century; for many individuals, reality dictated a rhythm of 'work – poverty – unemployment – crime'.[10]

Most of these, and other studies, have a pronounced industrial and urban, if no longer a metropolitan bias. Crime in the countryside has received uneven coverage, though fascinating attempts to demarcate between various categories have been attempted.[11] Protest crime, notably the misnamed coastal 'wrecking',[12] animal maiming and above all arson have received detailed coverage.[13] So too have social crimes, those technically outside the criminal law, but largely sanctioned by the bulk of rural communities, especially wood-stealing, poaching and smuggling.[14] Other dominant offences, especially sheep-stealing, have been shown to be very complex; sheep-stealers ranged from inadequate or hard-pressed or greedy farmers and butchers, to literally starving labourers.[15]

Chadwick also perceived linkages between crime, public disorder, notably that organic to social protest, and the deficiencies of countryside policing. In his estimation, there was a form of linear development, emanating from the social conflict in the post-war, poor-relief theatre, repeated during both the

[7] Esp. C. Steedman, *Policing the Victorian Community: The Formation of English Provincial Police Forces, 1856–80* (London, 1984), pp. 25–26.

[8] R. Wells, 'Social Protest, Class, Conflict and Consciousness in the English Countryside, 1700–1880', in M. Reed and R. Wells (eds), *Class, Conflict and Protest in the English Countryside, 1700–1880* (London, 1990), pp. 174–79.

[9] R. Wells, 'Popular Protest and Social Crime: The Evidence of Criminal Gangs in Southern England, 1790–1860', *Southern History*, 13 (1991).

[10] V.A.C. Gattrell, 'The Decline of Theft and Violence in Victorian and Edwardian England', in V. Gattrell, B. Lenman and G. Parker (eds), *Crime and the Law: The Social History of Crime in Western Europe since 1500* (London, 1980), p. 265.

[11] J.G. Rule, 'Social Crime in the Rural South in the Eighteenth and Early Nineteenth Centuries', above, Chapter 8, pp. 153–68.

[12] J.G. Rule, 'Wrecking and Coastal Plunder', in D. Hay et al. (eds), *Albion's Fatal Tree* (Harmondsworth, 1975).

[13] R. Wells, 'The Development of the English Rural Proletariat and Social Protest, 1700–1850', and J.E. Archer, 'The Wells-Charlesworth Debate: A Personal Comment on Arson in Norfolk and Suffolk', both reprinted in Reed and Wells (eds), *Class, Conflict and Protest*. J.E. Archer, *'By a Flash and a Scare': Incendiarism, Animal Maiming and Poaching in East Anglia, 1815–70* (Oxford, 1990).

[14] B. Bushaway, 'From Custom to Crime: Wood Gathering in Eighteenth and Early Nineteenth-Century England: A Focus for Conflict in Hampshire, Wiltshire and the South', in J.G. Rule (ed.), *Outside the Law: Studies in Crime and Order, 1650–1850* (Exeter, 1982), C. Winslow, 'Sussex Smugglers', in Hay et al. (eds) *Albion's Fatal Tree*. P.B. Munsche, *Gentlemen and Poachers: The English Game Laws, 1670–1831* (Cambridge, 1981).

[15] See below, Ch. 10, pp. 237–53. R. Wells, 'Sheep Rustling in Yorkshire in the Age of the Industrial and Agricultural Revolutions', *Northern History*, 20 (1984); idem, 'Social Protest, Class, Conflict and Consciousness', pp. 179–80.

Swing uprising and the next round of riotous rural protestations accompanying the critical implementation of the hated Poor Law Amendment Act in 1835–36. Chadwick went on to identify the urgent need for the termination of ancient system of amateur parochial constables by a fully professionalised *preventative* police. The centrality of the Old Poor Law to the Swing rising, with widespread parochial permutations of intimidation, negotiations and crowd enforcement of more generous social-security benefits, was speedily seized on by utilitarians to support their demands for radical reform of the Elizabethan relief system. In the infamous rural query fifty-three, respondents to the Poor Law Commissioners' questionnaire, circulated in 1832, were invited to evaluate Poor Law administration as a specific and major cause of Swing. After the implementation of the Amendment Act across much of rural England in 1835–36, Chadwick emphasised to Home Secretary Lord John Russell, in August 1836, the need for police to contain both the vagrants he perceived as among the primary authors of countryside crime, and the 'tumults connected with the administration of relief' under the new legislation.[16] The experience of Swing, rather than the current Chartist threat, was uppermost in the minds of many magistrates, including those in the predominantly rural southern counties of Wiltshire, Hampshire and East Sussex, who successfully supported the introduction of the permissory Rural Constabulary Act, when the topic was discussed at their Quarter Sessions in 1839–40.[17]

In some senses, the 1830s not only saw recurrent revolts in the countryside, but an interaction of revolt and state response, itself germinating renewed protest which served to stimulate further statutory intervention in the form of legislation facilitating professional policing. The principal periods of public disorder, dominated by the Captain Swing insurrection of 1830, have been described, analysed and debated.[18] The famous episode of the Tolpuddle Martyrs has been firmly placed in a broader context, as a rural reflection of buoyant urban and industrial trade unionism in the early 1830s,[19] while the entire question of rural

---

[16] P. Dunkley, *The Crisis of the Old Poor Law in England, 1795–1834* (New York, 1982), pp. 95–98, 106–7, 109–110. S.G. and E.O.A. Checkland (eds), *The Poor Law Report of 1834* (Harmondsworth, 1974), pp. 121, 123, 498, 410. A. Brundage, 'Ministers, Magnates and Reformers: The Genesis of the Rural Constabulary Act of 1839', *Parliamentary History*, 5 (1986), pp. 57–58.

[17] R. Wells, 'Implementation and Non-Implementation of the 1839–40 Police Acts in Sussex', *Policing and Society*, 1 (1991). R.D. Storch, 'Policing Rural Southern England before the Police; Opinion and Practice, 1830–1856', in D. Hay and F. Synder (eds), *Policing and Prosecution in Britain, 1750–1850* (Oxford, 1989), p. 82. D. Foster, *The Rural Constabulary Act of 1839* (London, 1982). R.E. Forster, 'A Cure for Crime? The Hampshire Rural Constabulary 1839–1856', *Southern History*, 12 (1980).

[18] E.J. Hobsbawm and G. Rudé, *Captain Swing* (Harmondsworth, 1973). A. Charlesworth, *Social Protest in a Rural Society: The Spatial Diffusion of the Captain Swing Disturbances of 1830–1831*, Historical Geography Series, 1 (Norwich, 1979). B. Reay, *The Last Rising of the Agricultural Labourers* (Oxford, 1990).

[19] R. Wells, 'Tolpuddle in the Context of English Agrarian Labour History, 1780–1850', in J.G. Rule (ed.), *British Trade Unionism, 1750–1850: The Formative Years* (London, 1988).

working-class consciousness in the early nineteenth century has been addressed.[20] Finally, the Chartist presence in the south has been described, with its initial extension to countryside locations, and subsequent apparent contraction to urban centres.[21] But to date there is no microstudy of any specific location, of the interaction of popular protest, social and other crime. Such a study is needed in order to examine, first, the relationships between these phenomena and, secondly, the participants. Among other things, it may identify whether there was a criminal class or subculture, and the link – if any – between these actors and those engaging in protest.

Burwash, in East Sussex, was a classic exemplar of the 'open' village. Heavily wooded, it was typically High Wealden, with a total acreage exceeding 7000. Land ownership was diverse. The two largest proprietors, the Earls of Ashburnham, and the gentry Fullers, who had made their fortune from the now virtually extinct iron industry, were both absentees. So too were several other owners, with more modest acreages, some of whom farmed at least parts of their estates directly, through bailiffs. The largest resident owners, the Haviland family, were also considerable owner occupiers, farming some 430 of their 550 acres. A handful of substantial tenants, or part tenant part owner-occupiers, cultivated over 190 acres. Rather more in a similar category farmed between 100 and 190 acres, and a larger number still occupied farms from fifty to one hundred acres. Numerous farmers represented that other considerable Wealden phenomenon, the small farmer with under fifty acres.[22]

A fair proportion of these lesser agricuturalists were dual-occupationists – another notable Wealden feature – with tradesmen, and after the 1830 liberalisation of the licensing laws, beerhouse keepers, who also farmed to degrees. Burwash, partially because of its status as a decayed market town, retained an annual fair. The village was the nature centre for farms widely dispersed outside the nucleated settlement at the heart of the parish, and it – and the lesser settlement at the Weald adjacent to the Common in the west – both lay on an important east-west highway, with a constant stream of foot and horse-drawn traffic. The parish also had a sizeable service industry. Most trades were represented, among them blacksmiths, builders, carpenters and joiners, wheelwrights, sadlers and harness-makers, publicans, butchers, bakers, and a range of other shopkeepers, including the ubiquitous general traders, commonly dubbed 'grocers and drapers'. Some merchants, of livestock and wood products, as befitting a woodland rural economy, ranged from modest capitalists to the petty entrepreneurs, notably the hucksters who dealt in especially perishable countryside produce with constant conveyance to urban markets at

[20] Wells, 'Social Protest, Class, Conflict and Consciousness'.
[21] Idem, 'Southern Chartism', above, Chapter 7, pp. 127–51.
[22] ESCRO, Land Tax/Burwash. C.J. Barnes (ed.), *The 1851 East Sussex Census Index*, x (Burwash, Ticehurst, Etchingham) (Hastings, 1989). Burwash, tithe schedule, 1842, Worthing Public Library.

places like Tunbridge Wells, Lewes, Brighton and Hastings. Higlers were essential middlemen in that burgeoning industry, chicken fattening, and Burwash lay in one major district of it, centred on the neighbouring parish of Heathfield. There was a little stone-quarrying, and several of those landed people with appropriate clays also diversified into brickmaking, some on an extensive scale. Thus, for a rural community, the economy – however depressed for much of the period under review – was very diverse.[23]

If all of these factors were essential ingredients in Burwash's 'open' categorisation, the final facet was the absence of any unambiguous squire. It is possible that the last resident modest landower from the Constable family, who was a county JP, did function as a squire until the end of the French wars in 1815, but the documentation is too poor for a definitive appraisal. Thereafter only the Havilands could realistically have aspired to such a status. However, while successive heads did periodically play a leading role in the parish vestry, their attendance according to the detailed records extant for the key period between 1819 and 1833, was too intermittent to ensure real leadership, and they narrowly avoided bankruptcy in 1849.[24] Two other candidates, again successive heads this time of the stable legal firm of Philcox and Baldock, who passed their interests down from fathers to sons, bought their way into land; but they remained very much men of business, and as this included the clerkship to the local Petty Sessions – dominated by the unambiguous gentry Courthopes of neighbouring Ticehust – and the receiver of tithes for the rectors of Burwash, this effectively disbarred themselves from any squirearchial aspirations they may have remotely entertained. Social leadership by default perhaps devolved on the Anglican rectors and their curates; one, the Rev. Egerton whose incumbency (with a short break) stretched from 1857 to 1888 certainly saw himself as the village 'boss', as he once privately put it.[25]

But the Anglican clergy's position was itself ambiguous. First, again, like so many Wealden communities, Burwash hosted a vigorous and probably growing Dissenting sector – the Wesleyans adding to non-Anglican churches within reach of Burwash folk with the erection of a new chapel on the Common in 1843 – who had little time, in the main, for either the Anglican Church or its incumbents. In this the tithe was but one, be it important element. Secondly, there was a healthy coexistence, sometimes amounting to combination, of general insubordination and political radicalism, which provided another source of anticlericalism. Although the Rev. Gould was resident, first as curate and then as rector, from 1824 to 1867, and was also something of both a paternalist and a low-keyed evangelical, he himself admitted that his influence was modest. As

---

[23] Barnes, *The 1851 East Sussex Census*, 1841 census, PRO, HO, 107/1108. Kelly's, *Directory of East Sussex* (1867 edition).

[24] Select vestry minutes, 1819–33, ESCRO. Par. 284/12/1. R. Tournay to J.W. Roper, 19 January 1851, Kent County Record Office (KCRO), U840/E692. *Sussex Weekly Advertiser*, 29 July 1793.

[25] R. Wells (ed.), *Victorian Village: The Diaries of the Reverend John Coker Egerton of Burwash, 1857–1888* (Gloucester, 1992), passim.

he put it publicly in 1859, he wanted to see 'less drunkenness, fewer il-
legitimate children, more religion' amongst his parishioners: and, he concluded,
not only had he been thirty-five years 'among them', but 'it grieved him to see
so little good from his labours . . . he could not say that his was a model parish,
he wished he could'.[26]

Although the sources are inadequate to any detailed analysis of Burwash's
economic history during the French Wars, there is no reason to doubt that its
experiences were in any way fundamentally different from other Wealden communities with woodland agrarian economic structures. Cereal production no
doubt expanded, possibly at the expense of pastoral, encouraged by the apparently irreversible increase in prices. And if farmers in the main prospered, some
of that wealth was spent in farm investment and personal consumerism, both
of which benefited local tradesmen. Meanwhile the labour supply, while depleted
by mobilisation, was largely adequate to demand, though shortages were beginning to slow down harvesting operations. Post-1815 evidence suggests that labourers' wartime wages did not rise commensurate with living costs, and that
farmworkers with large families were in receipt of allowances in aid of wages
under the Poor Law, for at least part of the year.
  Demobilisation and the baby-boom which began in the 1810s coincided with
the onset of agrarian depression, fuelled principally by cereal price collapses
from artificial wartime levels and the considerable fall in demand for meat, as
the armed forces were speedily run down. Burwash's population rose from 1603
in 1811 to 1937 in 1821. Although hop-acreages expanded from 143 to 381
between 1807 and 1821, the additional demand for labour – including women
and children – from this source, did not compensate for shrinkages in cereals
and less intensive farming. The village vestry, in common with Poor Law authorities across the region, struggled to contain the resultant oversupply of labour,
fierce downward pressure on wages and under- and unemployment. Farmers
preferred to give employment to married men, though this did not eradicate
the need for wage supplements for those with two, three or more children.
Finding work for boys and youths also devolved on the vestry, but of all the
problems faced this proved the most intractable and an entire generation of
young men became rebellious in the face of an uncertain present and prospectless
futures. They were the subject of various make work schemes, and were joined
by older men, especially during the winters when a high proportion of those
not considered 'the best description of Labourers', were turned off. Experimenta-
tion with the Roundsmen system, which distributed unemployed labourers on
a *pro rata* basis between farmers, were extended to journeymen craftsmen, who
were apportioned similarly among the master tradesmen. But this failed to solve
especially wintertime unemployment, and gangs were put to work on the roads,

---

[26] *Sussex Agricultural Express*, 24 May 1859.

in hired quarries and on the ninety-six acre Bough Farm acquired by the parish.[27]

Public authority engaged with the necessity to organise employment for adolescent and teenage girls, and usually resorted to paying premiums to such employers who would give them residential farmwork or domestic service. Other problems, especially housing shortages, also vexed vestrymen, who responded by guaranteeing and commonly part-paying inflated rentals in the private sector, and increasing densities in accommodation – including the substantial poorhouse – the parish owned or hired. Although migration and some publicly-funded emigration kept demographic growth down in the 1820s – the 1831 census revealed population growth of a mere 29 over 1821 – this levelling off did not stop the 1820s from witnessing acute social conflict in the critical theatre of poor relief. Bankruptcy repeatedly threatened the parish, forcing cuts in relief rates, in part achieved by the appointment of a salaried professional overseer of the poor, whose job was to investigate every claim minutely; to legitimise reductions; and where possible to rule against any assistance.

That conflict continued to hinge on the village vestry until 1835 when the radical Poor Law Amendment Act ended Burwash's virtual autonomy in social-security affairs, and placed the parish with eight others in a new Union centred on neighbouring Ticehurst. The Act's ostensible termination of all outdoor relief to able-bodied men and their families, except medical aid, may have been partly if covertly circumvented, but it did initiate fairly fundamental change for that sizeable component in the village workforce previously dependent to degrees on repetitive, if not invariably regular assistance from the rates, despite the almost unremittant economic gloom during the rest of the decade. Under the new system there was no protection for farmworkers from under- and unemployment, with the exception of road-work; and, despite theoretical pronounciations to the contrary, wages did not rise. The alternative, resort to the workhouse, was bitterly resisted by most men with families. As one said he 'don't like the thoughts of "breaking up his establishment"', namely surrendering the tenancy of his home, which meant getting out of the workhouse necessitated finding a new job *and* a new cottage. One ramification of this transformed reality was the claim of 'half starvation' made during early 1838. A number of workers, including journeymen tradesmen, confirmed that many subsisted on a 'diet . . . almost entirely of potatoes', and even then only through periodic pawning, including essential items of clothing. One emphasised that he was 'quite willing to work, but something to eat he *must* have'.[28]

Further departures for locations at home and abroad kept population growth to a minimum, rising to 2093 in 1841 and 2227 in 1851, but the oversupply of

[27] R. Wells, 'Social Conflict and Protest in the English Countryside: A Rejoinder', reprinted in Reed and Wells, *Class, Conflict and Protest*, pp. 67–72. BPP, 'Report of the Commission on the Poor Laws', appendix B, answer to rural queries, pp. 493–5a. *Sussex Weekly Advertiser*, 3 September 1821. Newspaper cuttings and miscellaneous documents, ESCRO, SAS, Co/C/230.

[28] *Brighton Patriot*, 13 March and 3 April 1838.

labour doggedly remained a perennial problem, if a marginally reducing one after 1840. 'There is scarcely any part of the year', it was said formally to the Poor Law Board in 1859, 'except at the Seasons of Haymaking, Harvest & Hoppicking that there are not Paupers' – a euphemism for farmworkers – 'out of employ in Burwash'. A little amelioration continued from traditional itinerancy of labourers during the summers, going off to Kent for haymaking, to Romney Marsh, and back to the South Downs for the earlier harvests there, before returning home for the local harvest; some men then went again to Kent for the hop-picking. And, in addition, the woods provided especially wintertime employment, and a modicum of employ for women folk, notably in shaving hop-poles, features unknown outside wooded districts. Even so, life remained a struggle, with family earnings during the again untypical twin harvests of corn and then hops, at best severely stretched, to make ends meet. When Sarah, the wife of labourer Robert Dann, was observed in her 'kitchen . . . counting the Tallies I have received for Hoppicking and also some Silver and halfpence', it may have looked 'a lot of Money', but as she observed, 'Yes I owe it in a great many places', no doubt to clear debts with village tradesfolk, the baker, the grocer and draper, and the shoemaker, and to pay the rent.[29]

Burwash's reputation had long been coloured by its participation in smuggling which went back at least to the days of the notorious Hawkhurst gang who terrorised much of the county and West Kent in the mid eighteenth century, and almost certainly before.[30] Smuggling seems to have continued unabated, as goods from the coast were passed through the Weald *en route* to London, but if Burwash was not the scene of any of the violent confrontations between revenue and excise men and smuggling parties which were common enough in the High Weald in the immediate post-war years, many inhabitants engaged in it, periodically at least. One man in the witness-box blandly admitted that 'There is smuggling in these parts'. A farmer paid in contraband gin for stolen lime-kiln fuel. Smuggled spirits were on sale at most licensed – and unlicensed – premises. The depression hit the drink trade, causing some proprietors to relinquish their licences, encouraging illicit retailers to offer a compensatory service. One example involved the Russell family; when the licence of the Wheel Inn lapsed in the mid 1820s, adjacent premises owned by one of the Russell kin supplied its place, generating confusion over which – if either – was legitimate.[31] But it was other developments, not ostensibly connected with smuggling, principally between the end of the war in 1815 and the 1840s, which

[29] Clerk, Ticehurst Union to the PLC, 5 February 1858 and 7 May 1859, PRO, MH 12/13146. Deposition, Sarah Dann, 12 September 1842, ESCRO, QR/E896. BPP, 169 (1839), xx.

[30] *A Handbook for Travellers. Kent and Sussex* (London, 1858), p. 232. P. Wragge, 'Social and Economic History', in W. Page (ed.), *Victoria County History of Sussex*, ii (1907), p. 200.

[31] Battle Petty Sessions minutes, 1825–32; deposition Keziah Collins, 8 December 1802; Land Tax, Burwash for the 1820s, ESCRO, PSBA 5; QR/E694; LT/Burwash. *Sussex Advertiser*, 31 July 1826.

gave the village a notoriety as the seat of 'Robbery, violence and lawlessness of all kinds', and 'the birth place or sheltering place of rick-burners, sheep stealers, and thieves'.[32]

In 1822 – perhaps the worst year of the recession – a petition formally stated that 'the labouring Class' was

> very dissatisfied and irritable, regardless of advice, disrespectful and insolent to their superiors, riotous and turbulent in their dispositions and behaviour, and appear to be quite ready for extreme acts of depredation.

A supportive catalogue of evidence included anonymous threatening letters, arson, malicious damage, assaults on overseers of the poor, and the forcible release of protesters taken prisoner by special constables unequal to the maintenance of public order. In 1821 a 'riotous' posse of protesters pursued prisoners being taken to the county gaol into Heathfield – a 'very daring outrage' – though on this occasion their object was defeated. Informers were also subjected to mob violence. On brothers Thomas and Henry Hicks 'leaving Church' on 14 December 1823, they 'were followed down Burwash Town by about fifteen young Men of the Place Laborers and Others who made a great Noise and hallooed them . . . for about a quarter of a Mile', and then they were assaulted. John Flurry, the domineering overseer of the poor, was one a notable victim of arson, with damages totalling £200 to his barn and its contents. The receipt of scores of threatening letters at this time suggested a campaign, which officials attributed to a 'combination of paupers'.[33] When the vestry ruled against traditional public expenditure on Guy Fawkes celebrations, a band of men raided the parish fuel store, openly carrying away faggots for the bonfire. Even a decision not to ring St Bartholomew's bells on Christmas Day 1820 was rudely challenged by an assembly determined on customary celebrations. Moreover, the local judiciary were not immune, as posses of social-security claimants had 'tumultuously and alarmingly beset the Magistrates on the Bench', who were reputedly only 'too well acquainted with the State of Burwash' in December 1821. Larceny rates were allegedly unprecedented. This picture of virtual social disequilibrium embraced forms of both open and covert populist protest, elements of what can only be regarded as class struggle, together with escalating scale of theft, which lumps together many components of what historians have been concerned to categorise, including social crime. Other incidents, including collective protests by lesser ratepayers, serve to complicate the picture. That

---

[32] J.C. Egerton, *Village Instruction: Twelve Sermons* (Tunbridge Wells, 1892), p. 115. C.F. Trower, 'Burwash', *Sussex Archaeological Collections*, 10 (1858), p. 113.

[33] Wells, 'Rejoinder'. Letters to Peel from C. Jenkins, and E.J. Curteis, Battle, enclosing Flurry's deposition, 11 and 13 November 1822, PRO, HO 64/1, fos 46–47, 307–12. Recognizance to keep the peace, Henry Blackford, 15 August 1816; indictment, J. Sellings jnr and snr, J. Langridge and S. Elliott, Epiphany Quarter Sessions 1820; deposition, Thomas Hicks, 27 January 1824, ESCRO, QR/E746, 763, 779.

these occurred simultaneously will not cause much surprise, but their inter-relationship warrants analysis.[34]

Perhaps the most elusive element in this scenario is the origin, diffusion, and continuity of Paineite or democratic radicalism from the 1790s. There is no suggestion of any organised grouping at Burwash, though the availability of Paine's *Rights of Man* must be assumed on the count of its universal circulation. Family and other interpersonal links were probably important. Jonathan Harmer, the 'ardent republican' and Heathfield mason who emigrated to the USA in 1794 to escape Prime Minister Pitt's so-called reign of terror against populist politicians, retained communications with 'Kinsman Harmer of Burwash' from the sanctuary of New York, only to return to Heathfield in May 1800 on inheriting his father's business. Harmer was thereafter a regular visitor to Burwash, and it is unlikely that his activities were restricted to trade.[35] As in other villages, there were demonstrations in favour of Queen Caroline in late 1820, though at Burwash this form of 'symbolic rebellion' – 'by Several Hundred people [who] paraded the Street accompanied by a Band of Music' – against the Tory state, had immediate targets in those 'respectable inhabitants', including the eighty-five year old rector, who refused to illuminate their premises. The crowd stoned recalcitrants' houses, demolishing 'above Ninety Windows' at the Rectory'.[36] Burwash was among several parishes in the hinterland of Battle known to be a centre of support for William Cobbett and, as we shall see, several inhabitants attended his lecture at Battle on 16 October 1830, rallying to his support when he was subsequently prosecuted for sedition.

Political motivation certainly played a part in stimulating, and broadening, Burwash's contribution to the Captain Swing rising in November 1830. Burwash was the third parish to rise in Sussex, as the insurrection spread into the county from Kent. Interestingly, the second, Brede, had strong smuggling contacts with Burwash, and the rising at the latter paralleled events at the former two days earlier. Both initially focused on their respective salaried overseers. At Brede the officer was literally carted by a triumphant crowd across the parish boundary. At Burwash 'the labouring population' led by three men, 'assembled *en masse*' on 7 November. Their target, Freeman, preemptively fled thirty miles to Rochester; frustrated, the assembly passed a motion 'with a threat of severe punishment if he was ever seen again in Burwash'.[37]

---

[34] Vestry minute, 1 January 1820; gaol calendars, Epiphany 1822, Easter 1824; depositions, S. Elliott, J. Westover, W. Eastwood, R. Button, and J. Cruttenden, 7 November 1821, and Thomas Hicks, 27 January 1824; G. Darby to the Clerk of the Peace, 25 December 1821, ESCRO, Par. 284/12/1; QR/E769–70, 779. *Sussex Weekly Advertiser*, 7 May 1821.

[35] P. Lucas, *Heathfield Memorials* (1910), pp. 104–6, 174–75. C.L. Remnant, 'Jonathan Harmer's Terroltas', *Sussex Archaeological Collections*, 100 (1962), pp. 142–45.

[36] *Sussex Weekly Advertiser*, 20 and 27 November 1820. Rev. Gouldsmith to the Clerk of the Peace, 11 January 1821, ESCRO, QR/E768. For the context and interpretation such incidents, see C. Calhoun, *The Question of Class Struggle: Social Foundations of Popular Radicalism during the Industrial Revolution* (Oxford, 1982), pp. 108–11.

[37] The standard authority is Hobsbawm and Rudé, *Captain Swing*. Their copious table of Swing

continued

Against a backdrop of several incendiary attacks in the district, the Burwash crowd reconvened on 8 November. One sector joined contingents from other parishes which formed a mass lobby of an emergency meeting of the judiciary at Battle, chaired by George Courthope. The Bench published its resolutions, condemning arson as unEnglish, evasively attributing it to the malignancy of strangers; the magistracy urged farmers in each parish to devise methods of creating full employment, and promised to enforce civil tranquillity. The crowd was in effective control of the town when the first troops arrived on the scene, but there was no confrontation with this cavalry detachment.[38] The other Burwash group went across the border to Robertsbridge, the scene of another indigenous rising against the professional overseer. He, like Freeman, fled, but a consider-able number of farmers had covened at the main inn, and the crowd – now swelled by groups from other places – proceeded to force them to concede wage increases. The crowd was flush with this victory when the lay tithe-proprietor, returning from the magisterial meeting at Battle, fortuitously ar-rived. Some clergymen had already, if grudgingly and parsimoniously, reduced tithes, in response to farmers opportunistically claiming that tithe exactions preventing them from upping wages. Now the Robertsbridge crowd chanting 'none of your paltry 10 p Cent', successfully demanded a 25 per cent reduc-tion.[39]

The genesis of two Swing crowds from one parish – be it to participate in grander assemblies in neighbouring locations – on one day is impressive. On 9 November Burwash activists convened again, to lobby their own vestry forcibly to agree to wage levels conceded at Robertsbridge, and more. The additional demands reflected recent relief cuts.They insisted on the restoration of child supplements payable from the third child, and eligibility for such payments was extended from current cut-off points, to fourteen for boys and twelve for girls, 'for under that age they are not able to support themselves'. In return, the protesters assured the 'Gentlemen' of the vestry that 'we will assist you in every extremity that ever may be required', and to this militant statement added the uncompromising assertion that, 'We do not intend for any more Tythe to be paid in the Parish of Burwash'. From this point two things are clear. First the politicised elements among the activists, the 'disaffected persons' and 'read-ers of Cobbett', had gained the upper hand. Secondly, Burwash was a district epicentre of the revolt. At this moment, one of the extensive Russell family,

---

continued

incidents comprised in appendix III, does not list this mobilisation, nor another on 9 November. For a brief reevaluation of the Swing crisis, see Wells, 'Social Protest, Class, Conflict and Conscious-ness', pp. 159–69. *Rochester Gazette*, 16 November 1830. Wells, *Victorian Village*, pp. 82, 254, 293.

[38] Sir Charles Webster, Battle, and fourteen JPs, Battle, to Peel, 9 and 12 November 1830, PRO, HO 52/10, fos 388–89, 394–95. *Hastings Iris*, 13 November 1830.

[39] *The Times*, 12 November 1830. *Brighton Herald*, 13 November 1830. R. Davenport, Robertsbridge, and E.J. Curteis, Battle, to H.B. Curteis, 8 and 10 November 1830, ESCRO, AMS 5995/3/10, 13. Webster, and J. Collingwood, Cranbrook, Kent, to Peel, 9 and 10 November 1830, PRO, HO, 52/8, fos 166–69; 52/10, fos 388–89.

almost certainly Francis the small-scale farmer (and current proprietor of the relicensed Wheel Inn where some key activists met to plan their next moves), slipped the parish border to warn that Mayfield was to be visited twice: once, immediately, to expel their overseer, and secondly on fairday, 12 November.[40]

Major tithe reductions – or abolition – now became a central demand in a rash of parochial mobilisations between 9 and 12 November in most neighbouring parishes, namely Etchingham, Ticehurst, Heathfield, Mayfield, Brightling and Rotherfield. Supportive elements came from other locations, including Burwash. At Etchingham the rector agreed to halve his tithe demands. By this stage, farmers, who had shown a distinct disinclination to fight their workforce and neighbours through refusals to become special constables, began to support the uprising. As John Baldock, the farming solicitor from Burwash, judiciously and later put it: 'Many of the Farmers . . . did not . . actually instigate the Labourers to rise, yet they evinced approbation rather than displeasure at their so doing.' Moreover, the strengthening political strand to the rising, some said spurred by both the recent continental revolutions, and the opening developments in Britain's own major crisis round the Reform Bill issue, became unmistakeable, and – briefly – very ominous. By the time the crowd containing Burwash folk reached Rotherfield, after a week of daily mobilisation, they were equipped with 'inflammatory Placards', entitled 'Nice Pickings', which stated the salaries paid to select sinecurists, and the incomes of senior Anglican clergymen. These High Wealden events comprised a central part of the intelligence which led the long-serving Lord Lieutenant of Sussex to describe the 'general prevailing opinion that all governments must now submit to the will of the people & Cannot resist redressing all real or imaginary grievances of the labouring population'.[41]

By this juncture, 14 November, justice Courthope was 'so fatigued & harassed that I can scarcely put two connected sentences together'. At the end of the month he reported local 'society in a very feverish state', by which time the jails were filling with Swing activists for trial at the approaching Assize and Quarter Sessions.[42] Only one man from Burwash appears to have been arrested, reflecting the attitude of the farmers, no doubt also worried about possible reprisals, together with the fact that little violence had accompanied action in the home parish. Even if Burwash people were responsible elsewhere, they were less likely

---

[40] Burwash petition, no date, forwarded by the vestry to H.B. Curteis, 9 November 1830, ESCRO, AMS, 5995/3/12. N. to W. Stone, 8 November 1830, PRO, HO, 52/10, fo. 525.

[41] Sir Charles Blunt, Heathfield, to Peel, 10, 11 and 14 November; Courthope to Egremont, enclosed Egremont to Peel, 7 and 9 November; J.C. Sharpe, Northiam, and Webster, to Peel, 9 and 12 November 1830, PRO, HO, 52/10, fos 386–87, 397–98, 523–24, 526–9, 619–9. BPP, 'Report of the Commission on the Poor Laws', appendix B, p. 495a, Baldock's answer to query 53. Resolution, Etchingham occupiers of land, 10 November 1830, ESCRO, AMS, 5995/3/14.

[42] Courthope to Home Office under secretary Phillipps, 14 November 1830, PRO, HO 52/10, fos 403–8.

to be recognised away from home by potential prosecution witnesses, who were much more likely categorically to identify violent personnel from their own parish.[43]

Nevertheless, parochial authority in the village was not slow to reestablish itself. On 16 December Freeman's formal resignation was accepted, and the intrepid local farmer Richard Button, who we will reencounter as a principal actor in the struggle against criminal elements, took over as assistant overseer. Swing victories were soon reversed. Child benefits payable on the third child were the first casualty before the old year was out; and in the first week of the new, wages for married childless and single men employed by the parish were reduced. Unemployed bachelors were soon to face the option of a derisory 2s. 6d. per week, or incarceration in the poorhouse. Thereafter the vestry, and Poor Law administration, resumed its centrality for fierce social dissension, again exacerbated by near-bankruptcy, with even vestrymen being summonsed for the non-payment of rates.[44]

If this continuation of problems remained unameliorated owing to unremittant agricultural depression, the unfolding Reform Bill crisis enhanced political awareness in Burwash in common with most rural communities. The crisis' resolution hardly answered the radicalism of the political positioning revealed by the Swing episode, for while many of Burwash's tenant farmers were enfranchised by the famous Chandos Clause, which extended the vote to tenants paying the low annual rental of fifty pounds, a large number of petty agriculturalists remained excluded from the parliamentary political forum, together with all working people. Opposition to this state of affairs was reflected by the foundation of a branch of the National Union of the Working Classes whose raison d'être hinged on further agitation to achieve manhood suffrage. Although the record is hopelessly defective, the sources do reveal that the Burwash branch comprised 'working men' and farmers – presumably the unenfranchised little variety – and we may also surmise that it facilitated the monitoring of political developments.[45]

The maintenance of the radical presence was no doubt responsible for further politicisation over the Poor Law Amendment Act. Because it was engineered by the Whigs, and supported by the Tories, most ostensibly during Peel's hundred days of government in 1834–35, which coincided with the first round of moves to actually implement the Act with the demarcation of the new Poor Law Unions, it not only, as Dr Bohstedt has written, brought the 'concrete significance of national policies right to the doorsteps of the working poor', it also comprised a massive indictment of the recently reformed political system. As one labour

---

[43] For considerations respecting the prosecution of Swing activists, see R. Wells, 'Rural Rebels in Southern England in the 1830s', in C. Emsley and J. Walvin, *Artisans, Peasants and Proletarians, 1760–1860* (1985), pp. 136–37.

[44] Vestry minutes, esp. 16, 23 and 30 December 1830, 8 January 1831 and April 1832, ESCRO, Par. 284/12/1. For Button, see below p. 191.

[45] M. Reed, 'Social Change and Social Conflict in Nineteenth-Century England: A Comment', reprinted in Reed and Wells, *Class, Conflict and Protest*, p. 107.

activist declaimed at a meeting in neighbouring Healthfield, the 'first reformed Parliament passed the poor Law', a 'despotic Measure', which through incarceration in the new workhouses punished those unable to support themselves like 'a common fellon'.[46]

In the event, neither Burwash nor other component parishes in the Ticehurst Union were seats of the mobilisations against the new Poor Law, despite Courthope's anticipation of universal 'formidable resistance'. Three reasons may be advanced. First, the Ticehurst Union did not commence operations until the autumn of 1835, some months after most other Unions in East Sussex, which galvanised the disturbances. Secondly, the date of Ticehurst's launch, coincided with the hop-harvest which engaged everybody with adequate health in an operation critical to domestic economic equilibrium, and moreover quickly followed the legal offensive against protesters from other Unions in the district. Thirdly, after representations that renewed rioting might commence in the autumn, army detachments were stationed in Battle with cavalry patrols through the entire district. But, if Swing is any guide, it must be likely that some Burwash folk participated in the earlier populist moves against the Act. These hinged on the adjacent Battle Union, with each of the initial meetings of the Board of guardians besieged by protesters, moves to 'march to London with a view of laying their Complaints' before the Poor Law Commission, riots in the neighbouring parishes of Ewhurst, Mountfield and Sedlescombe, and the foundation of a new agrarian trade union, the United Brothers, with its administration centred in the latter village. The Brothers are not known to have established a branch in Burwash, and indeed had been extinguished by a ferocious lock-out before the Ticehurst Poor Law Union started.[47]

The maintenance and possibly the strengthening of the radical, democratic movement in Burwash occurred in direct response to the horrors of the new social-security system. If this cannot be proved, it is suggested by subsequent events. First, the discussions respecting the creation of a friendly society in 1835, largely to make better provision for working men when sick than available under the Amendment Act, revealed great hostility to any charitable aid by paternalist subscriptions to the funds, expressed in the unmistakable language of class: the

> labouring Men appear to be so decided in confining themselves to their own views, that it is much to be doubted whether any Plan of a Sick Club would succeed with them which did not originate from their own Class, even if patronised by the principal Gentry.[48]

---

[46] J. Bohstedt, *Riots and Community Politics in England and Wales, 1790–1810* (1983), p. 220. J. Durant to W. Day, 25 July 1835, WSCRO, Goodwood 1575.

[47] Wells, 'Resistance to the New Poor Law', above, Chapter 6, pp. 91–125.

[48] Wells, 'Rural Rebels', pp. 155–56.

Secondly, the attempts to create a southern equivalent of the northern anti-Poor Law Movement, in response to parliamentary endorsement of the new measure following investigation by a select committee in 1837–8, rejected changes despite an impressive performance by hostile witnesses, received powerful backing from Burwash. On 23 February 1838 a public meeting, which went on to vote a petition to parliament, was addressed by seven working men, all of whom were married with between four and seven children, bar one bachelor. All detailed their sheer poverty to the crowd.[49] Thirdly, a 'Radical News Club' was created in the village; this seems to have derived from anti-Poor Law campaigning, but in 1838 it not surprisingly hosted a new Chartist branch. Although southern Chartist initiatives into the villages were speedily and effectively countered by the combined offensive of magistrates, Anglican clergymen and the bigger farmers, at least one public meeting was held in Burwash, and – it was said in April 1839 – that 'democratic principles continue to be held in this populous village'.[50] Fourthly, as the sources are so poor for the subsequent course of countryside Chartism, it is impossible to know whether any formal (or informal) grouping obtained, or if Burwash folk were among the subscribers to the Land Plan.[51] But the radical tradition remained: a local farmer spoke of

> much political activity among the agricultural labourers . . . created in a great measure by the general diffusion of cheap Republican journals. Every labourer became a politician, and his inclination began to bend towards equality, he began to look upon his employer as a tyrant, and the Throne and the Church as useless institutions.

and he went on the decry the attendance of 'most labourers' at an anti-Corn Law rally in 1843. The tradition subsequently, if occasionally, surfaced. For example, in 1870 the rector, John Coker Egerton, recorded an encounter and 'a long discussion' in the street, with

> a violent radical named Jesse Thompsett: who turned out to be a regular & old accustomed orator. His abuse of the 'bloody' aristocracy was vehement, if not to the point as regards truth.[52]

In stark contrast to the oscillations in patterns of social protest, and the incidence of populist politicising, crime – of all denominations – exuded perennial characteristics. Clearly, the most incessant, though relatively rarely prosecuted, was pilferage and more substantial theft by workers from their employers. Within

---

[49] *Brighton Patriot*, 13 March 1838.

[50] Ibid., 30 April 1839. T.M. Kenmitz, 'Chartism in Brighton' (unpublished D.Phil. thesis, University of Sussex, 1969), p. 174. Wells, 'Southern Chartism', above, Chapter 7, pp. 127–51. London Working Men's Association, *The Radical Reformers of England, Scotland and Wales to the Irish People* (n.d., 1839). I am indebted for this reference to Dr Malcolm Chase.

[51] Wells, 'Southern Chartism', above, Chapter 7, pp. 127–51.

[52] *Sussex Agricultural Express*, 6 April 1844. Wells, *Victorian Village*, p. 103.

this category, there was considerable conformity to one widely-articulated adage, that 'No labourer can be *honest* and feed a pig';[53] to this should be added chickens and rabbits, equally commonly raised by Burwash people. Cereals and straw comprised the principal targets. Corn and roots were also regularly stolen for human consumption, as were rotten hop-poles for home heating. Regular replacement meant piles of the used article left adjacent to hop-gardens, a feature creating a fertile arena for ambiguity, not least as old-poles were regarded by workers as perks, though not invariably so by farmers. Removal of old poles by non-employees, and the theft of new poles by any party, was less problematic.[54] There were many permutations on this theme. One farmer gave a worker permission to take rabbits.[55] Perks were not restricted to farm labourers; for example carters claimed hay, and coppice workers chips. Codes were somewhat fluid, but they were flouted by some employees, typified by allegations against two carters for recurrent and substantial theft of coal from consignments brought for different customers from a Lewes merchant.[56] Labourers in employment stole food for others when out of work. William Butcup approached Edward Valvick when hand-threshing just across the Etchingham border, with whom Butcup had worked three years previously, 'to let me have a Grist'. Although Valvick, when refusing, stressed his inevitable eviction from his tied cottage if caught, the real reason was that 'I did not know him well enough for that'.[57] Irrespective of the precise motive, in the main this was precisely the type of crime which eluded detection, thereby guaranteeing the 'impunity of depredators', and constituted the multitude of 'minor offences' which never came before the Bench so central to Chadwick's 1839 report.[58] There are strong implications that farmers, especially, expected to be the victims of relatively restrained pilfering by their workers; the paucity of Burwash cases before the courts across a half century is an eloquent testimony.

Wood-stealing retained echoes of customary rights. When Thomas Vidler pleaded guilty to the theft of twenty 'pieces' of hop-poles – valued at 3d. – he

---

[53] Alexander Somerville, *The Whistler at the Plough* (1852; 1989, reprinted, ed. K.D.M. Snell, London), pp. 335–36.

[54] For especially revealing cases see depositions, farmer James Noakes, 9 December 1817 and 26 April 1822, bricklayer Richard Reeves, 29 October 1839, professional policemen Banks, 29 November 1847, and Sergeant Peerless, January 1861; confession, labourer John Clifton, 30 March 1818, ESCRO, QR/E754–5, 777, 865, 928, 1012.

[55] *Sussex Agricultural Express*, 29 May 1847.

[56] Depositions, Walter Gower and others against labourers S. Waterhouse and James Luck, December 1816, ESCRO, QR/E750.

[57] The insight derives from the prosecution, undertaken in unusual circumstances. Butcup responded to the refusal by saying he would raid the place as 'there were not many Barns but what He could get into': Valvick told his employer; and when the barn was entered a week later, Valvick and the police followed footprints three miles across fields to Burwash. Depositions against Butcup, James and George Eastwood, by Valvick and others, 1 December 1847, ESCRO, QR/E928. For the Eastwoods, see below.

[58] BPP, 'Commission on the Constabulary', p. 3, deriving from the testimony of the Upper Division, Lewes Rape, Bench.

explained that 'he picked up the wood for fuel'. There was perhaps recognition of law deemed unjust, behind those parents who sent children out 'pulling hedges and carrying away the wood' in hopes that their age would save them from prosecution.[59] Something not dissimilar coloured perceptions about the legitimacy of helping oneself the vestry's faggot stocks.[60] Less ambiguous was the unmistakable 'social crime', namely poaching in a district particularly noted for the abundance of game. It is difficult to obtain more than the names of those convicted of poaching, before the press commenced more detailed reporting of cases heard at Petty Sessions after 1850.[61] Among those convicted were lesser farmers and their sons, dual-occupationists, master craftsmen and also on one occasion, a parish surgeon. If their motives were primarily sporting, they no doubt resented their exclusion under the Game Laws.[62] Many labourers were convicted, some of them repeatedly, who were able to meet the heavy fines imposed, a feature which suggests that the clandestine fund used to pay fines which the rector – after many years in the parish – got wind of in the 1870s, was operative much earlier.[63] If rabbits were consumed in poachers' families, the sale of hares, and especially partridges and pheasants on the black market, was facilitated by the numerous itinerant dealers in foodstuffs, the hucksters and higlers in contemporary parlance. Their legitimate trading covered illegal business deals, and enabled some poachers to add significantly to family earnings.[64] In 1792 a pair of 'dexterous poachers', Charles Leaney and George Hickmet, had a county-wide notoriety, as the latter had reputedly made a fortune of £1500 through a lengthy career black-marketing 'game for the capital'.[65]

Hucksters changed with the times, most notably when the law was amended in 1831, with the legalisation of the trade in game. Although game retail licences were restricted, their issue enabled hucksters to add legalised traders to their unlicensed customers of old, who continued their under-the-counter trade. Hucksters also acted as fences, encouraging the rural poor to steal, and buying what was thieved. Across the Ticehurst border, when Henry Wheeler was caught stealing fowls at night, red-handed by an armed farmer, Wheeler 'said if it had not been for the Higler he should not have got into such a Snare'. The sheer numbers of labourers raising a few chickens annually encouraged some to sell

---

[59] *Sussex Advertiser*, 25 May 1840. *Brighton Gazette*, 1 May 1851.

[60] Depositions, overseer James French, and innkeeper Edward Carman, 14 September 1818, ESCRO, QR/E757.

[61] An exception from 1830, in which the local Bench seems to have returned the minutes of evidence, rather than the standard summary conviction notice, reveals that very full hearings of the evidence were the rule when defendants pleaded not guilty. Case against H. Weston, 29 September 1830, ESCRO, QR/E805.

[62] Lucas, *Heathfield Memorials*, p. 2. Convictions, farmer Cane, 18 September 1818, farmer's son Baker, 12 November 1821, surgeon Evans, 9 December 1823, and blacksmith Weston, 29 September 1830, ESCRO, QR/E757, 770, 778, 805.

[63] Wells, *Victorian Village*, p. 50. Cf. Munsche, *Gentlemen and Poachers*, pp. 98–99.

[64] *Sussex Weekly Advertiser*, 21 September 1807, 7 November 1820 and 19 January 1826.

[65] Ibid., 30 January, 19 and 26 March 1792.

them in the nearer towns, and the same method was directly used by fowl thieves. The youthful Alfred Ellis and Samuel King, who stole two chickens and a duck from the farm next to the one on which they worked, aroused suspicion while hawking at Hastings, not because of the attempts to sell but because they asked too high a price, and then panicked and dropped it way below those current.[66] A considerable amount of this type of crime was literally grafted onto the huge, continuous, legitimate supply of perishable goods to urban marts. Non-perishable items also figured, though it was said that the 'strict Eye' maintained by urban police forces, notably in Brighton, regularly detected stolen goods; especially valuables offered to pawnbrokers. Nevertheless, the regular trade and those involved, notoriously 'the numerous Carriers and Vans', provided cover for illicit exchanges, including scrap metals.[67] A number of transactions in the late 1830s involved Thomas Dunford, a 'Dealer in Bones and Rags and Marine Stores' in Lewes, and Anthony Buss the driver of one regular cart between Burwash and the county town, owned by John Parsons, haulier, farmer and proprietor of the Bell. At that time, two youngish economically marginal men, Thomas Eastwood a collector and dealer in 'ashes', and Bill Shadwell, who 'goes about fairs', were also engaged in thieving leaden articles, including cisterns, which were cut up and put in sacks for picking up on the night run by Buss for sale to Dunsford.[68]

Yet the towns, and both crooked and legitimate dealers there, were not the only outlet for stolen goods. The range – however incomplete – is quite impressive. Leather stolen from a Mayfield shoemaker was used for shoes by Burwash cobbler Dann who 'made up Leather for any body', and was none too inquisitive about the origin of customers' raw materials.[69] Likewise, Richard Buss, who never quite rose in status from labourer to full-time haulier or carrier/huckster, willingly bought stolen oats at a knock-down price from a local chimney-sweep, who also owed Buss a shilling.[70] Other small-scale entrepreneurs able to mix stolen goods with the legitimately obtained article included the ubiquitous mealmen, whose range of disguises included mixing up hog corn with cereals from several different sources.[71] This evidence suggests a considerable black market linking Burwash with regional towns, but also a significant one within

[66] Depositions, farmer Farrace and 'yeoman' Snoad, 18 November 1839, against Wheeler; and professional constable Duly of Hastings, 12 November 1838, against Ellis and King, ESCRO, QR/E857, 865.

[67] See returns 1836–37 to the Constabulary Commissioners, from esp. Upper Division Lewes Rape, and Frant Petty Sessions, PRO, HO 73/5, pt 2.

[68] Depositions, Dunsford, 5 and 9 September the Rev. Gould's bailiff Carman, 6 September, Beadle Haymen, Lewes, 9 September, and labourer George Coppard, Burwash, 9 September; Buss, examinations, 5 and 9 September 1839, ESCRO, QR/E863.

[69] Depositions, innkeeper Vidler and cooper Best; statement by Buss, 4 April 1847, ESCRO, QR/E925.

[70] Depositions, cordwainer Zachariah King and constable Jenner, both of Mayfield, 19 November 1841, ESCRO, QR/E880.

[71] *Brighton Patriot*, 22 May 1838.

the local rural economy. By its very nature, details of disputes between those participating rarely – if ever – found its way into the records; though where villians gave evidence against their associates, it would be surprising if their motives were solely to escape punishment, and were never conditioned by vengeance in response to being exploited. There is some evidence that crooked middlemen were themselves thought to be legitimate targets. When black-marketeer and huckster Hayward of Heathfield collapsed in a drunken stupor in 1831, young men rifled his pockets, extracting over eleven pounds, observing that such a tidy sum was 'a pretty haul to keep the cricketing up with'.[72]

Burwash inns, and from 1830 the beershops, were central not only to working-class culture (of which many petty entrepreneurs were a part), but also to trade and its intermixture with criminal activities. Trading in the comfort of such places was commonly colourful. In a typical scene at the Bell in 1858, Burwash labourers and a couple of bell-hangers, on their way home from a job, looked on as a horse was bought by a local tradesman from a non-resident. People were also – illegally – gambling with dice; and once the generous quantities of ale on the table to finalise the horse deal were shared, coin-tossing – also illegal – determined who should pay for refills. The intervention of one of the inebriated bell-hangers in the horse transaction led to a dispute over the gold content of sovereigns, which were then pocketed, and a solution sought in a street fight between two of the men. Both were stripped ready for action when the police arrived on the scene.[73]

Nor was perennial gambling in the bars limited to coin-tossing for drinks and various games on 'gambling boards' openly left on tables. When Mary Elliott, an elderly widow from Ashburnham, joined a boisterous group, they immediately had 'a wager of a pot of beer . . . on the respective heights of myself and another woman'. Licensed premises also hosted lively social functions. When the Labour in Vain was raided by the police at 3 a.m. on Sunday 8 July 1842, they encountered diverse people – locals and visitors – 'dancing' in full swing. Although the Bear Inn emerged later as a 'hotel' aiming at the middle-class trade – notably commercial travellers all inns – and beershops provided accommodation for itinerant and temporary workers, who were joined by indigenous young males while they sought new lodgings. For this fluctuating group the bar became a home; and if debts derived from entertainment and promiscuous gambling, such people and other regular customers were also encouraged to incur further debts by the landlords. At the Bell, Parsons had 'a Book shewing the amount . . . owed', including the seven shilling debt of Burwash labourer Edmund Hawkins. When he came in for the second time on 7 August 1839 'to pay for a pot of beer he had that morning', he also paid off 'the old Score', a

[72] Depositions, higher Hayward and labourer S. Manwaring, 24 August 1831, ESCRO, QR/E809.

[73] Despositions, fruiterer Fuller, labourer Peter Sawyer, constable Maynard and bell-hanger Patsy Cunningham, 23 June 1858, ESCRO, QR/E1002.

sum exceeding half a farmworker's weekly wage. No doubt uncertain employment and low wages also underlay loans from publicans, and linkages between indebtedness and crime were often direct.[74]

The Wheel Inn was in a category if its own. Its reputation for 'roughness', in the 1830s, extended throughout the southern counties. The pub was the recurrent scene of disorder, drunkenness and crime – both on and off the premises – and remained largely unchanged and certainly untamed at mid century. Itinerant workers also put up there, often sleeping two or three in a bed. Drinking, notably under the auspices of one landlord's son, might begin at daybreak, followed by decisions against going to work, in favour of boozing the day away. Fights, not all of which had comprehensible origins but often involved women, and claims of theft, appear endemic. Other crimes were planned in the warmth of the bar, and perhaps executed with degrees of Dutch courage. Raids netting hop-poles, chickens, lambs and sheep are known to have occurred after drinking in the Wheel, and doubtlessly a much larger number of unsolved crimes originated here.[75] Customers who drank themselves into a stupor, and passed out either in the bars or the streets, fields or ditches afterwards, were regularly robbed while unconscious. One such scene occurred in the Labour in Vain in September 1848. Shoemaker Aaron Apps, who admitted (in something of an understatement) that he was 'the worse for drinking'; in fact, he passed out in the bar with his 'watch chain hung out' at ten o'clock and awoke at 3 a.m., without his watch. Apps was an ineffective prosecution witness against one of the several George Eastwoods, whose widowed mother lived with the proprietor. Under cross-examination Apps failed to identify the watch, or recall whether he had lost it in either June, July or September. As Apps informed a jury, 'he did not know except that he played cricket on the day after, and the day he played cricket at was five weeks ago (roars of laughter)'. Of one thing he was certain, 'He was drunk at the time'. Eastwood was acquitted and Apps' claim for prosecution costs disallowed.[76]

This incessant criminal activity was reflected in other ways, notably in the protective procedures adopted by the propertied. One of Jane Vigor's duties as 'housekeeper' for farmer Sam Cruttenden in the late 1830s was not only to lock up fowls in an outhouse overnight but to count them 'every night and morning'. Likewise, barns containing heaps of grain during machine-threshing were equally carefully locked, after labourers

[74] Depositions, John Parsons, 9 August 1837, H. Stiles, n.d., James Eastwood, 18 May 1841; summary conviction, Edmund Hilder, 20 August 1842, ESCRO, QR/E847, 875, 887. *Brighton Gazette*, 1 September 1842 and 2 August 1849.

[75] Wells, *Victorian Village*, p. 147. Confession, Clifton, 30 March 1818; deposition, farmer Thomas Ellis, 18 June 1838; statement, George Tyes, hawker, June 1855; summary convictions, farmer James Russell, for smashing the Wheel door off its hinges, 17 October 1856, ESCRO, QR/E755, 854, 992, 996.

[76] Apps' deposition, 13 October 1848, ESCRO, QR/E935. *Maidstone Gazette*, 24 October 1848.

before leaving off work . . . made a mark with the handle of a Rake in the Oats on the Barns Floor like the Letter E . . . there were two such marks . . . to see if any is gone.

Alternatively, piles of corn could be 'smoothed up towards the Bay Boards . . . and covered . . . with Hop Bags'. Even a relatively wealthy farmer, James Lade, scratched his name on his working 'half boots'. Interestingly, those who feared that they might be wrongfully accused of crime, unless they took precautions, did so; the notorious Mrs Chandler, pardoned after an unsafe conviction for her husband's murder, who remarried, once insisted that the sack marked with the name of grocer and draper John Fuller, be endorsed '"Sold by J.F." . . . for her protection' after she purchased it.[77]

If many minor crimes were committed individually, others involved the commonly shifting confederacies, identified as normal in a recent study of criminal gangs active in the southern countryside.[78] As both smuggling and much poaching were collective activities, other forms of organised crime probably – at least partially – derived from such associations. Organised crime and the operations of gangs were particularly feared. If they increased with the desperation in the post-war years, they escalated further with the coming of the Poor Law Amendment Act in the later 1830s and 1840s, notably across the winters. Complaints against 'nightly Depredators . . . we have been' the victims of 'for many past winters' were vigorously articulated in 1839. Crime became more violent, as the catalogue of petty criminality was overshadowed by the intensity of 'Burglaries and larcenies'. At least one gang eluded detection while they repeatedly stole sheep, allegedly committed about twenty burglaries, including raids on big shoemakers' workshops and the Bear Inn after linen and cloth stored by a travelling salesman; even preserved foodstuffs were stolen in considerable quantities during burglaries of farmhouses. Gangs of burglars also targeted local retailers, the grocer Stone being subjected to 'repeated attempts at robbery' in the late forties. 'Bats', customarily used in smuggling, were regularly carried by those responsible, and on occasion victims were savagely beaten. Relatively few of the perpetrators were caught during this period, and the documentary evidence – largely dependent on prosecution records – is hopelessly defective. Complainants, like those above, simply lumped together all manner of incidents, a characteristic shared with periodic press reports. Furthermore, Burwash-based gangs frequently operated across entire districts, and indeed their personnel were sometimes drawn from two or more parishes.[79]

[77] Depositions, Jane Vigor, 12 November 1838, carpenter Garner of Salehurst, 8 December 1841, yeoman John Pankhurst, 22 February 1842, John Fuller, 24 December 1858, bailiff John Russell and labourer Thomas Cramp, December 1860, ESCRO, QR/E857, 881–82, 1004, 1012.

[78] Wells, 'Criminal Gangs', passim.

[79] *Sussex Agricultural Express*, 1 July 1837; 10 and 17 February, 3 March, 16 and 23 June, 18 August 1839; 30 May and 27 November 1840. Indictments, Summer 1838, Assize, PRO, Assi, 35/278/3.

The lawyer John Baldock, replying to the Constabulary Commissioners in December 1836, commented in conformity with Chadwickian predelictions: annually elected constables 'are never upon the watch to see if felonies are committed and being generally persons in some Trade or Business they have no time to spare or go out to watch'.[80] Although this was not inaccurate in itself, it overlooked policing experiments aimed to combat pronounced social protest and crime. Between 1822 and 1830, the bankrupted farmer and butcher Robert Ellis tried to make a living from rewards and expenses by volunteering his services as headborough, a post which traditionally rotated. Although he had his failures, notably not securing the substantial reward for the conviction of those who fired Flurry's barn, and on another occasion was fined for letting a prisoner escape, Ellis figured prominently in many prosecution cases over this period.[81] Moreover policing deficiencies were partially compensated for by the enthusiasm of some propertied residents. The most intrepid was farmer and vestryman Richard Button. At 6.30 a.m. on one Sunday in 1824 Button 'was riding on Horseback' along the road to Brightling, when he saw somebody suspiciously 'stooping down' at the side of a gravel pit; Button 'called out to know who it was and not receiving any Answer . . . immediately rode up to him', recognised Henry Pettit – recently assigned to work on the parish farm – who 'threw a Sack upon his back' and made off. Button made a feint, but 'kept his eye upon the Man', accosted him again, 'insisted upon knowing what he had got', and wrested the sack which proved to contain a bushel of wheat, 'a pretty sort of Hog corn'. Having identified Pettit, Button released him and went off to the farm and established that the sack's contents clearly came from wheat being threshed on the farm. Pettit was quickly arrested.[82]

Although Button, and others, are subsequently encountered staking out repositories of stolen goods, and taking further anti-crime initiatives,[83] more formal experiments were tried. In August 1821 the vestry responded to the scale of disorder by committing hard-pressed funds to the erection of a two-cell 'Cage', and then financing a night watchman to deter people 'wilfully pulling down or injuring . . . the Cage . . . while building'. Special constables were introduced, and the night watch doubled in the following February; the sources are inadequate to establishing the role of the specials, but paid policing across the next eighteen years represented oscillating majority views on whether the expense was justified or not. Burwash paid for a watchman under an Act of 1830, passed in the immediate aftermath of Swing, giving statutory authority to this use of parochial funds, and also fitfully adopted the provisions of the

[80] Baldock's return to the Constabulary Commissioners, 6 December 1836, PRO, HO, 73/8.

[81] *Sussex Weekly Advertiser*, 13 August and 8 October 1821, 11 April and 24 October 1825, and 31 July 1826. Depositions, Baldock, and innkeeper Covey (of Waldron), 16 August 1825; indictment, W. Isted. Michaelmas 1825 Quarter Sessions, ESCRO, QR/E785.

[82] Button's deposition, 14 April 1824; East Sussex questionnaire re police proposals, 15 October 1839, ESCRO, QR/E782; QAC/1/E1.

[83] Button's deposition, 5 November 1825, ESCRO, QR/E786.

1833 Lighting and Watching Act, which extended the financial authority to daytime policing. After much argument in the mid 1830s, an annual and modest ceiling of £50 was put on such policing costs, with up to three men employed at times; it was claimed that these resources 'had a good effect in preserving the peace and preventing depredations'. The maximum was reduced to £32 in 1837, but this proved to be the last year as the reduced manpower was 'found not to be of sufficient use to Warrant the Expense', a decision forced by the smaller ratepayers who needed only a simple majority.[84]

Ironically, this termination of paid police coincided with the intensification of the activities of criminal gangs. In February 1838, Burwash in conjunction with neighbouring Ticehurst decided to hire a Metropolitan policeman, not an uncommon initiative for threatened rural communities; as procedures were not covered by the 1833 Act, sabotage by discordant ratepayers was impossible. However, Henry Sherwin's performance gave little return on the investment, as his principal contribution was to lose a case of lamb-stealing at the sessions. The amateur policeman, Ellis's successor as headborough, Harris of Ticehurst, proved the principal detective, ably assisted by Burwash special constables, butcher Vigor and grocer Stone, both of whom were repeated victims of crime. Although ludicrous incidents were not eradicated, one suspect escaping when left in the temporary custody of a seven year-old child, breakthroughs came from prisoners turning Queen's Evidence, and three villains were transported, though other suspects eluded indictment.[85]

Divisions among the ratepayers recurred nakedly over proposals for East Sussex to adopt the permissory 1839 Rural Constabulary Act. Rather than use the Quarter Sessions' arbitrary powers, the Earl of Chichester as chairman launched a campaign to convince his magisterial colleagues and the more substantial ratepayers of the Act's utility. He unwittingly stimulated one of the fiercest public debates ever seen in the county.[86] After personal lobbying by the curate, a petition arguing strongly for professional police was signed by thirty-four Burwash ratepayers, including most of the biggest, and a smattering of medium-sized farmers, together with several tradesmen not all of whom were the most prosperous. It stressed the inadequacy of the 1833 legislation giving 'the small Ratepayers the power of outvoting by numbers those who represented the principal Property', and additionally 'the low rate of Payment did not admit the employment of Officers fitted for the duty'. As Baldock and his legal partner Philcox both signed, the petition naturally condemned parochial constables for their

---

[84] Vestry minutes, 18 August and 8 December 1821, and 16 February 1822, ESCRO, Par. 284/12/1. Summary conviction of Ephraim Bond for 27 January 1836 assault on watchman James Relf, ESCRO, QR/E836. Button's return to Constabulary Commissioners.

[85] Depositions, B. Carley, 8 November 1837, E. Haycock, 5 September 1839, and G. Eastwood, 6 April 1841, ESCRO, QR/E849, 863, 875. Indictment, Summer 1838 Assize; Philcox and Baldock, to Lord John Russell, 13 January 1838, PRO, Assi, 35/278/3; HO 40/39, fo. 293. *Sussex Agricultural Express*, 16, 23 and 30 June, 31 July, 4 and 18 August 1838. *Brighton Patriot*, 31 July and 7 August 1838.

[86] Wells, 'Implementation and Non-Implementation', pp. 303–6.

total inefficiency . . . either to protect us from Losses by the depredations of depraved Characters, or detect the depredators after the Commission of Robberies – or after detection, to obtain such evidence of guilt as will procure their Conviction and Punishment.

They went on somewhat unrealistically to hope that the 1839 Act would be implemented before the ensuing winter to counter normal seasonal peaks in criminality.[87]

A general meeting of all ratepayers promptly and equally adamantly rejected the idea of implementation, clearly on the grounds of expense and impoverishment; 'many of the Parishioners would be distressed to pay'. The Act's stipulation that the entire force in aggregate should not exceed one policeman per 2000 inhabitants, enabled the opportunistic additional claim that Burwash's ostensible entitlement to a solitary policeman was manifestly inadequate. However, Sherwin's recent failures were ignored.[88]

In 1840 the East Sussex County Constabulary was created be it on the smallest possible scale. The tiny establishment led by Chief Constable Mackay, comprised three superintendents and eighteen constables, reflecting county-wide ratepayer hostility, and an amending statute passed in the same year, permitting the appointment of Local constables. These represented a revamped form of parish constable, except that the men were paid when on duty, directed by the professionals, and not compelled to serve outside their parish except for attendance at Petty Sessions. Local constables were thus intended as a cheap way of increasing the available manpower, though success would depend essentially on volunteers. The Hurst Green Petty Sessional division was one of the very few in which success was initially registered, with some nineteen men – divided into night and day shifts – available in Burwash alone.[89] Such apparent enthusiasm for the new policing establishment, which a majority of ratepayers adamantly opposed while a significant minority equally adamantly supported, would be paradoxical but for the increasingly violent crime associated with gangs.

The professionalisation of the police, and the extension of available manpower through the facility of local constables, certainly gave the forces of law and order an unprecedented profile in Burwash, though not one replicated across most of East Sussex. The Locals made their presence felt, and at least in the early days brought their local knowledge to bear. For example, on 16 May 1841 one Local 'on duty that night . . . for the purpose of watching', confirmed that a man initially suspected for burgling the Bell was in fact a lodger. On another occasion, Locals Sellings and King were 'requested' by professional constable Smith, 'to watch' one of the notorious haulage family of Eastwood and a suspect member of the Buss kin, 'who were travelling with a Horse and Cart along the

---

[87] Burwash petition, and Rev. Munn to G.C. Courthope JP, 7 and 14 October 1839, ESCRO, QAC/1/E1.

[88] Burwash, return to police questionnaire, 18 October 1839, ESCRO, QAC/1/E9.

[89] Wells, 'Implementation and Non-Implementation', p. 307. Foster, *The Rural Constabulary Act of 1839*, passim.

Road from Hurstgreen to Burwash' just after dusk on 10 October 1842. The pair were shadowed by the Locals, who saw them take several hop-poles from land adjacent to the road, but they wisely waited till the cart arrived in the village before arresting them and handing them over to P.C. Smith. Subsequent documentation reveals arrest made by the professionals during night watches in the village, including that of John Hicks whose outpacing of pursuing P.C. Peerless was useless, as Peerless bellowed after him, 'it was no use running for I knew him'. On another occasion, when two constables were called over bacon mysteriously filched from 'up the Chimney of the Taproom' of the Admiral Vernon, they 'got under a Waggon very near the House and watched', until a couple of customers emerged from the pub, retrieved the bacon and tried to make off. By the end of our period, it could be said of the professionals that those parishioners 'suspected of dishonest practices' were 'kept under the eye of the police' and were consequently very vulnerable to speedy arrest on convicing evidence when they reengaged in crime.[90]

But success was neither instantaneous nor complete, nor entirely attributable to more rigorous policing. Three Burwash men who went across the Ticehurst border in April 1861 to rob a barn took 'Bats' much like smugglers, and when surprised by the police used them ferociously, and seriously injured both constables. Local constables, and fearful property owners, responded to violence with violence: revealed, for example, by yet another attempted robbery at grocer Stone's when his gun was nearly knocked from his grasp by a 'violent blow' from a bludgeon; then Stone 'directly aimed at the fellow but his gun missed fire'.[91] Nevertheless, from 1850, there was an unmistakable reduction in crime levels at Burwash; policing efficiency, challenged on occasion,[92] was but part of the explanation, which is elusive yet seems to turn on the impact of more prosperous agriculture on rural communities, coupled with some reduction in the excess of farm labour supply over demand. In this respect, Burwash seems fairly typical of other rural communities in Southern and Eastern England.[93]

The foregoing account of crime, social and political protest, and policing, in Burwash between 1790 and 1850, has revealed endemic petty crime, interspersed with pronounced periods of more serious crime, some of it organised and violent. It has also established three major types of protest: the perennial petty variety,

[90] Depositions, Henry Stiles and John Parsons, 18 May 1841, Henry King and James Sellings, 22 October 1842, and professional constable Banks, 21 December 1855 and 2 April 1856, ESCRO, QR/E875, 888, 985, 993. *Sussex Agricultural Express*, 18 May 1850.

[91] Depositions, William Sewell, professional constables Company and Peerless, April 1861, ESCRO, QR/E1014. *Maidstone Gazette*, 14 December 1847.

[92] The police were lambasted for their conspicuous absence on Guy Fawkes Day 1850, despite formal notices issued by the Road Surveyor prohibiting the discharge of fireworks in the streets, who was roughed up for trying to enforce his own edict. *Sussex Agricultural Express*, 9 November 1850.

[93] Rudé, *Criminal and Victim*, pp. 10–11.

including insulting – and sometimes assaulting – vestrymen and their parish officers; major riotous episodes, principally associated with the Swing rising; and political organisation and protest, which by comparison achieved a lower profile, however alarming the objectives might appear to some, especially the wealthy and powerful. These final analytical sections aim to discuss the people involved in all of these phenomena, to see what the relationships were between them. For example, were Swing rioters and other social protesters the predominantly respectable though poor people, largely without criminal antecedents, claimed by Professors Hobsbawm and Rudé?[94] Were those who engaged in populist political movements uncontaminated by criminal activities? Or were both social and political protesters involved in social crime, pilfering from employers, stealing wood and poaching, but not more serious crime, including burglary and other forms of substantial larceny, which Rudé dubbed 'acquisitive crime'?[95] Finally how accurate were Chadwickian claims about a distinct criminal class, comprising work-shy, ne'er do wells, who existed principally on the proceeds of larceny of all types, where necessary using violence to terrify victims and non-professional policemen alike? Or was most crime essentially the product of the perpetrators' poverty, and the lack of alternatives, including stable employment?

Such an exercise, even at the parochial level, is beset by an alarming range of evidential problems. The distinction of sons from fathers, and from uncles and cousins, where the same combination of Christian and surnames occurs, is often impossible, where records do not include the date of birth. Such difficulties are not ironed out by the time-consuming method of family reconstitution, for several reasons. Underregistration of births was much greater than usually assumed,[96] and its effect was aggravated during our period by mobilisation. This resulted in many children being born elsewhere, who returned with their fathers after 1815. This feature partially accounts for the rapid rise in Burwash's population between the 1811 and 1821 censuses, and also means that the baptismal dates of adults living in the parish in the first half of the nineteenth century are unrecorded. Although family reconstitution has been attempted, the results are of overall restricted import, however valuable for some families. Different spellings of the same name – the Revd. Egerton noted that the Relfe family used three varieties of their common name when signing the parish register[97] – present additional problems.

The parish where a crime is committed is commonly given as the suspect's and the witnesses' place of abode. Greater accuracy is sometimes provided, be it inadvertantly; for example, when George Cole accurately described himself as a wheelwright of Horsted Keynes, his place of domicile was said to be Burwash

---

[94] Hobsbawm and Rudé, *Captain Swing*, pp. 208–11.

[95] Rudé, *Criminal and Victim*, p. 78ff.

[96] H. Mitcham, 'Infant Mortality in South-East England, 1813–1840: Chronological and Regional Variations' (unpublished MA thesis, University of Brighton, 1994), ch. 4.

[97] Wells, *Victorian Village*, p. 53.

by another witness to a crime in the village.[98] Labourer is repeatedly used to describe men not of at least farmer, or superior, status, including Henry Delia, when in fact he was not only a professional policeman, but an assault upon him was the reason for the documentation.[99]

The minutes of Petty Sessions were hardly models of accuracy, examples including summonses issued against two of the Blackford family being recorded as Blackpool, and John Hickens being attributed as the successful applicant for a summons, instead of Hicks.[100] Moreover, some clerks to Petty Session, seem to have adopted a lackadaisical attitude to their obligation to make returns of summary convictions to the county clerk of the Peace, though few were as obstructive as the Rye County Bench who went for fifteen years without making any returns, despite being 'written to over and over again'.[101]

Officials, even when drafting documents as potentially critical as witnesses' statements, could make fundamental mistakes, including on one occasion confusing members of the numerous Isted kin with those of the even more numerous Eastwoods.[102] When reporting court proceedings, the press regularly got details wrong, deriving from, as one journalist claimed, 'the very loose manner in which the names of prisoners and witnesses are generally made known to . . . reporters'. On this occasion the paper was forced to make an apology as it had juxtaposed the names of defendant and witness, but it added in self-justification, that 'the mistake was not very extraordinary'.[103] Another pressman simply said that a man accused of assault was a 'carpenter whose name we could not catch'.[104] Some mistakes are easily rectifiable, for example when calling John Vigor, Virgo.[105] Other misreportings can be corrected through complementary materials. For example, the *Brighton Gazette's* report on Hurst Green Petty Sessions, sitting on 29 January 1858, said that Charles Honeysett was cleared of opening the Bear Inn on the previous Christmas Day before 12.30p.m., but the summary returns made by the court clerk records Honeysett's conviction for selling beer at 11.25 a.m. on Christmas morning at the Rose and Crown, where he had been licensee since the previous August.[106]

Press coverage of the Assizes was cursory, irrespective of accuracy at the start of our period, but steadily improved not least owing to competition generated by the increase in titles before 1850. Spectacular cases, including murder, riot and arson, usually received more generous coverage than the more mundane

---

[98] Depositions, Cole, and victualler Parsons, 29 August 1837, ESCRO, QR/E847.

[99] Delia, deposition, February 1849, ESCRO, QR/E938.

[100] Battle Petty Sessions minutes, 28 May and 27 August 1816, ESCRO, PSBA. 7.

[101] *Sussex Advertiser*, 5 April 1864.

[102] Second deposition of Lewes Beadle Haycock, 5 September; examination of Anthony Buss, deposition of labourer George Coppard, both of Burwash, 5 and 9 September 1839, ESCRO, QR/E863.

[103] *Brighton Gazette*, 29 May 1858.

[104] *Sussex Agricultural Express*, 22 May 1869.

[105] *Brighton Patriot*, 28 February 1837.

[106] *Brighton Gazette*, 4 February 1858. Summary conviction, 29 January 1858, ESCRO, QR/E1001.

succession of petty property crimes before all courts. By the 1840s even petty sessional proceedings received at least intermitant reportage. The records of Assize and Quarter Sessions, despite their deficiencies, facilitate a parochial portrait of crime, though the exercise of caution ensures that it underrepresents, rather than exaggerates. So too does the obvious impossibility of tracing crimes committed elsewhere by Burwash folk, and here the recreated record may be hopelessly deficient. Occasionally, Burwash residents do crop up unambiguously in other jurisdictions, including labourer Benjamin Fuller who was bailed by Maidstone magistrates on assault charges for an incident at the fair on 20 June 1832, to appear at the Borough Sessions on 7 July. Here, unusually, the Petty as opposed to the Quarter Sessions records are extant, and Fuller disappears from the judicial paperwork. His case went unreported in the press; one paper simply reported that 'very little business' was done on the 7th, while its rival noted only that a 'few cases of assault were settled'.[107]

The criminal law for the entire first half of the nineteenth century provided for the transportation of many first offenders, and a subsequent conviction for felony almost invariably resulted in a sentence of at least seven years' exile. Given these legal conditions, the academic establishment of a criminal class is rendered even more difficult by the fact that those apparently on the verge of such categorisation were literally and irrevocably placed outside the environment where a 'criminal class' could be proved through the reasonably tight definition of recidivism. This criteria simply does not become available until the run-down in the system of transportation, and its replacement by short, medium, and long-term sentences of imprisonment in the second half of the nineteenth century. Conversely, where detailed evidence is available, notably in depositions, some picture of those who seem to have been habitually at the scene of crimes, or mixing with clearly suspect people in equally notorious places, builds up. On the other hand, dilemmas are posed where prisoners are not committed, or are found not guilty. No English historian ought to assume guilt, especially even where depositions are available – principally at the Quarter Sessions as opposed to the Assizes – as these are the basis of the prosecution's case, not the defence's whose cross-examination produced different stories from witnesses resulting in acquittals by juries, in trials receiving adequate press coverage.

William Cobbett had many supporters in Burwash, though how many subscribed to his notorious *Political Register* is unknown. In the autumn of 1830 Cobbett embarked on a lecture tour of south-eastern and southern England. He aimed to publicise the recent continental revolutions, to win support for their principally plebeian begetters, and argued that their success should encourage political action by their English counterparts. They could play a critical role – especially if backed by the middling orders – in forcing through parliamentary reform in

---

[107] Deposition, grocer J. Hollands of Sutton Valence, 20 June 1832, KCRO, PS/Md, Sd.1. *Maidstone Gazette*, and *Maidstone Journal*, both 10 July 1832.

Britain. To the latter end he supplied petitions for reform for distribution and signing by his supporters. A number of Burwash residents flocked across the border to hear Cobbett's lecture on 16 October 1830. His two-hour harangue, delivered in a hastily-rigged booth, made of poles and planking, and roofed by sails from Hastings, attacked the overthrown Bourbons, and emphasised the collections in Kent for those who had fallen while manning Parisian street barricades. Cobbett argued that the restoration of agricultural prosperity could only follow parliamentary reform, the prerequiste for the essential reductions of state pensions and taxes, and the abolition of the tithe. All this would enable the farmers to increase labourers' wages. He also referred, ominously, to the current incendiarism in Kent, and reiterated his well-publicised warning to the 'middle class', notably farmers, to make common cause with workers for reform. Cobbett lambasted the Game Laws, and the system of professional Poor Law overseers, responsible for drastic cuts in poor relief. A local *cause célébre* exemplified the latter, namely the Ticehurst grandfather who had been forced to sell two cottages in order to support his grandchildren.[108] Cobbett's speech was itself privately denounced by Lord Ashburnham as 'rank treason', though as yet the Home Office was merely monitoring Cobbett's speeches and his *Register*, hoping that an indiscretion would facilitate his prosecution.[109] That chance came at the end of the year on the conviction of the Battle arsonist Thomas Goodman: Goodman claimed that Cobbett's Battle speech had incited his incendiarism, coupled with a particularly fierce article in the *Register* on 11 December, embracing arson and reflecting on its causes.[110]

Part of Cobbett's defence hinged on a petition from members of his Battle audience denying that he had advocated 'any . . . act of violence', let alone the arming and arson alleged against him. Indeed the petitioners stressed that Cobbett had specifically argued that people should sign the reform petitions, and 'wait with patience for the[ir] Effects' as the 'most effectual way . . . of putting a stop to . . . fires and other acts of violence'. Fourteen men from Burwash signed this petition.[111] Clearly, all these people had attended Cobbett's lecture; while the audience no doubt contained opponents,[112] it is unlikely that those who put their names to the petition were among them, though there is a chance that the odd opponent did sign through pure honesty. The Burwash signatories comprised three farmers, four shoe-makers, a tailor, a saddler, a cabinet-maker, a carpenter, a mason, a clock-maker, a labourer and the grocer Joseph Sawyer.

---

[108] *Political Register*, 23 October 1830.

[109] Ashburnham to Lord Camden, 24 October 1830, PRO, HO 52/8, fos 231–32.

[110] R. Wells, 'Mr William Cobbett, Captain Swing, and King William IV' (forthcoming).

[111] Battle petition, undated, Nuffield College, Oxford, XI/8, fos 1–3.

[112] Ashburnham alleged that Cobbett was 'very indignant at the reception he met with', though this may be pure hyperbole or the product of misrepresentation by Ashburnham's informants. Ashburnham to Camden.

Sawyer must have been an ardent Cobbettite, for he attended the trial in July 1831, though in the event was not called to give evidence.[113] Sawyer was a relatively prosperous retailer. He had been a leading contractor supplying groceries to the parish, much of it on credit (thereby easing the parish's perennial financial problem during the 1820s), and was owed no less than £472 in May 1830. He repeatedly served as a juror at the Quarter Sessions, on one occasion being formally summonsed for non-attendance, but was seemingly never involved even as a witness in a criminal prosecution.[114] At least two of the shoemakers were masters, James Baker being described as a 'very old and respectable inhabitant' when his workshop was burgled in 1838, while Anthony Baker owned his house and garden in 1842. Not much is known about Samuel Newington, except that he owned his own house – which he in part let. John Payne was a well-known Dissenter.[115] So too was the clock-maker, John Noakes, who owned his own house, as did the cabinet-maker Richard Manktellow and the master harness-maker Stephen Brown. The properties of these four men rendered them liable to jury service. Labourer William Thompson appears to fall into the 'respectable' category; he was a recurrent allotment prize-winner in the 1840s.[116] Benjamin Wood, the carpenter, came from the dynasty of parish clerks, which extended back to 1734, to which Benjamin added the post of sexton from 1827.[117]

The three farmers, James Cane, Samuel Cruttenden, and John Honeysett (also a miller), were all relatively substantial. In 1842 Honeysett was the owner-occupier of 104 acres, Cane rented 291 acres, and Cruttenden farmed 112 acres while letting his freehold estate of thirty acres to another farmer. All three were important villagers: Cruttenden and Cane served on the select vestry, and all occupied parish offices during the period 1819 to 1850. Cane became a Poor Law guardian in the mid 1840s.[118] Predictably all were the victims of crime; and mounted prosecutions, not invariably successfully. But Honeysett and Cruttenden were not above taking action against lads for scrumping, some of whom were imprisoned; and poachers on their lands were also subjected to

[113] *Political Register*, 16 July 1831.

[114] Burwash vestry minutes, 6 July 1827, 7 January, 19 March, 16 June, 1 October and 24 December 1829, 29 May 1830 and 25 March 1831; East Sussex Quarter Sessions, jury lists, 1 July 1831, 23 April 1834, 16 October and 18 December 1839; ESCRO, QR/E808, 821, 864, 866; Par. 284/12/1.

[115] Burwash tithe schedule, 1842, Worthing Public Library. East Sussex Quarter Sessions, jury list, 23 April 1834, ESCRO, QR/E821. *Sussex Agricultural Express*, 16 June 1838.

[116] Barnes, *The 1851 East Sussex Census*. East Sussex Quarter Sessions, jury lists, 23 April 1834 16 October 1839 and 27 June 1842, ESCRO, QR/E821, 864, 885. Burwash Tithe schedule, 1842, Worthing Public Library. 1841 Census, PRO, HO 107/1108. *Sussex Agricultural Express*, 16 June 1838, 26 October 1844, 17 October 1846 and 23 October 1847.

[117] Burwash vestry minutes, 8 April 1824, 28 March 1825, 28 March 1826, 28 March 1827, 25 March 1830 and 25 March 1831. ESCRO, Par. 284/12/1. *Sussex Agricultural Express*, 9 June 1849.

[118] Burwash tithe schedule, 1842, Worthing Public Library. Burwash vestry minutes, 10 May 1819, 25 March 1820; 5, 8 and 28 December 1821; 31 January, 16 February, 12 March and 5 December 1822; 30 April 1823, 6 March 1824; 28 March and 24 December 1825; 28 March 1826; and 12 November 1831, ESCRO, Par. 284/12/1. Ticehurst Union, Guardians of the Poor, election returns, 1846 and 1847, PRO, MH, 12/13143. *Sussex Weekly Advertiser*, 29 November 1824.

prosecution. Conversely, Honeysett was fined for flour adulteration, and had at least thrice lost court cases over underpayment of wages.[119] These farmers' profiles over their relationship with their social subordinates are however ambiguous. As overseer in 1840 Honeysett was pilloried for making generous (and illegal) emergency payments to poor-law claimants, thereby usurping the probably parsimonious relieving officer. All three supported publicly-funded emigration; if containing longer-term poor-law expenditure costs was a primary objective, they might also have entertained altruistic beliefs, in that colonial living standards were much higher, and upward social mobility was a well-known possibility.[120]

With the exception of Payne, none of these supporters of Cobbett subsequently emerged as radical activists. Several already had the vote in 1830, and most of the remainder were enfranchised by the 1832 Reform Act. In common with many others of comparable socio-economic status, they were probably satisfied with the outcome of that prolonged process.

The leading radical in Burwash in the later 1830s and 1840s was John Fuller, who did not arrive until 1832. Born at Waldron, he ran a Burwash school from 1832 until 1843, when he took over a grocer and draper's shop. Sometimes road surveyor, and a newspaper correspondent – for the Liberal *Sussex Advertiser* – he was secretary to the Radical News Club in the village, whose inspiration came from the Working Men's Associations strong in parts of Sussex in the post-1832 years, and represented in Burwash. Several reemerged as Chartist branches at the end of the decade.[121] The clearest evidence of the identity of working-class political radicals derives from the six men who spoke at the anti-New Poor Law rally in 1838.[122] Only one, Joseph Blackford, a labourer aged eighteen, was unmarried, and no doubt gave evidence respecting the discrimination against youthful workers by local employers. Two men were skilled, John Harmer (thirty-two), and John Rich (twenty-four), respectively a bricklayer and a shoemaker, though both resorted to labouring on occasion. The remaining three were all agricultural labourers, namely Henry Budd and George Coppard (ages unknown), and forty-year-old William Kemp. Harmer was related to the Heathfield mason, whom we encountered as an emigrant to the USA in response to Pitt's terror in the 1790s, and the only one known to have radical antecedents. At the time of the meeting, only one (Budd) had any criminal record, and that

[119] Honeysett, summary conviction, 8 February 1825; summary convictions for theft of fruit, 15 August 1846 and 30 August 1841, and poachers 15 December 1843; cases against A. Ellis and S. King, 28 November 1838; Battle House of Correction records, custody of M. Elliott, October to November 1828, ESCRO, QR/E782, 789, 857, 877, 899; QDB/2/E1. Assize indictments, against C. Weston, Lent 1842, PRO, Assi, 35/282/3. *Brighton Gazette*, 4 April 1844, 25 June 1846 and 27 July 1848. *Maidstone Gazette*, 1 January 1839.

[120] Ticehurst Union minute, 15 October 1840, ESCRO, G10/1a/2. Burwash ratepayers' meeting, 4 March 1836, notification of proposed emigrants; emigration loan request, 21 February 1839, PRO, MH 12/13138, 13140.

[121] Wells, 'Rural Rebels', pp. 141–42, 153–54. 1841 census, PRO, HO, 107/1108. *Sussex Advertiser*, 3 August 1847; 13 and 27 August 1873. London Working Men's Association.

[122] The men are named in the report in the *Brighton Patriot*, 13 March 1838.

a poaching conviction and £5 fine,[123] though the same cannot be said of their family connections.[124] Conversely, Harmer and Kemp had appeared as prosecution witnesses, the former in a solitary case of poaching,[125] but the latter against indigenous burglars and an outsider for theft.[126] Kemp had also studiously refused to get involved in any way with the murdered publican Russell's thieving activities.[127]

If this evidence suggests that these men were largely 'respectable' in contemporary perception and parlance, this characteristic did not endure permanently for two of the five men who remained Burwash residents. Rich served three prison terms: fourteen days in 1839 for thieving straw; six months hard labour for potato theft in 1841; and a year for stealing a hymn book in 1851.[128] Ironically, Harmer – who had been a member of a vigilante patrol in 1841, and a prosecution witness in two larceny cases in 1840 and 1843 – was heavily implicated in the latter, though in the event he again appeared in the witness-box.[129] Blackford was fined for poaching in 1842, and for assaulting the police in 1843, and served nine months' hard labour for a vicious attack on the policemen who surprised him and two others while robbing a barn in Ticehurst in 1861.[130] Kemp kept on the right side of the law, though he was unemployed over the 1840–41 winter when his family was in 'extreme destitution', a situation aggravated by his wife's affair with an unnamed widower.[131]

The identity of only three from amongst the hundreds who mobilised during the Swing rising are known: forty-one-year-old stone-cutter Jesse Relf; agricultural labourer. William Weston (twenty-seven); and bricklayer's labourer Sam Lidbetter (twenty-one). Relf was a colourful character. A friend of publican

[123] Summary conviction, November 1827, ESCRO, QR/E794.

[124] For example, Joseph Blackford's father, had repeated altercations with parish officials, and had served a one-year prison term for assaulting poorhouse master Westover. Denounced, but not prosecuted, as a fowl thief in 1817–18, he escaped prosecution for sheep-stealing in 1820 by turning King's Evidence against co-defendant, Steven Langridge. Blackford was also involved with Ben Russell. Vestry minutes, 6 October 1821, 6 April, 3 May, 1 June and 13 December 1827; committal notices, 11 June 1816 and 29 May 1821, and recognizance to keep the peace, 15 August 1816; John Clifton, examination, 20 March 1818, ESCRO, QR/E748–9, 755, 768. Indictments, Lent 1820 Assize; deposition, labourer J. Oliver, 27 November 1826, PRO, Assi, 35/260/4(1); HO, 47/71.

[125] Summary conviction, J. Crowhurst, 22 March 1830, ESCRO, QR/E803.

[126] Assize indictments, William Baldwin, Lent 1826, and Stephen Langridge, Winter 1826–27, PRO, Assi, 35/266/5.

[127] Baldwin indictment. Deposition, William Kemp, 27 November 1826, PRO, HO, 47/71.

[128] *Sussex Advertiser*, 5 August 1839. Indictments, Summer 1839 Assize, and Summer 1851 Quarter Sessions, PRO, Assi, 35/279/2; ESCRO, QR/E877, 957.

[129] *Sussex Advertiser*, 2 and 16 March 1840. Indictment, George Eastwood, Lent Assize 1840, PRO, Assi, 35/280/3. Depositions, local constable Stiles, 13 May 1841, John Harmer, 20 January 1843, ESCRO, QR/E875, 890.

[130] *Brighton Gazette*, 13 October 1842. Summary convictions, 30 September 1842 and 25 July 1843; indictment, Blackford, J. and W. Isted, Summer 1861 Quarter Sessions, ESCRO, QR/E887, 945, 1015.

[131] Clerk, Ticehurst Union, to the Poor Law Commissioners, 17 February 1841 and 28 January 1842, PRO, MH 12/13141. Ticehurst Union minutes, 20 January 1842, ESCRO, G10/1a/3.

Benjamin Russell – with whom he had been caught poaching and fined in 1815 – he had also served a week in Battle House of Correction for bark stealing in 1824, and narrowly escaped prosecution for implication in a butter theft case in 1827. He later claimed to have been 'one of the 3 who began' the rising in 1830, giving a graphic account to the Rev. Egerton, who recorded its gist but not the details; however, as Relf lived on the Common, and patronised the Wheel Inn where at least some planning took place, there is no reason to doubt his assertion.[132] Weston (who was arrested at Mayfield during Swing, pleaded guilty and was merely bound over) had been cleared of thieving a pig at the Assizes in 1821, and had firmly resisted a chance to buy stolen wheat four years later; while working for Haviland three months before Swing he witnessed systematic theft of trusses of hay, and went on to give evidence against Richard Siggs, whom we shall encounter as a transportee on a different and more serious charge in January 1831.[133] Of Sam Lidbetter little is known, except that while working he saw the crowd making for Robertsbridge, tried to hide, was 'seen . . . summarily led down compelled to go with the rest, much to the amusement of the multitude'.[134]

Most other collective social protests were more mundane. The riotous assault in April 1820 on overseer Weston, by several parish-employed men frustrated at repeated refusals of the parish officers to provide food, saw indictments against John Sellings senior and junior, Stephen Elliott and James Langridge. All were convicted, the elder Sellings and Elliott being imprisoned for a year, with Langridge and younger Sellings receiving six and two month terms respectively. None of these men appear to have had criminal convictions, though Langridge had recently served a three-month term for refusing to work while in parish employ.[135] The decision to prosecute on this occasion probably derived from repeated threats – and some violence – towards parish officers, and reflected something of a determination to reimpose their authority. The posse of protesters against the vestry's 1821 decision not to provide faggots for the Guy Fawkes bonfire in 1821 produced eight prosecutions at the Quarter Sessions, and one at the Assize, at the ratepayers' expense. Indictments were secured against David (fifty-one) and his son Thomas Collins (twenty-eight), James Eastwood (thirty-two), George Hyland (thirty), Thomas Lidbetter (thirty-five), John Luck (twenty-two), George Page (thirty-one) William Thompson junior (twenty-five), and Charles Weston (fifty-one). All were labouring men, apart from Thompson, a

[132] Wells, *Victorian Village*, pp. 72, 90, 92. Summary convictions, Relfe, 12 December 1815 and 22 June 1821, and G. Pope, December 1827; Battle Petty Sessions minutes, 12 December 1815, 9 July 1816, 21 and 23 June 1824, ESCRO, QR/E746; QDB/2/E1: PSBA.2–3.

[133] Indictment, Lent Assize 1821, PRO, Assi, 35/361/4(1). Depositions, W. Weston, 5 November 1825 and 24 August 1831, ESCRO, QR/E786, 809. *Sussex Advertiser*, 15 November 1830 and 17 January 1831.

[134] He later emigrated. Clerk, Ticehurst Union, to the Poor Law Commissioner, 12 March 1837, PRO, MH, 12/13139. Wells, *Victorian Village*, pp. 202–3.

[135] Indictments, Easter 1820 Quarter Sessions, and undated, unsigned letter from one of the accused, addressed to 'Gentlemen', ESCRO, QR/E763.

somewhat wayward member of the master-building family. Stephen Elliott, recently released from prison, was also arrested, and doubtlessly concerned about a severe sentence; he escaped by turning King's Evidence. Only Weston, Page and Lidbetter were acquitted; the others were fined a shilling with seven days imprisonment, with the exceptions of Eastwood, who got a fortnight's jail, and Thomas Collins, who received a two-month term and a private whipping.[136] Thomas Collins had been whipped – publicly – only two years previously, when he admitted to stealing the faggots found in his father's house; both were named in the search warrant. The son's admittance probably reflected the strong possibility of his father's transportation if found guilty. David Collins had narrowly escaped prosecution as a fifteen-year-old lad in 1784 for thieving cherry brandy while employed at the Bear Inn, and a six month sentence – plus a public whipping – for stealing flour from his employer while working at a mill in 1808/9.[137] John Luck had been acquitted only a month previously for thieving flour, though one of his two alleged accomplices was convicted. While he was in prison awaiting trial, his wife was implemented in a fowl theft; a search of her home revealed no evidence.[138] James Eastwood had been arrested in July 1819 for assaulting the police, and had served a short prison sentence, but seems to have escaped indictment after committal to the county gaol on a charge of stealing hop-poles in February 1821.[139]

Although some of these men had minor altercations with the parochial authorities over the next few years,[140] none was subsequently involved in crime, with the exception of Thomas Clifton. He served two one-month sentences for non-payment of fines for wood-stealing and poaching in 1824; was fined again twice in 1825–26 for thieving potatoes and cabbages; and again he served a sentence for non-payment of the latter fine. In 1828 he was punished with loss of employ for another collective protest over parish work. He appears to have kept out of the dock prior to 1836 when it was reported that:

> Exertions have been made by the [Poor Law Union] Clerk for . . . [Collins's] family to emigrate & the Pauper [viz. Thomas] went round the Parish last year to obtain a Certificate of character but no one would sign it.

---

[136] Indictments, Lent 1822 Assize, and Epiphany 1822 Quarter Sessions; depositions of Elliott, R. Button, and J. Cruttenden, 7 November 1821; PRO, Assi, 35/262/3; ESCRO, QR/E770. *Sussex Weekly Advertiser*, 21 January 1822.

[137] T. Collins, indictment for 11 December 1815 faggot theft; D. Collins, indictment, and deposition, miller Skinner, 7 November 1808, ESCRO, QR/E623, 718.

[138] *Sussex Weekly Advertiser*, 22 October 1821. G. Darby JP to the constable of Heathfield, 24 December 1821, ESCRO, QR/E771.

[139] *Sussex Weekly Advertiser*, 19 February 1821. Vestry minutes, 3 and 17 July 1819, ESCRO, Par 284/12/1.

[140] Vestry minutes, 19 April 1823, 6 March 1824 and 14 July 1826, ESCRO, Par, 284/12/1.

(This was in contrast to his fellow defendent of 1822, John Luck, who emigrated in 1829.)[141] Collins stayed in Burwash and went into the workhouse in 1836. He lost his wife about 1841, when he received outdoor relief while unemployed to look after his three children. He served another six-month sentence for theft in 1841, and was fined in 1842, 1843 and 1852 for wood stealing. In the 1851 census he appears as an ageing lodger.[142]

The two men tried at the Assize in 1822 for firing Flurry's barn were acquitted, but the case reveals interesting details. Charles Weston, whom we have just encountered as a bonfire protester, was indicted together with George Eastwood, aged sixty-three. Both were in perennial conflict with the parochial authorities. Eastwood, in common with others, had had his relief stopped on 3 November 1821 until he got rid of his dogs; the same meeting first ordered Weston's two unemployed daughters into the poorhouse,[143] an equally regular condition. Both men's daughters were the subject of further wrangles in 1822: the vestry ruled that 'they had grown up daughters at home, dressed in a manner superior to their condition', and 'frequently' denied relief to the fathers until the daughters went into the house. Although Eastwood's youngest daughter, aged nineteen, had either complied or left home.[144] On 2 November, the six vestrymen present, including Flurry, salaried overseer Westover, and farmers G.F. Gilbert and Richard Button, ruled again that Weston's relief be stopped until his '2 Oldest Girls' went in. Weston tackled Westover at Gilbert's house one week later. He claimed that Flurry moved the resolution, whereupon Weston 'greatly . . . raged against' Flurry and went off to consult Eastwood. Thomas and Ann Clifton, who had been incarcerated in the poorhouse with their two daughters in 1819,[145] heard Eastwood say he was going to fire Flurry and Button's barns. That night the former's property went up, though both defendants were among the firefighters. The Cliftons were key witnesses. Given that Thomas Clifton was himself dependent on the vestry, and had recently been released from a nine-month term for his part in the riotous rescue at Heathfield, he probably came under strong pressure to give evidence. Arson was a notoriously difficult crime to prove and specific grudges against witnesses comprised the regular nature of evidence adduced.[146] Flurry had offered a £50 reward and the sum was increased by

---

[141] Vestry minute, 3 April 1829, ESCRO, Par, 284/12/1.

[142] Summary convictions, 11 April and 15 June 1824, 14 October 1825, 30 March and 20 June 1826, 28 March 1842, 31 March 1843 and 21 May 1852, ESCRO, QR/E780, 785, 788, 885, 893, 965; QDB/2/E1. Clerk, Ticehurst Union, to the Poor Law Commissioner, 5 December 1836 and 17 February 1841, PRO, MH. 12/131/38, 13141.

[143] Vestry minutes, 3 November 1821, ESCRO, Par, 284/12/1.

[144] Based on the fact that on 17 August 1822 the vestry ruled that Stephen Hezelden 'be not allowed the Parish Team to fetch his Wood in consequence of having his Daughters at home', whereas this was specifically granted to Eastwood, ESCRO, Par, 284/12/1.

[145] Ibid., 19 May 1819.

[146] According to one judge, case law dictated that the prosecution had to 'prove the existence of malice in the mind of the incendiary towards the victim', a criterion broadened once insurance legitimated evidence of an intention to defraud. *The Times*, 7 January 1831. Wells, 'Social Protest, Class, Conflict and Consciousness', pp. 164–65, 170–71.

subscriptions from others. This may help explain Clifton's motives, and no doubt accounts for Headborough Ellis's stirling efforts. The trial judge's summing up included two key elements: first the evidence was limited to threats: and secondly, in the event of a conviction, there would be no reprieve.[147]

During this period three Burwash men were hanged for felonies, and twenty more were transported. All – bar one – of them had criminal partners and criminal associates; some from both categories turned approvers. While their evidence did lead to convictions, juries were hostile to those who sought to save themselves from punishment at the expense of their companions in crime, and prosecutions ended in acquittals even in cases where corroborative evidence came from untainted witnesses.[148] There are also indications that some witnesses – including associates of convicted criminals and acquitted defendants – were subjected to intense pressure, especially from more affluent and powerful members of the community, to give evidence. The affluent were the principal employers and ran the social-security system, and were thus well-placed virtually to force reluctant prosecutors into the witness-box. This feature revises earlier provisional conclusions that criminals rarely, if ever, gave evidence against each other.[149] There was it seems, less honour among thieves than legend would have it, confirming one Assize judge's pointed remark that 'whenever the hour of difficulty arose . . . some were willing to sacrifice comrades . . . to extract themselves'.[150] Gangs were a recurrent feature of the criminal scene in Burwash, most notably during the post-war depression, and throughout the rest of the period reviewed here. Analysis of the available details of these fraternities, including those prosecuted, their known associates, and their criminal records, when addressing the question of criminal class or sub-culture, is critical, together with the profiles of transported felons.

Little is known about two of the three capitally convicted and executed. They were hanged before the radical reform of the capital code began in the 1820s. George Hickmett and Charles Leaney were indicted for highway robbery in 1792; they roughed up their victim, the substantial farmer John Cruttenden, stole his pocket-book containing £10, his silver watch and chain. Leaney – the notorious poacher encountered above – was acquitted, but Hickmett went to the gallows.[151] William King was sixty-four when he was executed for stealing a sheep from another prosperous farmer, William Baker, in 1805.[152]

---

[147] Indictments, Winter 1822–23 Assize; E.J. Curteis, Battle, to Peel, 13 December 1822, PRO, Assi, 35/262/3; HO, 64/1, fos 310–2. *Sussex Weekly Advertiser*, 30 December 1822.

[148] For example, the 1820 acquittal of Stephan Langridge for sheep-stealing after his partner, Joseph Blackford, turned approver; nine other witnesses appeared. Indictment, Lent Assize 1820, PRO, Assi, 35/260/4(1).

[149] Wells, 'Rejoinder', passim.

[150] Wells, 'Criminal Gangs', pp. 73–74.

[151] Indictments, Lent 1792 Assize, PRO, Assi, 35/232/9.

[152] Indictment, Lent 1805 Assize, PRO, Assi, 35/245/7.

In stark contrast, the third capital case emerged from a 1826 *cause célèbre*, the murder through poisoning of the unlicensed publican Benjamin Russell, allegedly by his thirty-two-year-old wife, and her teenaged lover Daniel Leaney. Benjamin was the son of labourer William, and nephew of Francis Russell, a quite substantial farmer and important member of the select vestry. The family disapproved of the marriage, but William gave substantial assistance to his son. He borrowed substantially from farmer Holloway to purchase 'a House and premises' on the Weald, which he let to Ben, while 'mortgaging' it to Holloway. Ben, who was also a prize fighter, and Hannah ran a bakery which provided a useful cover for an unlicensed pub. Ben appears to have half-accepted Leaney's relationship with Hannah; the two men were partners – along with others – in both social crime and theft. Ben was heavily in debt. Like other members of the Russell clan, he engaged in the smuggling trade, and sold contraband spirits at his establishment. As we have seen, Ben had at least one poaching conviction – with Jesse Relf – and in March 1821 served a one-month hard-labour term for thieving wood from Robert Ellis.[153] Leaney had at least two poaching convictions, serving three months in prison for non-payment of one fine in 1824.[154] He was one of a number of notorious young men, including Thomas and Nicholas Crowhurst and George Clifton, implicated in the theft of an expensive scarf at the Rose and Crown,[155] and was miraculously acquitted – along with James Crowhurst – for a barn break-in and theft of wheat in 1825, when they were caught almost red-handed.[156]

Despite this narrow escape, Leaney continued barn-breaking after corn, now with Ben Russell. Ben's father knew of these activities, and was also concerned over rumours that their arrest was imminent. On the night of 7 May 1826, Ben dropped dead some three miles from home in Glyddish Wood, while carrying a sack of wheat, stolen from none other than farmer Holloway's barn. On learning of his son's death, William's principal aim was to 'hide the shame of the family, in . . . stealing wheat', and preserve his relationship with Holloway; even though he did not suspect foul play, he perhaps surprisingly was anxious to protect Leaney from the probability of transportation. Together they moved the body and hid the wheat. William was still under the impression that Ben died from natural causes when he gave perjured evidence to the coroner. The autopsy established arsenic poisoning, and Hannah and Leaney were charged with murder. Subsequently, a general meeting of the vestry agreed by a majority of thirty-two to three to pay all 'reasonable expences (over and above what may be obtained from the county) in the prosecution', a decision which led to

---

[153] Battle Petty Sessions minutes, 12 December 1815 and 2 July 1816, ESCRO, PSBA, 7. Indictment, Lent Assize 1821, PRO, Assi, 35/261/4(1).

[154] Battle Petty Sessions minutes, 9 March 1824. Summary convictions, 31 May and 25 October 1824, ESCRO, PSBA, 2; QR/E782; QDB/2/E1.

[155] Depositions, Thomas Weeks, landlord of the Rose and Crown, and labourer John Manwaring, 8 October 1823, ESCRO, QR/E777.

[156] Depositions, R. Button, J. Vigor, W. Weston and others, 5 November 1825, ESCRO, QR/E786.

a large number of witnesses, several of whom were Ben's friends and probable partners in his and Leaney's crimes, some of whom were subjected to pressure.[157]

At the marathon twelve-hour trial, evasions and prevarications repeatedly generated 'considerable laughter in the auditorium'. William Russell was subjected to a battering over the disparities between his testimony to the coroner and his present evidence. John Woodsell, again under fierce cross-examination, admitted that 'if I heard of smuggling going on, I should not have told of it', while claiming that he 'should if' witness to a 'felony'. John Sheather, who refused to say 'whether Ben kept a public house', was more frank over his attitude: 'He should not tell about smuggling, nor do I know that I should of a felony.' Among the five other prosecution witnesses who regularly drank at Ben's were two from across the nearby Heathfield border, who therefore fall outside our survey, and Mark Blackford. Among other associates named, but not called to testify, were Joe Blackford, Thomas Parsons, Thomas Crowhurst and Thomas Luck. We shall encounter Parsons and Mark Blackford as transportees. Blackford's brother, Joe, had served one year in gaol for assaulting the workhouse master, and had been denounced as a fowl stealer; he had escaped from a sheep-stealing charge by approving.[158] Crowhurst who had served one of a three-month sentence for non-payment of a fine for malicious damage, was among the men at the Rose and Crown when the scarf was stolen. He was high on the list of suspects for the wheat theft for which his brother, James and Dan Leaney were acquitted, and had been recently released after two weeks spent in Battle House of Correction for wood stealing.[159] On the scaffold Leaney informed overseer Weston of 'some matters concerning persons connected with him in illegal pursuits, who have hitherto escaped suspicion'.[160]

Leaney's intelligence did not result in any major offensive with arrests and trials; although the details went unpublished, the gallows incident was known about, and this doubtlessly forwarned Leaney's confederates. Two of his neighbours were established villains: James French was an unforthcoming witness about his patronage of Russell's establishment; while his associate, the middle-aged higler Thomas Parsons did not appear against Russell's murderers, though Ben had asked him for a sack for thieved corn. If French had been acquitted of the theft of a halter from another publican in 1818, Parsons was named as one of six suspects by a Heathfield victim robbed of forty-two fowls in 1821, when a formal search proved positive. While he was imprisoned, his wife relied on poor relief after the vestry sold off some of their household goods. In June

---

[157] This and the following paragraph are based on trial reports, *The Times*, 29 July and 5 August 1826, and *Sussex Weekly Advertiser*, 31 July 1826, and from the trial judge Baron Graham, who enclosed resworn statements, PRO, HO 47/71.

[158] Blackford, committal, 11 June 1816; examination, J. Clifton, 30 March 1818, ESCRO, QR/E748, 755. Blackford, indictment, Lent 1820 Assize, PRO, Assi, 35/260/4(1).

[159] Summary convictions, Crowhurst and J. Vidler, 9 May 1825, and Crowhurst, 10 April 1826, ESCRO, QR/E784, 786; QDB/2//E1.

[160] *Sussex Weekly Advertiser*, 7 August 1826.

1824 he was convicted again – with French – for passing counterfeit money, and they both served six-month hard-labour terms. They were indicted again in 1826 for barley theft, escaping it seems because they were not seen near the mill from whence came the corn in their possession. Parsons maintained his criminal career. In 1827 the Brightling workhouse master received information from an undisclosed source about the theft of eight chickens, a charge brought home to him. At the age of fifty eight he was transported for seven years. In 1829 French, who had five children, was one of the few criminals who benefited from publicly-funded emigration.[161]

Other men led charmed lives, perhaps even conforming after a fashion to Chadwickian concepts of lengthy criminal careers before conviction. George Pope, born in 1804, was one such character. He was acquitted by an Assize jury for attempted house-breaking in 1822, and was fined no less than £50 when apprehended at Heathfield with ten items of game in 1825. He paid this enormous sum, and another poaching fine of £5 imposed in 1826, along with William Relf (twenty), John Buss (seventeen) and Thomas Vidler (nineteen). The same four were arrested for assaulting Headborough Ellis in the following January: Pope and Vidler were unable to find acceptable sureties, in contrast to the other two; all were sentenced to three-month hard-labour terms. Thereafter Pope was a marked man, notably by Ellis, who orchestrated attempts to bring home crimes to him: as one witness said, he 'frequently found his [Pope's] footprints about the land' in the vicinity of the scenes of offences. In December 1827 he was eventually arrested at Jesse Relf's cottage for the theft of nearly thirty pounds of butter from a dairy; but while being taken by Ellis to Heathfield for committal by Sir Charles Blunt, a sister and a friend lifted the butter from the cart. Pope was indicted nevertheless, but a Quarter Sessions' jury proved unreceptive to inadequate evidence, so he was acquitted. Within a fortnight he was again fined £5 for poaching, then was arrested in March 1829. He faced three separate counts at the Assizes, namely a barn break-in at Burwash, potato theft at Heathfield and a burglary at Mayfield. Ellis was involved in all three detections, but indictments were not found on the first two counts. He stood trial only on the most serious offence of burglary. Acquitted once more, he immediately recommenced his criminal career, only to be speedily arrested and indicted at the next Assize for a burglary at a Heathfield draper's, with Stephen Colvin, a Heathfield man. This time Pope did not escape, though the death sentences passed on him and Colvin were commuted to transportation for life.[162]

---

[161] Vestry minutes, 16 February and 20 April 1822, and 3 April 1829: search warrant, 24 December 1821, various depositions, May 1824, April and October 1827, ESCRO, Par, 284/12/1; QR/E770, 789, 793. *Sussex Weekly Advertiser*, 23 November 1818, 18 January 1819 and 31 July 1826.

[162] *Sussex Weekly Advertiser*, 18 November 1822, 16 March, 17 and 24 August and 5 October 1829. Indictment, Lent 1829 Assize, PRO, Assi, 35/296/5. Indictment, Epiphany 1827 Quarter Sessions; summary returns, Epiphany 1826, Epiphany 1827 and Easter 1828; depositions, E. Jenner and W. Willson, December 1827, ESCRO, QR/E786, 790–91, 795.

Three more Burwash men were transported at the same sitting. James Weston, had at least three poaching convictions, and one for minor theft, when he to was sentenced to death for burglary, reprieved and exiled for life.[163] William Relf (twenty-four) and William Hayler (twenty-one) were both transported for breaking into and stealing flour from a Wadhurst mill. Hayler, who came from an Etchingham family, had narrowly evaded prosecution for involvement with John Buss in the theft of tares while a lad in 1823, served a two-month sentence for wood-stealing in 1825, and was fined in 1827 for poaching.[164] Relf had been imprisoned for six months in 1824 with John Pennels (then seventeen) for thieving wheat, and had at least one poaching conviction. He was amongst those imprisoned in 1826 for assaulting Ellis; the vestry then ordered his prosecution for assaulting the assistant-overseer in 1827.[165]

John Buss was eventually transported for seven years at the age of nineteen or twenty in 1831, along with Richard Siggs (twenty) for opportunistically robbing the Heathfield higler and black-marketeer John Hayler on 23 August. Hayward had spent the day drinking in various Burwash pubs, treating any number of people, among them the youthful Betty Braban and Ruth Pilbeam, before collapsing in a drunken torpor in an alley. When he awoke he discovered 'several sovereigns' and a banknote missing. He initially suspected the women, and ironically asked Siggs to approach them and 'if I could', persuade them to return the money. Recriminations flew in a confused sequence of events, with Buss handing over his share of the booty to Hayward, while Siggs refused to admit to any role. Sixteen-year-old Stephen Manwaring, who had kept lookout while the other two rifled Hayward's pockets, not only wanted to evade punishment – transportation sentences were being publicly anticipated – but also knew that his brother, John, was involved in hay stealing with Siggs while the latter worked as 'Head Mate' of one of Henry Haviland's ox-teams. Richard Manwaring's approving ensured Siggs' and Buss's conviction. Hayward, as the victim, petitioned for Buss's sentence to be reduced; such action was quite common nationally, but this was the only example respecting Burwash. Hayward's motives can only be guessed at, though he told a pack of lies: first, that Siggs was significantly older; and that secondly he was the instigator of Buss, whom he represented as a 'Steady young man'. The gaolor's report gave a different account, specifically that Buss bore a 'Bad . . . Char[acte]r – Twice before in prison'.[166]

[163] Summary convictions, 18 July 1820, 1 January 1825 and 27 July 1829; Battle Petty Sessions minutes, 25 October 1825, ESCRO, QR/E765, 782, 801; PSBA, 3. Indictment, Summer 1829 Assize, PRO, Assi, 35/269/5. *Sussex Advertiser*, 17 and 24 August and 5 October 1829.

[164] Indictments, 1823; summary convictions, 1825 and 1827, ESCRO, QR/E776, 791.

[165] Indictment, Summer 1829 Assize, PRO. Assi, 35/269/5. *Sussex Weekly Advertiser*, 29 March 1824 and 30 April 1827. Summary convictions, 1826; vestry minute, 7 September 1829, ESCRO, QR/E790; Par, 284/12/1.

[166] Gaol calendar, October 1831; depositions, S. and J. Manwaring, and constable R. Weston, 24 August, H. Putland, H.H. Haviland, W. Weston, W. Whybourn, T. Waterhouse and G. Olliver; statements by Buss and Siggs, all 2 August 1831, ESCRO, QR/E809. Hayward, 'Barwash', to Earl Grey, 24 November 1831, HO, 17/46 (part I, Gq/69).

In fact, Buss had served three prison terms: first for the non-payment of a fine imposed for the tare theft mentioned above; secondly as one of Ellis's assailants in 1826; and thirdly for assaulting (with Frederick Siggs) gamekeeper Coppard in 1829. In the events preceding the latter incident, the pair confronted Coppard in the Bear Inn, dared him to try to take their wires, blandly told him that, as they 'had no more Hare money', they were off poaching, followed the gamekeeper into the street, where he was felled by a brick.[167] Buss had at least two poaching convictions (1826 and 1830), and another – with Richard Buss, William Waterhouse and Edward Leaney – for stealing apples in 1826.[168] In fact, it was Siggs who had no criminal record, though he had been implicated in the alleged theft of a spoon at a pub in 1828.[169] John Manwaring received a three-month hard-labour term for his hay-stealing in 1831. He, too, had a record; he had served six months after his 1824 conviction – with Nicholas Crowhurst – for assaulting alleged informers. He had also been present with the Crowhurst brothers in the scarf thieving incident at the Rose and Crown, though Manwaring had been forced to give evidence against Elizabeth Russell for receiving the scarf; it had been a present from her paramour, the pugilist George Clifton.[170]

Only Parsons from amongst these transportees is known to have been involved with Russell and Leaney, but there are strong implications that various criminal partnerships periodically flourished between some of them in the later 1820s and early 1830s. But the most spectacular subsequent event against organised crime came in June 1838 with the arrests of members of 'a gang of audacious robbers' responsible for the break-ins at various premises in Burwash and neighbouring parishes, including the huge burglary at William Pitt's Ticehurst warehouse. The arrests were triggered by George Langridge (twenty-four) who was having an affair with fellow gangster Thomas Funnell's (thirty-six) wife Lucy. In an attempt to get rid of Funnell, Langridge flamboyantly waved a hat taken in the Ticehurst raid to Pitt's face to give credence to his information that stolen goods were stored at Funnell's and Edward Elliott's (twenty-two) cottages. A formal search proved the point, whereupon both Funnell and Elliott confessed. Langridge's strategy collapsed when he was indicted as an accomplice on the evidence of the hat. George Eastwood (twenty-nine) was also taken, along with Ephraim (twenty-two) and Job Bonds (twenty-four) for another Ticehurst burglary, at Benjamin Buss's. Eastwood proved more slippery with a 'full confession to that, and several other burglaries', including one at Catsfield, which implicated Langridge. Eastwood also admitted to a barn break-in, again at Ticehurst, with two men who went unnamed in the documentation, but this exonerated the Bonds brothers, who were released. Another prisoner, Edmund Hawkins (twenty-six), who confessed to burgling the Bear Inn, escaped from

---

[167] Gaol calendar; depositions of Coppard and J. Skinner, 18 May 1829, ESCRO, QR/E800.

[168] Summary convictions, 15 August 1826, ESCRO, QR/E789.

[169] Depositions, T. Vidler and J. Pennells, January 1828, ESCRO, QR/E794.

[170] Depositions, J. Manwaring and others, 2 September 1823; gaol calendar, Easter 1824 Quarter Sessions; Battle Petty Sessions minutes, 27 January 1827, ESCRO, QR/E777; PSBA, 2.

custody while on remand in the ludicrous circumstances outlined above. Mark Blackford may have been an accomplice, as he was in the audience at the committal hearing, though he ended up being fined for drunkenly intervening. Finally, Charles Sands (twenty), domiciled at the notorious Wheel, was unsuccessfully charged with lamb theft. Transportation sentences of fifteen, ten and seven years were respectively imposed on Elliott, Funnell and Langridge. Eastwood received a year's hard labour for the bar break-in and Sands was acquitted. Hawkins was never recaptured. Eastwood's two accomplices remained at large. During the very week that this Assize convened, there were two break-ins after wheat in Burwash, and in the following week another farmer lost five bushels.[171]

Eastwood recommenced his criminal activities soon after his release in August 1839. On 25 February he was arrested for the theft of ten yards of calico, only to be acquitted at the next Assize.[172] Shortly after dark, on the 'very clear' moonlit night of 5 April 1841, farmer Packham encountered a horse and cart tethered in Turks Lane, just off Burwash Common; and on inspecting the vehicle read that it belonged to George's brother Stephen. Suspecting that 'the Cart was waiting for a Load of something .. stolen', Packham alerted the foreman at a nearby farm, and the two recognised George as one of two men carrying sacks of oats from a barn which had been broken into. They succeeded in apprehending George, though his companion escaped. George claimed to have been delivering 'a Load of beer' to an unlicensed pub, which he refused to identify, but he admitted getting 'very tipsy and laid down by the Side of the Road near the Cart'. This lame excuse symbolised the fact that his luck had finally deserted him, and he was sentenced to fifteen years' transportation.[173]

Eastwood's exile was presumably treated as a triumph for Burwash's propertied inhabitants. In January 1843 Robert (thirty) and Thomas Buss (twenty-five) somewhat euphemistically reported as 'two well-known characters' – were arrested for sheep-stealing. Robert had been heavily fined as a fourteen year old with five other adolescents, including Edward Leaney and John Buss, for a scrumping raid on farmer Cruttenden's orchard,[174] but the family subsequently moved to Salehurst where Robert was presumably involved in events generating his notoriety. Thomas is known to have been in trouble in Salehurst, Etchingham and Burwash. Fined for poaching in 1836, and again in 1837 for assaulting the police (with Thomas Funnell), he and John Isted were discovered drunk in a Burwash pub before licensed hours in 1838, for which the publican was fined. Thomas took up residence at the Bell in 1840, while it was run by James Eastwood. Accused of thieving an axe in that year, Thomas decamped to Essex, where he was arrested in undisclosed circumstances at Harvering in May 1841, but no

---

[171] *Brighton Patriot,* 7 August 1838. *Sussex Agricultural Express,* 23 and 30 June, 2 July, 4 and 18 August 1838. Indictments, Lent and Summer Assizes, 1838, PRO, Assi, 35/278/3.

[172] Indictment, Lent Assize 1840, PRO, Assi, 35/280/3. *Sussex Advertiser,* 2 and 16 March 1840.

[173] Gaol calendar, Summer 1841 Quarter Sessions; depositions, J. Gorringe, and J. Packham, and Eastwood's statement, all 6 April 1841, ESCRO, QR/E875.

[174] Summary convictions, 15 August 1826, ESCRO, QR/E789.

indictment was laid at the Sessions by the grand jury.[175] Thomas was acquitted on the 1843 sheep-stealing charge, principally for lack of the calibre of evidence which resulted in Robert's conviction. His home was searched; raw and boiled mutton – some of that 'hot' was hidden 'between the lattice and plaistering cover'; and 'two Skeleton Keys' were found in his pocket. Sentenced to fifteen years' transportation, his wife was the only one in the Ticehurst Union from Burwash or with Burwash connections, who petitioned in 1846 to join her husband in Australia with their four children.[176]

Two of the five men transported for offences in Burwash in the later forties represented those with Burwash connections, but who were not permanent residents. Henry Baker, born in 1818, had served a four-month hard-labour term for the theft of a sheep at Tonbridge, Kent, in 1841; in 1846 he was caught at the Bell by the landlord while attempting to steal a silk handkerchief from a customer's gig parked at the rear of the pub. Although the item was worth only half a crown, it comprised a second conviction and Baker was transported for ten years.[177] John Matthews, a carpenter born in 1807 and whose Burwash settlement was investigated in 1829, in common with many in his trade, probably travelled seeking work. In 1846 he was lodging in Burwash with labourer Edward Pankhurst (twenty-seven) when the pair stole a lamb apiece, clearly for their own consumption as the police discovered 'a crock' full of meat concealed under a wash-house brick floor. Matthews had legally returned from an 1838 seven-year transportation for thieving five ducks at Waldron. Perhaps Pankhurst, who had no known record, was harshly dealt with owing to his companion's past, as they were both exiled, respectively for seven and ten years.[178] James Eastwood, aged twenty, who had served a seven-day hard labour term for stealing a tame rabbit in 1845, was convicted in 1849 for the theft of four chickens from farmer Stevenson which he sold to a Heathfield higler; for which he was transported for seven years.[179] Mark Blackford, now aged nearly fifty, whom we have encountered as a criminal associate of Ben Russell, was repeatedly in trouble after his drunken intervention at the 1838 gang committal hearings; fined again for drunkenness in 1842, he served a two-month hard-labour sentence in the same year for thieving twopence worth of onions from a publican's garden; and in 1846 another of onions from a publican's garden; and in 1846 another

[175] Summary convictions, 2 December 1836, 26 September 1837 and 17 July 1838; depositions, J. Parsons, H. Stiles and J. Eastwood, 18 May 1841, ESCRO, QR/E846, 848, 875. *Brighton Gazette*, 27 May 1841.

[176] Gaol calendar, February 1843 Quarter Sessions; depositions, G. Ditch, J. Vigor, Inspector Plumb, and examinations of both Busses, all 20 January 1843, ESCRO, QR/E890. Petition of the wives of transportees from Ticehurst Union, June 1846, PRO, MH, 12/13143.

[177] Gaol calendar, Summer Quarter Sessions 1846; depositions, oastler Axell, publican Cane and constable Wood, 29 May 1846, ESCRO, QR/E917. *Brighton Gazette*, 2 July 1846.

[178] Vestry minutes, 7 February 1829, ESCRO, Par, 284/12/1. Indictments, Lent 1849 Assize, PRO, Assi, 35/289/9. *Sussex Agricultural Express*, 24 March 1849. *Brighton Gazette*, 22 March 1849.

[179] Gaol calendar, Summer 1849 Quarter Sessions; depositions, J. Stevenson, and others, April 1849, ESCRO, QR/E940.

of six months duration for stealing two chickens. He not surprisingly anticipated transportation in 1849 for a pathetic, drunken and opportunist attempt to lift a bag of oats from the Admiral Vernon. If his guilty plea aimed to generate compassion, he failed to evade exile, being sent to Australia for seven years.[180]

Definitive conclusions remain complicated if not elusive. Further difficulties derive from vagrancy, and the partly related sizeable annual influxes of hop-pickers. Convicted vagrants were, however, vulnerable to instant severe punishment. The pair of tramps who stole two donkeys at Burwash in 1791 were tried at the Assize, in front of a public gallery full of their 'vagrant fraternity', who contributed to the denunciation of a 'principal witness' when transportation sentences were handed down, which might have presaged reprisals.[181] Conversely, two young skilled male itinerants were transported in 1829 and 1830. 'Butcher' William Igglesden, indicted for breaking in to none other than the future transportee George Eastwood's cottage and stealing his £2 watch, and weaver James Smith for a burglary which netted goods valued at over £4, were both initially sentenced to death.[182] Joseph Sorrell, who captured an escaped mare valued at £6 and then insisted he owned the horse, was transported for life in 1833, the judge observing that the offence's recent removal from the capital code dictated the inevitability of the sentence.[183] The vagrancy problem first peaked with post-war demobilisation, and secondly after the implementation of the Poor Law Amendment Act.[184] But there were links between vagrants and indigenous criminals. Young Burwash men in the 1820s and early 1830s who refused to live in the poorhouse, a condition for receiving relief, commonly dossed down in barns, hovels and outbuildings.[185] Others took similar evasive action to keep out of Ticehurst Union workhouse after 1835, including Samuel Beney aged twenty-six 'Belonging to . . . Burwash but a vagrant', who 'died of Small Pox . . . While encamped on the Road'.[186] On his release from a three-month term for stealing a whip, William Sands (twenty-one) teamed up with two fellow inmates to burgle the affluent farmer Gilbert's farmhouse at Burwash; Sands turned King's Evidence to evade the transportation sentences imposed on his confederates.[187]

[180] Summary conviction, 15 August 1842; gaol calendar, Michaelmas 1849; depositions, J. Alchorne and others, 21 August 1849, ESCRO, QR/E887, 942. *Brighton Gazette*, 31 March 1842, 8 January 1846 and 20 September 1849.

[181] *Sussex Weekly Advertiser*, 16 January 1792. Depositions, W. Wood and W. Barnard, 2 October 1791; Quarter Sessions minutes, January 1792, ESCRO, QR/E650; QO/EW30.

[182] Indictments, Assizes Summer 1829 and Summer 1830, PRO, Assi, 35/269/5; 35/270/5. *Sussex Advertiser*, 7 and 14 September and 5 October 1829.

[183] Indictments, Winter Assize 1833–34, PRO, Assi, 25/273/5. *Brighton Gazette*, 5 and 19 December 1833.

[184] Wells, 'Social Protest, Class', pp. 153–54.

[185] For example, James Wood, who 'pulled . . . two Trusses' of hay in a loft 'to Pieces' for a bed; deposition, 17 October 1831, ESCRO, QR/E809.

[186] Burial register entry, 18 May 1839, ESCRO, Par, 284/1/5/1.

[187] Indictments, Lent and Summer Assizes 1831, PRO, Assi, 35/271/5.

Hop-pickers pitched tents and slept almost anywhere, including animal stalls. Drunkenness was rife, typified by William Simes of Stockbridge Hampshire, who emerged from the Bell at 6 p.m., walked for 'a short distance along the Road when I fell down and remained all night'. Simes was just one of many hoppers robbed by others of their paltry belongings, in his case a 'bundle' containing three sheets, trousers, a handkerchief, a kettle and twenty-eight shillings.[188] Other stayed in the countryside after hopping closed and, once their earnings were gone, resorted to crime; the three men responsible for the 'great many Hives . . . stolen', principally from labourers' gardens in the district in the autumn of 1837, stored the honey in a lodge, presumably to sell in their way home. They were apprehended by a posse of Brightling people 'out to watch for robbers'. Transporting all three, chairman Blencowe explained the court's severity as reflecting magisterial attitudes to 'cottage robbery', an identification repeatedly made at this time of year.[189]

George Eastwood's victimisation at the hands of cottage robbers, and his willingness to testify, probably reflects intolerance among working people of crimes committed against the poor by outsiders. In some contrast, indigenous informers ran very real risks. Even a reprobate like Nick Crowhurst, when 'remonstrated' with for not revealing that the pugilist George Clifton had lifted a scarf in the Rose and Crown, simply responded by saying that 'if he said anything about it Clifton would damn near kill him'. Carter's mate James Leaney explained his silence 'as he was afraid that . . . Waterhouse would flog him' if he informed that the driver had sold off the odd sack of coal from the two-caldron load the pair had collected at Newenden wharf. This case also exposed gatekeepers who split the toll-money in return for handouts of filched commodities. William Eastwood, who witnessed the 5 November raid on the parish faggot stack, 'cannot say who the Men were . . . nor did he have any suspicion' of their illegality. Interestingly, Crowhurst did offer to obtain the stolen scarf for ten shillings. This would have no doubt been shared with Clifton, in the event of a bargain, for mutually satisfactory deals were commonly concluded between criminals and victims. John Skinner was robbed of a bundle while resting at the Seven Stars in Robertsbridge. On his return to Burwash and 'asked . . . if he would make it up with the' thief, Skinner agreed that 'if the value of his property [15s. 6d.] was brought to him . . . he should be satisfied with that and think no more about it.'[190]

---

[188] Depositions, Sarah Dann, 12 September 1842, and W. Simes, 26 September 1856, ESCRO, QR/E886, 995.

[189] Indictment of W. King, H. and J. Talbot; depositions, shoemaker J. Fuller, and constable Mann, both of Mayfield, 28 November 1837, ESCRO, QR/E849. *Sussex Agricultural Express*, 2 September 1837. *Brighton Patriot*, 5 December 1837.

[190] Depositions, W. Eastwood, 7 November 1821, victualler Weeks, 8 October 1823, gatekeeper Nash of Salehurst, 6 April 1829, and J. Leaney, 4 and 6 April 1829, farmer F. Russell and miller J. Skinner, 1835, ESCRO, QR/E770, 777, 779, 827.

The irony of most of the evidence presented in the previous paragraph is that it should have been recorded at all, as what it represents militates powerfully against the possibility of prosecution for even detected crimes. There is no question that some affluent villagers were anxious to prosecute, as represented by the activities of Richard Button, aided by the likes of Robert Ellis, who tried to make an alternative career as a detective; in 1819–22 an unmistakable crackdown occurred with the thirteen cases prosecuted at the Assizes, in addition to those launched at the Quarter Sessions against minor protesters and thieves. This stands in stark contrast to the absence of any Burwash cases sent to the Assizes between 1806 and 1818.[191] This determination appears to have evaporated in the immediate aftermath of the firing of Flurry's barn and, if a recovery occurred subsequently, no comparable offensive was launched until that against the gangs in the late thirties. There is little local evidence to support one historical claim that the more generous public funding for victims and their witnesses available under Acts passed in 1818 and 1826 made much difference to the poorer victims of crime.[192] The arrival of the professional police in 1840, their local strengthening in 1846,[193] and the supportive role of the Local constables made little apparent immediate difference to a willingness by poorer victims to prosecute before 1850, despite further historical claims.[194] The extension of summary jurisdiction to offences against property by the 1847 Juvenile Offenders Act and the 1855 Criminal Justice Act, combined with the increasing willingness of the police to prosecute, may have had the presumed positive impact,[195] but the evidence is juxtaposed with the effect of the erosion of the transportation option. In 1860 East Sussex criminal statistics revealed a 'small decrease', which in one estimate was 'not too small for . . . congratulations' in view of population increase, 'and the retention of a large number of criminals who, under the old system would have been deported'.[196]

If one definitive conclusion emerges from this amorphous mass of commonly contradictory evidence, it is the apparent relationship between the intensification of post-war poverty and the escalating level of crime and protest. Yet this requires some clarification, as organised crime was certainly experienced both before and during the war.[197] The evidence from 1815 to 1850 suggests that there was a criminal sub-culture amongst a sector of the population,

[191] PRO, Assi, 35/246/7; 35/247/5; 35/248/5; 35/249/3/; 35/260 to 261/4; 35/262/3.

[192] Rudé, *Criminal and Victim*, pp. 89–90; cf. p. 26.

[193] *Sussex Agricultural Express*, 12 December 1846.

[194] See esp. Gattrell, 'The Decline of Theft', p. 250, where this assertion is made on the highly suspect evidence of the 1852–53 select committee on policing whose report led directly to the compulsory 1856 County and Borough Police Act.

[195] J.S. Davis, 'Prosecutions in their Context; The Use of the Criminal Law in Later Nineteenth-Century London', in Hay and Snyder, *Policing and Prosecution in Britain*, p. 400.

[196] *Brighton Gazette*, 8 November 1860.

[197] A gang allegedly led by John Beney robbed an Etchingham farmhouse in 1781, though none of the suspects were arrested until 1784, and the trial collapsed on the evidence of the approver. Greater success attended the posse led by the constable who staked out higler John Luck's house

principally the working class, but also amongst others marginally above them, notably those branches of the Luck and Eastwood kins, respectively hauliers and higlers. Other names from the labourers' ranks recur, the Blackfords, Buss's, Cliftons, Isteds, Popes and Westons amongst them, with some regularity. Moreover, this very recurrence derives from prosecution for crime, and especially conviction. It is underpinned only to a degree with people evidentially present in the vicinity of the commission of crimes, usually with suspicion extending to them. This all suggests a solid corpus who regularly stole in addition to the commission of so-called social crimes. It also implies that contemporary perceptions of a considerable degree of unprosecuted crime, committed by people who could enjoy durable criminal careers, had a concrete viability. This picture emerges from many of the detailed histories of criminals in the previous pages; as we have also seen, some led charmed lives across several years. Their ability to do so was probably aided by intimidation and restitution on occasions. The latter, especially, also means that detected wrong-doers were often let off by victims unwilling to prosecute, a feature which was central to the litanies of legal reformers. Tramps and vagrants were less likely to benefit from compassion. Many individuals were prosecuted for a single, and usually minor, offence; other working-class families, revealed by the censuses as stable residents, seem to have kept out of trouble. These phenomena imply that contemporary identification of 'roughs' and 'respectables' had a greater validity, in the countryside at least, than notions of a criminal class.

The vestry's commitment of considerable funding to emigration, in the 1820s and early 1830s, saw the departure principally of many family men, some with large numbers of children. Only very few of these had major convictions, and though some came from families unmistakably central to the sub-culture, the details show that the parish largely eschewed the opportunity to shovel out criminals along with the paupers, before its powers to do so were compromised by the rules introduced by the Poor Law Commission.[198] However, the removal of considerable numbers not only restrained demographic growth, it also removed those who might well have otherwise reinforced the criminal sub-culture, a probability rendered stronger by the fact that the majority of convicts were criminal activists from early adulthood if not their youth. Yet the context in which they lived suggests that their criminality was not a simple attribution to youth and male machismo – of which there are signs – but negative discrimination in the labour market. Transportation sentences militated powerfully against the development of a criminal class, but so too did other factors discussed above. Moreover,

continued
in 1806; but Luck's two accomplices escaped though he was transported for stealing geese. Indictment, Summer 1784 Assize, PRO, Assi, 35/224/10. Depositions, farmer J. Shoesmith of Heathfield, his labourer William Sands, constable John Ellis, collar-maker Noakes, blacksmith Weston and labourer Moore, all 1 November 1806, ESCRO, QR/E710. *Sussex Weekly Advertiser*, 19 January 1807.

[198] List of accepted emigrants, 3 April 1829 and 17 April 1832 (ESCRO, Par, 284/12/1) and their reconstituted profiles.

the transportees are encountered working when they could secure employment, and their offences were not uncommonly work-related. It could also be argued that Burwash was too small literally to conceal a Chadwickian criminal class. Even the local gangsters worked, and the few who were not labourers used their avocations as a cover for criminality. This cover was at a considerable remove from the nature of its urban counterpart in the rookeries of late Georgian and early Victorian towns. Chadwick certainly had a point about vagrants and countryside criminality; the 'gypsies' and 'tramps', from whose ranks came many of the personnel comprising criminal gangs, used itineracy as their form of disguise.[199]

Finally, what of the social criminals, and the social protesters and populist political activists? As the details emerging from the Russell murder case reveal, historians should beware, when categorising social crime, that they do not extend the classification to identify social criminals. Smugglers, and their ubiquitous associates, engaged in both organised crime and committed offences on their own.[200] Parallel observations apply to the equally ubiquitous poachers and wood-stealers. Social protesters of all hues, including those engaging in political activities, were relatively rarely unimpeachable members of the community, as revealed most tellingly by the plebeian speakers at the Anti-Poor Law rally. All of these people were trapped to degrees in the 'grim cycle' of work, unemployment, poverty and crime. If defining types of crime – social, acquisitive, and poverty-induced – has its analytical uses, extending the classification to individuals can only be done with *minimal* empirical underpinning. A deviant sub-culture, embracing criminals of most types, and social and political protesters, is sustainable by the evidence. This classifactory device neither directly confronts, nor is it coterminous with, the concept of 'roughs' and 'respectables'; the latter categorisation is far too neat to be sustained, though it has more validity than that of a rural criminal class.

---

[199] Wells, 'Criminal Gangs', passim.
[200] Cf. Winslow, 'Sussex Smugglers', in Hay et al. (eds), *Albion's Fatal Tree*, esp. p. 159.

Appendix

Crime in Burwash, 1790–1850

* Denotes non-resident

Date	Crime	Victim	Perpetrators	Verdict
2 October 1791	Theft, two donkeys	Edward Veness	Two tramps*	Guilty
10 December 1791	Theft, hop poles	Richard Carter	Stephen Pennells	Guilty
27 January 1792	Highway robbery	John Cruttenden	Russell Hickmott Charles Leaney	Guilty Not Guilty
1 May 1792	Burglary	Hab Wood		
31 May 1792	Burglary	Hannah Sutton	Francis Baldock	Guilty
27 December 1792	Theft, halter; theft, two faggots	James Vigor; Rev. Curteis	John Ford*	Guilty
31 December 1792	Theft, nine rabbits	Stephen Fendell and Edward Burtonshaw	James Beney	Not Guilty
28 January 1793	Burglary	Margaret Potton	Thomas Castle*	Guilty
19 March	Assault, and malicious damage	Robert Ellis	Thomas Sutton	Guilty
13 September 1794	Burglary	John Rabbit	Mary Goodwin	Guilty
5 March 1795	Theft, hay	Thomas Watson	John Beney	Guilty
1 January 1797	Theft, iron chain	Thomas Twort	Thomas Hyland	Not Guilty
23 January 1798	Theft, hay	John Payne	Thomas Kemp	Not Guilty

Date	Crime	Victim	Perpetrators	Verdict
10 February 1799	Theft, cash from till	George Newington	William Meopham	Guilty
September 1801	Theft, tools	Peter Pankhurst	William Lipscomb	Not Guilty
July-Aug 1802	Theft, lime-kiln faggots	Lord Ashburnham*	John Sutton	Guilty
			Henry Collins	Guilty
			Thomas Balcomb	Not Guilty
10 December 1803	Theft, spade	James Vigor	Daniel Collins	Guilty
23 February 1804	Breaking and entering	William and John Skinner	Richard Vidler	Not Guilty
11 February 1805	Theft, leather	Robert Ellis	John Bishop	Guilty
16 February 1805	Theft, sheep	William Baker	William King	Guilty
18 June 1805	Theft, planed wood	Edward Pilbeam, John Noakes, Edward Hilder	William Taylor	Guilty
10 April 1806	Theft, clothes	James Pont	Sarah Evans	Guilty
31 October 1806	Theft, geese, and resisting arrest	John Ellis, and John Moore	John Luck	Guilty
16 February 1806	Fraudulent obtaining cheese	John Ellis	Edward Fairhall*	Guilty
April 1807	Theft, loaf	James Kemp	Edward Relf	Guilty
21 March 1808	Theft, eggs	William and Joseph Hyland	Jesse Braban	Not Guilty
20 August 1808	Theft, flour	John Skinner	David Collins	Guilty
18 November 1808	Theft, scythe	Edward Payne	Stephen Pankhurst	Guilty
13 May 1810	Turnpike toll evasion	William Oliver	Thomas Francis Gorringe*	Guilty
4 March 1813	Horse stealing	John Cruttenden		

Date	Crime	Victim	Perpetrators	Verdict
17 September 1813	Horse stealing	Rev. Curteis		
15 May 1816	Theft, promissory note	James Napp Leaney	Thomas	Not Guilty
May 1816	Assault on police	John Westover	George and Mark Blackford	
11 June 1816	Assault on police	John Westover	Joseph Blackford	Guilty
23 August 1816	Obstructing police	John Westover	John Mills	Guilty
12 December 1816	Theft, coal	William Waghorn and five others	Samuel Waterhouse and James Luck	Not Guilty Guilty
October 1817	Theft, spud	William Waghorn	John Clifton	Guilty
19 December 1817	Horse theft	John Hilder		
December 1817	Theft, hop poles	James Noakes	Thomas Etherington, snr and jnr	Guilty
January 1818	Theft, bread	George Beal*	William Collins	Guilty
12 September 1818	Theft, faggots	Parish officers	George Hyland and Thomas Pennells	Not Guilty
20 October 1818	Theft, keeler	William Waghorn	James French	Not Guilty
12 December 1818	Assault, game-keepers	James Manser and Alex Baxter*	William Colvin*	Guilty
20 March 1819	Assault, parish official	John Veness	Nicholas Crowhurst	
25 March 1819	Assault	John Veness	Nicholas Crowhurst Thomas Crowhurst	Guilty Not Charged
1 April 1819	Theft, hay	Rev. Curteis	Thomas Buss	Guilty

Date	Crime	Victim	Perpetrators	Verdict
3 July 1819	Assault, police	Samuel Noakes and others	James Isted, William and George Hyland, John Summers	
20 July 1819	Theft, two geese	John Fry and Richard Stone	P Douff*	Not Guilty
11 December 1819	Theft, faggots	Joel Newington	Thomas Collins	Guilty
28 January 1820	Theft, one sheep	John Baldock and William Oliver	Stephen Langridge Joseph Blackford	Not Guilty King's Evidence
13 April 1820	Riot and assault on parish officials	John Westover, John Cruttenden and Henry Hone Haviland	Stephen Elliott, James Langridge, John Sellings, Snr and Jnr	Guilty
13 November 1820	Demonstration and malicious damage	Rev. Gouldsmith		
8 January 1821	Theft, hop poles	Messrs White and Newington	Thomas Fuller	Not Guilty
11 January 1821	Theft, planed wood	Robert Ellis	Benjamin Russell	Guilty
18 January 1821	Theft, ten gallons beer	Parish officers	William Elliott	Guilty
27 January 1821	Theft, hop poles	Robert Ellis	George Eastwood	Not Guilty
7 February 1821	Pig theft	John Baldock and William Oliver	William Weston	Not Guilty
8 February 1821	Theft, hop poles	Richard Button	Mrs Ann Clifton	Guilty
26 Mary 1821	Malicious damage	Edmund Carman	Joseph Blackford	
28 July 1821	Theft, gooseberries	John Flurry	John Jenner jnr and John Sellings jnr	Guilty

Date	Crime	Victim	Perpetrators	Verdict
8 August 1821	Theft, various items from waggon	William Manwaring	Thomas Eastwood	Guilty
12 August 1821	Highway robbery	Dallington carpenter*		
August 1821	Hop-bines maliciously cut	Henry Hone Haviland		
4 October 1821	Theft, eight bushels wheat	John Hodges	William Pope John Luck and Francis Ellis	Guilty Not Guilty
5 November 1821	Theft, faggots	Parish officers	Charles Weston and eight others	Six guilty, (see text)
22 December 1821	Assault, parish officer	John Westover	William Pankhurst	Guilty
December 1821	Malicious damage, to parish 'cage'	Parish officers		
11 January 1822	Assault on gamekeepers	James Marchant and Brightling colleague	Thomas Funnell and John Sellings	Guilty
Febuary March 1822	Assaults on police			
10 August 1822	Attempted burglary	John Langridge	George Pope	Not Guilty
10 March 1822	Arson	John Flurry	Charles Weston, George Eastwood	Not Guilty
25 April 1823	Theft, hop poles	James Noakes	Stephen Sands	Guilty
12 June 1823	Theft, sack	William Marchant	William Hayler	Not Guilty
12 June 1823	Malicious damage to growing crop	Robert Tournay	John Buss	Guilty

Date	Crime	Victim	Perpetrators	Verdict
2 September 1823	Theft, clothes	James Noakes and Sarah Bigg	Sussanah Pope	Guilty
4 October 1823	Horse theft	John Cruttenden		
4 November 1823	Theft, bottle of brandy	James Leaney	Mark Blackford	Guilty
4 December 1823	Riot and assault	Henry and Thomas Hicks	Nicholas Crowhurst John Manwaring, Samuel Cornford	Guilty Not Prosecuted
23 January 1824	Theft, wheat	Edward and Thomas Simes	William Relf and John Pennells	Guilty
February 1824	Wood stealing	Henry Hone Haviland	Thomas Collins	Guilty
25 March 1824	Riotous assembly	Vestry		
June 1824	Theft, bark	Edward Simes	Jesse and Peter Beney	
30 November 1824	Theft, goose	Walter Hicks	Henry Hinds and Richard Wickham	Guilty
11 December 1824	Wood stealing	Robert Tournay	Stephen Sands	Guilty
12 December 1824	Theft, wheat	Parish officers	Henry Pettit	Guilty
7 January 1825	Theft, faggot	Parish officers	Framfield labourer*	Guilty
10 January 1825	Wood stealing	James Lade	Mary Kemp, Sarah Rich and Mary Chandler	Guilty
13 October 1825	Theft, potatoes	Rev. Gould	Thomas Collins John Clapson	Guilty Not Guilty
5 November 1825	Theft, wheat	Robert Tournay	Daniel Leaney and James Crowhurst snr	Not Guilty

Date	Crime	Victim	Perpetrators	Verdict
30 December 1825	Wood stealing	Edmund Austin	Elizabeth Crowhurst	Guilty
January 1826	Theft, sheet	James Leaney	Ester Brown*	Guilty
3 February 1826	Theft, shirt	Mary and William Kemp	William Baldwin*	Guilty
20 March 1826	Breaking parish pound	Thomas Geer	Jesse Fuller	Guilty
27 May 1826	Murder	Benjamin Russell	Daniel Leaney	Guilty
			Hannah Russell	Guilty, Reprieved
June 1826	Theft, cabbage	John Park	Thomas Collins	Guilty
6 August 1826	Fruit theft	Samuel Cruttenden	Edward Leaney, William Ballard, John and Robert Buss, and William Waterhouse	Guilty
26 December 1826	Attempted burglary, poorhouse	Parish officers	Stephen Langridge	Not guilty
January 1827	Assault police	Robert Ellis	William Relf, John Buss, Thomas Fuller, George Pope	Guilty
7 September 1827	Assault, assistant overseer	John Freeman	William Relf	
30 September 1827	Horse theft	Joseph Hyland		
November 1827	Theft, straw	John Vigor	John Clapson	Guilty
December 1827	Wood stealing	Parish officers		
December 1827	Theft, butter	Joseph Meopham	George Pope	
January 1828	Theft, hay	William Hyland	John Crowhurst	Guilty

Date	Crime	Victim	Perpetrators	Verdict
January 1828	Theft, silver spoon	William Marchant	John Heasman*	
20 February 1828	Theft, wheat	William Stone and John Fry	Thomas Kemp	Guilty
21 March 1828	Attempted rape	Harriet Eastwood	John Lidbetter	Guilty
March 1828	Malicious damage to poorhouse	Parish officers	Samuel Thompson	Guilty
28 October 1828	Theft, turnips	Thomas Ellis	Mary Kemp and Elizabeth Braban	Guilty
13 December 1828	Attempted rape	Ann Relf	Robert Blackford	Guilty
30 January 1829	Theft, coal	Francis Russell	Thomas Waterhouse	Guilty
6 March 1829	Theft, wheat	James Bourner	George Pope	Not Guilty
15 March 1829	Theft, lime	Francis Russell	Thomas Hyland and Thomas Waterhouse	Guilty
13 April 1829	Assault, gamekeeper	John Coppard	John Buss and Frederick Siggs	Guilty
April 1829	Fraud, shopkeeper	Joseph Sawyer	John King*	Guilty
April 1829	Theft, distrained goods	Parish officers		
May 1829	Theft, gin	Henry Hone Haviland	John Crowhurst	Guilty
20 July 1829	Burglary	Edward Ellis	James Watson	Guilty
24 July 1829	Burglary	George Eastwood	William Igglesden*	Guilty
28 July 1829	Theft, peas	Richard Button	Thomas Pankhurst and James Weston	Guilty
28 September 1829	Theft, fruit	Henry Hone Haviland	John Crowhurst	Guilty

Date	Crime	Victim	Perpetrators	Verdict
6 December 1829	Theft, wheat	William Smith	Frederick Siggs	Not Guilty
December 1829	Fraud, shopkeeper	Parish officers	John Lidbetter and John Wood	
5 March 1830	Receiving stolen flour	William Peckham	Thomas Clifton	Not Guilty
13 May 1830	Breaking and entering	Richard Saunders	James Smith*	Guilty
4 July 1830	Theft, gooseberries, cabbages	William Hyland	Joseph Pennells	Guilty
24 January 1831	Theft, whip	Edward Simes	William Sands	Guilty
21 June 1831	Breaking and entering; demanding money with menaces	George Fagg Gilbert	William Sands	King's Evidence
			Two former prisoners*	Guilty
18 July 1831	Theft, fowls	John Pankhurst	George Langridge	Guilty
21 August 1831	Theft, fruit	Henry Hone Haviland	Samuel Eyles, William Bowles and George Ellis	Guilty
22 August 1831	Street robbery	John Hayward*	Richard Siggs and John Buss	Guilty
3 September 1831	Theft, bridle	John Vigor	William Paine	Guilty
7 October 1831	Theft, copper kettle	Matthew Howe	Samuel King	Guilty
14 October 1831	Theft, gun	Robert Tournay	John Bovis	Guilty
11 February 1832	Indecent assault	Mary Ann Whybourn	William Usherwood, William Bowles and Samuel Eyles	Guilty
10 July 1833	Breaking and entering	William Burgess	Thomas Bovis	Not Guilty

Date	Crime	Victim	Perpetrators	Verdict
20 November 1833	Horse theft	Benjamin Fuller and Joseph Sorrell	John Churchill*	Guilty
28 December 1833	Malicious damage		Mary Relf	
January 1834	Theft, harness	Sarah Clark*	Samuel Strace*	Guilty
22 April 1834	Theft, sacking	Samuel Smith	Tramp*	Guilty
3 September 1834	Theft, straw	John Marchant	Jesse Relf	Not Guilty
29 January 1835	Wood stealing	Thomas Marchant	James Etherington	Guilty
27 January 1836	Assault, police	James Relfe	Epraim Bonds, George Hyland and Stephen Elliott jnr	Guilty
3 August 1836	Malicious damage	William Thompson	William Twort	Guilty
23 October 1836	Assault, police	Henry Stiles, and John Vigor	James Forward* and William Bovis*	Guilty
22 April 1837	Assault, police	Henry Stiles	George Hyland jnr	Guilty
12 May 1837	Assault, police	John Cruttenden	Edmund Hawkins	Guilty
11 June 1837	Assault, police	Henry Stiles	George Freeman	Guilty
7 August 1837	Fraud	John Parsons	Edmund Hawkins	Guilty
28 August 1837	Malicious damage	William Thompson	Mark Blackford and George Cole*	Not Guilty / Not Charged
29 August 1837	Assault, police	John Vigor	Thomas Johnson jnr*	Guilty
11 September 1837	Theft, faggots	A.E. Fuller*	John Baker * and John Boswell*	Guilty

Date	Crime	Victim	Perpetrators	Verdict
7 November 1837	Theft, beehives	Richard Saunders	William King, James* and Henry Talbot*	Guilty
26 February 1838	Assault, police	John Vigor	Lucy Funnell, George and John Langridge	Guilty
12 May 1838	Assault, police	Henry Stiles	Job Bonds	Guilty
9 June 1838	Burglary	James Baker		
16 June 1838	Lamb theft	John Park	Charles Sands	Not Guilty
11 August 1838	Theft, wheat	John Cruttenden		
September 1838	Theft, oats	John Vidler		
September 1838	Theft, copper	Henry Hone Haviland		
7 November 1838	Theft, fowls	Samuel Cruttenden	Alfred Ellis and Samuel King	Guilty
2 December 1838	Theft, fowls	David Hyland		
2 December 1838	Theft, fowls	John Henty		
13 December 1838	Wood stealing	A.E. Fuller*	John Rich	Guilty
24 December 1838	Sheep theft	Samuel Cruttenden		
7 January 1839	Theft, bonnet	Jane Boulden	Frances Dann	Guilty
25 January 1839	Shooting at	George Waddle	Gamekeeper William Hairby*	Guilty
8 March 1839	Attempted burglary	David Hyland		
3 July 1839	Theft, peas	Rev. Munn	William Saunders	Guilty
14 July 1839	Theft, straw	John Sutton	John Rich	Guilty
23 July 1839	Malicious damage	National School Committee	John Barden	Guilty

Date	Crime	Victim	Perpetrators	Verdict
15 August 1839	Theft, lead	Rev. Gould	Thomas Eastwood, William Shadwell and Anthony Buss	Not guilty
4 September 1839	Theft, lead	Joel Newington	Same	Not Guilty
19 September 1839	Breaking and entering	William Snashall, Sarah Honeysett and Samuel Shorter	John Martin*	Guilty
23 September 1839	Breaking and entering	Robert and Kathy Weller	Robert Waite*	Guilty
26 September 1839	Theft, shirt	Stephen Brown	Robert Waite*	Guilty
28 October 1839	Theft, hop poles	Richard Reeves	Charlotte Meopham and Sarah Rich	Guilty
26 December 1839	Theft, wheelbarrow and moulds	Samuel Daw	Solomon Stubberfield	Not Guilty
25 February 1840	Theft, cloth	John Harmer	George Eastwood	Not Guilty
9 May 1840	Theft, hop poles	Edward Maynard	John Vidler	Guilty
26 May 1840	Burglary	John Marchant		
16 October 1840	Sheep theft	Henry Hone Haviland		
28 October 1840	Fraud	Thomas Stone	David Honeysett	Guilty
9 December 1840	Burglary	At Bear Inn		
8 January 1841	Cutting willow	Thomas Ellis	Henry Coppard and Thomas Parsons Jnr	Guilty
16 January 1841	Burglary	John Parsons	Thomas Buss	Not Guilty

Date	Crime	Victim	Perpetrators	Verdict
29 January 1841	Theft, spud	James Pilbeam	Joseph Meopham	Guilty
January 1841	Cutting timber	James Noakes	Edward Collins	Guilty
4 February 1841	Theft, sacks	Joel Meopham	Thomas Collins	Guilty
8 February 1841	Theft, sacks of peas	Francis Russell snr		
9 February 1841	Burglary	Agent for Roberts, bridge shoe manufacturer		
19 February 1841	Attempted highway robbery	Joseph Harmer		
5 April 1841	Theft, sixteeen bushels of oats	John Stapley and Charles Noakes	George Eastwood	Guilty
April 1841	Wood stealing	Joel Newington	George Relf	Guilty
12 May 1841	Disorderly conduct		Thomas Foord*	Guilty
13 May 1841	Passing counterfeit coins	Battle pie-seller	Henry Eastwood	Not Guilty
12 June 1841	Sheep theft			
27 June 1841	Theft, spud	John Vigor	Joseph Meopham	Guilty
13 July 1841	Malicious damage	John Baldock		
13 July 1841	Theft, garden produce	Henry Hone Haviland		
16 July 1841	Theft, tame rabbit	John Rich	John George Barden	Guilty
18 July 1841	Theft, milk	George Ellis	Ephraim and Abner Bonds	Not Guilty
28 July 1841	Theft, 3s. 6d cash	Richard and William Lamb	Augustus Bailey*	Guilty
August 1841	Theft, peas			

Date	Crime	Victim	Perpetrators	Verdict
3 October 1841	Theft, fruit	Benjamin Wood	Nelson Thompson,* Richard Horden* and Edmund Brown*	Guilty
7 December 1841	Theft, boots	James Lade	John Wiles*	Guilty
27 December 1841	Theft, spatterdashes	James Funnell	John Pankhurst	Guilty
19 January 1842	Theft, wood-rails	James Noakes	Edwin Collins	Guilty
7 February 1841	Wood stealing	John Blunden	Thomas Hawkins	Guilty
21 February 1842	Theft, ten bushels wheat	John Pankhurst	William Oliver	Guilty
13 March 1842	Theft, wheat	Samuel Cruttenden	Charles Weston, William Blackford and William Shadwell	Not Guilty
27 March 1842	Theft, fencing pales	Henry Hone Haviland	Thomas Collins	Guilty
29 May 1842	Stabbing	Joseph Harmer	Thomas Manser	Guilty
2 June 1842	Theft, boot	William Maynard	Richard Clifton	Guilty
26 June 1842	Receiving stolen goods	Mayfield victim*	Mary Buss	Not Guilty
22 July 1842	Theft, faggots	John Henty	Hannah Relf, Ellen Dann and Mary Ann Copper	Guilty
14 August 1842	Theft, onions	James Pilbeam	Mark Blackford	Guilty
14 August 1842	Destruction, pound	Hundred authority	Joseph Moate*	Guilty
11 September 1842	Theft, cash, gloves, bag	Robert Dann	Phoebe Chater*	Guilty

Date	Crime	Victim	Perpetrators	Verdict
11 November 1842	Wood stealing	John Hook	Joseph Clapson, William and James Pennells	Guilty
18 January 1843	Sheep theft	John and George Ditch	Robert and Thomas Buss	Guilty Not Guilty
30 January 1843	Fowl theft	Thomas Simes	Henry Eastwood jnr	Not Guilty
11 February 1843	Beastiality		William Saunders	Not Guilty
22 February 1843	Wood stealing	John and George Ditch	Thomas Collins	Guilty
30 March 1843	Malicious damage	Francis Russell	George Waddell	Guilty
May 1843	Wood stealing	Joel Newington	Thomas Hawkins	Guilty
4 October 1843	Assault, police	Inspector Plumb	George Copper jnr	Guilty
14 December 1843	Wood stealing	Edward Simes	John Hetherington	Guilty
2 January 1844	Theft, wood fencing	John Bullen and George F. Gilbert	Edwin Collins	Guilty
16 February 1844	Theft, beagle	James Watson	George Honeysett	Guilty
26 March 1844	Theft, 2s. and neckerchief	James and Mary Pope	James Hoad	Guilty
13 March 1845	Theft, tame rabbit	William Hempderi	James Eastwood	Guilty
4 May 1845	Burglary	Admiral Vernon Inn proprietor		
27 July 1845	Malicious damage	Thomas Bowles	Henry Petts	Guilty
25 October 1845	Theft, boots	James Russell	Samuel Evans*	Guilty
14 December 1845	Theft, fowls	John Maynard	Mark Blackford	Guilty

Date	Crime	Victim	Perpetrators	Verdict
2 February 1846	Theft, faggots	William Chandler	Alfred Smith	Guilty
6 February 1846	Theft, two bushels cabbages	Henry Playstead	Eliza Leaney, Margaretta and Harriet Price*	Not Guilty
April 1846	Fraudulent evasion of turnpike toll		William Bates	Not Guilty
20 May 1846	Theft, 10lbs bacon	William Manwaring	William Saunders	Guilty
29 May 1846	Theft, silk hankerchief	Benjamin Morris*	Henry Baker	Guilty
9 June 1846	Theft, bundles matchwood	John Maynard	Charles Weston jnr	Not Guilty
20 June 1846	Theft, planed wood	Thomas Leaney	Edwin Lusted	Guilty
8 December 1846	Theft, sack of corn	Edward Lansdell		
January 1847	Theft, butter and cheese	Stephen Pilbeam	James Collins	Not Guilty
1 April 1847	Theft, fowls	Francis Russell		
1 April 1847	Theft, potatoes	James Noakes		
4 April 1847	Receiving stolen corn	Etchingham farmer*	Richard Buss	Not Guilty
8 April 1847	Attempted burglary	John and John Buss Noakes		
29 November 1847	Theft, hop poles	Francis D Haviland	John Hilder	Not Guilty
29 November 1847	Receiving stolen wheat	Etchingham farmer*	James and George Eastwood	Not Guilty
12 December 1847	Attempted burlgary	Henry Stone		
29 January 1848	Theft, two bottles	William Nightingale	Thomas Hilder	Guilty
23 February 1848	Theft, ornaments; hop spud	John Blackwood and James Sawyer	John King*	Guilty

Date	Crime	Victim	Perpetrators	Verdict
7 June 1848	Theft, cash and watch	Thomas Sawyer	Thomas Kelly* and Timothy Nolan*	Guilty
14 June 1848	Theft, two razors	John Barnard	Richard Clifton	Guilty
July 1848	Fraud	Schoolmaster Cox	Itinerant*	Arrested
10 September 1848	Theft, watch	Aaron Apps	George Eastwood	Not Guilty
23 September 1848	Theft, spatterdashers	Stephen Fuller	James Relf	Guilty
24 September 1848	Theft, two ducks	Joseph Newington	Thomas Carsey*	Not Guilty
3 October 1848	Malicious damage	William Nightingale	James Cork* and Samuel Heathfield*	Guilty
5 January 1849	Theft, saw and axe	Henry Heathfield	Itinerant*	Not Guilty
16 February 1849	Assault, polie	Henry Delia	Richard Relf	Guilty
18 February 1849	Sheep theft	John Munn and Stephen Pilbeam	Edward Pankhurst and John Matthews	Guilty
27 April 1849	Theft, fowls	John Stevenson	James Eastwood	Guilty
5 July 1849	Theft, shirt	Charles Honeysett	John Brown*	Guilty
9 July 1849	Theft, mutton	John Park	John Brown*	Guilty
20 August 1849	Theft, bag of oats	Thomas Althorne	Mark Blackford	Guilty
20 October 1849	Attempted theft, planed wood	David Hyland	Itinerant*	
4 December 1849	Theft, hay	J.M. Durrant*	Thomas Hicks	Guilty
23 December 1849	Theft, geese	John Park		
4 February 1850	Theft, thirteen turnips	Stephen Pope	Harriet Cornwall	Guilty

Date	Crime	Victim	Perpetrators	Verdict
24 February 1850	Theft, sewing items	Hannah Paiger	Sarah French	Guilty
11 May 1850	Theft, fowls	Benjamin Thompson	John Thompson	Guilty
17 May 1850	Sheep theft	Benjamin Buss	Richard and William Holmes	Guilty
14 July 1850	Burglary	George F. Gilbert	John and James Pennells	Guilty
1 August 1850	Theft, one gallon potatoes	Thomas Luck	John Thompson	Guilty
7 September 1850	Theft, clothes; gun	James Philcox and John Coppard		
1 November 1850	Theft, two geese	James Beale		

10

The Manifold Causes of Rural Crime:
Sheep-Stealing in England, c. 1740–1840

John Rule

> Then I'll ride all around in another man's ground
> And I'll take a fat sheep for my own
> Oh I'll end his life by the aid of my knife
> And then I will carry him home.

(Dorset folksong)

To William Cobbett, poverty was the self-evident cause of increasing rural crime in the years following the end of the great French War:

> the tax gatherer presses the landlord; the landlord the farmer; and the farmer the labourer. Here it falls at last; and this class is made so miserable, that a felon's life is better than that of a labourer. Does there want any other cause to produce crimes?

He sneered at those who kept 'bothering our brains about education and morality ... who is to expect morality in a half-starved man? ... what education, what moral precepts, can quiet the gnawings and ragings of hunger?'[1]

Historians of the bleak period of English rural history which lies between the high-profit years of the French War and the middle of the nineteenth century have tended to follow Cobbett in linking desperate poverty among farm labourers with an increasing incidence of criminal committals in the rural counties.

The Hammonds pronounced the labourer's lot 'wretched and squalid in the extreme' and suggested that it was only through crime that he survived at all:

> He was driven to the wages of crime. The history of the agricultural labourer in this generation is written in the code of the Game Laws, the growing brutality of the Criminal Law, and the pre-occupation of the rich with the efficacy of punishment.[2]

More recently Professors Hobsbawm and Rudé have described the farm labourer in the years leading up to the risings of 1830 as not just pauperised but demoralised and degraded, becoming not 'merely a full proletarian, but an underemployed, pauperised one'. Especially so far as the southern and eastern

---

[1] William Cobbett, *Rural Rides* (Everyman edition, 1957), i, pp. 297–98.
[2] John L. and Barbara Hammond, *The Village Labourer* (1948), pp. 183–84.

counties are concerned, it is a verdict which is not easily disputed even by those with an ideological predisposition to do so.[3]

Like the Hammonds, Hobsbawm and Rudé emphasise the connection between this poverty and increasing crime in the rural counties:

> He could seek a relief from poverty in crime – in the simple theft of potatoes or turnips which constituted the bulk of the offences which he would himself regard as criminal, and in poaching or smuggling which he would not. It was, of course, not a mere source of income, but also a primitive assertion of social justice and rebellion.

Crime in the agricultural areas, they conclude, was 'almost entirely economic – a defence against hunger'.[4] For the eighteenth century Professor Beattie's study of Sussex and Surrey indictments tends towards a similar conclusion. He finds a 'strong suggestion' that property crime in the countryside was to a considerable extent a matter of hunger and necessity and varied in incidence with the price of food.[5]

Given the nature of the crimes which fill the Assize and Sessions calendars of the rural counties and accepting the serious level of poverty among farm labourers, either for a prolonged period as in the early nineteenth century or in years of harvest failure in the eighteenth, the linking of poverty and crime should perhaps seem as obvious to the social historian as it did to Cobbett. Indeed poverty must be assumed the underlying condition: but is it sufficient explanation of why rural felonies should have increased in one period or year over others? Some contemporaries were sensitive to the complexity of the issue and stressed a variety of causes. Sir Thomas Baring of Hampshire, who was regarded as something of an authority on rural crime, gave a list of reasons for its increase to a select committee in 1828:

- The increase in population.
- Increase of wealth of one class of the population and poverty among the other.
- Temptation caused by the exposure of property and its transit from place to place.
- The number of ale-houses and fairs.
- Want of control over lodging houses.
- The game laws.
- Transportation sometimes inducing rather than deterring crime.
- Too good treatment of prisoners in the hulks.
- The state of the poor laws, the bastardy laws and those relating to lewd women.

---

[3] Eric J. Hobsbawm and George Rudé, *Captain Swing* (Harmondsworth, 1973), p. xxii.

[4] Ibid., pp. 50, 54.

[5] John M. Beattie, 'The Pattern of Crime in England, 1660–1800', *Past and Present*, 62 (1974), p. 92.

- The state of the customs and excise laws.
- Payment of legal clerks by fees rather than salary.
- Frequent and unnecessary commitment of petty offenders by magistrates, such as husbandry servants for disobedience of their masters' orders or for not performing their work.
- Want of a uniform prison system.
- The Act for paying prosecutors and witnesses their expenses which had had a short term effect in increasing indictments.[6]

Without entering into a discussion of all of Baring's points, it is clear that he was well aware that the level of indictments could be determined by things other than 'real' movements in crime. Administrative changes (fees and expenses), multiplying of offences by laws (Game Laws and excise), defects in the methods of punishment, changing temptations and opportunities, and changing attitudes to what was considered serious enough to merit instituting proceedings, all exerted influence on the level of indictments and cannot be presumed constant over time without investigation.

Even if poverty was a fact, and accepting that rural felonies were increasing, several possible explanations exist. Crimes could have been committed by rural labourers not so much as a direct result of their poverty but rather as an expression of resentment against that condition. Felonies might increase not simply because poverty was extreme and widespread but because it coincided with a decline in social order, a decrease in morality, a loosening of traditional sanctions and restraints which had previously operated more effectively in keeping even hungry men from crime. Increasing indictments in rural courts may not have been at all the result of the actions of hungry labourers but accounted for by 'invading' townspeople (much poaching was of this kind) or vagrant groups like tinkers, beggars or gypsies. There is at least the possibility that a large proportion of rural crimes may have been perpetrated by a 'professional core' of country villains who lived by crime in the same way as many urban thieves did. This was at least the impression which Edwin Chadwick strove so hard to give in his loaded report of 1839 urging the desperate need for the establishment of a rural constabulary.[7]

In case-studying an individual crime like sheep-stealing we should reasonably expect to find instances which fit all of these categories. The problem is one of weighting the various motivations. Sheep-stealing offers good possibilities for investigation. As mutton is food, hunger motivation is possible; but since sheep are also a movable and transferable form of property so too are 'professional' motivations. As a capital felony, cases would finally come before the Assize courts and not be 'lost' to the historian in the areas of lower courts and summary jurisdiction. It was also a sufficiently common crime to have generated a good deal of documentation; and being covered by a specific Act it is

[6] BPP, HC, SC, *Criminal Commitment*, 1828, vi, *Minutes of Evidence*, p. 21.
[7] See Samuel E. Finer, *The Life and Times of Sir Edwin Chadwick* (London, 1952), pp. 167–74.

extractable from the statistical series. In this essay I have cast a wide net over regions and sources, although with a distinct bias to the western counties where most of my research was done. The wide cast was deliberate. It seemed necessary to get an idea of attitudes and assumptions on the matter of sheep-stealing rather than a detailed count of incidence in one selected area.[8]

Under an act of 1741 sheep-stealing was a capital felony without benefit of clergy – a hanging matter. The Act had followed the petitioning by farmers and graziers from Essex and Middlesex complaining of increasing night-time depredations on their flocks. A committee was appointed to hear the evidence of the petitioners and, within ten weeks from receipt of their petition, the farmers got their wish and the royal assent made stealing a sheep punishable by death.[9]

In 1801, the year of widespread hunger, sentences were passed at a single Assize at Salisbury which were to make six widows and twenty-nine orphans. One of six men hanged had been a highway robber, another a horse-thief, but the remaining four had all been sentenced for sheep-stealing. That was a year of exceptional hunger and of widespread unrest among the poor and fear among the propertied. In fact, most persons convicted of the offence during the ninety years it enjoyed capital status did not hang. More often they were reprieved for transportation. Even poor men convicted of stealing single sheep were not returned to their families and neighbourhoods. While apologists for the eighteenth-century penal code are apt to make much of the fact that most capital sentences were not actually carried out, it is worth bearing in mind the words which Jeremy Bentham put into the mouth of a judge passing sentence of transportation:

> I sentence you, but to what I know not; perhaps to storm and shipwreck, perhaps to infectious disorders, perhaps to famine; perhaps to be massacred by savages, perhaps to be devoured by wild beasts. Away – take your chance; perish or prosper, suffer or enjoy; I rid myself of the sight of you.[10]

Nevertheless, whatever the likelihood of reprieve, until 1832 men convicted of sheep-stealing even without any aggravating circumstances could be, and some in every year were, hanged. The notion that a man could be hanged for stealing a sheep or a lamb has not only passed into a popular saying but made a strong enough impression on the village mind for some traditions to rest on the assumption that sheep-stealing remained a hanging offence long after the repeal of 1832.[11]

---

[8] Roger Wells' later study of sheep-stealing in the north generally supports the argument of this article: 'Sheep-Rustling in Yorkshire in the Age of the Industrial and Agricultural Revolutions', *Northern History*, 20 (1984), pp. 127–45.

[9] *Journals of the House of Commons*, xxiii (1737–41) 572, 585, 690.

[10] *Hampshire Chronicle*, 30 March 1801; quoted in Alan G. Shaw, *Convicts and Colonies* (London, 1966), p. 57.

[11] See for example Bob Copper, *Songs and Southern Breezes* (London, 1973), pp. 11–20, where a

Official statistics do not make the measurement of sheep-stealing committals on a national basis possible before 1810. Between that year and 1840 committals in England and Wales averaged 207 a year. In terms of per 100,000 of the population, peak years were 1817, 1827, 1830 and 1837. For the eighteenth century the much less reliable conviction statistics are available for some circuits: the Western from 1770 to 1818; the Norfolk for the same years; and the Oxford from 1799 to 1818. These show an interesting consistency with evident peaks in 1782 and 1786 and a great vaulting leap in 1801.[12] Dr Hay's findings for Staffordshire also show the peaks of 1786 and 1801 but in 1783 rather than 1782; and for the earlier part of the century in 1742/3, 1766/7 and 1775.[13]

It is doubtful whether the repeal of the capital sanction in 1832 had a marked effect on prosecution levels. In theory reluctance to begin a process which might take a poor man to the rope, may have led to under-prosecution of known offences, while the removal of the sanction might have reduced this disinclination. This was the argument of the criminal law reformers but official statistics show 1231 committals in the five years leading to 1832 and 1320 in the five years following. Committals for horse- and cattle-stealing covered in the same repeal actually declined in the second five-year period.[14]

Not infrequently contemporaries expressed the view that, for the most part, sheep-stealers were hunger-driven men rather than hardened criminals. The peak years, coinciding as they do with years of high bread prices and widespread shortages, support this. Those of 1766/7, 1782/3, 1801, 1817 and 1830 all coincide. It is a reasonable assumption that hungry men steal when food prices in general are high; while 'professionals' would be likely to increase their activities when *meat* prices were high. The peak of 1837 is the only one which clearly coincides with a widespread scarcity of fat beasts.

In one of the few surviving folk-songs about sheep-stealing, the stealer was 'most wonderful poor'.[15] In a work of 1781 we read:

> Poverty alone can induce men to be guilty of it; and it is very hard that the same severity should be inflicted upon the wretched sheep-stealer, whose hunger and the cries of his family have driven him to the commission of this crime, as upon the hardened highwayman, who robs to support himself in luxuries, and to dissipate it in the most abandoned pursuits.[16]

---

continued

story is recounted which took place at the end of the nineteenth century and yet ends: 'and the penalty for sheep-stealing in the old days was hanging by the neck'.

[12] Statistics after 1818 are taken from the annual returns but up to that date from the appendices to BPP, SC, HC, *Criminal Laws*, 1819, viii.

[13] Douglas Hay, 'Crime, Authority and the Criminal Laws in Staffordshire, 1750–1800' (unpublished Ph.D. thesis, University of Warwick, 1975), p. 72.

[14] K.K. MacNab, 'Aspects of the History of Crime in England and Wales between 1805 and 1860' (unpublished Ph.D. thesis, University of Sussex, 1965).

[15] Albert L. Lloyd, *Folk Song in England* (1969), p. 239.

[16] George Parker, *A View of Society and Manners in High and Low Life* (2 vols, London, 1781), i, 162–63. *Commons Journals*, xxiii (1737–41) 572 (7 January 1740), 585 (14 January 1740).

In instances motivated by poverty several things might generally be expected to have been true: (1) the accused was not a member of an organised gang; (2) one or perhaps two sheep were taken rather than significant numbers; (3) that there was no record of a criminal past. In addition it would confirm results if sheep-stealers could be shown to have been men of the age at which family support pressures were likely to have been heaviest. A preliminary investigation of 1834 suggests this last may have been true. In that year 62.7 per cent of committals for sheep-stealing were of men between twenty-two and forty years and only 21 per cent younger than twenty-two. For all crimes the figures were 44.9 per cent and 41 per cent. Female convictions were very rare.[17]

Of thirty-nine cases reported in sufficient details in the Cornish press between 1811 and 1850, twenty-nine involved the stealing of only one sheep, nine of several sheep and in one case it is unclear. In two of the twenty-nine cases of single sheep-taking, lambs were taken and kept alive and so immediate hunger was presumably not the motive. In twenty-five of the twenty-nine no associates were mentioned. In the four cases where associates were implicated, in one the relationship between the two men is unclear; in another they were 'labouring men', perhaps work colleagues; in a third an accomplice with a butcher's knife was seen but not taken; in the last the pair were brother and sister. Only one of the twenty-nine seems to have had a previous record. Michael Stevens, convicted in 1820, was described as a 'very bad man' by the person he himself called on for a character reference. At his execution he attributed his loss of character to having been imprisoned before and 'hardened in guilt'.[18] One other was charged at the same time with stealing clothes, but the court accepted that he had become deranged since the death of his wife.[19]

Several pleaded poverty in their defence. One of these, a cottager on the common, said he had had no money to buy food. Another spoke of being driven by 'extreme distress' and for a third the man from whom he had taken the sheep spoke on his behalf of his wanting 'the necessaries of life'. Five had previous good character pleaded for them and in several cases the description of the discovered mutton as being cut up in 'an unbutcherlike manner' suggests consumption rather than resale.[20]

During the debate on the repeal of the capital Act, the feeling that sheep-stealing was not usually a crime of 'deliberate wickedness' was frequently and widely expressed. It was rather a crime which might be perpetrated without any 'combination' by a labourer in temporary distress. In general the Cornish evidence supports this view but there were nevertheless a number of cases in that county and elsewhere where the motivation was clearly different: there is even more uncertainty about the eighteenth-century evidence. Dr Hay has written of a black market in mutton operating in eighteenth-century Staffordshire

---

[17] Based on returns in BPP, 1835, Cmd 218, xlv, *Criminal Offences for 1834.*
[18] *West Briton,* 8 September 1820.
[19] Ibid., 5 August 1820.
[20] Ibid., 2 April 1824, 3 April 1818, 28 March 1828.

and of butchers who specialised in receiving stolen meat.[21] Alfred Peacock has uncovered an East Anglian gang in the 1830s who had an arrangement with local butchers for a rate of 10s. a carcass if the skin was cleanly removed. Some Bedfordshire sheep were so professionally skinned that they were thought to have been destined for the quality London market.[22]

Butchers appear as accomplices in four of the Cornish cases and one was strongly suspected in a fifth. Elsewhere in the west country they also appear. John Uppington, convicted at Ivelchester in 1799, was a master-tailor, schoolmaster and parish clerk, but even his varied skills were not thought up to the skill of butchering when he was caught and a butcher named Westcott was named as an accomplice although insufficient evidence could be produced to secure a conviction. A Devon butcher was hanged in 1798 and another charged along with a blacksmith in 1801.[23]

Unless for poaching, it is not easy to uncover individuals with recurrent criminal acts in their past. But as C.D. Brereton, one of Edwin Chadwick's most persistent critics and totally opposed to the idea of establishing a rural constabulary, pointed out:

> In cities the majority of thieves exist in gangs, practice fraud by profession, and live by a constant series of depredations ... criminals in the country only occasionally once or twice a year steal a sheep, pig, corn, hay, wood, turnips, poultry as the case may be.[24]

One of the Cornish committals for stealing a single sheep had a previous conviction. Another in 1818 had been in gaol before but as his character witness explained: 'it was not for felony, but for smuggling' and he was a man of good character. Perhaps not so was the butcher caught in the act on Hackney Marshes in 1742. He had been burned in the hand thirty years before for a similar act (before the capital sanction) and two of his sons had already been transported for highway robbery. Charles Rudman confessed at Salisbury in 1801 that he had been taking sheep and calves for many years; he was also suspected of murder. Issac Box, convicted at the same Assize, had been extensively engaged in sheep-stealing and had twice committed burglary and once highway robbery, besides innumerable thefts of poultry. In 1806 a shepherd and labourer convicted together in Salisbury were represented as having been engaged in the practice

---

[21] Douglas Hay, 'Poaching and the Game Laws on Cannock Chase', in Douglas Hay et al. (eds), *Albion's Fatal Tree: Crime and Society in Eighteenth-Century England* (Harmondsworth: 1977), p. 205.

[22] Alfred Peacock, 'Village Radicalism' in John P.D. Dunbabin, *Rural Discontent in Nineteenth-Century Britain* (London, 1974), pp. 43–44. A study of East Anglia, while recognising that gangs were sometimes involved, generally accepts that most sheep-stealing was poverty-induced, but points out that it fell rapidly after 1850 with the upturn in agricultural fortunes: John E. Archer, *'By a Flash and a Scare': Arson, Animal Maiming, and Poaching in East Anglia, 1815–1870* (Oxford, 1990), pp. 12–13, 16.

[23] *West Briton*, 15 August 1816, 3 April 1818, 27 March 1829, 13 August 1830, 5 August 1836; *Sherborne Mercury*, 18 February 1799, 16 April 1798, 30 November 1801, 13 April 1742.

[24] C.D. Brereton, *A Refutation of the First Report of the Constabulary Force Commissioners*, pp. 72–73.

for many years and received the death sentence. Levi Chivers, indicted at the same assize in 1815, had stolen 153 sheep from five different parishes; and in one parish alone from five different owners.[25]

Taking sheep in such numbers was clearly rustling for resale and, even if discovered in only one offence, men taking them cannot be assumed hunger-motivated. One commited to Maidstone Gaol in 1742 had driven thirty-seven sheep and two lambs to Smithfield. A farmer's servant stole twenty-five ewes near Winchester in 1773 and sold them for £15 at Petersfield Fair. 'Farmers should therefore be very cautious of whom they buy such small parcels of sheep, even at public fairs', cautioned the *Hampshire Chronicle*. William Rowe, executed in Cornwall in 1818, had stolen ten sheep on one occasion and fifteen on another. He sold them to a market butcher for 22s each. In 1828 the taker of sixty-one sheep from a fold of 554 offered them for sale at Devizes Fair the following morning. Such examples could be multiplied and clearly an approaching fair offered tempting resale possibilities.[26]

Sheep-stealing by gangs was widely reported. A man convicted at Winchester in 1773 of stealing wheat, confessed to having been one of a gang 'of desperate villains' who had stolen many sheep in that area. In the following year Hampshire was still being troubled by a gang of horse- and sheep-stealers who were killing sheep and leaving their skins, heads and entrails in the fields. Several committed to Ilchester gaol in 1799 were supposed to belong to a gang who had been taking sheep for some time. A gang of seven, of whom four, all local people, were taken in Devon in 1742, had stolen cider-apples, linen and lead as well as three fat sheep. Thomas Vardy, convicted at Dorchester in 1788 for returning from transportation to which he had been sentenced four years previously for sheep-stealing, had, since his return, 'terrorised' the village of Glanville Wootten with a 'gang of villians'. Dartmoor and Exmoor were in 1801 experiencing 'to a most atrocious extent [the] business (for as such in some parts of the county it seems to be almost exclusively practised) of sheep stealing'.[27]

These instances refer to persons grouped in a lasting sense for the committal of criminal acts, but sheep-stealing groups were often more informal associations of family or neighbourhood. Thus in 1829 in Cornwall four men, two of them brothers and one a butcher, met to plan a sheep raid. They took four rams but, on pursuit, one of the brothers fell into the sea and drowned. The involvement of the butcher suggests that they were intending resale of the meat, but at their trial there was no suggestion that they had combined other than for this one escapade. They cannot be described as a gang in the sense of an

---

[25] *West Briton*, 14 August 1818; *Sherborne Mercury*, 13 April 1742; William Dowding, *Fisherton Gaol: Statistics of Crime from 1801 to 1850* (Salisbury, 1855), entries for 1801, 1806, 1815.

[26] *Sherborne Mercury*, 30 November 1742; *Hampshire Chronicle*, 18 January 1773; *West Briton*, 14 August 1818; Dowding, *Fisherton Gaol*, entry for 1828.

[27] *Hampshire Chronicle*, 18 January 1773, 24 January 1774; *Sherborne Mercury*, 22 July 1799, 2 February 1742, 14 January 1788; Charles Vancouver, *General View of the Agriculture of the County of Devon* (London, 1808), pp. 366–67.

organised grouping of criminals. A 'gang' suspected in Somerset in 1801 consisted of a man and his three sons and two brothers. Three seamen who took a sheep in 1815 were father, son and son-in-law, while Robert and Betsey Percy, convicted in Cornwall in 1842, were co-residing brother and sister. Similar pairings took sheep elsewhere, although more commonly a wife than a sister; Charles and Ann Miners, convicted at Salisbury in 1817, were condemned by Charles's diary in which he had actually recorded: 'About home and night to L. mill after NARB and W prig'd two Sh'P'.[28]

Rarer than cases of taking for consumption or for immediate resale, but not unknown, were cases of stocking farms with stolen livestock. When in 1776 a Devon farmer was charged with cattle-stealing, investigation revealed that he had rented a farm at £100 per annum and that among his stock were six stolen horses and more than a hundred stolen sheep taken from different persons and places. A Herefordshire farmer who hanged himself in Gloucester gaol in 1785 had stocked a farm with over sixty head of sheep and cattle stolen from different parts of the country. A Cornish farmer was fortunate in 1849 that a jury could not agree when he was observed in the act of putting a strange lamb to one of his ewes.[29]

Clear cases of 'rustling' apart, the adding of stolen sheep live to existing flocks directs attention to the matter of strays. Some evidence suggests that in the minds of country farmers and shepherds there was a distinctively permissive attitude when it came to allowing strays to remain with their flocks. The execution of a thirteen-year-old boy at Ilchester in 1786 dramatically illustrates this. Edward Wiatt had been convicted along with another man of going into his own father's field and taking away what was in fact a stray, although he claimed not to know this but believed that it belonged to his father: 'as it was a sheep that had strayed from its own flock, into his father's from whence he took it'. The *Sherborne Mercury* made the lad's fate the subject of lengthy editorial comment:

> As sheep stealing appears to be a very growing evil, it would be well if the rigour of the law were more generally understood ... Boys and servants observe strangers among their flocks, and as by growth in size and of wool they are not to be discovered, the masters or parents take them as their own. This is observed by the whole family, who thinking it easy are induced to hire small farms or connect themselves with those that have such – and to cause strangers from flocks in a variety of ways which an open country is easy to be effected and success prompts repetition.

Masters and parents should refrain from setting such a 'dreadful and often fatal example'. Instead they should regularly search their flocks and advertise

---

[28] *West Briton*, 27 March 1829; *Sherborne Mercury*, 29 June 1801; *West Briton*, 7 April 1815; *Cornwall Gazette*, 25 March 1842; Dowding, *Fisherton Gaol*, entry for 1817.

[29] *Hampshire Chronicle*, 18 March 1776; *Sherborne Mercury*, 4 April 1785; *Cornwall Gazette*, 30 March 1849.

strays: 'so that it may be impressed upon the minds of servants and boys that the detaining or secreting the strayed sheep may be a means of much trouble and distress'.[30]

In the following year a farmer in the west country was convicted of stealing seven sheep found in his flock. He was worth £200 per annum and declared he had had no intention of taking them and indeed to have been in the act of driving them back when they were discovered to be another's property. One Wiltshire farmer was later remembered as having encouraged his shepherd to add others on the way when driving flocks to market. Such instances may lie behind the attitude which seems to be revealed in the oral traditions recorded by Bob Copper, W.H. Hudson, Alfred Williams and others in which sheep-stealers tend to figure more in the 'old rogue' than the 'damned villain' category.[31]

Public sympathy for a poor man driven to steal a sheep and suffering for it the extreme penalty of the law does not in itself imply that sheep-stealing was a 'social' crime in the sense of being popularly sanctioned, any more than does a permissive attitude towards strays. Hudson's informant, an old woman of ninety-four when he spoke to her in 1910, thought hunger made men indifferent to hanging and recalled one man hanged at Salisbury who, having a starving wife and children, had been 'maddened by want'. But this is excusing, not approving. More difficult are the fuzzy areas where shepherds' customary rights may have been involved. A young shepherd was convicted at Oxford in 1832 of killing and stealing a young lamb. The farmer had discovered a skin and found the lad's mother cooking the lamb. The shepherd argued that it was the custom for shepherds to have small lambs that died. This was accepted by the court but it was found that the lamb had not died but had been killed.[32] Such customs would have been very regionalised. None are mentioned in the standard accounts of William Marshall.

Clearly sheep-stealing cannot be regarded as a social crime in the sense that smuggling, wrecking or poaching can. These were endorsed by the community in most if not all cases. They were not actions considered in themselves 'criminal'. Sheep-stealing was, although the specific circumstances of its committal might in instances bring popular approval as well as sympathy. Such occasions might be those on which sheep were taken or killed as acts of protest against persons who had offended the community. In this sense of popularly approved act of protest or revenge, sheep-stealing could in some instances be viewed as 'social' crime. David Jones, who has made a study of incendiarism in East Anglia in the aftermath of the rural labourers' revolt of 1830, includes the stealing of livestock, along with incendiarism, poaching, animal-maiming, machine-breaking and the sending of threatening letters, as a 'traditional' form

---

[30] *Sherborne Mercury*, 24 April 1786.

[31] *Sherborne Mercury*, 9 April 1787; William H. Hudson, *A Shepherd's Life: Impressions of the South Wiltshire Downs* (London, 1910) p. 236.

[32] Hudson, *Shepherd's Life*, pp. 234–35.

of rural protest and argues that only further research can reveal to the historian when 'crime' became protest.[33]

The protest nature of many acts of arson speaks for itself, although doubt might remain as to whether the resentment expressed in flames was individually or collectively felt. Sheep-stealing is less obviously a protest action. However, a growing body of evidence suggests that in many instances it was of this nature. Alfred Peacock has suggested that criminal actions of a protest kind reached epidemic proportions in East Anglia after the revolt of 1830, when, according to Hobsbawm and Rudé, farm labourers 'waged a silent, embittered vengeful campaign of poaching, burning and rural horror'. Peacock has further shown that sheep-stealing was prominent among such activities. In several cases recorded by him, only choice portions of the beast were removed: 'skin, fat and entrails were left as an awful reminder of the power of the labourers'. He misleads us a little here. There are other explanations for leaving the head, skin and entrails. Basically it was good thieving. Discovery of concealed skins was one of the commonest causes of detection. The inquiry which had first led to the passing of the capital Act in 1741 had learned that many stealers came in the night: 'killing great numbers of sheep ... and stripping off their skins, and then stealing the carcasses of the sheep so killed, but leaving their skins behind to prevent discoveries'. It also refers to cutting open sheep and stealing 'their inward fat' and leaving the rest of the carcass behind. The tallow, the fine fat around the kidneys, had a high value to weight ratio and was easily disposed of.[34]

Peacock is on stronger grounds when he examples the posting of defiant notices, such as that affixed to a Bedfordshire gate in 1836:

> Sir, your mutton's very good
> And we are very poor,
> When we have eaten this all up
> We'll then come and fetch some more.[35]

Another note was pinned to a gate in Cornwall in the middle of a spate of sheep-stealing instances:

> Dear Sir William, do not weep,
> We've had one of your fat sheep,
> You are rich and we're poor.
> When this is done we'll come for more.[36]

---

[33] David Jones, 'Thomas Campbell Foster and the Rural Labourer: Incendiarism in East Anglia in the 1840s', *Social History*, 1 (1976), pp. 5, 11. On definitions of 'social crime', see above, Chapter 8, pp. 153–68.

[34] Peacock, 'Village Radicalism', pp. 40–44; Hobsbawm and Rudé, *Captain Swing*, p. xxiii; *Journals of the House of Commons*, 23 (1737–41), pp. 572, 585; Hay, 'Crime, Authority and the Criminal Laws', p. 67.

[35] Peacock, 'Village Radicalism', p. 44.

[36] Alfred K. Hamilton Jenkin, *The Cornish Miner* (London 1927) p. 300 n. 94.

It was not only in the 'sullen aftermath' of the 1830 rising that some instances of sheep-stealing can be viewed as protest. An interesting sequence of events in a Cotswold village in 1824 suggests a protest motivation. At the harvest of 1823 an attack by an armed mob of villagers had been made on an Irish harvest labour gang brought in by several local farmers. One of the leading farmers was Joseph Payne and, on 10 February following, two men, Robert Costin and James Hulet, were imprisoned for sheep-stealing. On 13 February Payne's barn was burned down and five days later a man was imprisoned for attacking one of the watches at the fire. On 11 March the two sheep-stealers, Costin and Hulet, were sentenced to be transported for life. On 16 March Dickens Prigmore and George Costin (same surname as one of the previously convicted sheep-stealers) were gaoled both for firing Payne's barn and for sheep-stealing; and next day Francis Hulet (same surname as the other of the first two sheep-stealers) was also gaoled both for the fire and for sheep-stealing. Ultimately the two Costins and the two Hulets were transported, Prigmore having turned King's Evidence. Clearly in such a case it is difficult to separate the strand of sheep-stealing from that of popularly-supported incendiarism. The perpetrators appear to have been the same men and the target the same farmer who is known to have incurred community resentment.[37]

Threats against flocks sometimes accompanied anonymous letters preceding food riots. Edward Thompson has provided two clear examples of this. The first from 1767 was pinned to a gate after a sheep had been stolen. It clearly shows that the stealing was intended as a protest against the farmer's charging of high prices for his grain:

> *Gentleman farmers*
> Farmers tack
> nodist from
> This time be
> fore it is to
> let
>
> Be fore
> Christ mas
> Day sum of
> you will be as
> Poore as we if you
> will not seel
> Cheper

The second reinforces this:

> This is to let you no We have stoel a sheep, for which
> the reason was be Cuss you sold your Whet so dear

---

[37] 'A Grave Digger's Diary', in John W. Robertson Scott (ed.), *The Countryman Book* (Idbury, 1948), pp. 156–64. The sequence of events described is on pp. 160–61.

and if you will not loer pries of your Whet we will
Com by night and set fiar to your Barns and Reecks
gentlemen farmers we be in Arnest now and that
you will find to your sorrow soon

A Northamptonshire farmer received warning in 1800: 'If you dornt lower the greain whe will destroy all your farm with fire, whe will destroy all your sheep and whe will pull all your turnips up.'[38]

Reports of sheep-stealing from Sir William Yeo near Taunton in 1778 followed reports of other incidents on his estate, including his being beaten up by a gang of masked men. One strongly suspects grudge-motivation here. A witness from the same county was to tell a select committee in 1819 when asked about horse-, cattle- and sheep-stealing: 'in some instances, where people are excessively vindictive, they are very liable to have their property stolen'.[39]

Historians have often suggested that the extent of pardons mitigates any description of the eighteenth-century penal code as 'bloody'. Indeed the figures show that few convicted sheep-stealers ended on the gallows. But before we get carried away in praising the goodness, kindness and mercy of the judiciary, we should bear in mind that the likely alternative sentence was long transportation. In the six years before the repeal of the capital Act (1826–31) when attitudes towards sheep-stealers might have been expected to have been softening rather than hardening, there were 935 convictions. Of these, execution followed in fourteen cases. Of those reprieved, however, 57.86 per cent were transported for life; 14.43 per cent for fourteen years; and 5.6 per cent for seven years. There were evident fluctuations in the ratio of executions to convictions with a greater likelihood of hanging in the eighteenth than in the early nineteenth century:

Ratio of Executions to Convictions:
Western Circuit[40]

1770–79	1 : 22.7
1780–89	1 : 12.9
1790–99	1 : 15.2
1800–09	1 : 4.8
1810–18	1 : 14.9

The striking increase in the period 1800–9 is largely accounted for by the single year 1801. No less than sixteen out of nineteen executions for sheep-stealing on this circuit during this period took place in that year. Official statistics for England and Wales show a noticeable decrease in the likelihood of hanging in the years leading up to the repeal:

---

[38] Edward P. Thompson, 'The Crime of Anonymity', in Hay et al, (ed.), *Albion's Fatal Tree*, pp. 281, 300.

[39] *Sherborne Mercury*, 10 March 1788; BPP, HC, SC *Criminal Laws: Minutes*, p. 105.

[40] Statistics for the Western Circuit from the appendix to ibid., appendix 9.

Ratio of Executions to Convictions:
England and Wales

1811–1817	1 : 32.5
1818–1824	1 : 21.1
1825–1831	1 : 61

In his brilliant study of the working of the law in eighteenth-century England, Douglas Hay has stated that the grounds for mercy were ostensibly that the offence was minor; that the crime committed was not common enough to need an exemplary hanging; or that the convict was of good character.[41] The grounds for choosing the victims, for that is the truer way of looking at the problem, may reasonably be presumed to be the obverse of these. Hay has convincingly demonstrated that pleading poverty alone was insufficient for reprieve. It needed to be accompanied by strong testimony of good character. He has also shown that, in the few instances where they stole property of sufficient value, the well-to-do might find their very affluence hurrying them to the gallows – so that the poor might continue to believe that all were equal before the law. Thus, in sentencing a prosperous sheep-stealer in 1787, a judge remarked that the law was tolerant of the trials of poverty but a 'rich rogue', who stole under the mask of a fair and upright character and was able to make depredations without being suspected, was not to be guarded against and was therefore more culpable than a poor man who committed a criminal act through real want.[42]

The case of Henry Penson of Teignmouth in Devon is interesting. A fifty-year-old farmer owning a large tract of land, he was indicted in 1801 for stealing a fat sheep belonging to one of his tenants. Parts of the carcass and skin were found badly concealed on his premises and he offered a £500 bribe to the arresting officer to let him escape. At his trial the court was crowded and in his defence Penson argued the improbability of one so well-off as himself stealing a sheep, claiming that the skin had been 'planted'. He could supply no alibi and when invited to call for character witnesses could produce only a servant girl who had been just three weeks in his employ. The jury found him guilty with unusual dispatch. In delivering sentence the judge lamented that a man though 'rolling in affluence' could not refrain from 'violating the property of his neighbour'. The verdict gave 'the greatest satisfaction' to a crowded court. So unpopular did the friendless Penson seem to have been that it crosses the mind that he might have been 'framed' by the planting of the skin. However his broadsheet confession survives and concludes with a not-unexpected plaudit to the English law:

The excellency of the English constitution in its impartial awards of punishment must excite the admiration of all who see the rich culprit, whose crime was aggravated by

---

[41] Douglas Hay, 'Property, Authority and the Criminal Law', in Hay et al. (ed), *Albion's Fatal Tree*, pp. 43–44.

[42] Ibid., p. 44.

the circumstance of his wealth, bend to an equally ignominious death with the meanest criminal.[43]

Other victims of the rope fit in well with Hay's suggestions. Two executions on the Western Circuit in 1786, one of a thirteen-year-old boy, took place in a year when sheep-stealing was prevalent enough to draw out editorial comment in local papers. One of these two, Tom Roberts executed at Bodmin, was clearly selected to serve as an example. The unfortunate man was of previous good character and had not even been concerned with the actual taking of the sheep, although he admitted being privy to the crime. Leaving a wife and four children, he went bravely to the gallows begging bystanders to take warning and not meddle with their neighbours' property. At that time seven men were in the county gaol awaiting trial for sheep-stealing.[44] William Rowe, executed in 1818 also in Cornwall, was a more obvious candidate for the fatal tree. He had stolen twenty-five sheep and the magnitude of his crime was compounded by a previous conviction, although that had only been for smuggling. In passing sentence, attention was drawn to the extent to which sheep-stealing had been taking place in the area.[45]

The desire to make exemplary sentences was especially evident in 1801 when in the Western Circuit sixteen of the nineteen executions for the offence carried out in 1800–9 took place in that one year. It was a year of such widespread food-rioting and industrial discontent in the south west that an historian has recently written of the 'revolt' in the south west.[46] Other examples confirm the 'choice' of victims. Michael Stephens, executed in Cornwall in 1820, was of proven bad character with previous convictions. So too were Charles Rudman and John Partingall, executed at Salisbury in 1800 and 1801.[47]

Although it seems most likely that most sheep-stealers, especially in the hardship period of the first half of the nineteenth century, were hungry labourers rather than professional or even semi-professional criminals (a conclusion also suggested by a very high ratio of acquittals to convictions), it is also evident that the case study of sheep-stealing warns against making any simplified view of the causes of rural crime. There seem to have been very few cases in which sheep-stealers were not local people. There is little evidence of stealing by migrants, although the 'floating' population of the bargees were said to take opportunities which presented themselves as they passed through the Midlands. Surprisingly, the traditional villain of the countryside, the gipsy, figures hardly at all. This so surprised W.H. Hudson that, when he researched the local press for *A Shepherd's Life*, he recorded what sounds almost like disappointment:

---

[43] Broadsheet in Exeter City Library and account in *Sherborne Mercury*, 20 April 1801.

[44] *Sherborne Mercury*, 24 April 1786.

[45] *West Briton*, 7, 14, 21 April 1818.

[46] See above, Chapter 2, pp. 17–51.

[47] *West Briton*, 11 August 1820; Dowding, *Fisherton Gaol*, entries for 1800 and 1801.

> In reading the reports of the Assizes from the late eighteenth century down to about 1840, it surprised me to find how rarely a gipsy appeared in that long, sad, monotonous procession of 'criminals' ... for stealing sheep and fowls or ducks or anything else.

He suggested that perhaps they were simply too skilled to have been caught and reported a communication from the *Salisbury Journal* for 1820 which claimed that gipsies would bury stolen sheep deep in the ground and then make their camp fire over the spot. If the sheep were not missed they could later return to dig it up.[48]

Hay has suggested that much sheep-stealing in the Black Country was done by persons for whom stolen mutton was a regular part of family diet over a period of years. Such men stole with great caution and never in large quantities. They were as likely to have been nailers, potters or other industrial workers as farm labourers. Such persistent thieves were sometimes suspected by their neighbours but managed to avoid detection for years; Hay suggests that perhaps 200 sheep in a decade might be accounted for in this way. It is indeed important to keep in mind that first offence really means first known offence. However, the nature of sentencing for a capital offence, at very least long periods of transportation, does not make it possible for there to be recurrent convictions. Evidence of earlier activities might come up in the proceedings but equally might not do so. I prefer to reserve judgement. Eighteenth-century Assize records survive only very poorly for the western circuit. The nineteenth-century evidence, although it clearly enough identifies hungry men, stealers for resale and social and individual protesters, has nothing to say about persistent stealing for family consumption. Without doubt it was not unknown but it is impossible to determine its significance as a percentage of total offences. When, and if, such offenders were taken, they had no incentive to confess to previous offences when nothing was more likely to mark them for execution than an admission of habitual depredation on the propertied.[49]

As most of my evidence has come from the counties of the western circuit, does this make my suggestions only regionally valid? I have found few disagreements with Douglas Hay's account of the crime in Staffordshire, but sheep-stealing in the northern moors and hills where flocks roamed unattended over vast tracts might have developed on a very different pattern from, say, Wiltshire, where sheep were herded in the day and folded at night.[50] In fact the west

---

[48] BPP, SC, HC, *First Report of the Commissioners on the Best Means of Establishing a Constabulary Force ... in the Counties*, 1839, cmd 169, xix, p. 3; Hudson, *Shepherd's Life*, pp. 269–70, but see BPP, 1839, xix, p. 17, where many of the gypsies around Salford were said to have been sheep-stealers.

[49] Hay, 'Crime, Authority and the Criminal Laws', pp. 71, 73–74. See also Jones, 'Thomas Campbell Foster', p. 11: 'Certain families, even sections of villages, virtually existed by crime – a yearly saga of stealing wood, turnip-tops, hay, food, farm animals and game'; and Brereton, *Refutation*, pp. 72–73, of 1839: 'I have known many persons transported from the neighbourhood in which I reside, but not one who had not some ostensible and legal occupation, and most of them were as constantly employed in that occupation as other persons of the same craft.'

[50] Roger Wells, 'Sheep Rustling in Yorkshire', pp. 127–45.

country offers an excellent cross-section of sheep-husbandry, for it included not only specialised raising areas like Dorset and Wiltshire but areas like Dartmoor, Exmoor and Bodmin Moor where sheep were kept in conditions little different from those of other upland areas of the country.

Index